Advance Praise for *Teardrop Diplomacy*

'Asanga Abeyagoonasekera's new book is essential reading for understanding the perils faced by Sri Lanka and other Indo-Pacific countries as they navigate between the major powers. It provides a front-row seat to Sri Lanka's China tilt under the guise of "neutrality" and the corrupt dealings that led to the country's economic and political collapse. The book is a stark warning for those who think that China's money comes for free.'

Dr David Brewster, senior research fellow, National Security College, Australian National University

'Asanga Abeyagoonasekera is an important voice from the trenches of the fight for liberty, democracy and justice, shining a light on the human cost of authoritarianism and corruption. I encourage everyone to read this book, not just to learn about Chinese influence in Sri Lanka but to acquire a general lesson on the existential importance of fighting to protect democratic values at this time.'

Daniel Sachs, founder, Daniel Sachs Foundation; senior advisor, Chatham House; and global board member, Open Society Foundation (OSF)

'What happened in Sri Lanka? If you want to know what is really going on, this book is one of the best in the world. This book covers both a big picture of US–China–Sri Lanka relations and real experiences in the island state. Therefore, I strongly recommend it.'

Dr Satoru Nagao, fellow (non-resident), Hudson Institute

'In *Teardrop Diplomacy*, Asanga Abeyagoonasekera does a masterful job in outlining China's engagement with Sri Lanka and the resultant impact on regional relations, "great power competition" and the security and economic stability of Sri Lanka itself. This work offers a cogent and balanced view from the Sri Lankan perspective, rightly reminding us of how decisions made can have unintended consequences for years to come. For students and experts on South Asian security and economic relations, this is a valuable and timely source.'

Dr Roger Kangas, dean, Near East South Asia Center for Strategic Studies, US Department of Defense, Washington, DC

'The Indian Ocean is one of the most contested regions in the world today. China, the US and India, and also Japan and Australia among others, are struggling for influence over Sri Lanka. Asanga tackles issues arising from these tussles, which are complex and require a nuanced approach and good judgement to secure Sri Lanka's best interests. The countries involved in the competition for influence in the region are the most powerful in the world [and they] all have significant stakes in promoting their interests at the expense of Sri Lanka's national interest. I congratulate Asanga on the research he has done and the learning he manifests in this book, which fills a lacuna.'

Dr Jehan Perera, executive director,
National Peace Council of Sri Lanka

'In *Teardrop Diplomacy* Asanga Abeyagoonasekera, one of the most perceptive amongst Sri Lanka's international relations experts, traces the geopolitical complexities that this island currently faces. Applying this geopolitical perspective, he incisively explicates Sri Lanka's ongoing politico-economic crisis. Indeed, the book carries an urgent message about how powerful nations can use their economic leverages to achieve their geopolitical objectives, especially so in the lingering post-pandemic precipice. Locating Chinese economic diplomacy and the Belt and Road Initiatives outreach into the Indian Ocean rim in the context of US–China great power rivalry in the Indo-Pacific, it illuminates interesting and evolving trajectories of its impact on Sri Lanka in specific and South Asia in general with clear implications for China's peer competitor, India.'

Dr Swaran Singh, professor of diplomacy and disarmament, Jawaharlal Nehru University, New Delhi, and currently visiting professor, University of British Columbia, Vancouver

'Through the lens of Sri Lanka, this book is a clear warning about how a democratically elected regime turned into an autocracy in a few months. Read it and learn. Democracy is hard to get and easy to lose.'

Lisa Witter, cofounder and CEO, Apolitical Foundation

'Asanga Abeyagoonasekera gives the world an extraordinarily rich geopolitical overview of the Sino-Indo-Pacific region with a very readable balance of historical context, current events and future possibilities.'

Jerome C. Glenn, cofounder and CEO,
The Millennium Project, Washington, DC

'Asanga Abeyagoonasekera is a serious, objective and unconventional analyst of Sri Lanka's strategic affairs. He has knitted an insightful narrative of Sri Lanka's dilemma in coping with the pressures of regional and great powers' competition in the Indo-Pacific region. He makes a valid point that without a credible democracy and stable economy led by honest and competent leadership, the island nation will not be able to remain afloat in the turbulent waters of the Indian Ocean.'

S.D. Muni, professor emeritus, School of International Studies,
Jawaharlal Nehru University, New Delhi, and former ambassador
and special envoy of the Government of India

'Few places in the world capture contemporary global strategic trends more sharply than Sri Lanka. In *Teardrop Diplomacy*, Asanga Abeyagoonasekera delineates the disastrous rise of the strongman rule in Sri Lanka, its intersection with China's power projection into the Indian Ocean and Beijing's rivalry with Delhi and Washington. *Teardrop Diplomacy* is a must-read for all students of the Indo-Pacific.'

C. Raja Mohan, Asia Society Policy Institute, Delhi

# Teardrop Diplomacy

# Teardrop Diplomacy

*China's Sri Lanka Foray*

Asanga Abeyagoonasekera

B L O O M S B U R Y
NEW DELHI • LONDON • OXFORD • NEW YORK • SYDNEY

BLOOMSBURY INDIA
Bloomsbury Publishing India Pvt. Ltd
Second Floor, LSC Building No. 4, DDA Complex, Pocket C – 6 & 7,
Vasant Kunj, New Delhi, 110070

BLOOMSBURY, BLOOMSBURY INDIA and the Diana logo
are trademarks of Bloomsbury Publishing Plc

First published in India 2023
This edition published 2023



ISBN: PB: 978-93-56401-17-4; eBook: 978-93-56401-18-1
2 4 6 8 10 9 7 5 3 1

Typeset in FournierMT by Manipal Technologies Limited
Printed and bound in India Gopsons Paper Pvt.Ltd., Noida

To Amma, my mother

and

To the fearless ordinary citizens
who rallied to change their collective future and to
re-democratise Sri Lanka

CONTENTS

*Acknowledgements* xv
*List of Abbreviations* xvii
*Introduction* xx

1 China in Sri Lanka 1
Sethusamudram to Samudra Manthan: Containing Chinese Influence in Sri Lanka 1
CCP Centenary and the Growing Chinese Footprint in Sri Lanka 6
America and China Dock in Sri Lanka 10
Before the Phoenix Nest: Questions Surrounding the Port City of Colombo 19
How China Won over Local Agency to Shackle Sri Lanka Using a Port City 25
The Rajapaksa Triumvirate and the CCP Backdoor in Sri Lanka 31
Political–Economic Instability and Wang Yi's Peripheral Diplomacy in Sri Lanka 36
Sri Lankan Crisis between Debt Trap and Strategic Trap: The Chinese Stake 41
The Trap: China's Debt Restructuring and Strategic Manipulation in Sri Lanka 47
Chinese Spy Ship and Lanka's Tilt towards Beijing 52
2 Geopolitics 58
Sri Lanka and the Return of Geopolitics in the Indo-Pacific 58
Sri Lanka and the Coming Biden Foreign Policy 63
Sri Lanka Facing the New Cold War in the Indo-Pacific Theatre 68

Joining the Chinese Bandwagon: Geopolitics of a Container Terminal in Sri Lanka 73
Russia and Sri Lanka's Role in Regional Security: Perspective from Sri Lanka 80
AUKUS, the Quad, China in Sri Lanka and India's Security Concerns 90
A World Challenged by Geopolitical Tensions: The Global Risk Report 95
China in Sri Lanka and the Solomon Islands: Role of Littorals in the Geopolitical Competition 98
3 Sri Lanka's Foreign Policy 109
Democracy and Equidistant Foreign Policy in the Majoritarian Government of Mahinda Rajapaksa 109
Perils of Power in Wounded Old Civilizations 113
Pakistan in Sri Lanka's Changing Foreign Policy 118
Sri Lanka's Rejection of the UNHRC Resolution: A Shift towards China? 130
One Country One Law, China Circumventing a Sri Lankan Fertilizer Hazard 135
Political–Economic Turmoil in Sri Lanka: Competing Interests of China and India 139
4 Domestic Political Environment 144
Sri Lanka's Parliamentary Election: International and Security Challenges for the Rajapaksa Government 144
The Coming Anarchy in Sri Lanka 153
Rajapaksa's Dysfunctional Regime in Sri Lanka and Its Impact on South Asia 158
Sri Lanka in Crisis: Repression, Protests and Geopolitical Tensions 163
Sri Lanka in 2021: Trouble Ahead for One of Asia's Oldest Democracies 167
Sri Lankan Economy Spiralling Out of Control: Requests IMF Assistance 173
People's Uprising in Sri Lanka: Sudden Rupture of the

Rajapaksa Regime 176
Economic and Political Crisis in Sri Lanka 180
The Sri Lankan Crisis: The End of the Autocratic Regime 184
5 Security 189
Twenty-Point Analysis of PCoI on Easter Sunday Attack 189
The Lynching of a Sri Lankan in Pakistan: Decluttering Religious Extremism 201
Fighting Economic Crime during the Pandemic: A Sri Lankan Perspective 204
The Wall of Strength against Aggression 212
Information Warfare between Ukraine and Russia 215
Ayman al-Zawahiri's Death and Political–Economic Fragility in South Asia 220

*Annexure 1*: Rajapaksa Family Rule in Sri Lanka 226
*Annexure 2*: Figure Showing the Most Severe Global Risk Factor 228
*Notes* 229
*Index* 289
*About the Author* 297

ACKNOWLEDGEMENTS

First, I must thank all the research think tanks that have given me the space to work and their staff for editing, and the researchers and senior academics who have taken the time to counsel and critique to improve my analysis. I also thank Jerome C. Glenn at the Millennium Project in Washington, D.C.

I thank the Observer Research Foundation (ORF), New Delhi; Millennium Project, Stimson Center, National Defence University NESA and Asia Society Policy Institute, all in Washington, D.C.; ISAS, Singapore; Cambridge University, UK; USAID, Sri Lanka; Social Impact, USA; KAS, Germany; NIICE and COSATT in Nepal; ISDP Sweden; and many other institutes that appreciated my writing and invited me to conduct research and present my work. I am grateful for their continuous support.

I thank senior advisors and government officers from many corners of the world who have recommended my work and allowed me to make presentations on Sri Lanka, Indian Ocean and South Asian political–economic, security and geopolitical challenges, to their government institutes and at research conferences. I also thank all the international media that has featured my work.

I have written this book by gathering information from many academics and practitioners of foreign policy and security studies; I thank them for providing me with valuable and timely insights and material.

I thank Bloomsbury India and Sanjiv Sarin, who copy-edited the book, for all the kind assistance in making this project a success.

Finally, I thank my wife Kumudu, and my two children, Avish and Arya, to whom I owe so much.

# ABBREVIATIONS

| | |
|---|---|
| ADB | Asian Development Bank |
| ASEAN | Association of Southeast Asian Nations |
| AVIC | China National Aero-Technology International Engineering Corporation |
| AUKUS | America, UK and Australia |
| BRI | Belt and Road Initiative |
| BRICS | Brazil, Russia, India, China, South Africa |
| CALMIT | Chinese Aerospace Long-March International Trade |
| CCCC | China Communications Construction Company |
| CCP | Chinese Communist Party |
| CHEC | China Harbour Engineering Company |
| China Exim Bank | Export–Import Bank of China |
| CIABOC | Commission to Investigate Allegations of Bribery or Corruption |
| CICA | Conference on Interaction and Confidence Building Measures in Asia |
| CICT | Colombo International Container Terminals |
| CMEC | China Merchant Engineering Corporation |
| CM Port | China Merchants Port Holdings |
| CNI | Chief of National Intelligence |
| CPA | Centre for Policy Alternatives |
| CPCEC | Colombo Port City Economic Commission |
| DMI | Directorate of Military Intelligence |
| ECT | East Container Terminal in Colombo harbour |

| | |
|---|---|
| EIA | Environmental Impact Assessment |
| FDI | Foreign Direct Investment |
| FOIP | Free and Open Indo-Pacific |
| HADR | Humanitarian Assistance and Disaster Relief |
| IPKF | Indian Peacekeeping Force |
| LTTE | Liberation Tigers of Tamil Eelam |
| MCC | Millennium Challenge Compact |
| MEPA | Marine Environment Pollution Authority |
| MOD | Ministry of Defence |
| NDP | National Defence Policy |
| NSP | National Security Policy |
| NTS | Non-Traditional Security |
| OHCHR | Office of the High Commissioner for Human Rights |
| OECCZ | Overseas Economic and Commercial Cooperation Zone |
| OETCZ | Overseas Economic and Trade Cooperation Zone |
| PCoI | Presidential Commission of Inquiry |
| PEIA | Pre-Environmental Impact Assessment |
| PLAN | People's Liberation Army Navy |
| PPP | Public Private Partnership |
| RCEP | Regional Comprehensive Economic Partnership |
| SAARC | South Asian Association for Regional Cooperation |
| SCO | Shanghai Cooperation Organization |
| SEZ | Special Economic Zone |
| SIS | State Intelligence Service |
| SJB | Samagi Jana Balawegaya |
| SLFP | Sri Lanka Freedom Party |

| | |
|---|---|
| SLOC | Sea Lines of Communication |
| SLPA | Sri Lanka Ports Authority |
| SLPP | Sri Lanka Podujana Peramuna |
| SLT | Sri Lanka Telecom |
| STARR | System, Timeline, Access, Resources, Re-evaluation |
| TRC | Telecommunication Regulatory Commission |
| UNHRC | UN Human Rights Commission |
| UN | United Nations |
| UNP | United National Party |
| US | United States of America |
| USIPR | US-Indo-Pacific Report |
| WCT | West Container Terminal in Colombo Harbour |
| QUAD | Quadrilateral Security Dialogue consisting of US, India, Japan and Australia |

# Introduction

1 October 2022

Sri Lanka, the teardrop-shaped island in the Indian Ocean is facing its worst political–economic crisis since its independence in 1948. In April 2022, thousands of ordinary citizens protested against President Gotabaya Rajapaksa asking him to step down. Mothers, children, youth, farmers, academics, lawyers, government officers and many more joined the protest against the deterioration of the economic conditions in Sri Lanka. On 7 May 2022, Sky News reported that 'Sri Lanka could descend into "anarchy" as it faces the risk of running out of fuel and food in the next month, the country's former energy minister has said . . . President Gotabaya and Prime Minister Mahinda Rajapaksa are accused of nepotism and blamed by many for a crisis that has seen Sri Lanka's usable foreign currency reserves dwindle to less than $50m.'[1] The country moved into an anarchic environment when the regime used brute force to dismantle the protests. The peaceful protests turned violent within hours, and Prime Minister Mahinda Rajapaksa resigned soon after. Two months later, on 9 July, Sri Lankans from all over the island got together at the nation's capital Colombo to join the protest and end the regime of President Gotabaya Rajapaksa. The unarmed protestors broke the military cordon, taking over the president's office and residence, followed by the prime minister's office. President Gotabaya escaped in a military aircraft to the nearby island-nation of the Maldives.

An year earlier, on 29 June 2021, I had written an article 'Coming Anarchy in Sri Lanka', describing the pattern of dysfunctionality of the regime and the dangerous autocratic path President Gotabaya Rajapaksa and the administration had chosen. I left Sri Lanka a few days later with my family since the authoritarian regime targeted many of its critics including me.

For the first time, Sri Lanka, one of the oldest democracies in Asia, had a regime which had siblings with heavy military footprints as heads in more than fifteen sectors, including Foreign Affairs, Economics, Agriculture, Health, Trade and Commerce, Disaster Management, Ports, Aviation and so on.[2] There were numerous extrajudicial arrests and instances of human rights abuse, as reported by UNHRC. One family controlled the entire country under a false pretext of national security, propagating ultra-nationalist sentiments, polarizing the community and building fear over exaggerated risks of losing sovereignty due to Western interference while allowing China to expand its strategic footprint. The US grant, Millennium Challenge Compact (MCC), through Millennium Challenge Corporation, and Indian port terminal projects were terminated under a guise of national security. Rajapaksa's foreign policy was tilted towards China but sometimes preferred to hedge between India and China. During the Covid pandemic, the regime found a favourable environment to further propagate its ultra-nationalist agenda, using constitutional amendments to enhance presidential powers and dismantle independent commissions and the existing checks and balances.

This book examines how a democratically elected regime turned into an autocracy in a few months. The inward looking, ultra-nationalistic policies that resulted in multiple policy blunders costing the nation heavily, leading to protests and a complete breakdown of the state machinery, have been captured in this book. The analysis raises questions such as—What are Sri Lanka's geopolitical challenges? In the context of the growing Chinese influence and the huge Chinese debt, is Sri Lanka in a Chinese strategic trap? Why did Sri Lanka pay the rejected fertilizer shipment from China two days before Chinese Foreign Minister Wang Yi arrived in Colombo? Is Sri Lanka sandwiched between China's Belt and Road (BRI) and the US's Indo-Pacific strategies? Why did the foreign secretary of Sri

Lanka defend China's human rights? Why did the regime, in rapid speed, approve a Chinese special economic, extra-jurisdictional zone in Colombo? Is there a long-term strategy for a Chinese military base operating in Sri Lanka? Is there a growing Chinese influence in strategic islands such as Sri Lanka and the Solomon Islands? What is Sri Lanka's role in the Indo-Pacific and Quad? How does Sri Lanka see Indian foreign policy and its sphere of influence? Why did Pakistan's former prime minister Imran Khan visit Sri Lanka in February 2021? Why were the recommendations of the Presidential Commission of Inquiry (PCoI) on Easter Sunday terror attack rejected by the Sri Lankan Cardinal?

The trust deficit between the public and the political institutions has grown. The high level of corruption, absence of accountability and the protestors' re-democratizing efforts demanding a complete 'system change' in political culture are data points captured in this book. Sri Lanka's political–economic challenges coupled with the foreign policy and the security challenges have also been analysed to present a broader picture and the strategic depth of the individual incidents.

In terms of presentation, this book is a compilation of essays on several themes, from the rise of the Rajapaksa regime in 2019 to the political–economic crisis in 2022. These essays and articles have earlier been published in various magazines and journals. There is some amount of repetition in the book since the articles needed the context to make them complete and several of them have the same context. The chapters frame the nation's journey from a democratic country to a completely autocratic, militarized nation.

This book will help the reader to understand the underlying political and social distress in everyday life in Sri Lanka and what brought this fragile state to this crisis within three years of the Rajapaksa regime coming to power. The crisis in Sri Lanka is a lesson for many developing nations, especially those under debt distress in the post-pandemic environment. I have travelled to many of these nations, from South America, Africa and Central Asia to South East

Asia. All of them are a part of the global big-power rivalry. High geopolitics has a significant impact on their domestic politics.

The US-India-China triangulation and its impact on Sri Lanka are captured in this book, with a unique Sri Lankan perspective. The importance of Sri Lanka to remain and commit to a rules-based international system, adhere to democratic norms and values, address human rights concerns, move forward as a nation along with democratic allies, and the challenges and impediments that remain to progress as a nation are all discussed in this book.

This book aims to identify the multiple policy miscalculations and challenges in the domestic political economy and foreign relations of Sri Lanka.

# I

# China in Sri Lanka

## ONE
## July 2020

### Sethusamudram to Samudra Manthan: Containing Chinese Influence in Sri Lanka[1]

Alfred Dundas Taylor, a civil architect to the Admiralty in the UK, head of the marine survey department, was the first to propose the Sethusamudram Shipping Canal Project in 1860.[2] This canal cuts across the Hindu God Rama's bridge, also known as Rama-Setu. According to Hindu belief, the bridge was built by Lord Rama, connecting the South Indian shore to the western shores of Sri Lanka. The 44.9 nautical-mile long canal would bypass ships navigating Sri Lanka's southern ports, opening up a shorter, continuously navigable sea route around the Indian Peninsula. Due to religious and environmental concerns, the canal dredging was suspended at intervals and has been revived due to political interest. At present, the project's nature has evolved into a geopolitical and security concern about Chinese influence over India's southern shores. A senior leader of the DMK and Lok Sabha member, T.R. Baalu, has written to Prime Minister Narendra Modi to revive the Sethusamudram Project,[3] citing security and geopolitical interests concerning China. The Tamilian politician from South India, mentioning China's huge investments in Sri Lanka, argued that there is a direct threat from the Chinese presence in Sri Lanka and requested the central government to prioritize a solution for this emerging threat to protect the southern part of India. While the Indian subcontinent faced a security threat recently in the northern border with China, now its focus is drawn to protecting the southern shores.

Tamil Nadu's political influence has been a distinct factor in the northern geography throughout Sri Lanka's history. It has usually been the southern shores of Tamil Nadu that have exported considerable threat to Sri Lanka. From the 2019 Easter Sunday bombers, who had a direct contact with a South Indian extremist cluster as discovered by the authorities, to narcotics trafficking and maritime terrorism, there are continuous security threats to the island from South India. But the strong influence of Tamil Nadu on Colombo and New Delhi has usually centred around the Tamilian grievances and not on China. Now the growing Chinese infrastructure diplomacy in the island is interpreted as a security threat to South India. This sort of reaction by the DMK politician could hinder the ongoing India–Sri Lanka bilateral security cooperation.

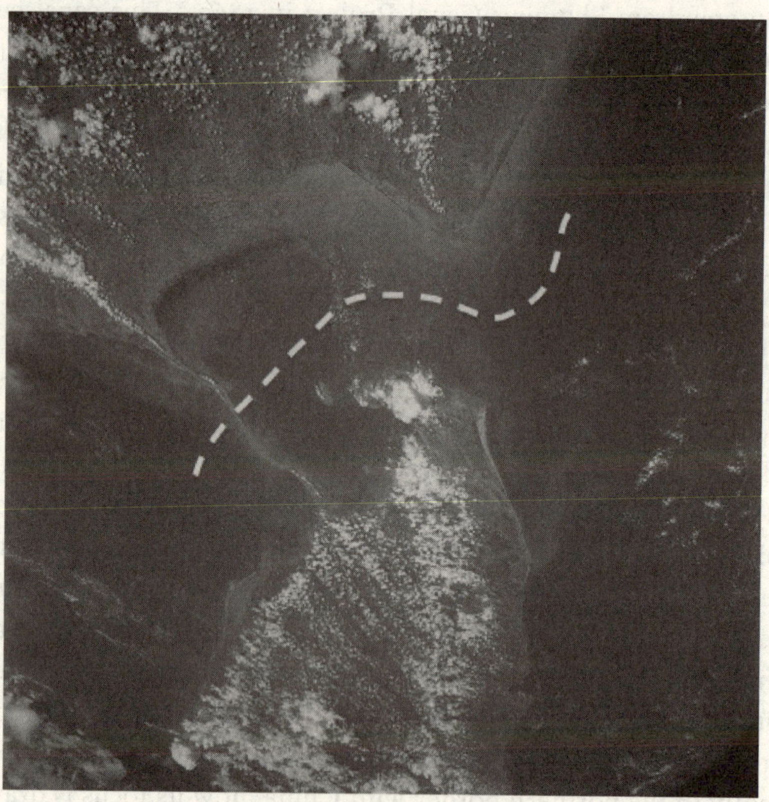

FIGURE 1.1: Proposed Sethusamudram Canal
(Source: Wikimedia Commons)

In the domestic political arena, discussing the importance of the Chinese built and operated southern port of Sri Lanka in Hambantota in an interview, Prime Minister Mahinda Rajapaksa's son Namal, who represents his father's previous constituency since 2010, explained, 'Hambantota will become the next commercial city in the island with highways, strategic port, international airport and all the logistics ready, we will make this happen.'[4] Namal Rajapaksa's long-term view is to continue where his father has left off, converting Hambantota into a modern city under his leadership, perceived as a difficult and unachievable task by many in Colombo.

When looking at the massive Chinese infrastructure diplomacy carried out at the two global connection hubs, the Hambantota port and Mattala airport, along with other ancillary infrastructure including an international convention centre, cricket stadium, highways, hotels and much more to come, this strategy of the next commercial city in the deep south could perhaps be achieved with Rajapaksa's leadership. The years of discourse about the political–economic history of the nation led to the shift of the western province dominated economic gravity towards the outer regions. Namal Rajapaksa has taken up this challenging task in his tenth year of political office. The political history of Sri Lanka is such that even the first prime minister, D.S. Senanayake, left his political legacy to his son Dudley Senanayake to continue at the age of 41 in 1952. While the context is different, the patterns could continue in the Sri Lankan political culture.

## STRATEGIC ALIGNMENTS TO THE QUAD

In the larger ocean space, the US is moving more of its military assets towards the Indo-Pacific. USS *Nimitz*, the largest of its aircraft carrier warships, arrived in the Indian Ocean for a passing exercise (PASSEX) with the Indian Navy off the coast of Andaman and Nicobar Islands in July 2020.[5] Together with USS *Nimitz*, two other US aircraft carriers were in the region, USS *Theodore Roosevelt* and USS *Ronald Regan*, to counter the People's Liberation Army Navy (PLAN). There is a triangular power projection in the Indian Ocean from the US, India and China, which is more prone to conflict as the US allies formed a NATO-like military alignments to contain China. In an interview in July 2020, Indian Minister of External Affairs Dr S. Jaishankar explained, 'The rise of China has impacted the entire world; more than any other nation, it has impacted its neighbour, India. China's significant growth is felt and understood by India.'[6]

The trilateral naval exercise could expand to a quadrilateral, bringing the Australian Navy along with that of India, US and Japan for the first time. This would push India towards a security tension with China as it is already negotiating its northern border dispute with it. India, at the same time, will bring Australia to engage in a wider containment strategy in the Indian Ocean. The quadrilateral exercise will be seen by China as a thinly disguised strategy of containment. The consequence was rightly assessed by analyst Abhijit Singh, who said, 'India should be cautious to such quadrilateral engagement without a cost–benefit exercise and commensurate gains in the strategic–operational realm. Further, this exercise could be ineffective in the long term.'[7]

The tense Indo-Pacific region provides a possible *casus belli* if containment of China intensifies. China may employ its newfound muscle to forcefully impose its will to resist even modest aggression in the region by the US. After four decades, there is a downward spiral in the relationship between US and China, escalating to the level of closing down the Chinese consulate in Houston. The US, for its part, will not abandon its allies who are opposed to Chinese expansion in the Indo-Pacific. In a recent statement, Chinese Foreign Minister Wang Yi said, 'Unilateralism and bullying are forcing their way in the world. An international disorder is more possible than ever.'[8] While the forces for contention remain, as explained by Minister Wang Yi, it is important to explore possible strategic space to minimize the tension.

China is already in the Indian Ocean, which is far away from its traditional ocean space. India has looked beyond Aden and Malacca choke points and has begun to make naval forays into the Pacific

Ocean, rightly assessed by C. Raja Mohan in his book *Samudra Manthan* (Churning of the Ocean).[9] Maritime strategic expansion requires allies and littorals who are strategically located. Sri Lanka was mapped by Beijing's strategic circle to facilitate the Chinese expansion in the Indian Ocean. In the same way, India is developing Australia and Japan as its close maritime partners to expand its presence in the Pacific Ocean. Military logistics agreements and military exercises are initial steps to cement these strategic alignments.

## US AGREEMENTS, ECT AND MATTALA AIRPORT

Sri Lanka has two important agreements with the US—the Status of Forces Agreement (SOFA) and the Millennium Challenge Compact (MCC) grant held up at the policy level in Sri Lanka. President Gotabaya Rajapaksa's expert panel, which reviewed the MCC agreement, released its conclusions to the public on 25 June 2020, at the height of the parliamentary elections. The review committee headed by Dr L. Gunaruwan drew the attention of the president towards examples of many other nations which had implemented the MCC and their economies had turned to worse after implementation.[10] According to Dr Gunaruwan, the report was compiled professionally and independently.[11] On page 10, the committee observed that a comprehensive analysis of the MCC was not presented by any authority in the past. Although the Institute of National Security Studies (INSS) under the Ministry of Defence has submitted a report of observations in 2019, but it was not made officially available to the committee. This was unfortunate and questions were asked as to why it was not made available. The US agreements will be on hold for some time due to domestic nationalist political constraints.

In another development, the Indian-led tripartite memorandum, along with Japanese and Sri Lankan governments, to develop Colombo Port's Eastern Container Terminal (ECT) is under review, and the Chinese-built international airport in Mattala, a proposed joint venture with India announced during the previous 2015–2019 regime, is held up. The new developments could be misconstrued as a pro-China position taken by the government, drifting away from Sri Lanka's balanced foreign policy. Amidst the radical alteration of the maritime environment through Samudra Manthan by the three powers—US, India and China—in the Indo-Pacific, the collective developments in Sri Lanka could signal the return of Chinese influence with a much stronger footprint in the new Gotabaya Rajapaksa regime.

# TWO
## January 2021

### CCP Centenary and the Growing Chinese Footprint in Sri Lanka[12]

The Middle Kingdom, as China was known in ancient times, played a global leadership role by creating a tributary system where nations like Sri Lanka paid tribute to it. China is far from that position today. Now, with its position in global multilateral institutions, it is playing a 'nation-state' role with its civilizational footprint. China would need to invest more in building trust, respecting diverse political models and following international norms and values.

The strategic neck of water that connects the Indian Ocean to the Pacific will be a highly contested area where China secures its energy-supply route. The suspected Chinese unmanned underwater vehicle (UUV) submarine drones found in these waters shows the significant investment China makes in undersea surveillance.[13]

Geopolitical fissures between India and China have further worsened as explained by Jagannath Panda,[14] 'China's desire to restrict India as a regional power has been further exacerbated by the latter's vocal criticisms of Xi's Belt and Road Initiative (BRI) and New Delhi's shift to an active foreign policy, which has seen it deepening partnerships with the US and other Indo-Pacific powers.'[15] The US strategic thinking on India's role in the region was published in a declassified US-Indo-Pacific report highlighting India as the primary regional counterweight to China and to deter Chinese 'predatory economic practices that freeze out foreign competition . . . [from] abet[ing] Chinese Communist Party (CCP) aspirations to dominate 21st century economy.'[16] India's closest neighbour, Sri Lanka, has been a point of reference in both these factors.

## US RALLYING DEMOCRACIES AND CCP CENTENARY

President Biden selected Jake Sullivan as his National Security Advisor (NSA). Sullivan is one of the youngest to serve in this position. Sullivan was quick to identify a present limitation of the US foreign policy, which was to ignore its allies whilst the 'US has gone alone in its trade fight with China.'[17] The new NSA has rightly identified the importance of 'rallying other like-minded democracies' to exert pressure on China rather than fight alone. For Biden, it is not too late to make up for the previous missed opportunities and build strong alliances with democracies. The NSA clearly says, 'It falls to the US to lead the way. No other nation has that capacity. No other nation is built on that idea.'[18]

In 2021, the CCP will celebrate its centenary and exhibit its achievements, especially on the economic front. The CCP, with its Leninist political structure, has not only influenced China from within but has also influenced several other developing nations who are hooked to its grand infrastructure strategy through the BRI, injecting development reforms in democratic nations. The China Reform Forum (CRF), an academic research institute affiliated to the Party School of the Central Committee of the Communist Party, is busy making inroads in Sri Lanka through Rajapaksa's political party SLPP[19] and with a local think tank advising the regime.[20] The local strategic circle being influenced to appreciate an alternative model to democracy will have a dangerous impact, particularly when it comes to upholding liberal democratic values and principles.

### *COLONIAL TO CHINESE INFRASTRUCTURE IN SRI LANKA*

One of the important accomplishments of the British Empire was the infrastructure it built. In 1820, five years after the British captured the Kandyan Kingdom in what was then called Ceylon (now Sri Lanka), commenced the challenging engineering task of constructing a road from the hills in the heartlands to coastal Colombo. Captain William Francis Dawson from the colonial Royal Engineers headed the project. He did not live to see the completion of Sri Lanka's first road network from Colombo to Kandy, an engineering marvel. The road was beneficial for accelerating trade logistics of coffee and tea, which were exported to the Empire. The road infrastructure also secured the Kandyan Kingdom, which until then was isolated from the coastal belt.

Now two centuries later, China is changing the Sri Lankan geography by adding highways, bridges, ports and airports; it is also reclaiming land through its Port City Development Project in the commercial capital of Colombo. The infrastructure development is tangible and visible to the locals in the rural areas as well as to the urban middle class. Several middle-class Sri Lankans are already engaged in subcontracts for providing material, importing it from China and selling it to the Chinese firms executing the projects here. The win–win situation has promoted China's image with the Sri Lankans and made it the country's largest trading partner.

The China Metallurgical Group Corporation has undertaken construction of a part of the central expressway from Colombo to Kandy at a value of US$1.164 billion.[21] This will be the third expressway the company will build in Sri Lanka. While China has massive development infrastructure projects within the country, other nations and schemes have limitations, such as the US MCC, which was highly politicized by a local committee, which might have misled the policymakers. Eventually, the nation lost the US$480 million grant to improve its transport and logistics infrastructure 'due to lack of partner country engagement'.[22] Similarly, the Colombo East Container Terminal (ECT), which involves India and Japan, has been held up and is under review. This terminal will operate adjacent to the Chinese-managed terminal, Colombo International Container Terminal (CICT).

Indian Foreign Minister Dr S. Jaishankar, who on his first foreign visit of the year 2021 arrived in Sri Lanka, highlighted the importance of commencement of some of the Indian projects, referring to the ECT, which was reported clearly in local media as, 'New Delhi's concerns that China was guiding the narrative . . . worried that the rhetoric around the ECT initiative was promoted by Chinese Intelligence, with the objective of having it blocked.'[23] Dr Jaishankar's assessment is correct about the blocking of ECT. The block is from Sri Lankan policymakers due to the China-tilt in Sri Lankan foreign policy. This is due to Sri Lanka's weak foreign policy stance regarding its strategic choices, where there is an irrational revisiting of past decisions to satisfy external powers such as China, limiting its strategic decision space. While Sri Lankan foreign policy has a deepening partnership with China and BRI promoted by it as opposed to the Indo-Pacific, foreign policy analysis has fallen into the psychological trap of 'false binaries'[24]—a clear miscalculation by the Sri Lankan regime's foreign policy establishment. The false binary, as explained by Singaporean diplomat Bilahari Kausikan and captured in Rory Medcalf's book, is the insistence that everything boils down to choosing between China as the future and US as the past.[25] Sri Lanka could explore and benefit more from close ties with the middle powers such as Australia, South Korea, Vietnam, Indonesia, Singapore, South Africa, UAE and several EU nations, rather than making most foreign policy decisions on binaries.

## UNHRC AND TAMILIAN GRIEVANCES

Unlike China, India has a much broader engagement with Sri Lanka, not limited only to infrastructure. India's concern about Tamilian grievances and their resolution not being adequately addressed was raised by Dr Jaishankar, mentioning the thirteenth amendment on the devolution of power in his official statement.[26] Sri Lanka has to face the UNHRC session in March 2021 and India will have elections in the state of Tamil Nadu then, a concern for New Delhi. Dr Jaishankar's statement bringing forth this disquiet about the long-delayed implementation and the state of Tamilian grievances a little before the UNHRC session, comes at the right time, as it can be seen to be a gesture to increase the pressure on Sri Lanka as it approaches the March UNHRC session.

Just a few days after Jaishankar's visit, the overnight removal of a Tamil war memorial in Jaffna University turned out to be diametrically opposite to the stated government desire to find space for and accomplish genuine reconciliation.[27] The accumulated load of Tamilian grievances will bring a huge pressure on India–Sri Lanka relations. C. Raja Mohan argues, 'India can encourage, but can't really force Colombo'[28]; but India will be pressurized to take the latter position due to repeated failure of Sri Lankan domestic policies. The Sri Lankan government should address the pressing issues of Tamilian grievances in a more humane and genuine manner, recalibrate its foreign policy and guard the values of democracy. The alternative will make it a cliche par excellence of a gradual democratic dysfunction in the coming years.

## THREE
## January 2021

### America and China Dock in Sri Lanka[29]

A week before the United States presidential election, US Secretary of State Mike Pompeo arrived in Sri Lanka to meet President Gotabaya Rajapaksa. Pompeo then told Gotabaya that '[t]he United States wishes to see the Indian Ocean remain a zone of peace'.[30] Sri Lanka's role as an enabler of 'Indian Ocean Zone for Peace' commenced in the 1970s as a part of Prime Minister Sirimavo Bandaranaike's non-aligned foreign policy vision. One of the significant areas where the littoral nation left a long-lasting imprint in international law was in its work on the United Nations Convention on the Law of the Sea (UNCLOS).

In his joint statement with Pompeo, Sri Lanka's Foreign Minister Dinesh Gunawardena highlighted this singular achievement and Sri Lanka's continuous commitment towards the norms and principles of the UNCLOS.

Sri Lanka has been a strong strategic partner of China's BRI since its inception. The sizeable volume of loans for infrastructure development projects has elevated and strengthened the Sino-Lanka relationship, especially with the Rajapaksas (Gotabaya and Mahinda) in power. The island-nation is sandwiched between China's BRI and the US's Indo-Pacific strategy. Colombo has preferred to continuously hedge its position to satisfy both, while rhetorically amplifying a 'neutral' and 'non-aligned' policy. Let us analyse the security aspirations of US and China in Sri Lanka and examine some pivotal security and foreign policy challenges for the Gotabaya regime.

The German geopolitical thinker Karl Haushofer first defined the confluence of the two marine bodies, the Indian ocean and the Pacific Ocean, in 1920, with the academic reference 'Indopazifischer Raum' (Indo-Pacific Space).[31] The term 'Indo-Pacific' gained prevalence in geopolitical discourse after Japanese Prime Minister Shinzo Abe's speech to the Indian Parliament in August 2007. With a rising China, American strategic planners over the next several years will not ignore the significance of the Indian Ocean and its littorals—Sri Lanka being a key geostrategic location in this equation.

The security aspirations of US and China have grown in the Indian Ocean region. The US, with its Indo-Pacific, and China, with its BRI, are two strategies accepted by Sri Lanka. A heightened Cold War has been visible between the US and Chinese diplomats in Colombo. In October 2020, the US warned of a binary choice in opting for a more democratic path over autocracy.[32] The Chinese embassy swiftly responded, stating it was 'busy promoting China–Sri

Lanka friendship and cooperation' and that it was 'not interested in [the US's] alien versus predator game invitation'. It added that the US 'can play two roles at the same time as always'.[33] This Cold War will continue as the US-China tension in the global arena persists with the next US administration.

Pompeo's visit to Sri Lanka, the Maldives and India in late October 2020 could be understood in geopolitical terms, taking into consideration the priorities of the superpower. The consistent US strategic interests in the Indo-Pacific and the regional power, India, will remain when the leadership changes from Donald Trump to Joe Biden. India is departing from its old 'Indira Doctrine', whose principles were to not allow foreign powers within its vicinity, akin to the US's 'Monroe Doctrine'. Strong US-India bilateral collaborations, from military to economic diplomacy, built in the recent years, will have a direct effect on its foreign policy posture in the region. India's power vortex will further increase with the Quadrilateral partnership (Quad) and continuous US support, converting a relationship based on quid pro quo to one based on strategic partnership.[19]

Indo-US strategic security ties have been strengthened with multiple military agreements, such as the Basic Exchange of Communication Agreement (BECA), an important defence pact signed in October 2020. This is in addition to two other previously signed security agreements—the Communications Compatibility and Security Agreement and Logistics Exchange Memorandum of Agreement. The BECA, a much-discussed agreement for several years due to India's sensitivity to geographical information, had also received impetus on being seen as a priority after the India-China face-off in the Western Himalayas. The US also strengthened its defence ties with the Maldives by signing the SOFA,[34] which was concluded with the support of India.

India, with its multiple defence agreements, now has a strong strategic relationship with the US, unlike Sri Lanka, which has frozen several US agreements, including the SOFA. While the US focuses on strategic-level security collaboration with India and the Maldives, Beijing has identified a containment strategy to keep the footprint of US out of the region, including from Sri Lanka.

## BILATERAL MILITARY RELATIONS: THE US AND CHINA IN SRI LANKA

To support the security aspirations of the US and China in Sri Lanka's waters, both nations have donated two patrol vessels. The US Navy donated high endurance cutters, earlier used by their Coast Guard, through the Excess Defense Articles Program while China gifted a P625 frigate,[35] which is used for offshore patrol and anti-piracy combat operations in the Sri Lankan waters. Sri Lanka has taken benefits from both the US and China and strengthened its navy.

The burgeoning relations with US and China focus primarily on maritime cooperation to promote their larger strategies of the Indo-Pacific and the BRI. Sri Lanka, as a strategic littoral, has received many US Navy and People's Liberation Army Navy (PLA Navy) port calls and maritime assistance. The PLA Navy submarine visits to Colombo, however, became a security concern for New Delhi during the last stage of the Mahinda presidency in 2014. According to Brahma Chellaney, 'Rajapaksa could have made serious miscalculations in challenging India's interests' by inviting Chinese submarines, threatening India–Sri Lanka security relations despite India's National Security Advisor (NSA) Ajit Doval's warning to the Sri Lankan Defence Secretary Gotabaya that any presence of a Chinese submarine in Sri Lanka would be unacceptable to India.[36] Due to the strong Sino-Lanka strategic ties during the Rajapaksa regime, the warning from New Delhi was ignored. Another policy decision by President Maithripala Sirisena's regime—the handing over of the Hambantota port to China on a ninety-nine-year lease—became a security concern to India, the West and their allies due to China's military ambitions in the Indian Ocean.

## SRI LANKA'S NEUTRAL FOREIGN POLICY

Gotabaya articulated a 'neutral' and 'non-aligned' foreign policy.[37] Stemming from Jawaharlal Nehru and Bandaranaike's commitment to a policy of non-alignment during the Cold War, both India and Sri Lanka took the moral high ground to stress 'non-interference' in their foreign policy imperatives. In recent years, India and Sri Lanka, in their rhetorical acceptance and belief in non-alignment, have used the principles of Chanakya (King Ashoka's prime minister and strategist) to maximize their gains through cooperation with extra-regional powers. India's security relationship with the US and Sri Lanka's strategic partnership with China during Mahinda's presidency during 2005–2015 (which is continued by his brother, Gotabaya) are examples of a realist foreign policy at play, as opposed to a non-aligned or neutral policy.

The Rajapaksa administrations have shown clear indications of a tilt towards China rather than the US. This is due to two factors—China's steady and large financial assistance and its assurance to support Sri Lanka at the United Nations Human Rights Council (UNHRC). Three days before Pompeo's visit, Sri Lanka's Foreign Secretary Admiral Jayanath Colombage altered his foreign policy position from 'India first'[38] to 'Sri Lanka first',[39] while Gotabaya tweeted from his official Twitter account about his 'neutral foreign policy' position amidst the great power rivalry.[40] The foreign secretary reiterated that Sri Lanka was a 'neutral' and 'non-aligned' country. He said, 'We don't want to be caught up in this power game',[41] during the visit of a Chinese high-level delegation headed by Yang Jiechi, weeks before Pompeo's visit.

The statements revealed Sri Lanka's hedging strategy despite the rhetoric of neutrality and a non-aligned foreign policy. Hedging has worked well for Sri Lanka as a secondary strategy, but it weakens the country's credibility by failing to articulate a clear foreign policy position. It also fails in building strong partnerships by gaining the trust of the global powers. The new regime will be obliged to defend the foreign policy of being neutral and refrain from taking actions which will question or compromise its neutrality. Sri Lanka's commitment to its UNCLOS position on China in the South China Sea; the UNHRC co-sponsored resolution and the reconciliation process; the rule of law and democracy; its relationship with the state, minorities and the diaspora; and its contribution to a rules-based order in the Indian Ocean are some pertinent commitments that it should engage in and voice in its foreign policy.

The Sri Lankan foreign policy establishment continues to refer to the outdated non-aligned policy due to its past success in steering the country away from big power rivalry during the Cold War. This is stated even by the present regime, although there is no clear correlation between its foreign policy and the actual practice of neutrality. Sri Lanka's neighbour, India, successfully managed to transition from the past non-aligned to a broad power-realist vision.[42] It established strong partnerships with external powers for the benefit of its economy. In the same manner, Sri Lanka needs to reset its strategic outlook by maximizing its options in the long run by picking strong strategic relationships in the short term and expressing a clear, realist foreign policy.

## SRI LANKA'S COMMITMENT TO A RULES-BASED ORDER

A three-directional power projection by China, US and India is taking place in Sri Lanka's maritime domain. Sri Lanka should anchor itself to its past commitments of establishing a rules-based order in the Indian Ocean and beyond. Its earlier contribution at the UNCLOS and commitment to preserving the Law of the Sea are strong steps in the right direction to navigate its foreign policy. The past foreign policy positions and achievements of a nation cannot be easily discarded. Sri Lanka's initiative which formulated the piece of legislation advocating the importance of a rules-based maritime order and continued commitment to UNCLOS is a convenient, beneficial and tactful strategy to adopt to balance the three-sided pressure from China, India and US.

Just like Singapore, Sri Lanka should also use UN and multilateral institutions to create a balance while furthering its own interests.[43]

Sri Lanka should anchor itself to its past commitments of establishing a rules-based order in the Indian Ocean and beyond.

Engagement with the regional security architecture and voicing concerns along with the twenty-one members of the Indian Ocean Rim Association should be the highest priority for Sri Lanka. Sri Lankan policymakers often quote Singapore as a shining example of a country which fulfils its commitments to the UNCLOS and also maintains its position on the South China Sea. Like Singapore, Sri Lanka should also widely participate in multilateral institutions. George Yeo, Singapore's former foreign minister explains, 'As a small country, Singapore is very reliant on multilateral institutions for its political and economic well-being.'[44] Singapore has adhered to the values of the UNCLOS by not taking China's side while still managing its bilateral trade relationship with Beijing. It has assisted China to transition from its past and embrace an open economic policy. Singapore even managed to train its armed forces in Taiwan and sign trade agreements with the latter without upsetting its relations with China. Sri Lanka should emulate this approach and work with both sides of the binary divide, but at the same time strongly articulate and protect its democratic and liberal values and recognize its achievements, rather than passively freeze one agreement after another. The Sri Lanka–Singapore free trade agreement (FTA) was one such opportunity, which is now inactive after having been, unfortunately, politicized by alt-right ultra-nationalists.[45]

## CHINESE LOANS, SECURITY CONCERNS AND CHINA TILT

An economic crisis, years in the making due to Sri Lanka's high debt obligations, has crippled the country's economy. China has been to the nation's rescue with multiple loans, which are questioned due to their opaqueness. With a downgraded 2020 credit rating and reduction of tourist arrivals after the Easter Sunday bombing in 2019, followed by the Covid-19 pandemic, the island-nation will be strained in fiscal debt management in the coming years. A further loan of US$500 million was pledged and accepted after Yang visited Sri Lanka. There is a trend of departure from more structural loans, such as those from the International Monetary Fund (IMF), towards China, which come without spending or end-use conditions. Sri Lanka's limitation to practise a neutral foreign policy is due to its weak domestic economic position and its heavy dependence on China, which has raised concerns of 'predatory loans' or a 'debt trap'.

This further threatens the security of the regional power, India. New Delhi's strategic autonomy and China's encroachment on its regional primacy are concerns for India. The US sees India as a strong strategic and security partner in the Indo-Pacific. Further, as stated by Anja Manuel, 'Only a strong, confident India can take a more prominent diplomatic and, if necessary, military role in the world. A strong India can help moderate China's more extreme international behaviour, for example, by pushing back on China's encroachment into the Indian Ocean.'[46]

Indian scholar Srikanth Kondapalli describes this encroachment as, 'A large-scale encirclement design by Beijing, which is actively roping in Nepal and Sri Lanka, besides provoking Pakistan to open a second front against India.'[47] The failure of the Sri Lankan foreign policy apparatus to assess this important factor of China's actions in South Asia will become a heightened security issue in India–Sri Lanka relations. Accurately projected by India's former national security advisor Shivshankar Menon, the Chinese desire to be involved directly or indirectly in the internal politics of the South Asian countries is reflected in its clear expression of preference for one particular candidate in the Sri Lankan elections.[48]

By only being neutral rhetorically in its foreign policy posture and allowing China to make inroads, Sri Lanka's relationship with India and the Western countries will deteriorate. Already, the present government's tilt towards China, witnessed in political discussions between Sri Lanka's ruling party, the Sri Lanka Podujana Peramuna

(SLPP), and the Communist Party of China (CCP)[49]; a review of India, Japan and Sri Lanka tri-party ECT; suspension of Japan's Light Rail project; and freezing of US MCC grant and the SOFA have raised serious concerns in Western quarters.

## THE NEW US REGIME AND SRI LANKA'S UNHRC RESOLUTION

There are hopes that Biden will end tribalism and the US's isolationist position followed at multilateral forums and restore the US's liberal footprint around the world. There are discussions in political circles in Colombo of a possible revival of UNHRC pressure on Sri Lanka with a US co-sponsored resolution. Sri Lanka's withdrawal from the resolution by the Gotabaya regime will take a difficult turn under Biden's leadership. There could be a possible rise in the Tamilian diaspora grievances, especially after the election of Vice President Kamala Harris, who is of Tamil descent. Harris has even stressed placing human rights at the centre of her approach to India on Kashmir.[50] She is more likely to revisit and support the long-ignored Tamilian grievances at the UNHRC. The continuous failure of the government in Colombo to devise a genuine reconciliation process and a political solution with devolution of power could transform and brew into another security issue domestically in Sri Lankan society. This itself is a priority for New Delhi, which has already raised concerns regarding the Rajapaksas' silence on the agenda of devolution of power. Sri Lanka's minister in charge of provincial councils has opposed the devolution of power, thereby giving it little hope of success.[51] While China would back Sri Lanka at the UNHRC, the US, along with India, could put pressure on Sri Lanka on Tamilian grievances.

The security aspirations of the US and China in Sri Lanka are heightened by the larger geopolitical strategies at play, such as the Indo-Pacific and BRI. Sri Lanka's neutral foreign policy under Gotabaya is key to balancing pressures from the US and China, but it prefers to hedge and seems to limit its neutrality to rhetoric.

Sri Lanka requires a more realistic approach, like its neighbour, India. The alt-right, ultra-nationalist political elements have a tight grip on government policy, which would shift the nation towards semi-autocracy and malign mercantilist economic policies. Some of these policies have a correspondingly strong tendency to pull Colombo towards China. This could, however, reduce Sri Lanka's democratic footprint and ability to practise a 'neutral' foreign policy. Sri Lanka's departure from the secular space will shrink many opportunities with the new US administration. The nation should gather its principal values from its past and move towards a realistic foreign policy posture, addressing its challenges and securing its democratic values.

## FOUR
## May 2021

### Before the Phoenix Nest: Questions Surrounding the Port City of Colombo[52]

Sri Lanka is in a quandary. Its present government has approved China's extra-jurisdictional Special Economic Zone (SEZ) in Colombo Port City, right next to its commercial port. The Colombo Port City illustrates how China has rapidly gained an economic foothold in many nations entangled in the BRI. SEZ or Overseas Economic and Commercial Cooperation Zones (OECCZ) are the *primum principium* of 'building a nest to accommodate the phoenix', according to Lin Yifu, chief economist and former senior vice president of the World Bank.[53] It was Lin Yifu who convinced former Ethiopian president Meles Zenawi and submitted a report to Omar Guelleh, the president of Djibouti to follow the OECCZ model.[54] Have all these Chinese OECCZ in Africa and elsewhere considered the host countries' needs? The twenty zones already established (Table 1.1) raise a question about the extent of their contribution to the host nation.

TABLE 1.1: The Twenty OECCZs and Their Dates of Certification

| | |
|---|---|
| Sihanoukville Special Economic Zone (Cambodia) | 2006 |
| Thai-Chinese Rayong Industrial Zone (Thailand) | 2006 |
| Haier-Ruba Economic Zone (Pakistan) | 2006 |
| Zambia-China Economic & Trade Zone (Zambia) | 2006 |
| Lekki Free Trade Zone (Nigeria) | 2006 |
| Longjiang Industrial Park (Vietnam) | 2007 |
| China-Egypt TEDA Suez Economic and Trade Cooperation Zone (Egypt) | 2007 |
| Russia Ussuriisk Economic & Trade Cooperation Zone (Russia) | 2007 |
| China-Russia Tomsk Wood Industry & Trade Cooperation Zone (Russia) | 2007 |
| Eastern Industry Zone (Ethiopia) | 2007 |
| Kawasan Industry Terpadu Indonesia China (Indonesia) | 2007 |
| Peng Sheng Development Zone (Uzbekistan) | 2009 |
| China-Russian Modern Agriculture Industrial Cooperation Zone (Russia) | 2010 |
| Asia Star Agricultural Industry Cooperation Zone (Kyrgyzstan) | 2011 |
| Sino-Hungarian Borsod Industrial Park (Hungary) | 2011 |
| Central European Trade and Logistics Cooperation (Hungary) | 2012 |
| Vientiane Saysettha Development Zone (Laos) | 2012 |
| Russia Longyue Forestry Economic & Trade Cooperation Zone (Russia) | 2013 |
| Indonesia Morowali Industrial Park (Indonesia) | 2013 |
| China-Indonesia Julong Agricultural Industry Cooperation Zone (Indonesia) | 2016 |

Source: MOFCOM at http://fee.mofcom.gov.cn/article/jwjmhzq/article01.shtml

## COLOMBO PORT CITY

'This is a new PPP model, this is not a Chinese project, this is an international project, we will have international developers, we are willing for a joint venture with Indian and US companies,' said Houliang Jiang, managing director of Colombo Port City, who was interviewed by this author on 22 February 2019. During the interview, the biggest concern raised by Houliang was the delay of the government, 'Government is far behind, we are ahead of schedule . . . the government have not given land title and no favourable investment climate . . . we provide the world-class infrastructure the "Hardware" part, but the "Software" part, the policy part, is missing, so how to do this project?' Unlike the previous regime, the Rajapaksa administration approved the missing 'software' component from the Port City Bill on 23 March. A backchannel was in motion taking the bill forward during the Sinhalese and Tamil New Year's Day.

Member of Parliament from the government, Wijeyadasa Rajapaksa, accused the government of creating a 'Chinese colony and foreigners can acquire that land and sell it'.[55] Explaining further, he said that though the former government had given the Chinese-built Hambantota port on lease for ninety-nine years, but handing over the Port City to China through an Act would be more dangerous than the Hambantota port lease. Twenty petitions were filed in the Supreme Court by all major opposition parties and civil society activists challenging the constitutionality of the Port City Bill due to its threat to Sri Lanka's sovereignty. Ikram Mohammed PC, who appeared for the president of the Bar Association of Sri Lanka (BASL) argued that the Colombo Port City Bill 'paves the way for the creation of a federal state'.[56] Does the bill transfer presidential powers to an unknown commission to bypass the country's financial regulations? There are vital and relevant questions raised by the petitioners. The Port City Bill would facilitate setting up of Sri Lanka's first OECCZ with special jurisdictional rights, separate from existing laws. This unique Chinese model has been introduced in many other nations to create jobs and foreign investment as a 'nest to attract the phoenix'.

Rajapaksa's political party (SLPP) supported trade unions had earlier rejected development projects such as the US MCC grant of US$480 million and the recent swapping of ECT to WCT, projected as a threat to the sovereignty of Sri Lanka, playing to their voter base with high nationalist sentiments. The same administration does not see any threat to the island's sovereignty from the Chinese port city. This is a clear indication of Rajapaksa's China-tilted foreign policy.[57]

There are several reasons for this China tilt. First, high-level diplomatic visits reaffirming the success of the Chinese political model during the CCP centenary—the October 2020 visit of

Senior Ambassador Yang Jiechi, followed by China's Minister of Defence PLAN, General Wei Fenghe's visit this April—strengthened Sino-Lanka diplomatic and security relationship. Second, China's open UNHRC support to the Rajapaksa regime. Third, China's vaccine diplomacy in Sri Lanka—as the Chinese Ambassador in Colombo, Qi Zhenhong said, '[Let] Sri Lanka and China build a great wall of vaccines.'[58] Fourth, the recent loans of US$1 billion as well as the US$1.5 billion currency swap where Sri Lanka, a weaker economy, is already shackled by a heavy Chinese economic grip. These incremental shifts in the Sino-Lanka relationship have increased the Chinese sphere of influence under the Rajapaksa regime.

The importance of the Colombo Port City project was discussed between President Gotabaya and President Xi during their last telephone conversation. China will use Sri Lanka's inner politico–social weakness, such as inadequate addressal of human rights concerns, to its advantage as it has no concerns in this regard. While China pushes its BRI agenda, the 'pull factor' from the Gotabaya Rajapaksa regime is positive and welcoming. The same pull factor of inviting China was seen during the Mahinda Rajapaksa era when the Colombo Port City was inaugurated in 2014. The Sri Lankan strategic community would need to do a deep study and assess the long-term strategic implications from the new Chinese PPP (public private partnership) model since Colombo Port City development exceeds more than twenty-five years. A comparative case to Colombo Port City is Djibouti, and both nations welcome the Chinese model.

## DJIBOUTI SEZ

Geostrategically well-situated like Sri Lanka is the Horn of Africa on the Gulf of Aden and the Bab-el-Mandeb at the southern entrance to the Red Sea in Djibouti. The 23,200 square kilometre nation has already become a Chinese colony. What attracted the Chinese was Djibouti's geography. China's large-scale infrastructure development connected the country to neighbouring landlocked

Ethiopia. Africa's first fully-electrified transnational railway stretched 752 km, from Addis Ababa to Djibouti port.[59] Multiple loan packages allowed China to extend its sphere of influence and shackle Djibouti's economy, keeping it firmly in Beijing's grip. Import dependent, its service sector, including logistics and transhipment, is more than 70 per cent of its economy. The country has become a lucrative new market for Chinese exports.

One clear ingredient in the Sino-Djibouti cooperation projects in the Horn of Africa is the Chinese SEZ. China has helped launch a pilot zone as a part of the first phase of Africa's biggest free-trade zone—Djibouti International Free Trade Zone (DIFTZ), a US$3.5 billion project that spans an area of 4,800 hectares.[60] The US$370 million, 240-hectare pilot zone is led by a global alliance including Djibouti Ports and Free Zones Authority (DPFZA), China Merchants Group, Dalian Port Authority and the IZP group. The DPFZA already offers 100 per cent foreign ownership, full exemption from direct and indirect taxes, 100 per cent repatriation of capital and profits, no currency restrictions and flexible recruitment laws.

Most of Djibouti's fourteen major infrastructure projects, which have been valued at a total of US$14.4 billion,[61] are being funded by Chinese banks. On 27 January 2014, China and the Djibouti government signed a memorandum of understanding (MoU) to build a SEZ aspiring to achieve success by following the models of Shenzhen and Shanghai in China. The government wished to build Djibouti into an African version of Singapore and Hong Kong by creating this SEZ, which had extra-jurisdictional rights and tax incentives. Touchroad, the Chinese multinational group that engaged in this operation, has promised that the SEZ will be different from a regular development zone or an industrial park, more like a fully-functional port city with residential areas, hospitals, schools, shopping centres and office facilities, which promises the locals thousands of jobs, just like the promises in Sri Lanka. Since Touchroad has already obtained the land and special administrative rights, it bypasses the Djibouti government's approval process, similar to the Colombo Port City. Touchroad Djibouti SEZ will function as a Chinese special colony in Djibouti catering for the Chinese market and the Chinese exports to Africa.[62]

President Xi's new 'dual circulation' economic model needs new markets. The Chinese PPP model in Djibouti and Sri Lanka will help Xi's 'dual circulation' model, flooding the countries with Chinese imports rather than increasing local exports. Many African SEZs have failed to deliver what was promised. An assessment of failures and what challenges the other SEZs faced would help nations like Sri Lanka who have accepted the Chinese PPP model, amending their laws to fit the model.

## MILITARY DIMENSION

Not limiting itself to economic development, a few months after opening the Chinese-funded SEZ, China established its first overseas military base in Djibouti at an expense of US$20 million a year. It is located closer to the foreign multi-base operation site. China justified its military base in Djibouti as its international obligation to achieve stability in the region. The economic gains and local jobs are one side of the coin. The other is the strategic dimension of China's geopolitical influence on such nations in the long run, converting the economic development model to a hybrid dual-use model with People's Liberation Army Navy's expansion.

China's economic and strategic intent in Djibouti and Sri Lanka is huge. China is using its economic influence to advance its security interests with stealth and precision. Sri Lanka is a well-positioned island for international counter-piracy operations. In the US-India-China maritime power triangle, China wishes to adopt the strategy of careful selection, low-key actions, cooperation first and then slow penetration to gradually promote the expansion of its sea power in the direction of the Indian Ocean, according to an article from PLAN-affiliated Chinese Naval Research Institute.[63]

The slow penetration to establish Chinese presence has a higher degree of success after establishing Hambantota, as assistance for the ailing economy is a priority for Sri Lanka. Beijing's uses its financial muscle in Colombo to thwart US's Indo-Pacific ambitions and reduce the Indian influence. China's actions will open up the nation to a geopolitical battleground. Just as China justified its military base in Djibouti as its international obligation to achieve stability in Africa, there are clear signs it could transform its port projects in the island-nation into dual use, claiming to want to achieve stability in Indian Ocean waters. The vision Djibouti 2035 is to transform itself into a commercial trade hub, similar to Sri Lanka's vision, elevating its geographical position along with China's.[64] It's time the nation calculates its geopolitical implications before building the 'phoenix nest'.

# FIVE
# June 2021

## How China Won over Local Agency to Shackle Sri Lanka Using a Port City[65]

In early June 2021, in an executive order President Biden essentially blacklisted several Chinese firms by prohibiting US investments in Chinese firms that 'undermine the security or democratic values of the United States and our allies'.[66] The port city developers China Harbour Engineering Company (CHEC) and the mother company, China Communications Construction Company (CCCC), were in this list. On its China policy, the US stands firm with its bipartisan consensus. This would raise concerns in nations like Sri Lanka, which has a large, constantly growing Chinese infrastructure portfolio in the country.

### REGIONAL POWERS AND THEIR PERIPHERY

The banned Chinese firms do not exclusively operate in Sri Lanka. In fact, they also operate in the US's own backyard along the 82 km Panama Canal. The Panama Canal was built for the strategic expansion of the US, connecting the Atlantic–Pacific Ocean route, and is today surrounded by Chinese infrastructure projects. Chinese firms such as CHEC and CCCC are also involved in infrastructure development in Panama. In 2017, Panama ended its diplomatic relationship with Taiwan and embraced Chinese BRI assistance for infrastructure projects, amounting to billions of dollars.[67] China is involved in a bridge project over the Canal for US$1.4 billion[68] and a US$4 billion rail project. It is also involved in the power sector, mining and a telecom infrastructure project with Huawei, including a digital free trade zone in San Miguelito.[69]

Panama's shift to Beijing had a domino effect, with fifteen Latin American nations welcoming China's BRI subsequently. However, the present Panamanian regime has managed to rebalance and scale back its Chinese infrastructure including the bridge,[70] considering the Chinese 'debt trap' and the US geopolitical security concerns.

In a similar manner, in the backyard of the regional power India, Sri Lanka has invited the Chinese BRI with several projects that are of concern to India. Colombo has fallen into the premeditated scheme of a Chinese debt trap, paying off its loans in varied ways, from leasing its strategic assets through debt–equity swaps to creating an extra-jurisdictional SEZ. Like Panama, the Sri Lankan government would need to backtrack its China bandwagoning foreign policy and bring a balance, and develop a considered perspective on the geopolitical and regional security concerns which its close relationship with China brings. The interwoven regional geographical alignments, such as India–Sri Lanka and the US with its immediate periphery in Panama, cannot be outweighed by the strategic interest drawn by an extra-regional power, China. The same *Monroe Doctrine* is applicable in China's periphery.

## CHINA'S PORT CITY VICTORY IN COLOMBO

The Speaker of the Sri Lankan Parliament, Mahinda Yapa Abeywardena, inked the Colombo Port City Economic Commission

Bill on 27 May after it had received approval, with two-thirds of the MPs supporting the government. Sri Lanka's Supreme Court ruled several clauses of the bill to be unconstitutional. The praetorian regime under excessive political influence of the military, with its Parliament majority, passed the Port City Bill in a hurry, ignoring its threat to the nation's sovereignty. Justifying the passing of the bill during the lockdown due to the pandemic, the Speaker of the House said, 'There were precedents that Parliament sittings have been conducted without any hindrance even during World War II and also when the Sri Lankan Parliament came under a bomb attack.'[71] What was left unsaid was that the environment was conducive towards suppressing the democratic mechanisms of public protests and discussions, and to bulldoze the bill through. There are ample mechanisms in the Sri Lankan government's political toolkit to turn down the bill, but they were simply not used against China. In other cases, such as India's ECT project[72] or for the US MCC grant,[73] there were public protests and experts committees of inquiry. China's strength in handling the local agency to manoeuvre projects is clear through all this.

Revisiting the article of Robert Putnam, 'Diplomacy and Domestic Politics: The Logic of Two-Level Games',[74] considering how diplomacy and domestic politics are entangled in Sri Lanka, the present Gotabaya regime has crushed the domestic decision-making and negotiation space. The government mechanism of bargaining for a better deal at different bureaucratic levels with a foreign party is no longer there. When the decisions are made and concluded at the highest level (Gotabaya with Xi), there is no space for bargaining.

The acceptance of Chinese proposals without any negotiations will have serious consequences. Tagging along with China's BRI and bandwagoning with the Middle Kingdom without any negotiations minimizes the fallback options with other players, especially Sri Lanka's closest neighbour, India. Gulbin Sultana warns, 'Given the dynamics of India–China relations, Sri Lanka should not expect that India will shut its eyes and keep mum over the developments in the Colombo Port City, which is just 290 kilometres away from its mainland, even though unlike the US, it has not raised any official concern.'[75] The president's decision to favour China and lose the foreign policy balance will significantly impact India–Sri Lanka relations.

The China tilt strengthened President Gotabaya's win at the political level within the SLPP coalition, securing his presidency. The same coalition, which had successfully created fear amongst the public over the US MCC project by depicting it as a threat to sovereignty, has used China's port city to secure a domestic political victory after passing the bill. What the present regime failed to recognize was the foreign policy fallout, even though it is necessary for Sri Lanka to sustain a balanced foreign policy. The belligerence of China and Sri Lanka's defence of China in an unusual manner, such as by the foreign secretary speaking on Xinjiang,[76] has invited multiple levels of external pressures on Colombo's foreign policy.

An assessment of the recent developments in the country reveals a subversion of democracy and a weakening of the neutral agencies that would otherwise ensure checks and balances in an effective democratic set up. The elected office bearers maintain a veneer of democracy and rhetorically accept the unbalanced foreign policy while eviscerating its substance by endorsing an alternative Chinese model.[77]

In China's CCP model, President Xi has nothing to worry about over Sri Lanka's port city project. The Sri Lankan government's acceptance and passing of the bill is another victory for President Xi's BRI strategy. It is a victory more for his foreign policy than for Sri Lanka's domestic policy. Gotabaya has a different measure where the passing of the bill has become more of a domestic political concern due to the democratic nature of governance in Sri Lanka. If the bill fails to muster support, it could even cost him his presidential seat while President Xi has no such concerns. The majoritarian win-set created and used to play the China card can switch its position, making the democratically-elected leader vulnerable.

There are two reasons the government hurried the Port City Bill in just under a month. *First*, Sri Lanka's economic situation had worsened with the pandemic. The country's foreign inflows had been impacted and debt management became a serious concern, with accumulated 'total outstanding external debt at US$35.3 billion by end of August 2020'.[78] P.B. Jayasundara, secretary to the president, justified the port city by pointing out that 'this is why the Port City law matters . . . Port City legislation enables Sri Lanka to create a service centre with an incentive structure that will encourage the FDIs on a much stronger footing.'[79] He further explained the government's position on foreign loans, asking 'to refrain from getting foreign loan-funded projects in the future'. While the government's fiscal position has deteriorated, China's port city is seen as a promise to restart the ailing economy. *Second*, the political security guaranteed at the UNHRC by China to the regime was proven by China's support and its vote against the UNHRC resolution to look into human rights violations during Sri Lanka's long civil war that ended in 2009. The phone call to President Gotabaya Rajapaksa after the UNHRC vote was well-timed by the Chinese leadership.[80] For the Rajapaksas, this political security is an essential ingredient for survival. China openly backs Sri Lanka on human rights issues, as was reaffirmed by the high-level official visit of Chinese State Councillor and Minister of National Defence, Wei Fenghe, who said, 'Chinese side appreciates Sri Lanka's position on issues relating to China's Taiwan, Hong Kong Special Administrative Region and Xinjiang Uygur Autonomous Region, and will as always support Sri Lanka's stance on issues relating to human rights.'[81]

While China would defend the Sri Lankan government's human rights posture and accept whatever form it takes, Western democracies will be obliged to highlight the long-delayed minority concerns in the island. The recent resolution from the US House Foreign Affairs Committee (HFAC) on Sri Lanka is a clear indication of pressure on the Sri Lankan government to establish some credible, transparent, domestic process to resolve the matter.[82] The Sri Lankan ambassador in Washington has denied what the resolution has concluded and stated, 'Calling an international mechanism at this juncture was sinister, at a time the present government had provided such mechanism.'[83] This 'state of denial' is a common trend in sync with the UNHRC resolution denial[84]; the absence of a credible mechanism is evident in the Sri Lankan society. The new European Union Parliament adopting a resolution to withdraw the Generalized Scheme of Preferences (GSP+) is a clear warning to the Sri Lankan regime. The resolution highlights Sri Lanka's 'alarming path towards the recurrence of grave human rights violations'.[85]

Being sheltered by only China's financial muscle and security is a clear miscalculation. For China, pushing this port city deal is high on the agenda, especially at a time when there is significant global pressure over their belligerent behaviour in their neighbourhood and elsewhere. Bringing Colombo into its sphere of influence is a considerable victory in its larger BRI game plan.

The agreed period of the commitments under Port City Bill exceeds the time span of the present government. Could a future government re-open the bill or default on the deal? A similar revisit was discussed by the former government after signing the Hambantota port deal. If a revisit regarding the port city deal is feasible, then Sri Lanka would be grateful for such transformative infrastructure. But President Gotabaya's election promise to revisit the Hambantota port deal that has been signed for ninety-nine years was never fulfilled. History tells us that there won't be much difference in Chinese flexibility for revisiting the Port City Bill. The fast-track approval for the Port City Bill shows the strength of the Chinese sphere of influence in dominating and dictating the local agency. Sri Lankan foreign policy today is in the shape of a doughnut, focused on the external interests of China. Worryingly, it is hollow at the centre, with national interests and safeguarding sovereignty lying completely neglected. This foreign policy will begin to shake once the external partner intervenes in domestic affairs and the Sri Lankan regime loses its domestic political grip.

# SIX
# August 2021

## The Rajapaksa Triumvirate and the CCP Backdoor in Sri Lanka[86]

The Sri Lankan regime has further moved away from democratic norms. There was a *triumvirate* of power centres amongst the three Rajapaksa brothers—Basil, Gotabaya and Mahinda Rajapaksa. For the first time in Sri Lankan history, the country's finance, economic and defence ministries are led by three brothers. The ruling family is further extended by adding five other members; thus a total of six family members serve as ministers, another as a member of parliament and two others as government officials, making it a political dynasty with the largest number of ministers, anywhere in the world. The entire family in politics is not anything new in South Asia, but it has never been seen on this scale at any one particular political moment. The new appointment of Basil Rajapaksa as the finance minister would further consolidate power amongst the Rajapaksa family members,[87] further departing from democratic norms and seeking alternative political models to justify their existence.

Apart from the existing autocratic nature of the government, there is yet another danger. The government has opened the floodgates and has allowed autocratic quintessence to flow into its political system. Other autocratic nations, especially China, can use the fertile ground prepared by the Rajapaksa brothers to advance their agenda.

### CCP CENTENARY, THE GREAT FIREWALL AND ITS SURVIVAL

In front of a 70,000-member audience in Beijing, President Xi sent a clear warning in his centenary speech: 'Chinese people would no longer allow any alien powers to bully and oppress and anyone who tried to do so would be badly battered by the Chinese nation's perseverance. . . . No one should underestimate the Chinese nation's will and power to fight against foreign power.'[88] China will fight in multiple geographies, including land, sea, space and cyberspace. The warning comes when China is propelling its ambition to be a great power with its own characteristics. The new world order that China wishes to create has its own Chinese flavour backed by the CCP. The belligerence in the South China Sea, the human rights issues in Hong Kong and Xinjiang, and the infrastructure loans in Sri Lanka, the activities in cyberspace and 5G technology are all coated with these Chinese characteristics. The world order that China envisions is through the CCP's political ideology. Its stance at the UN Human Rights Council makes it evident that China deems economic rights to be way more critical than individual civil liberty.

The CCP celebration is about the political values and its ideology, despite keeping the window open for reform. As Chinese reformist Deng Xiaoping said, 'If you open the window for fresh air, you have to expect some flies and mosquitoes to blow in.'[89] To keep such 'flies'—the political dissent and liberal ideology—away, CCP has used multiple mechanisms. One such tactic was unleashed by the Ministry of Public Security that initiated the firewall Golden Shield Project in 2000.[90] While the internet is a tool in China's economic development, its existence also undermines political stability since the internet encourages diversity of ideas, propels information and is an instrument for democratizing a society. The great firewall, thus, effectively carried out CCP's efforts in suppressing liberal ideology.

With a quarter of the human population living in China, the second oldest one-party authoritarian rule, has managed to sustain the communist system for seven decades. According to Rana Mitter, there are two reasons why the Marxist Communist system has survived for so long in China. First, the CCP continues to be ruthless. The Leninist strand of use of coercion continues to be a necessary factor that sustains the CCP model. Second, it practises flexibility—a trait uncharacteristic of authoritarian regimes. China's willingness to change from the Soviet model of Mao's time and open up economically during Deng's time points to that flexibility.[91] It is as if the Communist Party has implemented a capitalist revolution with Chinese characteristics.

## CHINESE BACKDOOR IN SRI LANKA

The CCP's Leninist model will navigate easily in nations that have suppressed liberal democratic values. In these cases, the external support will flow from China to sustain the autocratic government, as in Sri Lanka. The Rajapaksa *triumvirate* has already endorsed China and its CCP model of development. China will assist and use the Rajapaksa brothers to push the Chinese development and strategic agenda through its BRI. However, the efforts will not be limited to BRI. The Rajapaksas' power consolidation in Sri Lanka will have a long-term impact on the country's democracy.

At first glance, the CCP's political ideology with Leninist characteristics may not interest a democratic nation such as Sri Lanka and the promotion of the Chinese Communist model in nations along the BRI track will seem as an impossible task; however, that might not be the case in the long run. Currently, Sri Lanka might be predisposed towards a democratic model; however, this may change over time due to structural reforms to the nation's foundational elements, such as the Constitution. Administrative policy preferences may change due to import of autocratic values and norms from the CCP model, justifying as an alternative to the existing one, claiming more efficiency for economic development. China will push the CCP agenda, camouflaging it with a promise of an economic miracle, to many nations, including Sri Lanka.

Prime Minister Mahinda Rajapaksa praised the CCP's role saying, 'China has successfully eradicated poverty of 900 million people under its open economic policy. . . . I am confident that China will bring back the economic strength that Asia had 500 years ago through this Silk Road. China always believed that improving infrastructure will provide new ways and new strengths for the people. Therefore, we have constantly invited China to help develop the infrastructure of our country.' Rajapaksa was speaking on the 6 July CCP and World Political Future summit.[92] He also expressed his gratitude to China for the development and generous donation of the Sinopharm vaccine, saying, 'It is further admirable that China has approved for the production of the Sinopharm vaccine in countries like ours. During a global pandemic such as this, decisions initiated by the CCP will be respected as those taken for the benefit of humanity.'

The prime minister's praise of China shows clear signs of a dependence on China to ensure the regime's survival. The regime's decision to pass the Port City Bill and acquire large-scale Chinese infrastructure, even if it has negligible returns, is due to Prime Minister Rajapaksa's informal relationship with China.

However, many experts do not share this enthusiasm. Jonathan E. Hillman rightly observes in his book *The Emperor's New Road*, 'If Chinese loans were cigarettes, Sri Lanka's Hambantota Port would be the cancerous lung on the warning label.'[93] Sri Lankan leaders have raised the BRI spirits, ignoring economic returns, depending on the Chinese infrastructure development outcomes with high political expectations in order to sustain power. With economic woes and the rising cost of living, the public will have difficulty digesting the large-scale development projects with no returns as it requires a considerably more time than the regime's timespan to generate profit and jobs in projects, such as the Colombo Port City.

The Sri Lankan government completely ignored the strategic dimension of China's actions. Like in Europe, where China has built a '*Balkan Backdoor*' to enter the European Union through the Balkan states,[94] China will enter South Asia from autocratic states, such as Sri Lanka. The '*Sri Lankan Backdoor*' that China has created for its strategic expansion is not visible to government policymakers, who remain blinded by the Chinese economic miracle, which they accept for their own political survival.

*SYMBOLISM AND SLPP ENDORSEMENT*

CCP's significance was highlighted by the Sri Lankan government by issuing a special coin to commemorate the CCP centenary. The coins, which were perhaps minted in the Middle Kingdom and sent to Sri Lanka,[95] were a clear sign of Rajapaksa regime's China dependence. For the first time, Sri Lanka deviated from its usual practice of issuing commemorative coins to mark diplomatic relations milestones with foreign countries by extending it to a political party. The public displeasure was evident on social media. One such post was from a local aviation engineer who wrote, 'It is not even to honour a foreign country but a dictatorial, single party that rules the country. Is this what is in store for Sri Lanka?' While the CCP pushes its governance and economic model, the Sri Lankan public will reflect on the danger of losing its prized democratic values and freedom and view it as a threat to their civil liberties.

Another symbolic gesture by the government was the illumination of the Chinese-built Lotus Tower in Colombo. This tallest tower in Sri Lanka was built by China, and was declared open during the last regime, with no access to the public as of now.

The political group to which the Rajapaksa regime belongs, the SLPP alliance, includes many leftist political parties. Further adding to the list of CCP endorsements, Sri Lanka's leftist political parties and the ruling Rajapaksa SLPP conducted a joint conference online with China to support the CCP centenary. The Sri Lankan Prime Minister Mahinda Rajapaksa also attended the conference and said, 'The friend will always be there, both in sorrow and pleasure. Like the murals on a wall, they never look away . . . we appreciate the commitments made by the Chinese government for our independence during and after the war, forever.'[96] At the conference, eleven political parties recognized the CCP as a steadfast champion for developing countries through the BRI, helping to improve infrastructure and production, while respecting sovereignty. The Rajapaksa regime also signed a joint statement initiated by China at UNHRC,[97] raising concerns about the human rights situation in UK.

The Sri Lankan government went all out to promote the CCP centenary despite the prevailing pandemic when the public was struggling with the vaccine drive. The CCP's and Rajapaksa's publicity campaign failed to catch public attention due to the country's severe health and economic woes.

The arrival of Basil Rajapaksa is viewed with hope in the government quarters as an attempt to kick-start the economy. The *triumvirate* must, however, remain cautious in acts which are viewed as suppressing democracy, like further expanding the CCP agenda in Sri Lanka.

# SEVEN
## February 2022

### Political–Economic Instability and Wang Yi's Peripheral Diplomacy in Sri Lanka[98]

To ease the pressure from Beijing, the day before the Chinese Foreign Minister Wang Yi visited Sri Lanka, US$6.9 million was paid to Qingdao Seawin Biotech Group.[99] A few months ago, the Economic and Commercial Office of the Chinese Embassy in Sri Lanka blacklisted a local Sri Lankan bank over the payment for the rejected Chinese fertilizer shipment to Sri Lanka. Colombo's neutralizing effort reduced the Chinese pressure, especially from Wang Yi's bilateral agenda. During the foreign minister's visit, Sri Lankan President Gotabaya Rajapaksa requested that 'it would be a great relief to the country if attention could be paid on restructuring the debt repayments as a solution to the economic crisis',[100] which will give Beijing an ample and comfortable space to expand its sphere of influence in the island.

An economic crisis overshadowed the unseen strategic implications of such moves. Sri Lanka has to repay US$7 billion in debt in 2022[101]; the ailing economy with plummeting foreign exchange reserves is facing a worsening economic crisis day by day. To ease the economic crisis and the island-wide power cuts, Sri Lanka's Finance Minister Basil Rajapaksa requested assistance from India's External Affairs Minister S. Jaishankar through a credit facility of US$1.5 billion.[102]

Chinese loans to Sri Lanka account for more than US$5 billion. The amount was invested in infrastructure. Unfortunately, it failed to produce the expected revenue, through no fault of the lenders. A range of issues, including domestic corruption, investment in non-productive projects along with high debt-servicing costs, have caused this burden. Wang Yi visited the Colombo Port City, a large-scale infrastructure project that is a part of the BRI. At present, there is a limited foreign investment and foreign investors have shown little interest, though the Port City Managing Director Houliang Jiang had stated to this author during an interview in 2019 that 'there will be international investors, especially from India and many other nations'. However, little progress has been made on that front.

Achieving the Chinese project goals as well as supporting the ailing Sri Lankan economy will be a daunting challenge, especially in the present political conditions and Rajapaksa's foreign policy posture, which is to hedge between New Delhi and Beijing. Three weeks prior to the Chinese foreign minister's visit, the Chinese Ambassador Qi Zhenhong's visit to the northern province was approved by Colombo. Sri Lanka's hedging foreign policy in the context of alignment strategy, forging protective ties with India and China simultaneously, was clearly visible. Welcoming Chinese assistance to the northern Tamil community, while an all-out support articulated to India by 'India first' posture is an example of Colombo's hedging exercise. Some analysts who assess that a smaller state like Sri Lanka can play both countries against each other in the hope of finding more sustainable investments and to get some respite from further debt-trap diplomacy,[103] have missed China's stealth and security dimension. China's interest in developing the northern province, the closest geography to India's immediate periphery in the south, is not without its own agenda.

South Indian geography directly influences Sri Lanka's north. New Delhi has voiced Tamil grievances, including a political solution since the India–Sri Lanka Accord in 1987. At present, for the first time, China has strategized a dual approach to satisfy the majority Sinhalese and minority Tamil community at the same time. The Chinese ambassador's visit and the substantial assistance from China to the Northern Province is a strategic move by China to expand its footprint, by initially targeting an important stakeholder stressed by South India—the fisheries community.

Beijing's strategic circle orchestrated the ambassador's visit. It was not something the Chinese embassy in Colombo could decide alone due to the highly sensitive nature of the initiative. Carrying out Hindu rituals at a famous temple, inspecting northern waters with the Sri Lankan navy, and stating 'this is just the beginning'[104] were scripted exercises by Beijing aimed at sending a signal to New Delhi, on China's interest in Sri Lanka's northern province despite the Sri Lankan government's rejection of the Chinese wind power project due to New Delhi.

The timing of this visit was well calculated. It came only a few days after Finance Minister Basil Rajapaksa signed the agreement for bilateral economic assistance in New Delhi,[105] and the Chinese contaminated fertilizer consignment was rejected, where India filled the gap. Following this, Chinese renewable energy projects in the three northern islands were cancelled.[106] All these events, collectively, pushed Beijing to look for an alternative strategy to reduce the growing Indian influence in Sri Lanka.

After cancelling the Chinese renewable energy projects in the northern islands due to India's security concerns, Colombo kept projecting to Beijing that this was beyond its control. In the past, India has not given significant attention to her South due to its passive foreign policy posture. Unfortunately, the ground reality in the present context has changed, and India needs to understand the significant security threat to its immediate marine periphery. The visit of the Chinese ambassador to the north is a signal to both Sri Lanka and India that China is ready to take the extra risk of reaching out to the

Tamil geography and intervening in India's southern sphere. Beijing has read New Delhi and Colombo well, and it knows the limitations of India and Sri Lanka and the consequences of the ambassador's visit.

Usually, China maintains that it will 'not comment' on Sri Lanka's internal affairs. It did not support the UNHRC process to address the human rights concerns of the Tamil community in Sri Lanka. The Chinese ambassador's visit is also an early warning that China could use an alternative strategy and depart from supporting the Rajapaksas at the UNHRC and not use the veto against the resolution. It is also a direct message to India that China is ready to give a voice to the Tamil community and support it.

The space for the Chinese to manoeuvre in Colombo has become larger with a regime tied to the Chinese 'strategic trap', supported by the Rajapaksas who are not ready to approach the IMF for economic assistance. Dr Ganeshan Wignaraja observes, 'China can usefully add its powerful voice to calls for Sri Lanka to seek IMF assistance',[107] but instead, China has chosen to take advantage of the semi-autocratic political environment in Sri Lanka to promote an alternative model to the democratic model and expand its economic assistance. In this high-intensity environment, the Chinese foreign minister's visit to Colombo is a clear sign of China displaying its grip and reassuring the Rajapaksas' of its support in return for their commitment.

The Chinese foreign minister visited four other nations before coming to Sri Lanka, including Eritrea, Kenya, Comoros and Maldives, all of which have debt crises that are slowly turning into 'strategic traps'. Wang Yi, known as the 'Silver Fox' in Chinese diplomatic circles, has ample experience in peripheral diplomacy in China's vicinity to consolidate regional hegemony, a strategy advanced to fulfil President Xi's vision to create a 'Community of Common Destiny'.

Wang Yi is now exercising peripheral diplomacy in India's vicinity. The recent design of a new forum for Indian Ocean Island nations is a counter grouping strategy against India's existing Indian Ocean littoral network, impacting India's periphery.[108] Beijing has built its strategy by selecting Sri Lanka as a perfect launchpad to pitch the idea of the forum, given Sri Lanka's geography and the

Rajapaksa regime's clear China preference. Evaluating this macro geopolitical viewpoint is essential for Colombo's foreign policy; unfortunately, it is misread most of the time. Trilateral India–Maldives–Sri Lanka security dialogue held in early December is an important initiative, but it is inadequate to address a rising power in India's vicinity.

The dynamics of the relationship between India–China and China–Sri Lanka have changed completely in recent times. China spends four times as much on defence than India and China's GDP is more than five times that of India. India would need a more active foreign policy, expanding the strategic dimension in its outreach to blunt Chinese presence in its immediate periphery.

While course correction of foreign policy is required, internal cracks emerge in Rajapaksa's political circle. The ousted minister Susil Premajayantha with decades of experience in legislature and judiciary warned, 'The internal weak policy decisions with the absence of an inclusive approach for constitution-making, departure from democratic norms, and a weak foreign policy will invite a significant threat to nation's sovereignty.'[109]

President Gotabaya exposed his heavy autocratic rule, depending on his inner circle of confidants, bypassing the senior ministers, which will directly concern the prime minister who has engaged in politics for decades with his senior political peers. The cracks will run deep and spread throughout the regime's core in the months to come due to the aggressive style of the autocratic rule. The internal political dysfunctionality was further explained by former president Maithripala Sirisena,[110] signalling a possible departure of Sri Lanka Freedom Party (SLFP) from the coalition government. While domestic politics will take centre stage in the coming months, the underlying critical foreign policy concerns should also be prioritized. Colombo should see the larger geopolitical context and invest more in the right partnerships to push back against hostile foreign influences and sustain a balance in its foreign policy.

# EIGHT
# April 2022

## Sri Lankan Crisis between Debt Trap and Strategic Trap: The Chinese Stake[111]

There have been multiple debt trap myth-busting articles; the Chinese embassy in Sri Lanka has endorsed some.[112] The article by Deborah Brautigam clarifying there is no debt trap in the island-nation, was one of them. Brautigam says, 'Critics invariably point to a single case—the Chinese takeover of Sri Lanka's Hambantota Port—as proof of this strategy. Yet the evidence for this project being part of a Chinese master plan is thin.'[113] Today, the Sri Lankan political economy is in a crisis, and China is largely responsible for this. I have predicted the coming dysfunctionality of the political economy[114] and the danger inherent in Colombo's China tilt in my previous writings.[115]

People are out in the streets today with slogans seeking dismissal of the Rajapaksa regime. One of Asia's oldest democracies is now struggling to survive another day. The protest at the president's house[116] had a ripple effect and extended to the entire nation. Political dysfunctionality and the economic crisis, with long power cuts and the unavailability of essential goods further aggravated the anger of the protesters. The entire Cabinet crippled the Executive by submitting its resignation. The president immediately appointed a four-member Cabinet, but the finance minister resigned the next day.[117] A few weeks later, another seventeen Cabinet ministers were appointed.[118]

### BEHIND THE CRISIS

Behind the crisis was an external power intervening in the Sri Lankan economy and political space. Looking at the dynamics, I can clearly say that the Chinese have carried out 'strategic-trap diplomacy' in Sri Lanka, a more dangerous act than 'debt-trap diplomacy'.

Sri Lanka has a severe liquidity crisis with foreign reserves down to a bare US$500 million.[119] It is also facing an insolvency crisis and is unable to repay its large borrowings. As much as 70 per cent of the island's infrastructure projects have been constructed by China using commercial borrowings; some Chinese loans for Hambantota port development are at a higher rate of above 6 per cent, compared to other nations such as Japan, whose loans are at less than 2 per cent. And there was opaqueness in the Chinese loan process and conditionalities. Chinese debt of around US$3.38 billion is around 10 per cent of Sri Lanka's staggering foreign debt.[120] The growing financial dependence on China of Sri Lanka and other South and Central Asian countries is depicted in Figure 1.2.[121]

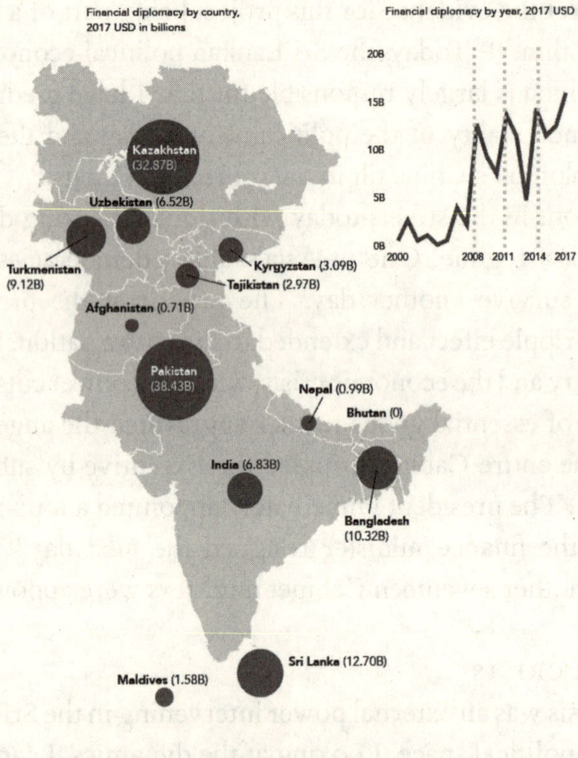


FIGURE 1.2: Financial Dependence on China

(Source: Samantha Curtis et al., *Silk Road Diplomacy: Deconstructing Beijing's Toolkit to Influence South and Central Asia*. Williamsburg, VA: AidData at William and Mary, 2019.)

Notes: The map visualises China's total financial diplomacy to all SCA countries from 2000 to 2017, including commitments for infrastructure, budget support, debt relief and humanitarian assistance. The line graph presents Chinese financial diplomacy by year from 2000 to 2017.

Sri Lanka needs to make nearly US$7 billion in payments for foreign loans this year itself.[122] The amount is more than the country's foreign exchange earnings and the government tax revenue. China has said it will provide a US$1 billion loan to Sri Lanka,[123] rejecting its restructuring request, where the funds will be utilized to settle previous loans from Chinese banks. Another US$1.5 billion buyer's credit to import material from China was also provided by China. The interest rate of these loans has been long debated and unclear to the public. For Pakistan, the rate charged by China is 3.76 per cent.[124] In comparison, OECD's interest rate is 1.1 per cent.

There are large borrowings from China on financially unprofitable projects in Sri Lanka and many other countries. The Mattala airport,[125] built near a wildlife sanctuary and not operating for many years, is just one example. Further, China has built this ancillary infrastructure for long-term civil–military use to support their ninety-nine-year leased Hambantota port.[126] All these projects are under the BRI, seen as an ambitious foreign policy strategy to bring the developing world under the Chinese orbit.

## BETWEEN DEBT TRAP AND STRATEGIC TRAP

The phrase 'debt-trap diplomacy' has been quite aptly discussed by the Indian academic Brahma Chellaney since 2017,[127] describing how the Chinese government leverages the debt burden of smaller countries for geopolitical ends. A debt-trap situation is one where 'the creditor country is said to extend excessive credit to a debtor country with the intention of extracting economic or political concessions when the debtor country becomes unable to meet its repayment obligations'.[128] Sri Lanka's Hambantota port was a case that highlighted debt-trap diplomacy where a large amount of loan was given by China, and when the Sri Lankan government was unable to repay the borrowings, China took over the port on a ninety-nine year lease in 2017.[129] In 2018, at Hudson Institute, US Vice President Mike Pence warned of the ongoing debt-trap diplomacy in Sri Lanka and said it 'may soon become a forward military base for China's growing blue-water navy'.[130] The Biden administration also accuses 'China of using loans to entice borrowing countries into a "debt trap" that gives Beijing sway over strategic assets and natural resources when governments can't repay'.[131] However, several academics debunked this assessment of debt-trap diplomacy, especially in the Sri Lankan case, as being inadequate.

Lee Jones and Shahar Hameiri authored the Chatham House paper 'Debunking the Myth of "Debt-trap Diplomacy" ',[132] pointing to five misconceptions. Here is what he said and the rebuttals:

First, the Hambantota port project was not proposed by China but by the government of Sri Lanka.

Although it is viewed as a request by the Sri Lankan government to develop Hambantota, it was more of a personal request of Mahinda Rajapaksa due to the port's location in his political constituency.

Second, it was a commercial, not a geostrategic, venture; it was one of several 'white elephant' projects and unsustainable developmental programmes.

One cannot dismiss the project as only a commercial venture and not geostrategic due to it being an unprofitable or unsustainable development. That the port could not generate the targeted revenue up to now is reason enough to label it geostrategic and a long-term venture. China also managed to secure the ninety-nine-year lease because Colombo could not repay the large borrowings.

Third, Sri Lanka's debt distress was unconnected to Chinese lending; it was the result of excessive borrowing on Western capital markets.

In another Chatham House paper, Ganeshan Wignaraja et al. argue that there is no debt-trap diplomacy. They say, 'Sri Lanka is not in a Chinese debt trap. Its debt to China amounts to about 6 percent of its GDP.'[133] This probably is the most widely-used claim, that Sri Lanka's debt distress is unconnected to Chinese lending as all other commercial borrowings are much higher than the Chinese borrowing, which is less than 10 per cent of the total debt. This view ignores China's strategic hold, limiting the argument to quantitative figures dismissing the 'strategic-trap diplomacy'.

Fourth, there was no debt-for-asset swap. Instead, after bargaining hard for commercial reasons, a Chinese SOE (state owned enterprise) leased the port in exchange for US$1.1 billion, which Sri Lanka used to pay other debts and boost foreign reserves.

But clearly there was a debt-for-an asset swap, and there was no hard bargaining. China did not restructure the debt nor assist in this regard. Sri Lanka's inability to pay the Chinese debt allowed the Chinese to lease the port. The ninety-nine-year lease agreement was in actuality an acquisition of the port and its surrounding facilities, rushed and signed on a weekend behind closed doors.[134] The agreement has still not been disclosed to the public, and China's opaqueness has always been prominent in Sri Lanka. Further, the lack of transparency was proven when the Sri Lankan foreign minister revealed, 'There is a provision for a further 99-year extension of the lease.'[135]

Fifth, Chinese navy vessels cannot use the port, which will instead become the new base of Sri Lanka's own southern naval command.

The argument that Chinese navy vessels cannot enter the port is incorrect. The former director-general of the national security think tank and I have discussed this topic multiple times and concluded that the Chinese navy could enter the port as well as provide logistics facilities to the People's Liberation Army Navy (PLAN), clearly highlighted by the 2021 Pentagon Report.[136]

Hambantota port was initially handed over for construction in 2008. China's large-scale military assistance during the last phase of the civil war surpassed other nations, which contributed to ending the three-decade war. This was the primary factor that gave China the opening to win Mahinda Rajapaksa's confidence. Hambantota port was awarded to China, and a few years later, CICT[137] terminal operations were also awarded to China.[138]

Strategic-trap diplomacy describes a scenario beyond debt-trap diplomacy where human rights, political and security aspects are added. In the case of a strategic-trap, the creditor country not only focuses its assistance on credit and excessive loans but simultaneously intervenes in the nation's human rights, political and security spheres. China provides financial loans to trap nations like Sri Lanka and offers protection in multilateral forums against action for human rights violations, support to alter the existing democratic political model to an autocratic model and military assistance.

In Sri Lanka, strategic-trap diplomacy was carried out as an extension to the debt-trap diplomacy. First, in the political dimension, China involved itself in installing an alternative model, different from the existing democratic model, that is, an authoritarian model. China provided assistance to Rajapaksa's political party including funding support. Second, in the human rights dimension, China supported the Sri Lankan regime on human rights concerns of international agencies.[139] The Sri Lankan government had no other option but to reciprocally support China's human rights violations in Xinjiang.[140] Third was a military dimension,[141] added to the strategic-trap, where China favours a heavily militarized system.[142]

The quantitative economic data falls short of capturing the strategic depth of these actions. All the Chinese projects have a long-term strategic design that could comfortably bring a 'hybrid model' of civil–military activity to the country concerned,[143] which is a security issue for Sri Lanka and the region. Calculating the value of loans provided by other foreign nations and sovereign bonds for private commercial loans vis-à-vis that from China is an oft-quoted argument to refute the theory of debt-trap diplomacy, but it does not dismiss China's strategic-trap diplomacy.

Debt-trap diplomacy is a severe concern for developing countries like Sri Lanka. Beyond this, a strategic-trap is another dimension to consider in many other BRI nations that could fall into the same political–economic crisis as Sri Lanka.

# NINE
## August 2022

### The Trap: China's Debt Restructuring and Strategic Manipulation in Sri Lanka[144]

China's BRI isn't quite as advantageous as often portrayed. Ten projects located in six nations—Vanuatu, Indonesia, Myanmar, Tajikistan, Pakistan and Hungary—could not generate sufficient revenue to justify the cost.[145] Projects in Mongolia and Azerbaijan face the same problem, despite gross gains. It falls on these countries to pay the difference from their earnings from other sources to repay the debt instalments.

Several of the would-be BRI beneficiaries have found themselves forced to transfer resources to service their debt. Experts such as Nicholas Casey and Clifford Krauss explain the other facet behind the BRI logic, and note that 'China gets to keep 80 percent of Ecuador's most valuable export—oil—because many of the contracts are repaid in petroleum, not dollars.[146] In Zambia, where Chinese creditors hold a third of the national debt, China has taken over mining assets of the country as collateral.

### SRI LANKA'S FALL AND THE TRAP

Sri Lanka was an even a more dramatic case. As Elizabeth C. Economy described in her book *The World According to China*, 'The country could not service its debt and instead granted China a 99-year lease on its Hambantota port.'[147] It was a senseless decision. Sri Lanka's political elites had only their political survival in mind; China saw, in this fragile and corrupt political culture, a historic opportunity. The newly elected prime minister, Dinesh Gunawardena, understands this as well as anyone. As the foreign minister earlier, he had warned that the ninety-nine-year Hambantota deal 'can extend for a further period. Which means it can go on for any number of years after 99 years or for another 99 years.'[148] Even today, as the prime minister, he knows he can never revisit this agreement nor investigate any Chinese project for corruption, just as his predecessor Ranil Wickremesinghe was unsuccessful in 2015.

At the Aspen Security Forum, CIA chief Bill Burns assesses Sri Lanka today is heavily indebted to China having 'made some really dumb bets about their economic future and . . . suffering pretty catastrophic, both economic and political, consequences as a result'.

'The Chinese have a lot of weight to throw around and they can make a very appealing case for their investments,' says Burns. He adds, 'That, I think, ought to be an object lesson to a lot of other players – not just in the Middle East or South Asia, but around the world—about having your eyes wide open about those kinds of dealings.'[149]

It's a timely warning for many other nations in BRI which have largely unsustainable borrowings and China as their major creditor. Field research in Sri Lanka in 2021 made it clear that China has effectively laid two traps in the country—the classic debt trap and a strategic trap.[150] The now-disgraced President Gotabaya Rajapaksa, who fled public anger to the safety of Singapore, contributed to the latter trap, tilting the formerly balanced foreign policy of Sri Lanka towards China. The trap has three levels—a political party level with the CCP, a human rights stance dictated by China and Chinese military assistance. All three dimensions have worsened significantly during Gotabaya Rajapaksa's regime. Today, several other South Asian nations follow the same trajectory, with heavy borrowings and need to support China's policies (Table 1.2).

TABLE 1.2: Chinese Debt to South Asia

| *Country* | *Public and hidden debt exposure to China* | *Value of Chinese construction contracts in BRI* | *Support for Chinese stance on Hong Kong National Security Law* | *Support for Chinese stance on South China Sea arbitral ruling* | *Support for Chinese stance on Xinjiang policies* | *Support for Chinese stance on Huawei 5G* |
|---|---|---|---|---|---|---|
| Sri Lanka | >10% | 10.01 bn | Yes | Yes | Yes | Yes |
| Pakistan | >20% | 49.38 bn | Yes | Yes | Yes | Yes |
| Bangladesh | >7% | 22.94 bn | Yes | Yes | Abstained | Yes |
| Myanmar | >5% | 3.33 bn | Yes | Neutral | Yes | Yes |
| Maldives | 1–5% | 1.12 bn | Abstained | Abstained | Abstained | Yes |
| Nepal | 1–5% | 2.57 bn | Yes | Abstained | Yes | Yes |
| Afghanistan | 1–5% | 210 mn | Abstained | Yes | Abstained | Yes |

Sources: https://www.aei.org/china-global-investment-tracker/; https://asia.nikkei.com/Spotlight/Belt-and-Road/385bn-of-China-s-Belt-and-Road-lending-kept-undisclosed-report; https://thediplomat.com/2020/10/2020-edition-which-countries-are-for-or-against-chinas-xinjiang-policies; https://thediplomat.com/2016/07/who-supports-china-in-the-south-china-sea-and-why/

## IGNORING THE EARLY WARNING

It should come as no surprise what Aid Data's findings suggest, 'The most corrupt governments among Chinese borrowers seem to leave office shortly after the onset of an IMF program.' Will the Chinese loans be the underlying reason for the Rajapaksa regime's end? After all, multiple IMF warnings had gone unheeded by the government; the conditions of Chinese loans, and their link to kickback schemes that directly benefited Rajapaksa and the political elites in Sri Lanka, cannot be ignored.

Sri Lanka's new president, Ranil Wickremesinghe (appointed by lawmakers, not elected by the people), is now in an awkward spot. He cannot negotiate with the IMF without cooperation from his opaque major creditor, looming over him like a ghost, rattling its promissory notes like chains. After its default in May on the instalment of its international debt totalling US$51 billion, Sri Lanka needs funds, and will also need restructuring of its loans if it wants IMF funding.

One of the conditions of IMF is to get the current lenders to restructure the loans. Negotiations with China, however, have made no progress. China's loans are opaque and the issues involved are unknown. According to Sri Lankan Central Bank figures, Chinese debt stands at 10 per cent of the country's US$51 billion in total external debt. But some economists argue that China's share totalled 20 per cent at the end of last year, including public and publicly-guaranteed debt, commercial lending and loans to Sri Lankan state-owned enterprises. Umesh Moramudali, a Sri Lankan researcher, says, 'Sri Lanka's [debt] to Chinese creditors comes to about 20 percent, not 10 percent. So, all the 20 percent will have to be restructured. That means you'll have to look at how the China Development Bank and China's Exim Bank will deal with restructuring.'[151]

### BEHIND THE FIGURES AND CHINA

Speaking at the G20 finance officials meeting in Indonesia, US Treasury Secretary Janet Yellen said, 'Sri Lanka is clearly unable to repay that debt, and it's my hope that China will be willing to work with Sri Lanka to restructure the debt.'[152] Zambia, Ethiopia and Chad have applied for help from IMF on their debt too, but their efforts have stalled, 'largely due to foot-dragging by China'. It was 'quite frustrating' that China was not stepping up on the debt issues, explained Yellen.[153]

This push for G20 creditors (including China) to finalize debt restructuring is likely to prove the most important step to stabilize nations like Sri Lanka and other developing countries facing debt distress. IMF Managing Director Kristalina Georgieva explained, 'Strong global leadership is also needed to tackle the scourge of high debt, which has reached multiyear highs.'[154] More than 30 per cent of emerging and developing countries are in or near debt distress;

for low-income countries that number rises to 60 per cent. With tightening financial conditions and exchange rate depreciation, the debt service burden is a harsh, sometimes unbearable burden, says Georgieva. In Sri Lanka, for instance, the high inflation rate is unbearable, not only for the low-income earners but also for the middle class. The lack of essential food and medicines in an import-driven economy like Sri Lanka means that people have no recourse at all but the kindness of others.

India, for one, has spent close to US$4 billion on currency-swaps and aid to stabilize its neighbour.[155] China, on the other hand, has delayed action. It has not offered any specific response, according to Palitha Kohonna, the Sri Lankan ambassador to China, except to offer a new loan to settle the existing debt. Sri Lanka has requested China for a loan of US$1 billion to repay an equivalent amount of Chinese debt becoming due this year; a US$1.5 billion credit line to pay for Chinese imports and activation of a US$1.5 billion currency-swap. This amounts to a total of US$4 billion. Sri Lanka's creditors will want the IMF to treat all of Sri Lanka's creditors on par, including China. For that to happen, the detailed terms of the secretive loans of China will have to be revealed to everyone, including international agencies. That is not going to happen easily.

This is no mere provincial squabble. Sri Lankan economists Anushka Wijesinha and Aquilah Latiff argue, 'What Sri Lanka could feasibly expect and indeed push for is that China joins a multilateral creditor committee and supports a harmonized effort for debt restructuring talks.'[156] Samantha Power, the administrator of United States Agency for International Development (USAID), posited, '[The] biggest question of all is whether Beijing will restructure debt to the same extent as other bilateral creditors.'[157] Sri Lanka is just one among many other developing countries where, between 2000 and 2017, debt to China increased tenfold, from US$500 billion to over US$5 trillion.[158] If more nations like Sri Lanka default, China would have to bear this extra burden and re-evaluate its BRI strategy. The consequences of such a shift could redefine the future of the BRI nations.

## Ten
## August 2022

Chinese Spy Ship and Lanka's Tilt towards Beijing[159]

Colombo had initially denied permission to the Chinese spy ship *Yuan Wang 5* to berth at the Hambantota port.[160] However, it later changed its position clearing berthing rights, before reversing it again by denying access to the Chinese vessel.[161] Foreign Minister Ali Sabry explained to the Cabinet that the Chinese vessel had only asked for a refuelling visit,[162] while Prime Minister Dinesh Gunawardena downplayed the threat of the Chinese visit with an India balancing act, calling it an 'approach of friendship'.[163] On 16 August 2022, however, the Chinese vessel was given clearance by Colombo to enter the Hambantota port despite the security concerns raised by New Delhi.[164]

The Chinese dual-use spy vessel, *Yuan Wang 5*, was heading towards Sri Lanka's Hambantota port on the southern coast on 11 August to berth for seven days. The vessel operates under China's Strategic Support Force (SSF) of the People's Liberation Army (PLA). The PLASSF bring in civilian assets such as *Yuan Wang 5* to augment the military capabilities and capacities. This gives it a certain leverage to hide its military agenda and project its commitment to civilian research. Elizabeth C. Economy, a senior fellow at Hoover Institute, explains in her book *The World According to China* that the 'SSF is designed to serve as a coordinating body for military and civilian research and development: nine universities have signed a cooperation agreement with it.'[165] The vessel, used for space and satellite tracking with specific usage in intercontinental ballistic missile launches. The ship was not supposed to deploy some instruments which could be construed as spying in the Sri Lankan waters in Hambantota port, but there was no guarantee the Chinese would limit the ship to its official purpose during the visit.

## CHINA'S INCREASING INFLUENCE

The PLASSF mandate is space, cyber and electronic warfare. The ship *Yuan Wang 5* will focus on all three domains, gathering information from Hambantota port in Sri Lanka from where Kanyakumari in India's Tamil Nadu is 451 kilometres away.[166] While India has fully blocked Chinese technologies such as Huawei's 5G, and acquired real-time intelligence and information capabilities allowing India to piggyback on American geospatial information to hit enemy targets with pinpoint accuracy,[167] China has managed an alternative route to build its space in India's immediate periphery, expanding its communications networks in Sri Lanka and other South Asian countries.

The PLASSF has used the same tactic in many nations, including Sri Lanka, in the past through submarine port calls at crucial times, especially during internal political challenges. The October 2014 visit,[168] for example, took place when President Mahinda Rajapaksa was three months away from his presidential election. The same pattern was seen in Australia before the Australian elections in May 2022 when the *Haiwangxing*, the intelligence collection vessel of PLAN,[169] was navigating as close as 50 nautical miles from the Harold E. Holt Communication Station that provides Very Low Frequency (VLF) communication transmission services for Australian, US and allied submarines.[170] The strategic manoeuvres were well calculated by Beijing and they deployed military assets in the waters of the Indian Ocean to create pressure on New Delhi and Canberra during the last few months.

Spying is a two-way street. The Chinese exposed their vessel *Yuan Wang 5* to India's advanced land-based monitoring systems, an opportunity India would never have had in the normal course. The *Yuan Wang 5* visit only demonstrated the Chinese hold over Sri Lanka.

The denial or acceptance of such Chinese manoeuvres by littorals like Sri Lanka has a consequence and heavy burden on their foreign policy establishment, which requires strengthening the bilateral relationship with China. Beijing usually oscillates between its soft power, sharp power,[171] and hard power from time to time, testing the genuine interest and power alignment of the new regime in Colombo, especially to understand Colombo's foreign policy toward New Delhi. The enthusiastic welcome to *Yuan Wang 5*, waving of Sri Lankan and Chinese flags and the presence of several parliamentarians depicts the Chinese influence in Sri Lanka.

In the past, Beijing's objective was obvious when a Chinese submarine port call was requested in May 2017, at the time when Indian Prime Minister Narendra Modi would be visiting Sri Lanka and President Maithripala Sirisena denied the Chinese request.[172] While the refusal was given a few days after the request, there was clear tension and pressure on President Sirisena. Chinese Defence Attache Senior Colonel Xu Jianwei, in a meeting with this author in Colombo, stated, 'The rejection was nothing for us [China], we used Pakistan's Gwadar instead of Colombo,' hinting at the multiple strategic options that China has in the Indian Ocean besides Sri Lanka. While India, Sri Lanka and the Maldives have a close mini-lateral arrangement on security issues, there are extra-regional powers such as China that test their security cooperation. The giving of permission by Sri Lanka in the first place, being well aware of the Indian objections in the past, and then the inability to even get the visit delayed, leave alone cancelled, shows China's power to override any mini-lateral security arrangements.

The spy ship's purpose of gathering intelligence will become effortless when China dominates the telecommunications infrastructure of countries like Sri Lanka. The Huawei proposal lying on President Sirisena's table in 2017 at the same time when he rejected the submarine visit is another example of China's intentions. Sirisena stood against Huawei's proposal to assist law and order, including surveillance cameras to monitor traffic and police in Sri Lanka, where the law and order ministry was not under the President at that time. There was a clear warning of Chinese backchannel entry into Sri Lanka's intelligence and communications network.

Steven Feldstein explains that through such projects, Huawei alone becomes responsible for providing AI surveillance technology to at least fifty countries worldwide and many BRI nations.[173] Uganda's USD$126 million CCTV project by Huawei is another evidence of China's plans.[174] The capture of more than 80 per cent of the entire telecommunications backbone by Chinese hardware was visible in Sri Lanka which agreed to Huawei's 5G expansion during the previous Gotabaya Rajapaksa regime.

The *Yuan Wang 5* visit is taking place when Sri Lanka is in the midst of a political–economic crisis, with limited strategic options against China's demands. The past strategic blunders made by President Wickremesinghe regarding China when he was the prime minister are well known. In 2015, it was Wickremesinghe who was a strong critic of Chinese projects and promised investigations to expose the corruption of Rajapaksa, but the promises remained unfulfilled. Today, Wickremesinghe does not want to go through the same exercise. His focus is to bring in USD$4 billion of financial assistance from China.[175] According to Dr Jehan Perera, a senior Sri Lankan academic, 'Sri Lanka needs financial assistance, and it would not want to displease China by revoking the permission.'[176] The heavy dependence on debt and financial assistance from China has increased Beijing's strategic manoeuvring space in the island. By approving the permission for the Chinese vessel, Wickremesinghe made a strategic miscalculation.

## PLASSF'S STRATEGY

There are three reasons for the PLASSF to engage in the strategic manoeuvre of deploying *Yuan Wang 5* in Sri Lanka. First, the dismantling of the pro-China Rajapaksa regime sent a message which was not favourable to China but more favourable to India. The Chinese-tilted foreign policy followed by the past regime could lose traction with the new leadership of Wickremesinghe. China wishes to sustain the same foreign policy privileges in the Wickremesinghe regime and has clearly understood Wickremesinghe's Achilles heel—the Rajapaksa majority that appointed the new president. Wickremesinghe has to depend heavily on the Rajapaksas' political support to stay in power. Since the present Sri Lankan president is appointed by the Parliament and not elected by the people, the internal manoeuvring through the Rajapaksa group is much easier for China, which already has a sway over the political elite of the country.

Second, close to USD$4 billion of economic assistance by India to the island during the crisis has enabled New Delhi to regain its position of influence which it lost during the Rajapaksa regime and win public trust as a neighbour that supported Sri Lanka at the most pressing time, especially when China was dragging its feet on its debt restructuring support to the island. *Yuan Wang 5* in India's immediate periphery will make New Delhi become aware of China's power and influence despite the change of the pro-China Rajapaksa regime.

Third, the timing of the *Yuan Wang 5* visit is just three months before the meeting of the Communist Party to re-elect President Xi as the party leader and head of the military commission, which requires a necessary projection of Xi's strength and forces him to be an ultranationalist, defending Chinese PLASSF strategy in two strategic theatres—the East China Sea and the Indian Ocean.

The docking of the Chinese vessel sends a strong message to Beijing that the new regime will continue the Rajapaksa pro-China policy.

The visit of *Yuan Wang 5* will not limit China's ambitions in these waters and China will have little inclination to modify its hard power posture and behaviour. Beijing's display of hard power by deploying military vessels has undermined its soft power, adding to the high levels of popular distrust for it in various nations. In the post-pandemic era, with its stance on 'Wolf Warrior diplomacy' and hard power, many nations will view China as a 'revisionist power' that intends to take over their regions and add them to its sphere of influence. With the financial crisis and debt unsustainability, especially due to the far lower returns than projected from Chinese projects, China's benign and benevolent image would further erode with hybrid civil–military activities in nations like Sri Lanka.

# 2

# Geopolitics

## ONE
## October 2020

### Sri Lanka and the Return of Geopolitics in the Indo-Pacific[1]

The term '*Indopazifischer Raum*' (Indo-Pacific Space) coined by German geopolitical thinker Karl Haushofer in 1920, is perhaps the first academic statement on the Indo-Pacific. Haushofer observed the marine space interlinking the two-great civilizations in Asia—India and China— separated by land by the geography of Tibet. Japan in the Indo-Pacific was identified by Haushofer, who contrived the German–Japan axis during the Second World War, with its similar interest to defeat Britain and the US in the Pacific theatre. The contemporary revival of the term has gained prevalence in geopolitical discourse after Japanese Prime Minister Shinzo Abe employed it in his speech to the Indian Parliament in August 2007.

#### GERMANY IN THE INDO-PACIFIC AND QUAD

German Foreign Minister Heiko Maas explains, 'It is already foreseeable today that, more than anywhere else, the shape of tomorrow's international order will be decided in the Indo-Pacific. Germany should not be an observer and thus play an active role, a rules-based order should be the ethos of the German foreign policy on Indo-Pacific.'[2] For the first time, the German government has released a seventy-page strategic policy guideline for the Indo-Pacific. While Germany is not an Indo-Pacific nation, many European states are joining the Indo-Pacific axis to exploit the enormous trade potential in Asia, a departure from the Atlantic axis which is security oriented. The European Union (EU) perceives China as a '*systemic rival*'[3] promoting alternative models of governance.

Today, the *Quad* (India, Japan, US and Australia) is being institutionalized and possibly broad-based to include more partners with a special focus on upholding a *rules-based order* for a *free and open Indo-Pacific*. As stated by US Secretary of State Mike Pompeo at the Quad meeting in Japan in October 2020, 'The ministers who gathered in Tokyo all came to understand the shared threat and the opportunity for us to work together not just diplomatically, but on the economic front to partner to fight back against Beijing.'[4] It is a fact that China's investments and presence in the Indian Ocean have increased, and there is no economic and financial match for Beijing in the present day. China's involvement in island-states has grown considerably, and Sri Lanka is an example of this, having received a large number of loans from China. Secretary Pompeo will visit Sri Lanka towards the end of the month and is certain to align Sri Lanka with the *rules-based order* of the Indo-Pacific along with India and the like-minded allies, directly targeting Chinese predatory infrastructure projects.

### OPAQUE LOANS IN WEAK ECONOMIES

Henry Kissinger warns that if the present US-China tension continues, 'We will slide into a situation similar to World War I.'[5] The US administration has accused China of spreading Covid-19, economic espionage by companies ranging from Huawei to TikTok, aggression in the South China Sea and its opaque loans to many nations. Sri Lanka has been cited multiple times with regard to Chinese loans which lack transparency. The US Ambassador to Sri Lanka, Alaina B. Teplitz, said, 'Sri Lanka should engage with China. It should do so in ways that protect its sovereignty and generate real prosperity for everyone, not just elites. It's not about choosing between countries, it's about transparency and charting a path that truly benefits all Sri Lankans.'[6] The ambassador's warning is pretty straightforward. Sri Lanka, counting on China, has fewer fallback options. There is too much of a China-centric dependence which limits the Sri Lankan government's inclination to look at alternatives. While successive governments have proceeded to borrow money and lease national assets, sovereignty will inevitably be threatened in every case. The Chinese embassy in Colombo reacted in its '*Wolf Warrior*' style to the ambassador's comments. 'The US has no power or obligation to lecture on China–Sri Lanka relations. Such naked hegemony, supremacy and power politics will neither be tolerated by the Chinese nor be accepted by the Sri Lankans.'[7]

Sovereignty of weak nations or failed states will always be under a threat. The US, with its '*liberal hegemonic*'[8] mission legitimising intervention or China's debt-trap diplomacy, are both directed more towards weak nations. A few weeks earlier, in October 2020, Moody's Investors Service had downgraded the sovereign rating of Sri Lanka to Caa1, or 'very high credit risk', equal to the rating of Iraq, Mali, Angola and Congo,[9] from the earlier B2 rating. There is a brewing economic crisis amidst the Covid-19 induced global economic meltdown with Sri Lanka expected to face a heavy debt repayment schedule in the coming years.

## NO MORE LOANS AND CONTRADICTORY POLICIES

Absence and disengagement of the US from the regional security architecture will not only embolden a new form of security threat—it could enable a departure from a *rules-based order* in the international system, threatening the very basis of international affairs. How does Sri Lanka, sandwiched between US's Indo-Pacific strategy and China's BRI, carve out a balanced foreign policy? In an interview in August 2020, the newly appointed Foreign Secretary of Sri Lanka, Jayanath Colombage, stated, 'President has said no more loans, our external debt to GDP is as high as 86%, if we earn $100, we have to pay $86.'[10] Explaining further, he said, 'We will not allow others to play football in our field, at least we should become a member of the team.'

Considering recent developments, it seems that Sri Lanka has joined the Chinese team due to the large amount of financial assistance and dependence, borrowing a further US$500 million on a ten-year concessional loan.[11] Another multi-million-dollar grant was made after the recent high-powered Chinese delegation's visit. Whilst accepting Chinese grants, the US MCC grant was heavily politicized and frozen. This position will threaten Sri Lanka's usual foreign policy of hedging or external balancing,[12] which involves carrying out a mix of a contradictory policy of closeness with China and the US at the same time.

## CHINESE DIPLOMACY OF BRI

Two high-powered Chinese delegations headed by Yang Jiechi and Wang Yi travelled in two directions this month. They visited South Asia, Middle East, North Africa, the Balkans and four East Asian countries. Senior diplomat Yang's delegation was to visit three maritime nations—Sri Lanka, UAE, Algeria—and one landlocked nation, Serbia. These nations play a substantial role in China's BRI.

Serbia sits at the crossroads of central and south eastern Europe and the largest share of 56 per cent of Chinese investments in the region are directed towards it.[13] Algeria has become China's fifth-largest trade partner in Africa with a trade of close to US$10 billion.[14] UAE is a key strategic partner in the BRI, linking China with Asian and European markets. China has a bilateral trade (nonoil) of US$50 billion with UAE.[15] In South Asia, Sri Lanka, with its geographically unique position in the Indian Ocean and with a strong BRI partnership established during the presidency of Mahinda Rajapaksa, has once again become a key player in the region. Yang Jiechi's visit was the first high-powered Chinese visit to South Asia after the pandemic and Sri Lanka was the first destination. The Rajapaksa sibling regime has assured Beijing of continuity of its support towards BRI and has invited further Chinese investment and funding to kickstart the ailing economy.

With Gotabaya Rajapaksa's victory followed by his brother Mahinda Rajapaksa's parliamentary victory, China has swiftly revived its earlier *Rajapaksa 1.0* (2005–2015) diplomatic relationship. This was visible with the large amount of financial assistance provided and reassurance to support Chinese infrastructure projects during the *Rajapaksa 2.0* regime. Yang Jiechi's visit will further bolster the Sino-Lanka relationship as the Chinese diplomat assured Beijing's continuous support from funding to backing at international forums including UNHRC.

President Gotabaya's development policy framework, '*Vistas of Prosperity and Splendour*',[16] was thus appreciated. 'We will support not from words but by action,' said Jiechi. President Gotabaya has welcomed further Chinese assistance in developing Sri Lankan villages, just like China has brought prosperity to many economically deprived Chinese villages. The successful Chinese visit amplifies Rajapaksa's foreign policy direction, tilting towards China in spite of his pledge to carve an equidistant foreign policy.

While 'equidistant' is merely a rhetoric for an ailing economy, external geopolitics continues to threaten the region. As Indian scholar Srikanth Kondapalli correctly highlights, there is 'a large-scale encirclement design by Beijing, which is actively roping in Nepal and Sri Lanka, besides provoking Pakistan to open a second front against India.'[17] Unfortunately, the Sri Lankan foreign policy apparatus has not assessed this external factor and the new phenomenon of China in South Asia. This is also noted by Ambassador Shivshankar Menon,[18] who points at the Chinese willingness to be involved directly or indirectly in the internal politics of South Asian countries, referring to the clear expression of preference of a particular candidate in Sri Lankan elections.

For a regional security architecture to function, there should be a cooperative security concept to anchor. What you see are *exclusive alliances* built to counter Beijing's belligerence. India,

Sri Lanka's neighbour and a main Quad partner with multiple defence cooperation agreements with the US, extending further towards *Basic Exchange and Cooperation Agreement* (BECA) to share geospatial defence intelligence, will see the emerging patterns in Sri Lanka and the Chinese influence, as unfavourable. Missing the bigger picture, an increasingly outdated scholarly tradition of *non-aligned* or *neutral* foreign policy which prevails in the country, takes comfort and repeats the rhetoric, ignoring the actual geopolitical vectors dragging us towards instability. The heavily indebted 'Sri Lanka's *conundrum*',[19] is unwittingly falling into a trap and stands to miss many opportunities if left out of the *rules-based order.*

## TWO
## November 2020

### Sri Lanka and the Coming Biden Foreign Policy[20]

Former US secretary of state Mike Pompeo's message to the Sri Lankan people to choose a 'more democratic path than tyranny'[21] has fewer implications in the post-US presidential election 2020 environment. It has been delegitimized by Pompeo's defeated leader Trump questioning the US's democratic values and procedures while refusing a peaceful transition of power and decapitating the Pentagon. It is as if President-elect Biden has the initial task of restoring and instilling dignity and integrity in the White House.

In the last few years, with the leadership of President Trump, the US lost direction and departed from multilateral institutions built with US leadership. In domestic politics, unpleasant racism, xenophobia and sexism engulfed the society and deeply polarized the community. President Biden has a Herculean task of bridging the gap and uniting the two divergent mindsets living within the same geography. To 'heal the nation, not to divide but to unify, stop treating our opponents as enemies'[22] was Biden's initial message as he clearly understood that there were millions who still believed in the Trumpian message and

Trump was most unlikely to retire in the coming years. Biden will ascend to office at 78 years of age and Trump, if he returns in 2024, will also be 78. Biden will have two daunting challenges—to restore peace in his polarized society and return the US to its global leadership role. For the domestic role, there is one positive sign. His own Vice President Kamala Harris, being the first South Asian American to become vice president in the history of US politics, could open the envelope sealed by Trump on diversity and begin to build racial harmony, an essential ingredient missing in the US society.

Warning of the dangers of Trump's rather messed-up foreign policy, former defence secretary Chuck Hegel has explained that the way out of the one-way street of Trump's foreign policy is to make it a two-way street of mutual benefit. Trump's 'America First' policy brought isolation and an overall reduction of liberal values in the international arena. The 'Trumpian structural disruptions, America First and isolationist foreign and security policies have provided China with opportunities to expand,' assesses Shrikanth Kondapillai.[23] China has grown and further strengthened its global reach with US allies, filling the vacuum created from narrow trade wars and the weakening of the US Atlantic axis, which Europe was deeply concerned with as Trump's deteriorated foreign policy was supposed to function as the guarantor of regional security. This perhaps echoes the moment when the powerful British empire failed to secure its allies, such as in Singapore, during the Japanese occupation.

### BIDEN FOREIGN POLICY AND SRI LANKA

The year 2020 began with the assassination of General Qasem Soleimani of Iran, followed by a virus which altered global geopolitics, resulting in a US-China Cold War and an unprecedented economic instability. US foreign policy had taken a dramatic shift during the Trump administration—withdrawing from the Iran nuclear agreement, TPP, UNHRC, Paris Climate Summit, to just name a few pivotal strategic decisions altering important previous policies.

South Asia will have prominence in the US grand strategy due to the significant Chinese sphere of influence in the region. China, the main competitor of the US, was seen as a *revisionist* and an aggressive power during the Trump administration. Chinese geopolitical influence in eight South Asian countries is too significant for the US to ignore. China, seen as a predator in certain countries such as Sri Lanka, is a concern for the US and its allies. The last high-level bilateral act of the Trump administration was the signing of the Basic Exchange and Cooperation Agreement for Geo-Spatial Cooperation (BECA) with India, enhancing the bilateral security relationship between the two largest democracies of the world. US foreign policy towards India would be further strengthened as Biden is committed to convening a *'summit of democracies'* in his initial year, to take on autocratic regimes. The Sri Lankan regime, which is close to China, will have to navigate stronger geopolitical headwinds with the new Biden administration.

There will be three key areas which will directly impact Sri Lankan foreign policy:

*First*, Biden will re-engage strongly in multilateral institutions and strengthen US engagement and its role. In 2015, the UNHRC resolution, co-sponsored by the US and the former Sri Lankan government, was hardly implemented due to domestic pressure and subsequent withdrawal by Sri Lanka. The Gotabaya Rajapaksa regime, which withdrew from the country's own co-sponsored resolution, will face significant pressure from the new US administration. Tamil Nadu, a state where Modi lost all the seats in the last parliamentary election, could engage with the US to voice the Tamilian issue on which the Indian government has made multiple attempts to gain attention of Colombo. After the conclusion of the war in Sri Lanka in 2009, a permanent political solution such as devolution of power has been shelved by successive governments. Unlike India, Sri Lanka has not spoken of devolution even during the last bilateral discussion between PM Modi and PM Mahinda Rajapaksa.

*Second*, the US position on the Indo-Pacific and China will have an impact on Sri Lanka's foreign policy. Many scholars assess that there is a bipartisan consensus on US-China policy. Biden will continue Trump's China posture on trade, the pandemic, technology transfers, Taiwan, South China Sea, economic and tech espionage, and North Korea. While the Covid-19 pandemic exacerbated anti-China sentiments, there was a fresh opening in 2021 for the Biden presidency to move away from Cold War 2.0 and *'Wolf Warrior'* responses to a realistic diplomatic posture and the untraversed path of mutual cooperation. The importance of multilateralism was rightly highlighted at the recent SCO summit by President Xi when he stated, 'We should take history as a mirror, practise multilateralism, improve global governance, follow the principle of extensive consultation, joint contribution and shared benefits, build a governance system, and share the benefits of development with all countries.'[24] This could be an avenue to explore peaceful cooperation and the easing of India–China border tensions.

*Third*, after losing the election, Trump issued a presidential executive order against China on 12 November, which will be effective from 11 January 2021. Thirty-one Chinese companies were targeted. The order said, 'President of the United States of America, find that the People's Republic of China (PRC) is increasingly exploiting United States capital and resources to enable the development and modernisation of its military, intelligence, and other security apparatuses.'[25] Trump's strategy is to pass to Biden, the agglomerated national security pressure on China built during his tenure. Nevertheless, due to the US '*vetocracy*' model of government, most executive decisions do not get executed. For example, the TikTok ban was held up by the commerce department.

Sanctions on Chinese companies by the US State Department will impact Chinese projects in countries like Sri Lanka. The twenty-four Chinese state-owned enterprises, including subsidiaries such as China Communications Construction Company (CCCC) that are involved in Colombo Port City and BRI-related projects in the island, faced pressure from the Trump regime. Would sanctions continue under the Biden Presidency and if they do, to what degree? This would include Huawei's 5G network where a rollout was planned by the previous Sirisena government but the overall project was not approved. Considering Colombo's close ties with Beijing and Huawei's recent strategic approach to sway policy,[26] the project is more likely to be implemented now. With India taking stern measures to ban TikTok and meet US security concerns, how will Sri Lankan policy navigate the situation? These are some important questions to ponder.

## CCP–SLPP SEMINAR AND BIDEN'S SUMMIT OF DEMOCRACIES

The CCP seminar was a peculiar development in Sri Lanka. The CCP and SLPP virtual meeting took place in November 2020 in Colombo[27] after SLPP leader Basil Rajapaksa's remark in July saying, 'SLPP party's vision is to develop similar to the Chinese Communist Party (CCP),'[28] which was a clear sign of preference for the Chinese development model.

A Sri Lanka benefiting from China should also engage in Biden's 'summit of democracies', amplifying Sri Lanka's democratic values and suppressing the semi-autocratic strains to introduce the third Rajapaksa brother to Parliament, making a triumvirate of power centres. Sri Lanka does not need to join the US and its allies to 'contain' or 'constrain' China as Shashi Tharoor prescribes for India,[29] thus articulating its principles of commitment to an international law and a rules-based order.

It is as if 2021 will begin with two different norms, presenting nations with only binary choices—between the BRI and Indo-Pacific; divided into two blocs dominated by China and the US. Let us hope that Biden's presidency will reduce the US's China drift and instead search for a compromise, with a shared value of mutual cooperation in a 'a two-way street' that will benefit the entire South Asian region.

# THREE
## December 2020

### Sri Lanka Facing the New Cold War in the Indo-Pacific Theatre[30]

Sri Lanka was never at war with Japan during the Second World War. Japan was at war with the Allied forces and Sri Lanka (then Ceylon) happened to be a base for operations of the British Eastern Command. Four months after the surprise attack on Pearl Harbour by the Japanese in the Pacific theatre which altered US's approach to the War, a similar attack took place in the Indian Ocean. On Easter Sunday morning of 5 April 1942, Sri Lanka came under attack. The geostrategic locations of Hawaii and Sri Lanka were identified and correctly assessed by the Japanese–German strategic officers—such as Vice Admiral Nomura and Admiral Kurt Fricke, Chief of Staff of the German Maritime Warfare Command (Seekriegsleitung)—as the perfect launchpads and a springboard for increasing their sphere of influence.

British Prime Minister Winston Churchill remarked that the Japanese attack, carried out on Sri Lanka (Figure 2.1)[31] by their Fast Aircraft Carrier Strike Force under the command of Vice-Admiral Chuichi Nagumo, was a decisive moment in the Second World War. This was due to the significant threat Allied Forces would face from losing Sri Lanka—a clear geographical advantage will fall to the enemy and enable them to expand to India, the Middle East and Africa. This was explained by historian, Sir Arthur Bryant, 'A Japanese Naval victory in April 1942 would have given Japan total control of the Indian Ocean, isolated the Middle East and brought down the Churchill government.'[32] Unlike Pearl Harbour, which was a surprise attack, the British Eastern Command in Sri Lanka was prepared ahead of the attack. The westward Japanese expansion strategy was suppressed and it ended in Sri Lanka, marking a decisive moment in the Second World War.

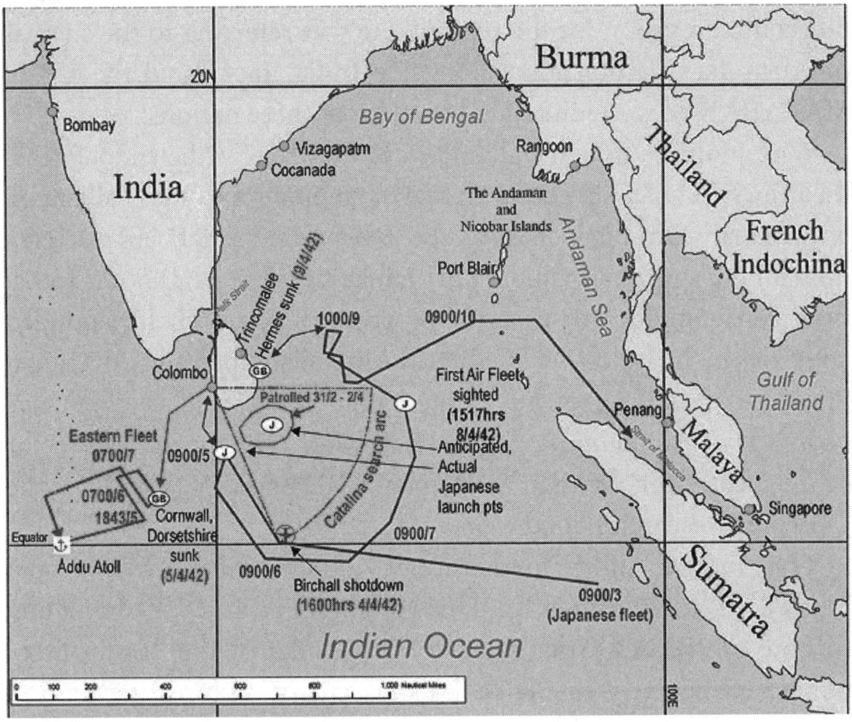


FIGURE 2.1: Japanese Raid on Ceylon in 1942

(Source: Data by ESRI Corp. 2007. Cartography by C.E. (Terry) Warner. Content is the intellectual property of ESRI and is used here with permission. Copyright © 2022 ESRI and its licensors. All rights reserved.)

At present, though in a different context, there is another westward strategy from the Eastern Pacific theatre. This is from the US Pacific Command (USPACOM) in Hawaii along with Japan, Australia and other like-minded allies who subscribe to 'shared values' of a rules-based order, against a rising China—where Sri Lankan geolocation is revisited with its strategic importance.

In view of China's acts of aggression and to protect the shared values, Admiral Philip S. Davidson, commander of the USPACOM, sends a clear message from Hawaii, 'Maldives and the US recently agreed to a security cooperation framework to deepen engagement and cooperation in support of maintaining peace and security in the Indian Ocean. India's support for this new effort is just one example of how like-minded nations can support one another in pursuit of our common vision for the region.' He was referring to the success of Australia's participation alongside India, Japan and the US in MALABAR 2020, a joint naval exercise of these nations.

With multiple military alliances taking place in the Indo-Pacific theatre, Sri Lanka also has a choice of stepping into these alliances, with a clear warning to abide by the 'rules-based order' and not team up with the aggressor China.[33] Sri Lanka's closest neighbour, India, 'has also entered into a series of partnerships with like-minded countries in the Indo-Pacific, such as Australia, Japan and the United States, to offset the growing Chinese influence as well as to enhance India's own capabilities', argues Rajeswari Rajagopalan, Director of the Centre for Security, Strategy and Technology (CSST) at the Observer Research Foundation.

The Indian high commissioner to Colombo, H.E. Gopal Baglay, in an interview in December 2020, said, 'I am happy to note the recent articulation by Sri Lanka of the "India-first" policy, particularly in the realm of security.' Expressing India's commitment to a rules-based order in the Indo-Pacific and appreciating Sri Lanka's view, as 'a free, open and inclusive Indo-Pacific [is] as important for Sri Lanka as it is for India. It is a matter of great happiness to hear similar views articulated in the senior echelons of the Government of Sri Lanka, including at plurilateral occasions.'[34] It is also worth noting that the senior echelons have also prescribed to China's BRI and recently endorsed the CCP model of development,[35] which is not really a free and open model. Sri Lanka executes a binary foreign policy and it is important to understand the implications of being part of both—one for economic benefit and another for security. A hedging foreign policy could weaken its alliance posture with external powers and gravitate towards an external conflict not by choice but by default. Sri Lanka needs to move beyond the binary choice between the US and China, disaggregating strategic competition, case-by-case.

One way is to establish strategic alliances with 'middle powers' to be able to move out of the binary path.

## GEO-INTELLIGENCE ALLIANCES IN THE INDO-PACIFIC

The US has expanded its intelligence budget according to the Director National Intelligence, and is clear on the Chinese threat as he stated, 'If I could communicate one thing to the American people from this unique vantage point, it is that the People's Republic of China poses the greatest threat to America today.'[36] Multiple alliance geo-intelligence pacts will be signed in the coming months and the Five Eyes structure revisited. From the Pacific theatre, Japan—an important partner—will join the Five Eyes intelligence-sharing network. The new Japanese Prime Minister Suga has pushed Japan to do so where, for the first time, a nation from the eastern theatre will join the military-intelligence alliance. The Five Eyes, established in 1941 with Australia, Canada, New Zealand, the United Kingdom and the United States, played a key role in signal intelligence gathering and analysis during the Cold War. In the present context, Japan's entry as the sixth eye would complement the strategic alliance as the other five, including Australia, anticipate increasing security concerns vis-à-vis China. This was further strengthened through the recent military partnership, the Reciprocal Access Agreement (RAA) with Japan and Australia.

Promoting India's subregional agenda with the critical island littorals in the Indian Ocean, the 4th NSA-level trilateral Maritime Security Cooperation meeting between India, Sri Lanka and Maldives was successfully concluded in November 2020.[37] Its previous meeting in 2014 was stalled due to strong bilateral relations of the littorals with China. At the November 2020 trilateral in Colombo, an important intelligence-sharing agreement identified the areas of terrorism and cybersecurity as 'common security threats'. This was a definite improvement since in the last high-level Indo-Sri Lanka Defence Dialogue held at the Defence Ministry in Colombo between the two defence secretaries, the subject area of terrorism or extremism was excluded from the agenda.[38] It is significant that the particular meeting was held on 8 April 2019, weeks before the 21 April Easter Sunday attacks.

The head of the delegation for the trilateral from India was the country's National Security Advisor Ajit Doval. On the sidelines of the trilateral, a meeting between President Gotabhaya Rajapaksa and Doval took place, where the multitudes of security challenges facing both nations were discussed. It was Doval who, back in 2014, flagged to then Secretary Defence Rajapaksa that the Chinese submarine presence would be a threat to India's interests.[39] Since then, there has been a strong personal-level connection between the two. Institutionalizing this relationship is an important step for India–Sri Lanka security ties. Due to India's strong security alliance with the US which includes multiple security agreements, Sri Lanka will be made a partner in the future, similar to the Maldives, with a view to share intelligence not only on counter-terrorism but also to keep (the US threat number one) China deterred.

## CIVILIZATIONAL POWERS

In the Great Powers rivalry, where several geographical theatres could be used, from Central Asia, the Arctic, the Middle East to the Indo-Pacific, there are indicators that the US-China tension would be more visible in the Indo-Pacific. During the Cold War, the pivotal defending geography for the Soviets was Berlin in Europe and today it is about defending Taiwan in East Asia.

Three ancient civilizational powers in Asia—India, China and Iran—will directly impact the geopolitics of the Indo-Pacific. These nations have a civilizational imprint on their geographies where neighbouring nations are overshadowed by their influence.

Iran holds a pivotal position in the Middle East. Their year began with the assassination of Iranian top military officer Soulamani and ended with the killing of the architect behind Iran's nuclear programme, Mohsen Fakhrizadeh-Mahabadi. The coordinated assassination of Fakhrizadeh in Teheran was a direct signal to the incoming US President Biden to stay away from the Iran nuclear deal and to continue the status quo. The assassination was aimed to secure the recent 'Abraham pact' with the UAE, Israel and Bahrain, backed by Saudi Crown Prince Mohammed bin Salman. The attack came days after the covert Israeli–Saudi–US meeting that reportedly took place in Neom.[40]

Two geopolitical pressure points will impact two regions in the coming year. First, the Middle East with its Abraham pact to deter Iran. Second, in the Indo-Pacific region, to deter China. If sanctions are relaxed, Iran would play a much larger economic role in the oil trade and support its proxies in the same manner. If China is not contained by the US and its allies, it will continue to influence through its economic, security and CCP–political model. From multiple military intelligence agreements crisscrossing geographies, expanding towards the sixth eye to contain China, with binary choices to nations like Sri Lanka, the year 2021 will begin with an elixir to the global populace suffering from a pandemic and an active Cold War in the Indo-Pacific theatre.

## FOUR
## February 2021

### Joining the Chinese Bandwagon: Geopolitics of a Container Terminal in Sri Lanka[41]

It is rather unusual for trade union leaders to talk of geopolitics. 'Geopolitics should not be a determinant factor for us to lease our own East Container Terminal (ECT) to India,' said Sanjaya Kumara Weligama, president of the Progressive Workers Association for Commercial Industry and Services (PWACIS) in an interview, along with secretary of the Trade Union Association, Shamal Sumanarathna.[42] Praising the shadow behind their strength—Prime Minister Mahinda Rajapaksa—he added, 'It was Mahinda Rajapaksa who saved our port . . . these were all to be privatised.'

Justifying the patriotism of the twenty-three unified trade unions at Colombo Port, he stated, 'None of the patriotic forces in the country wants to overthrow the government but help direct the government on the right path.'[43]

President Gotabaya Rajapaksa's earlier wish to proceed with the tripartite memorandum of cooperation (MoC) signed in 2019 with India and Japan, for a 51 per cent government majority, was turned down after the tense protest from the trade unions. President Rajapaksa was on a progressive path, pointing out at a trade union meeting that a 51:49 tripartite agreement is the most suitable geopolitical decision. The politically-influenced trade union victory denotes further inward protectionist policies of the government, departing from the liberal economic values propagated so far.

This action was deliberate, as the same fear did not exist when the government leased out a port to China for ninety-nine years. The contrived fear of external powers taking over Sri Lanka's strategic assets hyped up by ultra-nationalists will further drag the ailing economy into a narrow corridor of very few opportunities, thereby impacting individual lives. Apart from geopolitics, another factor reported in the media was the proposed Sri Lankan High Commissioner to India's involvement in misleading the president to make an illicit payment.[44]

Days after Indian Foreign Minister Dr S. Jaishankar's successful bilateral visit to Sri Lanka, the popular newspaper the *Sunday Times* discussed the ECT port deal, referring to Chinese intelligence as the only hindrance to moving the agreement forward. What the newspaper picked was the most critical underlying factor, the Chinese geopolitical push towards the island's strategic decision-making process where Beijing has become the largest source of influence. At the same time, when the ECT contract was refused to an Indian company, the Adani group, the Sri Lankan Cabinet decided to award a renewable energy joint venture project worth

US$2 million to China,[45] which is a concern to India's security due to the geographical proximity of the project to the Indian shoreline.

Geopolitics has been playing a multivariate role in determining Sri Lanka's relations with India, China and the US. Geopolitical dynamics vis-à-vis India's China stance has a direct impact on Sri Lankan foreign policy that prefers to hedge between China and India.

Sri Lanka's growing Chinese influence has affected the India–Sri Lanka relationship significantly. The danger of port geopolitics is still not understood by the hedging policy circle, where they have preferred to join the Beijing bandwagon, forgetting that a single submarine visit to Colombo port could alter India–Sri Lanka bilateral security relations, impacting domestic politics of Colombo in a similar manner as the Chinese PLAN submarine port call did in 2014.[46]

President Gotabaya Rajapaksa is shackled by an invincible geopolitical grip by an emerging extra-regional power in the form of China. The Beijing factor cannot be discounted when it comes to the nation's strategic ports. It has altered the western and southern shoreline, making two entry points—the Hambantota port in the deep south and the Colombo Port City in the west. In addition is the reclaimed seafront next to the main economic artery of the nation—the Colombo port and its CICT terminal. China already operates and has full control of the CICT terminal next to the ECT in Colombo port.

Geostrategic significance of Sri Lanka is determined by its ports, which are the entry points to the island. China strategically carved its path thirteen years ago, tagging Sri Lanka to its larger strategic map, the BRI. The strategic thinkers in Beijing snaking a path to invest in Sri Lankan ports were clear that even if there were minuscule monetary returns, they would remain in the island, as staying for a long duration was the priority. Thinking long term, China established its presence at the third strategic geographical corner of the Indian periphery, the other two port access points from land and sea being Pakistan and Myanmar—these two countries have been a major focus in China's BRI with the China–Myanmar Economic Corridor (CMEC) and the China–Pakistan Economic Corridor (CPEC).

In the backdrop of growing Sino-Pak and Sino-Myanmar dynamics, India's bilateral and multilateral interests including connectivity with other South Asian nations have been hampered. Indian foreign policy would have to consider more cautiously the Chinese sphere of influence in this regard. It is as if the ancient Chinese board game Wei Qi is played at three points—moving the power balance to dominate its opponent in a non-linear strategy. Sri Lanka, Myanmar and Pakistan have preferred to hitch themselves to the Chinese bandwagon, with China seen as the strong future power, departing from their balancing strategy with India.

On assessment, it is safer for Sri Lanka to work against aggression with like-minded allies than to join the bandwagon. Stephen M. Walt, in his book *The Origins of Alliances*, says, 'The weaker the state the more likely it is to bandwagon rather than balance.'[47] Deteriorating economic conditions with several miscalculated strategic choices have weakened the Sri Lankan state, and it is now bandwagoning with China. The government of Sri Lanka has revisited its own strategy decisions many times, either yearly or regime-to-regime, which raises questions about the weakness of its inner strategic circle.

In 2015, when the Sirisena–Wickremasinghe government came to power, a decision was taken to investigate and halt all Chinese projects. Several months later, they recommenced the projects but added some extra financial burden. When Gotabaya Rajapaksa came to power at the end of 2019, he promised to revisit the ninety-nine-year lease of Hambantota port, seeing it as a huge loss of a strategic asset. He said he would claim back the port from China.

A few days after ECT was cancelled, several questions were raised on Hambantota–Chinese agreement by the Chairman Ports Authority, General Daya Rathnayake,[48] sending a signal to New Delhi that even agreements with the Chinese could be questioned. The US MCC grant, SOFA and Japanese LRT, which were secured during the previous regime were all frozen and cancelled by the current dispensation. Most of the reviews of the past decisions were done with a weak strategic foresight. They were all politicized and the risks exaggerated out of proportion to the public. They were projected as actions to secure national assets, protect sovereignty and ensure national security, all of which had little actual relevance in the decisions. The losses from these progressive partnerships that were also PPPs are immense. From an economic point of view, the cancellations were actions of an island moving against the global norms of trade and introducing malignant economic practices. The change of decisions from the East to the West terminal at a weekly Cabinet meeting depicts inconsistency, which will impact investor confidence.

## A TURNING POINT AT UNHRC

Sri Lanka faces another daunting challenge at UNHRC in the months of February and March 2021. The 'Human Rights Watch Report 2021' has presented the picture of a deteriorating human rights footprint in the Gotabaya Rajapaksa regime, questioning militarization, forced cremation of people who died due to Covid-19, long-neglected Tamilian grievances and a few other areas of concern.[49] Further, the UN High Commissioner for Human Rights, Michelle Bachelet, has warned that the council would make a 'critical turning point' in its dealings with Sri Lanka at the upcoming session due to Colombo's long overdue commitments and present developments of the regime, especially the militarization factor (Table 2.1).[50]

While Sri Lanka has signalled last year to withdraw from UNHRC, this year the government is more likely to dismiss the allegations and follow the same path as earlier. The Sri Lankan foreign secretary, in an interview, highlighted that these allegations are coming from the global North towards the global South, and that the South will help Sri Lanka.[51] This is an incorrect assessment which will further distance the nation from the global North—not realizing that the UN Human Rights High Commissioner Michelle Bachelet is from the global South. She is a Chilean and a respected individual for her commitment to human rights. Sri Lankan policymakers continue to hope that nations like China would come to their rescue, but it is important to understand that Beijing's focus is different from Sri Lanka's and China's larger geopolitical interests would overshadow local Sri Lankan issues.

A massive protest rally was held in the northern province with thousands of participants. According to Tamil National Alliance (TNA) MP Sumanthiran, 'The march was held to protest the Government's constant restrictions on minorities, land grabbing in the North, and to demand the release of Tamil political prisoners, against the government's forced cremation policy of Covid-19 victims and all other human rights violations in the country.'[52]

It is time that Sri Lanka works on its commitments at the UNHRC, implements the recommendation and reverses the earlier decision to withdraw from the UNHRC.

It has been thirty-four years since the Sri Lankan state has spoken of devolution of power. The thirteenth amendment is still an unfulfilled commitment by subsequent governments. These concerns need to be addressed and the nation has to return to a genuine reconciliation process. A delicate balance in domestic policy—increasing the democratic footprint—and in foreign affairs is vital. A recalibration to balance rather than to bandwagon is the need of the hour.

## TABLE 2.1: Militarization in Sri Lanka

| *Date* | *Description* | *Institution/Body* | *Sector/Thematic Area* | *Type of Action* | *Position/Designation* |
|---|---|---|---|---|---|
| 2019-11-19 | Major General Kamal Gunaratne has been appointed as Defense Secretary | Ministry of Defence | Defence | Appointment of a military official (retired) | Ministry Secretary |
| 2019-12-04 | Retired Major General Jagath Alwis appointed as Chief of National Intelligence Service | National Intelligence Service | Defence | Appointment of a military official (retired) | Chief |
| 2019-12-18 | Major General (Rtd.) G.A. Chandrasiri appointed the new Chairman of the Civil Aviation Authority of Sri Lanka | Civil Aviation Authority | Civil Aviation | Appointment of a military official (retired) | Chairman |
| 2019-12-19 | Admiral Prof. Jayanath Colombage appointed Additional Secy. to President for Foreign Relations | President's Office | Foreign Relations | Appointment of a military official | Additional Secretary |
| 2019-12-23 | Former Army Commander Major General Daya Ratnayake made chairman of the Sri Lanka Ports Authority | Sri Lanka Ports Authority | Ports Authority | Appointment of a military official | Chairman |
| 2020-01-03 | Maj. Gen. (Retd) Sudantha Ranasinghe has been appointed as the Director General of the Disaster Management Centre (DMC). | Disaster Management Centre (DMC) | Disaster Managment | Appointment of a military official (retired) | Director General |
| 2020-01-24 | Major General (Retd.) Nanda Mallawarachchi assumed duties as the Director General of the Department of Multi-Purpose Development Task Force | Department of Multi-Purpose Development Task Force | Develoment | Appointment of a military official (retired) | Director General |
| 2020-01-14 | Major Geneneral Darshana Hettiarachchi was appointed as the Rehabilitation Commissioner General | Bureau of Commissioner General Rehabilitation | Rehabilitation | Appointment of a military official | Commissioner General |
| 2020-02-24 | Sri Lanka Corps Military Police personnel deployed to assist the Colombo City Traffic Division | | | Deployment of Military Personnel | N/A |
| 2020-02-25 | Maj. Gen. Vijitha Ravipriya appointed Customs DG | Sri Lanka Customs | Trade | Appointment of a military official (retired) | Director General |
| 2020-03-18 | Acting Chief of Defence Staff Army Commander Lt. Gen. Shavendra Silva appointed as Head of National Ops. Centre to counter COVID-19 | National Operation Centre for Prevention of COVID-19 Outbreak (NOCPCO) | Health | Appointment of a military official | Head |
| 2020-03-24 | Former Air Force Commander Roshan Goonetileke appointed Western Province Governor | Governor's Office | | Appointment of a military official | Governor |
| 2020-03-28 | Retired Maj. Gen.Sumedha Perera appointed Poverty Eradication Task Force Co-Chairman | Task Force for Poverty Eradication and Livelihood Development | Develoment | Appointment of a military official (retired) | Co-Chairman |
| 2020-04-16 | Appointment of Capt. Themiya Abeywickrama as the Director General of Civil Aviation/Chief Executive Officer | Civil Aviation Authority | Civil Aviation | Appointment of a military official | Director General |
| 2020-04-22 | One-fifth of the members of the presidential task force formed for post-COVID economic response are from the armed forces | Presidential Task Force in charge of Economic Revival and Poverty Eradication | Economy | Appointment of a military official, Appointment of a military official (retired) | Head Members |
| 2020-04-27 | Army replaces police for external security of the parliamentary premises | Parlaiment | Security | Deployment of Military Personnel | N/A |
| 2020-05-11 | Major General Sanjeewa Munasinghe, the Director General of Army Health Services, assumed duties as the new Health Secretary. | Ministry of Health | Health | Appointment of a military official | Ministry Secretary |
| 2020-05-11 | Retired Major General Sumedha Perera appointed as Secretary to the Mahaweli Ministry | Ministry of Mhaweli, Agriculture, Irrigation and Rural Development (Irrigation Sector) | Agriculture, Develoment | Appointment of a military official (retired) | Ministry Secretary |
| 2020-05-23 | Proposed Presidential Task Force headed by the Defence Secretary to protect archaeological sites | Presidential Task Force for Archaeological Heritage Management in the Eastern Province | Archaeology | Appointment of a military official | Head |
| 2020-06-02 | Establishment of a Presidential Task Force for Archaeological Heritage Management in the Eastern Province | Presidential Task Force for Archaeological Heritage Management in the Eastern Province | Archaeology | Appointment of a military official | Members |
| 2020-06-02 | Establishment of a Presidential Task Force to build a Secure Country, Disciplined, Virtuous and Lawful Society | Presidential Task Force to build a Secure Country, Disciplined, Virtuous and Lawful Society | Law and Order | Appointment of a military official, Appointment of a military official (retired) | Head Members |
| 2020-10-18 | Retired Major Anura Pandithage appointed as CEO of Lanka Sathosa | Lanka Sathosa Limited | Provisions | Appointment of a military official (retired) | Head |
| 2020-10-18 | Wing Commander Primal Paragahawatta (Retd.) appointed as DGM – Human Resources and Administration of Lanka Sathosa | Lanka Sathosa Limited | Provisions | Appointment of a military official (retired) | Deputy General Manager |
| 2021-01-01 | Appointment of senior army officials to each district for the coordination of COVID-19 prevention measures | National Operation Centre for the Prevention of COVID-19 Outbreak | Health | Appointment of military officials | Head Members |
| 2021-06-19 | Retd. General Daya Ratnayake appointed as the new Secretary to the Ministry of Industries | Ministry of Industries | Commerce | Appointment of a military official (retired) | Ministry Secretary |
| Miitary in key government positions during President Gotabaya Rajapaksa regime 2019-2022. | | | | | |

- Foreign Affairs
- Economy
- Health
- Law and Order
- Trade and Commerce
- Disaster Management
- Ports
- Civil Aviation
- Agriculture
- Archeology
- Provisions -Sathosa stores
- Department of Multi Purpose Development Task Force
- Task Force of Poverty Eradication and Livelihood Development
- Task Force Economic Revival
- Beureau of Commissioner General Rehabilitation
- Governor

Credit: Sachini Perera[53]

# FIVE
# June, 2021

## Russia and Sri Lanka's Role in Regional Security: Perspective from Sri Lanka[54]

### RUSSIA AND SRI LANKAN GEOGRAPHY

Sri Lanka is viewed today as an important strategic hub in the larger strategic maps of BRI and Indo-Pacific. Sri Lanka's geography has been discussed by many scholars of international relations due to significant Chinese infrastructure projects in the island, including the Hambantota port—a large-scale seaport built by China. While there are many references in literature about the Chinese explorer Zheng He who made seven voyages to the Indian Ocean region between 1405 and 1433, not much has been written about the great Russian voyager Afanasy Nikitin, who reached India in 1469.[55] Russia has 1,500-year-old rich history and a unique culture. This year, in 2021, Russia celebrated the seventy-sixth anniversary of victory in the great patriotic war over the Nazi Germany. Russia's role in restoring and stabilizing global order cannot be discounted.

Although Russia does not have a direct connection with Indian Ocean, its geographical position in the world map drew attention of many geopolitical thinkers such as the British geographer Halford J. Mackinder, in the early twentieth century, who depicted Russia as the 'heartland'. Mackinder's heartland theory portrays Russia's geopolitical influence over its vicinity and the surrounding regions and Russia's role in the global geopolitical theatre. I have cited Mackinder's work in my book *Sri Lanka at Crossroads* which refers to Mackinder's map and compares Sri Lanka, facing the Indian Ocean, to the other two islands—UK and Japan, facing the Atlantic and the Pacific—situated at the outer crescent of the rimland.

### RUSSIA–SRI LANKA DIPLOMATIC RELATIONSHIP

Russia today has re-established its global strategic and defence roles with new partnerships. We in Sri Lanka view Russia as a partner, with decades of diplomatic relationship established since 19 February 1957. Our relationship has been built in the past with Sri Lanka's commitment to non-aligned principles and its socialist values post-independence. Russia has assisted Sri Lanka in terms of security and defence throughout Sri Lanka's history. Its assistance in counter-terrorism and intelligence-sharing needs to be strengthened further. While the Intergovernmental Commission on Trade, Economic, Scientific and Technological Cooperation is a significant step in the development of our economic ties, it is important to develop defence and security cooperation between Russia and Sri Lanka.

Russian exports to Sri Lanka have been around US$400 million and imports almost US$290 million. While Russia plays a larger role in its multilateral arena including BRICS, SCO, ASEAN, CICA and Asia Cooperation Dialogue, and Sri Lanka is also an active member in these multilateral forums, there is so much potential that both countries could explore in trade, defence and other sectors. The minister of foreign affairs of Russia, Sergey Lavrov's visit to Sri Lanka on 14 January 2020 strengthens our bilateral relations further through track-one diplomacy. Russia and Sri Lanka have signed bilateral agreements in fisheries, tourism, culture, space research and many other areas. But there is a lot to be done in areas of track-two diplomacy.

### RUSSIA IN ASIA–PACIFIC

According to the HE Yury Materiy, Russian ambassador in Colombo, 'South Asia and Asia–Pacific region remains one of the key priorities of our foreign policy. Russia is not only a European but also an Asian country, due to its geographical position.'[56] Correctly prioritized, Russia in Asia at the time of the Asian century in the making, along with China, India and East Asian economies, will propel a more significant growth than any other time in history. Security cooperation and maintaining stability in the Asia–Pacific is a key ingredient for future progress. Cooperation and consultation with Russia as an external power to littorals like Sri Lanka is essential in maintaining its balanced foreign policy.

The Sri Lankan regime presently and in the past has articulated a balanced non-aligned foreign policy. My work in the recent years has been on researching on Sri Lanka's foreign policy and its impact, when losing the balance affects domestic security. Both my recent books—*Sri Lanka at Crossroads* which was published before the Easter Sunday terror attack, and *Conundrum of an Island*, which explores the security dimensions after the Easter Sunday terror attack—highlight the strategic vulnerabilities that have impacted Sri Lankan foreign policy and national security. With three spheres of major influences on the island of Sri Lanka—India, US and China—Sri Lanka requires extra-regional powers to balance and maintain its strategic balance. In this equation, Russia is an important player. In the evolving regional security environment, Russia should include Indian Ocean as a priority region.

## STRATEGIC AMBIVALENCE OF POLICIES

When exploring the EU strategy document released in April this year which clearly highlights the importance of EU's role in the Indo-Pacific, but takes a more diplomatic role with China and does not name it as an assertive power makes EU's strategy unique from other countries such as France, Germany, UK and US.[57] In the EU strategy, the elephant in the room—China—was not mentioned even once in the report. Frederic Grare questions, 'What message will the EU Council's words convey to China given that they do not even describe China as a "competitor, systemic rival and partner" in the way that the EU strategy does?'[58]

Due to fundamental ambivalence in UK and EU strategies on China, where the reports highlight the importance of trade with China but at the same time question China's security concerns from trade, '[It] falls to the Commission and the high representative to clarify the meaning of an EU Indo-Pacific strategy and make sure it does not fall into irrelevance,' argues Frederic Grare. This strategic ambivalence and the quixotic nature of the policy prescriptions could lead to confused policies. In this regard, Russia has a role as an important power in Eurasia and Asia–Pacific to set the norms in security for stability.

The problems confronting our international community cannot be addressed by one country alone as we are in a multipolar world. The UK government's policy on Indo-Pacific in its 'The Integrated Review of Security, Defence, Development and Foreign Policy' released in March 2021 highlights the importance of working with middle powers due to the multipolarity of the emerging world order.[59]

### BIG POWER RIVALRY AND BILATERAL TRADE

We require an inclusive and broader consultative process to resolve our global challenges. The unpredictability of the actions of big powers and the big power rivalry has increased today, calling it another 'Cold War'. The current deterioration of relationship between Russia and the West should be addressed to bring about global stability. The recent bilateral meeting between President Biden and President Putin gives strength and hope for this stability. If the instability at global level is not managed, it will be transmitted to the regional level and especially to the most vulnerable countries like Sri Lanka. The terrorism in Syria travelled all the way to Sri Lanka and killed more than 250 innocent people in the Easter Sunday terror attack.

Despite the global power competition, bilateral security trade could grow with Russia. In geopolitics, the static variable geography cannot be ignored, and Russia and China are a part of both Indo-Pacific and BRI mental maps. NATO may expand its mandate to Asia or Indo-Pacific due to big power rivalry in the coming years. NATO and Quad should consider the role their members play with Russia and China. India is purchasing Russian S400s, ASEAN weapons trade with Moscow is increasing.[60] While nations may endorse a rules-based order and Indo-Pacific in principle, they will continue to develop and maintain bilateral trade. Russia and Sri Lanka could build their bilateral relationship despite Sri Lanka supporting both BRI and Indo-Pacific strategies. Sri Lanka's defence capacities, especially on maritime security, should be built and Russia can support Sri Lanka in this regard.

## THREE CAVEATS FOR A POST-COVID WORLD

I have explored few caveats for post-pandemic stability for security and cooperation.

First, Russia's balancing role to provide stability at the global level and building mutual confidence should be a top priority in the post-pandemic world. The pandemic taught us how interconnected we are and the systemic risks we have all ignored in our global system.[61] The developed nations will not be safe without making the developing nations safe as well in terms of vaccinations. We need to think of the global ecosystem as one. The assistance of Russia and many other nations to save lives in Sri Lanka by donating vaccines has to be appreciated, especially at a time of economic slowdown in the country. Stability at a global level can be achieved with multilateralism and inclusive approach rather than isolation. The June 2021 meeting between President Biden and President Putin is in the right direction. As Biden explained, US has a 'predictable and rational' relationship with Russia and that US and Russia were 'two great powers,' a notable elevation of Moscow's status on the world stage.[62] An isolationist position elevates multiple levels of security threats to the world. Russia's role in the global order needs to be recognized.

Second, Sri Lanka could play a leading role as a neutral partner in the Indian Ocean. Sri Lanka's geographical position could be used by regional and extra-regional powers to bring stability to the Indian Ocean, especially in maritime security, HADR operations, drug trafficking, piracy and terrorism. Sri Lanka has faced almost a three-decade civil war, extremist terror threats and the recent environmental catastrophe by the chemical spill in Sri Lankan waters.[63] All these depict the vulnerability of nations like Sri Lanka in the NTS threat sphere.

At the regional level, guidelines can be developed with standard operating procedures on civilian–military cooperation in disaster relief operations. Military assets present in the Indian Ocean to sustain maritime security operations could be launched from Sri Lanka. The country is in a position, due to the significant threats to the island, to invite capacity-building mechanisms and technical assistance to develop its capability to play a larger role in the region. Sri Lanka's geographical position. Its trained security forces can possibly be used for regional peace building and stability. Projects like CRIMARIO from EU[64] in the Indian Ocean and Russia's future maritime security assistance could be positively viewed by Colombo. As Sri Lanka strengthens its mini-lateral security cooperation such as the India–Maldives–Sri Lanka agreement on security and intelligence, these mini-laterals could be further strengthened through extra-regional assistance such as from Russia to strengthen defensive security measures in the Indian Ocean.

Sri Laka's neutrality in its foreign policy is a key to bring all these projects and assistance to the island-nation. Unfortunately, Sri Lankan foreign policy has not maintained its balance, as several scholars argue. Tilting towards China is seen as a loss for the country in achieving this role as a regional stabilizer. The China bias has also constrained the relationship with India. As Sreeradha Datta explains, 'To take the relationship to a higher level it is imperative that Colombo understand and adequately address Indian apprehensions about Colombo's lack of adequate sensitivity towards India's security interests.'[65] Sri Lanka–India relationship is a key area to develop as India could propel such future aspirations of Sri Lanka's role in the Indian Ocean.

Third, track-two diplomacy is an essential ingredient in diplomacy. The term was introduced by Joseph V. Montville, who was also instrumental in developing the 'two track' diplomatic process.[66] In the post-Covid world, this should be given a priority.

Track-two involves a non-governmental approach with inputs from academia, think tanks and researchers. The preparation of confidence-building-measures and addressing multiple psychological barriers for peace building are done at the level of track-two. According to the New Zealand diplomat Suzannah Jessep, 'The need for diplomacy and Track II—as we contend with large-scale, complex challenges like Covid-19—is only going to increase over time. . . . Like all forms of diplomacy, the point of Track II is ultimately to steer us clear of conflict and disorder. Or to put this another way, to strike a balance between competing national interests.'[67] Giving less appreciation to track-two makes for weaker decisions at track-one and leaders become vulnerable to multiple NTS treats. The investment in track-two and its prioritization is an essential component to achieve track-one success and achieve a balance. Leaders would need to invest in this area for a better result in the post-Covid environment to maintain a regional security balance.

The three areas discussed could expand Russia's security role and cooperation in the global arena and in the Asia Pacific, including in nations like Sri Lanka.

# SIX
## September 2021

### Remembering a Military Quagmire: The Exit of the United States from Afghanistan and the Impact on Small States[68]

R.W. Apple Jr wrote way back in 2001, 'Like an unwelcome specter from an unhappy past, the ominous word "quagmire" has begun to haunt conversations among government officials and students of foreign policy, both here and abroad. Could Afghanistan become another Vietnam?'[69] It took another twenty years for the entire world to witness the US exit from Afghanistan. Shocking pictures of Afghan civilians clinging onto a US C17 military aircraft appeared in the media. Some of them shockingly perished in mid-air at the Kabul airport in Afghanistan. The US had to live another Saigon moment. Pictures of US withdrawal in Saigon circulated in the media—including the famous image of a man with a white shirt reaching down to grab a person at the top of a staircase to board the helicopter.

On the afternoon of 29 April 1975, CIA officer Oren Bartholomew Harnage was assisting the fleeing refugees at 22 Gia Long Street (not the US embassy). This was photographed by Dutch journalist Van Es. Back then, President Nixon's exit from Vietnam had 130,000 South Vietnamese evacuated to the US bases in Guam and the Philippines. Then the evacuees were resettled in the US. Just like refugees who fled Communist rule, today the same obligation to protect Afghan refugees fleeing Taliban's clutches has fallen on the United States. According to ORF scholar Harsh Pant, 'The hard-won rights for women and minorities and democracy have already been sacrificed at the altar, reaching a modus vivendi with the Taliban.'[70] The US withdrawal was depicted as a humiliation and a loss, falling short of not capturing the precise strategic dimensions. There was a discussion how the exit would impact India and the regional security of South Asia, especially the smaller South Asian neighbours like Sri Lanka, Bangladesh and the Maldives.

### THE FAILURE OF NON-MILITARY INSTRUMENTS OF POWER

Robert M. Gates, in his book *Exercise of Power*, admits, 'It is probably true that Brent Scowcroft and I as National Security Advisor and deputy should have at least devoted some time to focus on how the U.S. and others might help Afghanistan after a decade of war ... we certainly sent the wrong signal when we closed our embassy after the Soviets left. After helping the Afghans defeat the Soviets, we presumably had the foundation of at least some goodwill.'[71]

The lost opportunity in 1989 was due to the US focus on Eastern Europe and not on Afghanistan. With the US absence, between 1996–2001, Osama Bin Laden established camps in Afghanistan that trained an estimated ten thousand terrorist fighters. Afghanistan became a state sponsor of terror, and a state sponsored by terror, wrote President George W. Bush in his memoir *Decision Point*.

Exactly 26 days after the 9/11 attack, US military began its airstrikes in Afghanistan. Taliban and al-Qaeda were ousted from Afghanistan by early 2002, with 27 American lives lost and US$20 billion spent. After 20 years, the nation-building cost was nearly US$ 2 trillion. Gates observes, 'We and Afghans would have been better served had our military departed in 2002 and had we thereafter relied on our non-military instruments of national power and patience,' believing that lasting change would come with a more realistic projection. Georgetown scholar Christine C. Fair rightly assesses, 'After clearing Afghanistan of Al Qaeda, which happened in 2004, the United States should have withdrawn. When the United States decided to declare war on the Taliban and enter into a highly ill-devised state-building fiasco, it should have realised that this would be a disaster absent any policy to stop Pakistan from supporting the Taliban.'[72] According to Sarah Chayes, while Pakistan was a key factor for the Taliban's tentacles to grow in Afghanistan, the Afghan government's corruption was another important factor.[73]

### TALIBAN AND CHINA

The US has faced multiple exits and several cycles of proxy wars since the end of the Cold War when the hammer and the sickle flag fell in Kremlin. US exit from Afghanistan was a decision of the previous Trump administration, taken forward by President Biden.

The withdrawal strategy leaves China, the emerging power in Asia, with more responsibility to balance the Taliban occupation, making China's western frontier of Xinjiang open to multiple security threats. A month ago, Taliban leaders assured China 'that they will not allow anyone to use Afghan soil against China'[74] and promised to support China to maintain security in their border areas in the Wakhan corridor. However, China's BRI still remained vulnerable when the US left Afghanistan, a geographical pivot state wedged between Central and South Asian regions.

The calculated exit from the unending war in Afghanistan was a strategy that was in the making for many years in Washington. It was wholly executed by Biden. The danger of the US exit is not the Taliban's hold, but that their tentacles and extremist agenda will expand through their proxies to multiple geographies in the region, threatening the regional security balance.

### TALIBAN AND THE SMALLER SOUTH ASIAN NATIONS

There is a clear danger present to India from the Taliban. India, which focused its security concerns in the recent past towards north (China) and west (Pakistan) would need a broader spectrum of focus towards the south (Sri Lanka and the Maldives) and east (Bangladesh). Taliban's proxies in Bangladesh, which include Jund al-Tawheed Khalifa, Harkat-ul-Jihad-al-Islami (HuJI-B), AQIS, and Jamaat-ul-Mujahideen Bangladesh (JMB), will have a new lease of life with the Taliban's grip in Afghanistan. The Maldives, in comparison to other South Asian countries with its highest per capita contribution to foreign terrorist fighters, will be another nation that will be vulnerable. Radicalized extremists in the country will see an opportunity to spread their agenda with the Taliban's emergence to power.

In Sri Lanka, the burqa ban, madrasa regulation and forced cremation of Muslim victims of Covid-19 are clear factors to push Muslims towards further radicalization, which the Taliban will exploit. Jihadist movements, such as National Tohweed Jamath (NTJ), with contacts with South Indian cells, will get their energy back with the return of Taliban. Smaller South Asian nations with weak security structures will be fertile grounds for the Taliban to push its extremist agenda and suppress secular movements. Sri Lanka, which faced its most significant terror attack in April 2019, is vulnerable to security threats in the future due to its the weak political environment.

Pakistan will be a breeding ground of terrorism due to its support of Taliban terrorists to spread their activities. Pakistan Prime Minister Imran Khan's view is that Taliban's capture of Afghanistan is a moment of freedom for the country. He says, 'Afghanistan has broken the shackles of slavery.' The Taliban's grip and expanse will directly threaten India as well as many smaller South Asian nations. The radical Islamic elements will flow across borders easily due to a lack of infrastructure to counter the threat. The multi-jurisdictional structures for intelligence sharing and counter-terrorism in South Asia are underfunded and underdeveloped. The Sri Lankan Easter Sunday attack proves this.

### TALIBAN 2.0 AND THE INDO-PACIFIC

Greater Pakistan-China and Sri Lanka-China collaboration and Chinese projects, such as CPEC or Hambantota Port City, are development projects to accelerate economic growth. The security challenges from the Taliban can have a large destabilizing effect on these projects and cause severe delays. China's inroads in South Asia are well established in pro-China nations within the BRI. Many of these nations did not view the US presence in the region as a positive factor, depicting it as a potential threat to national security, mainly projected from miscalculated policy decisions. The US withdrawal from Afghanistan is a direct message to the regional powers to look after their own regional security concerns rather than depend on Washington. The Western allies will draw another strategy for Taliban 2.0, perhaps inclined more towards Indo-Pacific. Thus, filling the gap after the withdrawal of the United States will be a challenging task for India, China and Russia. Maintaining the regional security of Central Asia and South Asia is going to be highly contested. China is far from filling the gap and perhaps will not focus on wider security concerns. Russia is monitoring the situation, leaving the burden to India, which will face a clear, direct security threat from all directions including the smaller South Asian nations.

# SEVEN
# October 2021

## AUKUS, the Quad, China in Sri Lanka and India's Security Concerns[75]

Alliances gives a new meaning to political boundaries on physical maps and empower coalitions with similar political preferences to work together. President Biden does 'not seek a new Cold War', as he clearly expressed at the UNGA. Many world leaders are with Biden, including the Indian Prime Minister Modi. If the world is divided into two rigid blocks as in the past, it will only limit progress and prosperity of many nations. In reality, Cold War structures will resurrect if the rules-based order is threatened, and robust partnerships will be required at that time.

President Biden established a more structured alliance, the AUKUS,[76] a week before the first-ever in-person Quad Summit in Washington, D.C. on 24 September 2021.[77] AUKUS, the security alliance, will enhance the capability of the US, UK and Australia on deterrence. There will be an expansion of underwater warfare capabilities of the nuclear-powered submarine fleet which will be used for extended patrols. With more military capacity in the Indo-Pacific and substantial naval presence, the like-minded nations in the new security alliance will deter China's aggressiveness in the South China Sea and the surrounding waters. Many like-minded nations with democratic values, who subscribe to Free and Open Indo-Pacific (FOIP), will be a part of the AUKUS security structure in the future.

While the security alliances are usually heavily structured, the primary informal structure with a non-militaristic space will be the Quad. Michael J. Green from the Centre for Strategic and International Studies (CSIS) argues, 'It's like a dimmer, not an off-on switch. . . . It's a flexible tool, including who joins. It's flexible for a Korea or a New Zealand or the UK. If they decide they're upset with China, they can send a frigate to the next exercise.' The flexibility of the Quad made it easier for nations like Singapore to join military exercises a few years ago with the Quad and many other nations to follow bilateral or trilateral naval exercises to support the critical Quad goal—to maintain a free and open Indo-Pacific (FOIP).

In the Western diplomatic toolkit, Quad is in the forefront due to the aggressiveness of China in the Indo-Pacific—military expansion, economic takeover with stealth and 'strategic trap' to shackle nations under Chinese BRI orbit. 'The Quad has come together due to China's assertive behaviour . . . and economic dependence of some countries,' explains ORF scholar Dhruva Jaishankar.[78] The Quad is a non-security arrangement due to India's appeal to leave security out of its core agenda. In the last meeting, securing supply-chain security, semiconductors and vaccine diplomacy was the primary focus. China was not mentioned during the summit due to the Biden administration's idea that Quad should project a positive vision towards vaccines, climate change and critical technologies, and not be seen as a grouping to contain China.

However, C. Raja Mohan from ISAS Singapore observes, 'China's peaceful rise has not been peaceful, a concern to many nations . . . having bitten once [by China] people are finding alternatives.'[79] China's aggression with military expansion, the lack of concern for human rights and coercive economic practices with takeover of strategic assets by stealth, promoting alternative governance structures with more militaristic regimes such as in Sri Lanka, would alter the core agenda of the Quad. India, which preferred a non-military configuration for the Quad, would perhaps be forced to bring security issues to the Quad agenda in the future to defend and protect the regional balance in its immediate neighbourhood, which has been disturbed by China.

Quad, initiated in 2004 in the post-Asian Tsunami period, has been at the forefront during the pandemic to 'play the role of a force for global good'. Explains Prime Minister Modi, 'I'm confident that our cooperation under Quad will ensure prosperity and peace in the Indo-Pacific and in the world.'[80]

The informal structure of Quad to protect and bring democratic nations together will give protection to nations that have become victims of China's 'debt trap', such as Sri Lanka. Quad will also be a balancing counterweight to Chinese expansion. The Hambantota port and Colombo Port City are the best examples of Chinese strategic expansion. While accepting and expanding the Chinese loans, Sri Lanka rejected substantial grants such as the US MCC. Recently, at Carnegie Endowment,[81] the Sri Lankan foreign secretary explained the rejection of the US MCC grant of US$480 million by the government. He said it was 'democracy and people's power' that scrapped the project, maintaining that there was no China hand behind. The foreign secretary forgot about the presidential expert commission report. US MCC was rejected by the Sri Lankan government after the presidential expert committee falsely misinformed the public that there was a national security threat from the MCC project. The four-member committee headed by Professor Lalithasiri Gunaruwan submitted an interim report which said, 'There were clauses and conditions in the agreement that would negatively affect national goals and objectives, sovereignty, and national security, and were inconsistent with the legal framework and Constitution.'[82]

The Chinese sphere of influence has now enlarged and entered Sri Lanka's democratic space, where the Sri Lankan regime defends the Chinese abuse of human rights in Xinjiang. This is a clear sign of a reciprocal arrangement to receive assistance from China to defend the grave human rights concerns in Sri Lanka raised by the UN High Commissioner at the 48th UNHRC session a few weeks ago. The response of Foreign Secretary Jayanath Colombage was, 'We wish to remain neutral in our foreign policy,'[83] which contradicts the Chinese bandwagoning foreign policy posture taken by the government. Colombage further explained that Chinese warship arrivals in Sri Lanka are far lower than those from India and Japan, whose 563 warships have visited since 2009, trying to project a lower significance of Chinese presence and interest, using the quantum of warship arrivals as a criteria. This illogical view does not capture the broader strategic danger to the island-nation and its neighbour, India.

India will have two responses to the Chinese aggression and the strategic takeover of its neighbouring nations. The first response will be to strengthen its external alliance structure, such as Quad, to nudge nations like Sri Lanka towards the norms and values of the international system rather than drift from a quasi-democracy to a military-controlled autocratic regime. This drift towards China will pose a direct threat to India's security. While economic practices and standards are also a part of Quad dialogue, the focus on supply chain security shows the group's intention to work together in the economic arena, where China's place in the world economy would limit how much success the Quad can achieve in bringing in standards to economic practices.

The Biden administration's focus on the B3W (Build Back Better World) initiative will complement the economic infrastructure standards and supply chain security in the coming years. The Biden administration will focus more on Quad and the G-7, the two core organizing bodies that will focus on the global international system to achieve tangible results. India has a strong position and a strong voice in both of these platforms, more than any other South Asian nation. As mentioned by PM Modi, India is a 'natural ally for the G7 countries in the fight against authoritarianism, terrorism and violent extremism, disinformation, and economic coercion, among other threats'.[84]

The second response from India will be to partner and support security alliances. A more formal structure such as AUKUS will be of India's interest since the mini-lateral complements India's vision towards achieving a rules-based Indo-Pacific. ORF scholar Rajeswari Pillai Rajagopalan aptly captures this and says, 'AUKUS is an important development because it signifies the capability augmentation of one of India's closest strategic partners, with whom it has just started a 2+2 ministerial dialogue. A strong and capable Australia is in India's interests, that of the Quad and the broader Indo-Pacific region.'[85]

These mini-lateral platforms will crisscross the Indian Ocean, where Sri Lanka, an important maritime nation located geo-strategically in the Indian Ocean, will be a crucial partner to consider. Unfortunately, in the present context, it is drifting away from such platforms towards the Chinese orbit. Nations like Sri Lanka are essential due to their open access to the Indian Ocean, where naval exercises and maritime security will be primary drivers for sustaining the mini-lateral military arrangements. Sri Lanka's security trilateral signed by the Gotabaya Rajapaksa regime with India and Maldives is a mini-lateral in the right direction and will benefit Sri Lanka.

India would require a two-pronged strategy—one for its northern borders and another for its southern ones—the Indian Ocean. India, the only nation among the Quad nations that shares a physical geographical border with China, is more vulnerable than the other Quad members in case of a direct confrontation. India's challenges from its western flank, from Af–Pak, will grow with the Chinese footprint expanding in Afghanistan. From India's south, the security balance of the Indian Ocean will be of primary interest where Sri Lanka, Maldives and other littorals cannot be ignored. The efforts of mini-lateral democratic alliances such as Quad should focus more on nations like Sri Lanka, targeted by the Chinese 'debt and strategic trap'. The Sri Lankan regime seeping away from democratic norms to a militarized rule has drifted from the Indo-Pacific configuration, a geographical flashpoint in India's vicinity. The Quad should actively engage and seek commitment from nations like Sri Lanka, pulling them towards the norms and values of a rules-based order. The country-specific strategic push from the Quad will assist Sri Lanka to recalibrate its foreign policy towards a more balanced and progressive path and follow international norms and values.

## EIGHT
## January 2022

### A World Challenged by Geopolitical Tensions: The Global Risk Report[86]

The seventeenth edition of the Global Risk Report by the World Economic Forum was published on 11 January 2022 at a time of significant global geopolitical tension.[87] The Global Risks Perceptions Survey (GRPS) reported that they 'believe the world will follow a fractured trajectory in the medium term with a higher percentage of 41.8% observed the global outlook for the next three years will be "consistently volatile with multiple surprises", and

61.2% feel concerned'. The Global Risk Report 2022 is a valuable guide to comprehending the risk factors and designing strategies to formulate solutions for governments and other stakeholders. The pandemic has pushed many nations out of multilateral agenda into inward-focused, ultra-nationalist postures, triggering geopolitical tension in different geographies. Geopolitical and geoeconomics tension among the big powers will create a difficult environment to tackle shared global challenges such as in climate, health, economic, social and other areas highlighted in the report.

From Russia's periphery in Ukraine and Kazakhstan to India and China's periphery to the Indo-Pacific, geopolitical undercurrents have raised tension to a significant flashpoint which could impact the entire globe. The Global Risk Report mentions 'geopolitical and geopolitical tension' in more than sixty places, highlighting its importance and making it among the top ten most severe risk factors in the next ten years.[88] These risk factors include natural resources, climate, social, geoeconomics and debt crisis, all of which raise concerns in multiple geographies. The peripheral diplomacy carried out by big powers to stabilize their own regions has shifted from a passive posture to aggression, a factor visible in Russia, China and India's immediate geographical periphery, and the US in the Indo-Pacific theatre.

'[The] key global and regional powers are testing boundaries of international law and cooperation by conducting military exercises around tense areas, such as the Russia–Ukraine border and the Taiwan Strait.'[89] Also, apart from land, sea, air—the traditional domains of geopolitics—cyber and space are given attention in the report, which says, 'Competition is intensifying in newer dimensions and geographies, as evident in the militarisation and weaponisation of space and in developments in cyberspace, where already sharp tensions between governments impacted by cybercrime and governments complicit in their commission will continue to rise.'[90] This is a critical assessment that requires investment and commitment from individual nations to strategize a holistic approach to minimize the tension. The same evaluation is given by Dr Rajeswari Pillai

Rajagopalan, who explains, 'The absence of earnest multilateral discussions could send more states down the path of space weaponisation, making access to space tricky.' Major space powers need to recognize the urgent need to start multilateral negotiations.

The risk report highlights that geopolitical competition increases in exercising 'soft power'.[91] For example, the Chinese vaccine diplomacy and China's external financing strategy will 'continue to expand its influence throughout the developing world'.[92] The developing nations will seek China's assistance in the post-pandemic world, especially in the financial sector. The request on 'debt restructuring'[93] made in January 2022 by Sri Lanka during Chinese Foreign Minister Wang Yi's visit to the island-nation is a clear example of seeking Chinese assistance to address the present economic crisis in Sri Lanka. The global risk report states that many other developing countries will seek Chinese help. China will comfortably expand its influence in these nations using its BRI.

Protectionist measures due to US-China geoeconomics tension will be a significant risk factor. As highlighted in 'geoeconomics confrontations', it is a critical medium- and long-term threat. The geopolitical and geoeconomics tensions will make it more difficult to tackle shared global challenges highlighted in the report. The report states, 'Brazil, Indonesia, Mexico, and Turkey are among the top buyers of Chinese Covid-19 vaccines, and net debt payments to China rose by 62% in 2020.'[94] With the increasing debt default risk in many nations, geopolitical competition will further exacerbate among US and China.

The South Asian regional power, India, will be concerned about its immediate geographical periphery where most nations could move closer to the Chinese sphere of influence, threatening stability and India's security. The US exit from Afghanistan has increased the risks in South Asia's regional security, and US focus on Indo-Pacific will shift geopolitical fissures to a marine theatre. Multiple security alliances such as Australia-UK-US (AUKUS) will heighten the geopolitical competition in Indo-Pacific with nuclear submarine capability developed by Australia in the years to come. Chinese diplomat Qi Zhenhong observed, 'Establishment of AUKUS is like holding up a "Sword of Damocles" on the heads of countries in the Pacific–Indian Ocean regional countries' which will propagate an arms race and create further regional instability.[95] The competition could extend to other countries as 'other states, such as Russia and Turkey, are also showing greater capability and willingness to project power abroad'.[96] These are critical areas for serious attention.

As Klaus Schwab and Thierry Malleret explain in their book *The Great Narrative*, 'There is as little chance of emerging power abandoning their value system to be more like the existing power would like them to be as there is of American leaders abandoning theirs to become more like the Chinese would like them to be and in the coming years a peaceful coexistence between the two rivals and the demonstrable ability to collaborate on some global issues like climate change would be the best possible outcome, but it is not given.'[97] Individual nations must contribute and assist in easing the geopolitical tension to find a collaborative space to reduce the rising geopolitical competition.

# NINE
## July 2022

### China in Sri Lanka and the Solomon Islands: Role of Littorals in the Geopolitical Competition[98]

Zbigniew Brzezinski pointed out, 'Neither the US nor China can lead on their own. US power has diminished, and China is not yet ready or able to step up to the plane and may never be prepared to take on the role.'[99] Smaller nations such as Sri Lanka and Solomon Islands have become pawns in the geopolitical chessboard. Smaller yet strategically important island states are critical for their role and geographical position in the accelerating competition between

China–US, China–India and China–Australia. Chinese influence in Sri Lanka, distressing its close neighbour India, has a pattern that matches China's actions in the Solomon Islands, who have Australia as their neighbour. With the tense geopolitical competition between US and China, the geostrategic littorals will play a pivotal role in the security balance in the Indian and Pacific Ocean.

On 30 May 2022, China released a position paper on its relationship with Pacific Island Countries.[100] 'China's position paper on mutual respect and common development with Pacific Island Countries' highlights the significant economic and infrastructure assistance provided to these countries. Further elaborating, the paper says, 'China has signed Belt and Road cooperation MoUs with all the 10 Pacific Island Countries having diplomatic relations with China.'[101] China-Pacific Island 'community with a shared future' is in the making.[102]

The position paper was well-timed, released when Chinese Foreign Minister Wang Yi was visiting South Pacific Islands, including Solomon Islands, Kiribati, Samoa, Fiji, Tonga, Vanuatu, Papua New Guinea and East Timor. China's strategic expansion is evident with the ten Pacific nations, where it wishes to enter into arrangements ranging from security and law-enforcement cooperation to jointly develop fisheries, run the region's internet networks, and set up cultural Confucius Institutes and classrooms.[103] In Papua New Guinea (PNG), Wang Yi discussed salvaging an economic and security deal amidst the national election in the country. In PNG, a Chinese construction firm, China Civil Engineering Construction Corporation (CCECC), has created a considerable infrastructure footprint.[104]

The 'Pivot to Asia' introduced by the Obama regime and continued subsequently, including by the Biden administration, failed to calculate the Chinese strategic manoeuvres, especially the hybrid civil–military nexus strategy adopted by China. The absence of US diplomatic missions in several Pacific Islands for decades contributed to the Chinese expansion. The same Chinese expansion in the Indian Ocean littorals, such as in Sri Lanka, was due to the failure of the India–US policy in the Indian Ocean.

Canberra and New Delhi would need to take a much tougher posture on Chinese expansion and strategic manoeuvres in their immediate periphery. Washington would require a more active IndoPacific strategy and country specific commitments aligned to the Indo-Pacific norms, values and economic framework. Chinese activities in the Solomon Islands and Sri Lanka are clear wake-up calls for Washington, New Delhi and Canberra to reassess their strategic ambiguity which has been utilized by China in its grey zone tactics.[105]

## RAJAPAKSA IN SRI LANKA AND SONGAVARE IN SOLOMON ISLANDS

Solomon Islands Prime Minister Manasseh Songavare and Sri Lankan President Rajapaksa are political survivors—Songavare is a four-time prime minister and the Rajapaksa dynastic rule in Sri Lanka is in its second term. Both islands were geostrategically critical battlegrounds during the Second World War. The Allied forces' first significant land offensive with the Japanese troops was in the Guadalcanal battle in the Solomon Islands.[106] In Sri Lanka, British Prime Minister Winston Churchill saw defeating the Japanese air attack as a decisive turning point, putting an end to the Japanese expansion.[107]

Sri Lanka and the Solomon Islands sit on vital shipping lanes. Rajapaksa and Songavare have entered backdoor dealings with the Chinese that have shaken the regional security balance and created ripples, alarming US's Indo-Pacific strategy. Sri Lanka's Chinese BRI footprint with largescale strategic infrastructure is significant, just like the strategic infrastructure in the Solomons and many other littorals.

Most Chinese agreements, such as long-term agreements for Chinese loans, are opaque and non-transparent, with little information available in both countries. Both leaders faced protests, in Solomons back in November 2021 and in Sri Lanka in the recent days. The Solomon Islands protest was mainly about the logging industry where 'China is the destination for more than 90 percent of its timber exports'.[108] Increased political favours by Chinese foreign investors were visible in Solomon Islands. The same was seen in Sri Lanka, where the protestors highlighted unprofitable infrastructure projects by the Chinese and the loans with extremely high interest rates, with high-level corruption. Prime Minister Mahinda Rajapaksa resigned in May 2022 with public protest turning violent and the protestors burning residences of parliament members.[109] China's economic entanglements with the regime were an important factor in Rajapaksa's downfall. Songavare and Rajapaksa are also threatening their close neighbours, Australia and India, by bandwagoning with China, a dangerous tilt that invites an extra-regional power to the region.

### CHINESE AND US MILITARY LOGISTICS AGREEMENTS

While Quad leaders are busy making promises in the Indo-Pacific theatre, they would also need to focus attention on small littorals. Both Sri Lanka and the Solomon Islands face similar Chinese pressure due to their strategic location. Sri Lanka sits in India's immediate periphery facing the Indian Ocean; the Solomon Islands sit in Australia's immediate periphery facing the Pacific Ocean. Both islands became a threat to their immediate neighbour due to the growing Chinese influence and the strategic manoeuvres of the Chinese. The Chinese military logistics agreement with the Solomon Islands signed in April 2022,[110] which became a primary concern in the Australian elections, is similar to the effect of the Chinese influence through BRI projects, submarine visits, capture of strategic infrastructure and numerous hydrographic survey vessels that routinely arrive in Sri Lanka. This has directly impacted India's security as China is a direct aggressor on India's northern border.

Security and logistics agreements with small nations such as Sri Lanka became a concern as they affected their internal political stability since political factions that benefited from these agreements came to power. The Rajapaksas allegedly used and abused these agreements. They weaponized them by using them to spread discord regarding the US security agreements, during the 2019 elections and attacked the previous government, saying that the agreements threatened the nation's sovereignty. After coming to power, the narrative changed, and the security agreements continued.

When Sri Lanka received the Status of Forces Agreement (SOFA) in 2019 from the US,[111] this author, as the head of the national security think tank in Sri Lanka, obtained the Chinese view on the US agreements. During a one-on-one meeting with the Chinese defence attache Senior Colonel Xu Jianwei in Colombo, the Chinese position on SOFA was explained. The reply was swift, 'You may sign whatever with the US but tell the defense secretary not to disappoint us when we also want to sign a similar agreement with Sri Lanka in the future.'[112] The message was clear from the Chinese that there would be a future agreement and Sri Lanka should not treat China differently from the US. The Hambantota port acquired for ninety-nine years by the Chinese for a forward military logistics base will be fully operational when such an agreement is made with the Chinese.[113]

### BRI IN SRI LANKA'S EASTERN PROVINCE

Chinese ambassador Qi Zhenhong's visit to Sri Lanka's eastern province on 24 May, giving donations to low-income families and discussing the expansion of China's investment portfolio to the east with the Governor Anuradha Yahampath,[114] is a strategic manoeuvre to escape the growing criticism from protestors against China's underperforming infrastructure in the south of the island. The focus now is on a new geography, targeting Sri Lanka's resource-rich eastern province, which harbours the strategic Trincomalee port. The ambassador visited the port,[115] took a boat ride and presented a map to the governor. The map depicts the ancient Maritime Silk Road, where China played a dominant role with many nations, including Sri Lanka. According to Chinese scholar Wang Jian, 'President Xi's requirement officially linked the Maritime Great Power strategy to the Belt and Road initiative.'[116]

The mission of the Chinese Ambassador in Colombo was to include Trincomalee and the Eastern Province in the modern-day

BRI. This is a vital province with significant Indian investment and security-sensitivity for New Delhi. China's calculated manoeuvres reflect clear strategic directions from Beijing. Previously too, China had tried to make inroads in the Eastern Province. During the presidency of Mahinda Rajapaksa (2005–2015), the Chinese mining investment company ZXJOY had an interest in the mineral resources of the Eastern Province when they negotiated with the government.[117] The same Chinese company was present in Niger, extracting thorium. In the past, the Chinese interest in getting mining licences in the Eastern Province and in the present, the Chinese business chamber's investment in the east,[118] are clear signs of Chinese expansion towards a valuable strategic province of Sri Lanka. Brigadier General Robert Spalding's book *Stealth War*, explains, 'It is clear that China didn't exactly help Sri Lanka improve its infrastructure—it swamped the country in debt and has now gained significant economic control over the struggling but strategically placed nation.'[119] Despite multiple criticisms of Chinese BRI projects in Sri Lanka, Beijing's BRI agenda continues.

## EXPLOITING FRAGILE DEMOCRACIES

Most of the littorals, such as Sri Lanka and Solomon Islands, are fragile democracies. Sri Lanka has moved from a fragile state into a crisis state with both economic and political instability. The instability in Sri Lanka could be seen as a disadvantage. So China, as the country's largest trading partner and the largest contributor to the development of infrastructure, uses its local agency by influencing the political elites to navigate during instability. Even in the Pacific, China is aware of the fragile democracies with high risk of instability which are fertile grounds for its economic expansionism, with the goal to establish 'strategic-traps' in three domains—political, human rights and military. The long-term lease agreements for strategic infrastructure have further cemented China's position in these islands, regardless of regime change. In Sri Lanka, the ninety-nine-year lease agreements with the Chinese were not revisited by subsequent regimes and perhaps will not be revisited by future regimes also, due to the already established, strong, strategic relationship with China.

## PLA OPERATIONS IN INDIA'S AND AUSTRALIA'S MARINE SPHERES

At China Aerospace Security Institute (CASI) inside the National Defense University compound in Washington, D.C., I was listening to former Australian prime minister Kevin Rudd explain his analysis of China, referring to his new book, *The Avoidable War*.[120] He said, 'While there is a bipartisan consensus on AUKUS, how do we read China and the modern global PLA in the conflictual environment, hinting of a possible PLA takeover of Taiwan by 2027?' Chinese PLA operation is hybrid; a stealth operation takes place in many geographies aiming at like-minded allies so that the US does not capture the significant danger.

Rudd's assessment is accurate as the PLA has been developing a series of ports across the Indian Ocean region to support the long-term projection of Chinese naval power. This is consistent with the evolution of China's naval doctrine under Xi to protect Chinese overseas interests not just in the near seas but also in the far seas. Cambodia (Koh Kong), Bangladesh (Chittagong), Myanmar (Kyaukyu), Sri Lanka (Hambantota), the Djibouti naval base, and the Gwadar port project in Pakistan are examples highlighted in Rudd's book. 'The long-term lease agreements in Koh Kong, Hambantota, Gwadar, and Djibouti suggest that the Chinese navy will likely construct dedicated resupply, repair, and maintenance facilities to sustain a larger Chinese Indian Ocean naval presence in the future. If both the US and China fail to buy in as indispensable partners, such an order cannot take hold globally, the concern is the two giants are moving in opposite directions. . . . In the absence of a common narrative shared by the US and China, the two nations are likely to drift more rapidly apart. Trust builds on itself just as distrust builds on itself and compounds into deep enmity over time,' says Rudd[121] who had decided to scuttle the then-nascent Quadrilateral Security Dialogue in 2008 when he was in office.

While the outgoing Australian Prime Minister Scott Morrison made efforts to 'patiently restore trust and confidence following the Rudd government's policy to disconnect from the Quad',[122] the new Prime Minister Anthony Albanese is from Kevin Rudd's Labour Party. Rudd discussed the Chinese military pact with Solomon Islands at the Quad summit, and expressed 'the need for the Quad to engage more in the Indo-Pacific . . . push our shared values in the region at a time when China is clearly seeking to exert more influence'.[123] The heightened Chinese belligerence with Australia, India and in Japan's immediate periphery will provide a clear window for the US to expand its security measures in the Indo-Pacific in the coming months. If Prime Minister Albanese were to request more efforts to contain China, it would be natural since the US containment strategy has not reduced Chinese strategic expansion in the Indo-Pacific.

### IPEF AND QUAD

With 60 per cent of the world's population in the area, the Biden administration has prioritized the Indo-Pacific theatre as the most prominent economic contributor to the US economy in the next thirty years. US foreign direct investment has nearly doubled in the last decade and was more than US$969 billion in 2020, supporting more than three million US jobs. In Tokyo, the Indo-Pacific Economic Framework (IPEF) was launched by President Biden, partnering Australia, Brunei, India, Indonesia, Japan, Republic of Korea, Malaysia, New Zealand, Philippines, Singapore, Thailand and Vietnam.[124] This grouping represents 40 per cent of the world's GDP, and most of these nations have a large China's BRI economic shadow and dependence on trade with China. The IPEF will assist in setting economic standards for many countries in BRI which are struggling with Chinese opaque loans, corruption, bypassing environmental clearances, transparency in processes and debt-trap-to-strategic-trap concerns.[125]

The IPEF has four pillars:

Connected Economy, to set high-standard trade rules in the digital economy;

Resilient Economy, for mapping and setting up an early warning system on supply chain disruptions;

Clean Economy, for setting and following environmental standards; and Fair Economy, by strengthening systems for anti money-laundering and fighting corruption.

Sri Lanka and many other Indian Ocean littorals, including Maldives, Comoros and Pacific littorals such as Solomon Islands, are facing issues in Chinese BRI projects and are saddled with unsustainable debt.

The IPEF framework should not be limited to the initial countries but expanded to include nations from the Indian Ocean and Pacific theatre. IPEF could engage with non-member nations in the economic dimension. This is similar to what Tanvi Madan and Dhruva Jaishankar argue for Quad. They say that the Quad should diversify its engagement with other likeminded partners, 'Quad does not need to add more members to accomplish this; it could instead involve other countries in existing Quad activities based on their needs and comfort levels, or participate in their initiatives to enhance regional security and resilience.'[126]

President Biden announced the most unpalatable crusade against China, persuading Quad partners and US allies that the Chinese belligerence was an immediate threat, rousing them to be prepared to fight back. At the Quad summit, Biden pledged the US would 'intervene militarily if China attempts to take Taiwan by force',[127] a warning that appeared to deviate from the deliberate strategic ambiguity traditionally conveyed by Washington's One-China policy. Biden's warnings on two geographical theatres, Ukraine and Taiwan, is a move towards a two-theatre confrontation, similar to what happened during the Second World War. Unlike in the past, the context is different given the advanced military configuration and stronger power axis of Russia and China, backed by Chinese economic muscle. Zhu

Fenglian, China's Taiwan Affairs Office spokesperson, says, 'We urge the US to stop saying or doing anything in violation of the One-China principle and the three China–US Joint Communiqués.... Those who play with fire will certainly burn themselves,'[128] a direct warning, not to be downplayed as there are many countries in Asia taking China or Russia's side due to their strategic, economic and military dependence.

## QUADRILATERAL STRATEGIC INTELLIGENCE FORUM

In September 2021, intelligence officials from the US, India, Japan and Australia took part in a Quad strategic intelligence forum. This was an essential step since inter-agency intelligence sharing among the Quad had significant lapses in the past, triggering terror attacks, illegal arms trade and multiple security concerns in India's immediate periphery. When Sri Lanka faced its largest terror attack in 2019, the inter-agency intelligence provided by India was not shared with the US prior to the attack. Had a multipronged Quad intelligence security architecture been in place, we could have averted the terror attack in Sri Lanka, since multiple channels would have given the same signal to the Sri Lankan authorities and it would have been taken seriously by them. The Indian intelligence was not trusted by the Sri Lankan authorities and downplayed as 'mere information'. With political and economic dysfunctionality in the littorals, there is a growing security concern which requires consideration.

## CONCLUSION

The Solomon Islands security pact with China has become a cause for concern due to the failure of Australian and US policy in the Pacific Islands. The quick reactive tactics in Washington to undo the Chinese agreement in Solomon Islands only depicts the Chinese strength and prior calculated victories in other areas, achieved in the Pacific Islands. The US requires a more active and long-term, robust policy in these littorals, such as targeting the supply chain competition. Willy C. Shih from Harvard Business School, testifying before the US-China Economic and Security Review Commission, accurately posited, 'Step aside and see how China's top-down model will work facing the challenges in the years ahead. Their zero Covid strategy provides a lot of insight. . . . That also means we need to address our [US] weaknesses and penchant for watered-down short-term solutions . . . a little long-term planning would benefit us all.'[129] The US IPEF could assist the littorals in detaching themselves from supply chains entangled in China's economic coercive tactics and allow them to reposition themselves with the US.

The Quad and its like-minded partners require immediate diversification and expansion to many Indo-Pacific nations, some of which are undergoing economic distress. A broader framework, such as IPEF, is essential to pull these most-vulnerable littorals towards the FOIP. Otherwise, the US-China distrust will only widen with geopolitical flashpoints in these littorals where PLA's deeds of stealth and hybrid civil–military activity are already multiplying. What is required is a proactive country-specific commitment towards IPEF and Indo-Pacific from nations like Sri Lanka and the Solomon Islands to set standards to align towards a global rules-based order.

# 3

# Sri Lanka's Foreign Policy

## ONE
## August 2020

### Democracy and Equidistant Foreign Policy in the Majoritarian Government of Mahinda Rajapaksa[1]

Namal Rajapaksa, eldest son of Prime Minister Mahinda Rajapaksa and member of Parliament from Hambantota, says, '*Sri Lanka's strong capacity for exercising its franchise remains untouched even in the times of pandemic. Regardless of the party each of us supports, we can stand proud as one democratic nation.*'

'How many politicians truly feel the call to serve their nation? How many are utterly selfless in their desire to bring about change? The answer is probably not many,' writes Ajita, daughter of the erudite foreign minister Lakshman Kadirgamar in her book *The Cake That Was Baked at Home, the Only Biography of Kadirgamar.*[2] Having entered politics at the age of sixty-two, Kadirgamar made a significant stride in the nation's foreign affairs until his tragic assassination on 12 August 2005. His last official act as the foreign minister, on the day he was shot at his residence by a sniper, was a scholastic endeavour. This was the launch of the first international relations journal at a diplomatic academy in Colombo called the BCIS, along with the high commissioner of Sri Lanka's closest neighbour India, Nirupama Rao. The foreign minister was the editor-in-chief of the journal *International Relations in a Globalized World*, promoting and recognizing research as an integral component in the formation of the foreign policy of the nation. Patriotism, selfless desire to serve one's nation and respecting democracy, the ethos practised until his last breath, perhaps could be a value to reflect on by the newly-elected representatives to the nation's Parliament.

Making political history, the victorious Mahinda Rajapaksa secured more than half a million votes for his premiership. The parliamentary election 2020 was held amidst the pandemic with more than 70 per cent voter turnout as the public trusted the government's successful management of Covid-19. Sri Lanka was the first nation in the South Asian region to hold elections in this challenging environment. Rajapaksa secured two-thirds of parliamentary seats with 145+5 seats, leaving 54 to Samagi Jana Balawegaya (SJB), a breakaway faction of the grand old political party, the United National Party (UNP). The UNP, under the leadership of former prime minister Wickremasinghe, was reduced to one seat, a considerable defeat in its seven-decade political history. President Rajapaksa's political party, SLPP, founded in 2016, secured this mandate in a short period, perhaps due to the political strategist behind the curtain, President Rajapaksa's brother Basil Rajapaksa.

The break-up of Sri Lanka Freedom Party (SLFP) was the lead story during the last parliamentary election in 2015 due to President Maithripala Sirisena's move to make an alliance with the UNP. In the present context, it is as if the whole exercise turned against the UNP itself, breaking into two, eroding its voter base and paving the way for the constitutional amendment to repeal Article 19A passed during the previous Sirisena–Wickremasinghe government, which impeded Mahinda Rajapaksa's return to power. Mahinda Rajapaksa, who was ousted five years ago, came back not with a slight majority but with a historic political victory. This displays the futile experiment of the Sirisena–Wickremasinghe bipartisan model and the high volatility of the preferences of the Sri Lankan voter, which can swing from one end of the spectrum to the other in a short period of time.

This is the first time in Sri Lankan politics that the executive and legislative branches of the government are headed by biological siblings, Gotabaya and Mahinda Rajapaksa. The centralized, excessive power of the two branches will create the initial political challenge to uphold democratic values and the practical operations of the prevailing checks and balances. While separation of powers in the Sri Lankan *trias politica* model of executive, legislature and judiciary is explained in the Constitution, in practice the two branches—executive and legislature—for the first time will be headed by two brothers. The prime minister, with two-thirds majority, would need to exercise his mandate with more responsibility, safeguarding the independence of the individual branches and leaving aside sibling-preference biases. It is therefore vital to strengthen the checks and balances from the initial stage itself of a sibling-run regime in order to further strengthen democracy.

The eighteenth-century political thinker Montesquieu highlighted in his work *The Spirit of the Laws* (1748) that the distribution of political powers among the branches is an essential element for a government whose powers were not excessively centralized in a single ruler. He wrote, 'When the legislative and executive powers are united in the same person, or the same body of magistrates, there can be no liberty.'[3] There is prediction of a possible sibling rivalry due to the forthcoming Constitutional amendment. Analysts say, 'President Gotabaya Rajapaksa pushing for changes that will strengthen presidential power at the expense of those of the prime minister may trigger sibling rivalry.'[4]

The separation of powers, however, between the two siblings will be smooth and will not turn towards a rivalry due to the close understanding between them. This was demonstrated during the battle against the Tamil Tigers. The close bond and understanding between the duo was a primary contributor to the victory in the war in 2009. Having foreseen the importance of the separation of powers, Oxford-educated professor of law G.L. Peiris, who is the chairman of the SLPP and was the foreign minister of the post-war Mahinda Rajapaksa government, rightly cautioned that having obtained the coveted two-thirds majority did not give the government a blank cheque to act in a 'short-sighted and selfish manner'. The two-thirds majority also comes attached with significant responsibilities, Peiris noted.[5] Further explaining on the checks and balances, having a weak opposition will force the incumbent government to review their own performance, he claimed, pushing it to essentially police its own decisions and policies. 'This will force the government to self-critique. I believe we will need to empower the oversight committees in Parliament. We believe that the opposition members in these committees will ensure stronger accountability.'

The professor is right to focus on stronger accountability with checks and balances at a time of a majoritarian mandate, winning 18 of the 22 electoral districts and almost 60 per cent of votes going to one political party. In the Sri Lankan political history, there have been incidents of abuse of power after securing two-thirds majority, such as in 1978 by president J.R. Jayewardene. The nation does not need to walk the same path and the Rajapaksas should improve and further enrich the democratic institutions of the nation.

There will be four challenges the Rajapaksa duo will face with their overwhelming election victory. First, with much negative reporting from many Western media outfits predicting that the country will lose its democracy due to the majoritarian mandate received, they will need to disprove this with their actions. The domestic political mandate received was to enrich democratic values and not to pave a path towards autocratic rule. The constitutional amendments would need to be carried out with precision equalling brain surgery, thinking long term, keeping in mind separation of powers, improving checks and balances, strengthening individual liberty and securing the sovereignty of the nation. Second, they will need to quickly revive the economy, which is currently growing at a rate below 3 per cent, in the face of global recession. Third, they need to address and face the human rights discourse in the international arena and strengthen the reconciliation process. And finally, they need to exercise a balanced 'equidistant' foreign policy articulated by the regime, in a highly-contested global power struggle.

Sri Lanka is an important partner in Indian Prime Minister Narendra Modi's 'neighbourhood first' policy. Mahinda Rajapaksa's positive rhetoric identifying India as a close friend and balancing China policy, especially on BRI projects, will be crucial to Sri Lanka's foreign policy.

While Rajapaksa does not wish to get involved in the India–China or US-China power struggle, these powers may not leave the Rajapaksas alone, as already cautioned by several analysts of a possible China-centric tilt due to an unmatched, continuous volume of assistance from Beijing. Sustaining domestic democratic practices in a majoritarian government and keeping a balance between China, India and the US in the face of China's infrastructure diplomacy will be a daunting challenge for the new regime, with heightened external geopolitical fissures in the region.

## TWO
## September 2020

### Perils of Power in Wounded Old Civilizations[6]

In *Making India Great: The Promise of a Reluctant Global Power*, Aparna Pandey writes, 'India has yet to find the balance between philosophical debates and conversation on practical matters. Getting carried away by emotions about other people's beliefs or views on history often comes in the way of determining a course of action in the present moment.'[7] Religion and cultural beliefs and disputes have hampered and could end up reversing India's success, says Pandey. This analysis can be extended to several South Asian nations including Sri Lanka. It seems that some people in Sri Lanka are tied up in a time capsule, immersed in ancient glories of our magnificent civilization and constricted by religious conservatism. The shrill Sri Lankan overplay of ethno-religious sentiment and India's focus on Hindutva are examples of similar behaviour.

V.S. Naipaul describes the copious number of missed opportunities as a crisis of a 'wounded old civilization' due to shackles of this very entrapment.[8] To let go of such baggage requires, first and foremost, recognition and embracing of diversity. Policies and constitutional reform should secure this essential ingredient, to propel economic and social progress. While these nations are bogged down in their domestic constraints, they miss the economic reform opportunities, such as the fifteen years delay of economic liberalization missed by India, as compared to China, which started the process in 1978. India did that only in 1991. This was accurately captured by the current Indian Minister of External Affairs Dr Subrahmanyam Jaishankar in his new book *The India Way* in which he writes, 'The delayed economic reforms were undertaken a decade and a half after those of China. And far more ambivalently. The fifteen-year gap in capabilities continues to put India at a great disadvantage.'[9] Jaishankar further explains, 'Actual policy in a large country is a parallel pursuit of multiple priorities, some of which could be contradictory. Neither abstention nor hedging are always answering to their pulls and pressures. Choices had to be made, not just debated. And they cannot be without a cost.' India's choices on Sri Lanka have gone through rough terrain; the cost for some of these choices lingers, still to be paid, as a reminiscence directly touching the relationship, challenging the present political leadership.

## DEVOLUTION OF POWER

Jaishankar understands the complexity of the Sri Lankan political dynamics as he had first-hand experience, serving as First Secretary and Political Advisor for the Indian Peacekeeping Force (IPKF) at the Indian High Commission in Colombo. This was during the turbulent 1988–1990 youth insurrection that killed thousands of people in the island.

It was a twofold battleground in Sri Lanka at that time. The Tamil Tigers on the one hand and the youth insurrection on the other, both at the same time. Following Indian Prime Minister Rajiv

Gandhi's visit to Sri Lanka to ink the India-Sri Lanka accord in 1987 with President J.R. Jayewardena, the thirteenth amendment to the Constitution was introduced to create provincial councils as a follow-up action. The thirteenth amendment was designed to devolve power. It was supported by the ruling UNP and opposed by most of the opposition parties except for Sri Lanka Mahajana Party (SLMP) founded by Vijaya Kumaratunga, the famous politician assassinated in 1988 for his position on devolution.

The devolution of power has been discussed by subsequent leaders for thirty-three years with multiple promises such as '13 plus' during the presidential tenure of Mahinda Rajapaksa. In the present government of Gotabaya Rajapaksa, the minister in charge of provincial councils, Rear Admiral Sarath Weerasekera, in a recent interview explained, 'I am personally not in favour for provincial councils nor devolution of power' but he would still function as the minister of the provincial council. The government, with its unitary essence as the political ethos, not accepting the devolution of power and the ultra-nationalist position, could take a different turn at the constitution-making process on devolution of power, which will be a turning point in Sri Lankan political history.

## SHIFTING POWER

Within a month of appointing new Cabinet ministers, President Gotabaya Rajapaksa, with two-thirds majority in the Parliament, approved a major constitutional amendment, taken up by Parliament, 'the original draft was passed at the second reading with a two-thirds majority in Parliament on October 22nd 2020'.[10] The twentieth amendment was to revert the power from the legislature back to the executive, reversing the previously passed nineteenth amendment. 'Out of two hundred and twenty-three parliamentarians including the Speaker, one hundred and fifty-six MPs voted in favor while sixty-five voted against. Former president Maithripala Sirisena was not present in the House when the vote was taken'.[11] President Sirisena, who curtailed his powers through the nineteenth amendment five years earlier, was elected to the legislature as a member of Parliament, joining the Rajapaksa regime.

Shifting power back-and-forth is a dangerous exercise. President Gotabaya's move is seen as the fulfilment of the promise that the executive would make swift and efficient decisions. But the twentieth amendment could turn into a nightmare if power falls in the wrong hands. Such was the case in Pakistan under General Muhammad Zia-ul-Haq, who in introducing the eighth amendment to the Pakistan Constitution, shifted the balance of power towards the executive, which plunged the entire nation into an abyss of autocratic rule.

While Gotabaya is looked upon by the majority of the country as a benevolent president promising the much-required reforms to modernize the economy and introducing a new political culture, it is also important to comprehend the consequences of this amendment beyond his tenure, in the long term. Such constitutional reforms have broken many nations. A stronger executive branch would be able to operate quickly and efficiently. It would, however, have a very low degree of accountability, without checks and balances. Former president Sirisena regime installed more checks and balances, limiting the executive power, which resulted in creating commissions with strong bureaucratic power, including a veto. This was seen inefficient and less result oriented, with excessive constraints on fast decision making. Too many checks and balances will create a 'vetocracy', as explained by Francis Fukuyama.[12] It also helps the political party that dominates the Parliament to moderate the will of the majority and force it to pay greater attention to minorities. Sri Lanka would need to find an equilibrium between strong checks and balances and a strong executive.

The twentieth amendment to the Sri Lankan Constitution comes in the backdrop of the culmination of recent events that took place, threatening national security. The weakening of the executive was seen as an impediment to national security and to implement useful reforms in the previous Sirisena–Wickremasinghe government. The restoration of power to the executive will settle the existing debate in several quarters of the West which questions democracy under the Rajapaksa regime. As every solution brings more challenges, the Rajapaksa siblings regime would need to navigate its political journey with care, projecting its democratic values in the narrow space constructed from the constitutional changes it makes.

### BOYCOTT CHINESE COMPANIES IN SRI LANKA

China's territorial expansion is viewed as the modern-day equivalent of the East India Company by David R. Stilwell, the assistant secretary of state for the Bureau of East Asian and Pacific Affairs of USA. The developments in a distant place in the South China Sea is directly affecting Sri Lanka. US Secretary of State Mike Pompeo said, 'The Chinese government cannot be allowed to use the China Communications Construction Company (CCCC) or other state-owned businesses as weapons to impose an expansionist agenda. The United States will act until we see Beijing discontinue its coercive behaviour in the South China Sea, and we will continue to stand with allies and partners in resisting this destabilizing activity.'[13] The CCCC, which developed the Sri Lankan Port City Project that reclaimed the ocean-front, altering the coastal geography of Colombo city, and several other Chinese companies, were targeted by US sanctions. This would further weaken the US-China relations and impact projects under China's BRI. Colombo Port City developers market this venture as a global project, built to attract international firms who are expected to lease out most of the developed space.

The brewing Cold War between the US and China would hurt many economies and could interfere with domestic policymaking in the coming years. In a related development, Japan has expanded a subsidy programme that helps Japanese companies move out of China. Japan's supply chains diversification programme acknowledged India and Bangladesh as eligible destinations for companies leaving China. Assessed as a move targeting China, at the recent US-India Strategic Partnership Forum, Prime Minister Narendra Modi said that the pandemic has 'shown the world that the decision on developing global supply chains should be based not only on costs. They should also be based on trust.' In East Asia, China is pushed out from the KRA Canal Project in Thailand,[14] another geographical alteration seen earlier as an answer to the Malacca dilemma.

The 'Malacca dilemma' was a term coined in 2003 by then-Chinese president Hu Jintao.[15] Most of China's imports derive from the Middle East and Africa, 'Currently, eighty percent of China's oil has to pass through the Strait of Malacca, a narrow stretch of water between the Indonesian island of Sumatra and the Malay Peninsula. With Singapore, a major US ally that frequently participates in US naval drills, located at the mouth of the strait's eastern opening, the Strait of Malacca becomes a natural strategic chokepoint. In the event of a conflict, the Malacca Strait could easily be blocked by a rival nation, cutting off China from crucial energy resources.'[16]

The US sanctions, Japanese supply chain adjustments and the scrapping of KRA Canal Project would push China to look for alternatives and readjustments of its strategy to secure its interests in a more aggressive manner. This aggression and further US-China decoupling will see many nations, including Sri Lanka, pay a hefty price. This is also a huge opportunity for whichever country can provide goods to replace Chinese products. While nations are busy readjusting their domestic power balance and glorifying inward-looking values, they could miss the opportunity to grow, modernize, reform and embrace liberal democratic values.

# THREE
## April 2021

### Pakistan in Sri Lanka's Changing Foreign Policy[17]

On 23 February 2021, Pakistan's Prime Minister Imran Khan visited Sri Lanka with Foreign Minister Shah Mahmood Qureshi,

Commerce Adviser Abdul Razzak Dawood, Special Assistant Syed Zulfikar Abbas Bukhari and forty leading Pakistani businessmen. However, the visit was overshadowed by the challenges faced by Colombo at the UNHRC where the UN High Commissioner for Human Rights Michelle Bachelet submitted a resolution.[18] The Sri Lankan government rejected the UNHRC resolution and has sought assistance from China, Russia, Pakistan and other member-states to defeat it. China has given its unconditional support to Sri Lanka. Regardless of the ultimate fate of the UNHRC resolution, what is certain is that the China–Sri Lanka axis will be further strengthened, and Pakistan's support will add extra weight to it. Khan's remarks reflecting his desire to connect the BRI infrastructure to the Hambantota port in Sri Lanka suggests Pakistan's long-term ambition of generating more revenue from the China–Pakistan Economic Corridor (CPEC) than is currently being collected for the debt-ridden country. This 'infrastructure axis' between Pakistan, Sri Lanka and China will become fully operational when projects such as the CPEC are completed.

India, meanwhile, faces a three-sided security challenge after being surrounded by Chinese BRI infrastructure on three sides—with the CPEC in Pakistan, the China–Myanmar Economic Corridor in Myanmar and Hambantota port in Sri Lanka. The recent Chinese power project in Sri Lanka, and the consequent objections it elicited from India due to its proximity to the mainland, offer clear signs of India's mounting concerns about China. Tensions are likely to grow, as there is no clear regional security architecture to mitigate mistrust and uncertainty. Pakistan's growing ties with China and India's strong relations with the United States have triggered regional geopolitical competition due to which the BRI and the Indo-Pacific of the US are being executed simultaneously.

Sri Lanka rhetorically and politically supports both strategies. However, its allegedly 'balanced' foreign policy is experiencing a China tilt, seen in its preference to bandwagon with China, as demonstrated by the recent decisions taken by the Gotabaya Rajapaksa government on the US MCC grant, Japan's Light Rail Transit and India's ECT. China's growing sphere of influence, bolstered with help from Pakistan and Sri Lanka, will further heighten India's security concerns. Sri Lanka should recalibrate its foreign policy to 'balance' and benefit from both India and China while still strengthening its regional relationship with other nations, such as Pakistan.

Pakistan—which is wedged on four sides by India, China, Afghanistan and Iran—has its own unique geopolitical complexity that has contributed to large levels of distrust by its neighbours. On its western border, 'Afghans still view Pakistan with deep mistrust, blaming it for the resurgence of the Taliban and for giving the insurgents a safe-haven from which to operate,'[19] while towards its east, on the border of Jammu and Kashmir, historical tensions with India continue. China–India, with continuous border disputes and China–Pakistan's strong economic and defence cooperation is visible. Iran–Pakistan, with historically close relationship until Pakistan slowly began to drift away from Shia Iran to the Sunni Arab countries such as Saudi Arabia, are clear factors in the geopolitical complexity surrounding Pakistan.

Just like Pakistan, Sri Lanka, placed in a vital geostrategic location in the Indian Ocean, faces its own geopolitical challenges. The island is a part of the conceptual map of China's BRI and the US's Indo-Pacific strategy. The India-Sri Lankan mistrust originates from the Indian intervention in Sri Lanka, both pre- and post-civil war, that sought to address Tamilian grievances, a concern that remains unresolved to the present day. In addition, China is expanding its sphere of influence in both Sri Lanka and Pakistan. This has increased the bilateral trust deficit between India and Sri Lanka. On India's northern borders, a two-front confrontation with China and Pakistan is brewing. In India's south, the recent US$12 million Chinese energy project in Sri Lanka, close to the Indian shore, has become a security concern for India.[20] President Gotabaya Rajapaksa's government approved the joint venture for the energy project with the Chinese company Sinosar–Etechwin.

Weeks before this decision, an important trilateral agreement along with India and Japan on the Colombo East Port Terminal (ECT) was cancelled and repositioned to the Western Container Terminal. It was against this tense geopolitical backdrop that Prime Minister Imran Khan visited Sri Lanka in February 2021.

## KHAN'S VISIT TO COLOMBO AND SRI LANKA AT THE UNHRC

Khan is the first head of government to visit Sri Lanka since the pandemic began. His arrival occurs at a significant juncture when Sri Lanka is facing international pressure from the UNHRC resolution. While the government has rejected the resolution, it will require the support of the member-states to defeat the resolution in the coming weeks. With eighteen nations in support—along with China, Russia and Pakistan—Sri Lanka will need more votes to defeat the resolution.[21] India's vote will be decisive in understanding New Delhi's political posture towards its domestic Tamil community in South India and how strongly it will seek to addresses the concerns of the Tamils in Sri Lanka.

This time Sri Lanka will face a firm resistance from many member-states due to its failure since 2009 to fulfil its commitments of genuine reconciliation, aggravated further by the government's decision to withdraw from its own co-sponsored resolution in 2015. The 2021 resolution highlights the concerns of the minority, along with the country's growing militarization.[22] Pakistan's support will be an important factor in winning the Islamic members' support. The narrative against the resolution, as articulated by the Sri Lankan foreign secretary, positions the Global North teaming up against the Global South. He says, 'We fear whether they (the Global North) will hijack the agenda of the UNHRC to target Sri Lanka,'[23] reflecting the government's alignment with its domestic ultra-nationalist voter base. Even if the vote is passed against Sri Lanka at the UNHRC, the government could effortlessly weaponize its ultra-nationalist agenda to satisfy the domestic majoritarian Sinhalese-Buddhist constituency.

## KHAN'S PARLIAMENTARY SPEECH AND FORCED CREMATION

The last foreign leader to address the Sri Lankan Parliament was India's Prime Minister Narendra Modi during his visit in 2015.[24] Khan was initially scheduled to speak in the Sri Lankan Parliament, but his address was cancelled. Between the announcement of the speech and the cancellation, another major political development took place between Prime Minister Mahinda Rajapaksa and his Pakistani counterpart. This involved Rajapaksa's comment in the Parliament granting permission for Islamic burial of Muslim Covid-19 patients. Khan responded by tweeting, 'We welcome Sri Lankan PM Mahinda Rajapaksa's assurance given in Sri Lankan Parliament today allowing Muslims to bury those who died from Covid-19,' endorsing the move as the right decision. Sri Lankan Prime Minister's assurance to the Muslims was ignored by his own government. This further aggravated the sentiments of the Muslim community. Rauf Hakeem, leader of the Sri Lanka Muslim Congress and a parliamentarian, explained, 'Our government embarrassed our own Prime Minister first. Now they are embarrassing the Prime Minister of another country visiting us. [T]his is pathetic. They [the government] are going back on their own positions and statements repeatedly, like they did with the assurance on burials. This sort of blowing hot and cold, especially in diplomacy, reflects a lack of maturity and could impact our relations with our long-term friends and partners.'[25] The consequence of the unpleasant environment caused by the forced cremation of Muslim Covid-19 patients could become a heated event in the Parliament. This could possibly be the reason for cancelling the speech by Khan in the Parliament and not the official announcement which cited Covid-19 preventive measures.

This forced cremation of Muslim Covid-19 patients has also become a concern at the UNHRC, where Michelle Bachelet, UN High Commissioner for Human Rights, has raised concerns regarding Muslim minority rights,[26] questioning forced cremations in addition to the past issues of Tamilian human rights. Human

Rights Watch has made a clear reference regarding forced cremation and suppression of minority rights in its latest report.[27] In this regard, Pakistan's point of view and support will be essential for Sri Lanka to win the support of the Islamic nations in the battle at the UNHRC.

The same applies to India, where Tamil grievances are a serious concern. Since the end of the civil war in 2009, Sri Lanka has failed several times to deliver a solution of this problem. India has raised concerns in this regard, including during the visit of India's Foreign Minister S. Jaishankar to Colombo in January 2021, when he stated that the Sri Lankan government needed to make its position clear on the devolution of power. There was silence on this matter from both the Sri Lankan president and the prime minister, while Provincial Council Minister Rear Admiral Dr Sarath Weerasekera rejected the thirteenth amendment and the power-sharing arrangement, questioning India's moral right to intervene.[28] This leaves little or no space for a constructive avenue to address Tamil grievances.

Both Muslim and Tamil grievances depict the Sri Lankan state's continuous failure, due to its policy circle's non-addressal of the issue, to produce any comprehensive solution for the minority communities. In the process, there is little reason for the global community to support Colombo's rejection of the resolution. Pakistan's unwillingness to voice its concerns on forced cremation, unlike India's vocal concern for Tamil grievances, explains the former's passive foreign policy and desire to avoid getting entangled in Sri Lanka's domestic affairs, much like China. Although in terms of rhetoric, by refusing to make the forced cremation of Muslims an issue, the Pakistan government will be tacitly accepting Rajapaksa's tilt away from India towards China, perhaps opening a significant backdoor for it to provide military assistance to Sri Lanka in the future.

## PAKISTAN—SRI LANKA MILITARY ENGAGEMENT

In 2006, the Liberation Tigers of Tamil Eelam (LTTE) attempted to assassinate Pakistan's High Commissioner Bashir Wali Mohmand.

He was the only high commissioner targeted by the rebels. The strong Pakistan–Sri Lanka military ties became a critical factor during the war. The Pakistan military arsenal, including fighter jets and multi-barrel rocket launchers, contributed to the government's victory in the war. During the Mahinda presidency from 2005 to 2015, the Pakistan–Sri Lanka military relationship grew strong. During Khan's recent visit, a US$50 million credit line was offered to Sri Lanka for the purchase of military hardware to strengthen bilateral partnership in combating terrorism, drug and narcotic trafficking and intelligence sharing.

Sri Lanka faced its largest-ever terrorist attack on a single day on Easter Sunday in 2019, galvanizing the succeeding Gotabaya government to take a strong position by appointing a PCoI to bring the perpetrators to justice. Sri Lanka has also fallen victim to Pakistan's narco trade, where massive amounts of drugs were confiscated by the authorities during former president Maithripala Sirisena's administration as a part of a full-swing war on drugs months before the Easter Sunday attack.[29] Pakistan's assistance in intelligence sharing and combating terrorism and the narco trade will be essential to Sri Lanka, since drugs have been at the core of terrorism in the region and have also contributed to facilitating acts of terror. Pakistan–Sri Lanka military engagement—from the training of military officers to weapons purchases—would continue uninterrupted under the present Gotabaya regime, just like during the Mahinda presidency.

### ONE BILLION DOLLAR TRADE TARGET AND SAARC

In addition to economic ties, several memorandums of understanding (MoU) were also signed between Sri Lanka and Pakistan in tourism, education, sports and technology. A target of U$1 billion on trade, which now stands at less than US$500 million, was set.[30] Both countries will need to invest more through conducive economic policies in order to fully reap the benefits of the Pakistan–Sri Lanka Free Trade Agreement which has been in operation since June 2005.

However, on the contrary, Sri Lanka recently introduced heavy restrictions and more inward-looking economic policies. With Sri Lanka's reserves dipping to US$4.8 billion in January 2021, and increasing concerns over pending debt repayments, the government has undertaken measures such as requiring exporters to immediately convert 25 per cent of foreign exchange proceeds into Sri Lankan rupees. This action is being heavily criticized.[31] This strictly regulated environment is likely to continue due to the ailing economy and it would impact trade with many nations including Pakistan.

A joint communique was issued in Colombo projecting the success of the high-level visit and underscoring many areas of cooperation, including resurrecting the South Asian Association for Regional Cooperation (SAARC), where Pakistan and Sri Lanka emphasized their 'commitment to the principles and objectives of the SAARC Charter' and 'stressed the need of SAARC member countries to build on convergences for the greater good' so as to 'take forward the SAARC process for further strengthening regional cooperation'.[32] Departing from bilateralism, Pakistan pushed for its South Asian neighbours to revive the SAARC process. Assessing Khan's visit to Afghanistan in November 2020, it is clear, that a Pakistan foreign policy, which is proactive and regional is gradually in the making and that Sri Lanka was its second stop.

## CONNECTING THE CPEC WITH HAMBANTOTA

Sri Lanka and Pakistan established close strategic relations with China by joining the BRI from its inception. Altering Pakistan's geography through a 3,000-kilometre-long corridor slicing through the mountains, the BRI created a bridge with China through the China–Pakistan Economic Corridor (CPEC) starting at Kashgar in China and ending at Gwadar port in the Indian Ocean. To compare, Sri Lanka has the Hambantota port (the Chinese built the port and Sri Lanka leased it back to them), which is located along the world's busiest sea lanes. Thus, the BRI projects are expected to bring economic benefits to both nations. In addition, the twin projects have set the background for the expansion of the Chinese sphere of influence in the region and beyond, through the connections the CPEC will create with Central Asia.

Both infrastructure projects carried out by China have raised India's security concerns. Further, the China–Myanmar Economic Corridor at the eastern front of India would surround the Indian periphery on three sides by China's BRI infrastructure projects. Pakistan's growing ties with China and India's strong relations with the US are, therefore, creating regional geopolitical competition whereby two larger strategies are being executed simultaneously—the BRI of China and the Indo-Pacific of the US.

Tension between the US, China and India in Sri Lanka has heightened due to clear signs of the Sri Lankan government tilting its foreign policy towards China. In this competitive environment, the Pakistan-Sri Lanka-China infrastructure axis will connect and become fully operational when projects such as the CPEC are completed. China's large sphere of influence, due to its all-weather strategic partnership with Pakistan and the loans and economic assistance it provides to court the support of Sri Lanka, outweighs any other sphere of influence in which they participate independently. As testament to this, Khan proposed close collaboration between the two Chinese infrastructure projects. He said, 'Pakistan is part of the Belt and Road initiative of China, and [the] CPEC is one of its flagship programs, (which) . . . means connectivity, and it will help enhance Sri Lanka's connectivity right up to Central Asia.'[33]

With billions of dollars spent on these infrastructure projects, both Pakistan and Sri Lanka will be forced to find avenues to generate revenue to repay existing loans. This has become a burden in the present context due to the difficult economic conditions.

Connecting the CPEC's port in Gwadar with Hambantota will also raise a security concern for India if the usage of ports is for dual purpose, that is, for both civilian and military. A submarine port call incident in Sri Lanka is an example of such fears.[34] When Prime Minister Modi visited Sri Lanka in May 2017, a Chinese submarine requested a port call in Sri Lanka, which the then president Sirisena denied. The Chinese submarine was subsequently received by Gwadar in Pakistan. Pakistan and Sri Lanka's strategic partnership with Beijing could thus accommodate military submarines from the People's Liberation Army Navy, heightening New Delhi's security anxieties. The apprehensions would increase as China's sphere of influence in the region expands through the support of its allies.

This is made even more significant due to the absence of any countervailing regional security architecture, thereby becoming a source of serious concern for all South Asian nations. Due to heavy infrastructure debt and need for financial assistance, Sri Lanka has chosen to bandwagon with China rather than support India, the balancing power in the region. Its weak economic condition, with continuous need for loans like the US$1,500 million currency-swap loan from China in February 2021, is the obvious reason of Sri Lanka's preference for China.[35] As Stephen M. Walt explains in his book *The Origins of Alliances*, 'The weaker the state, the more likely it is to bandwagon rather than balance.'[36] Pakistan is also heading in the same direction.

Weeks before Khan's visit, Gotabaya terminated an important trilateral agreement between India, Japan and Sri Lanka on the ECT, which was signed in 2019. The tense protest by twenty-three trade unions demanding an end to the earlier agreement signed by the Sirisena–Wickremesinghe government, took centre stage. The cancellation was seen as a victory by the government in protecting its strategic assets and moving in a direction away from liberal economic practices. Against this backdrop, a simple public–private partnership could not be executed due to the ultra-nationalistic position taken. Alongside the domestic political concerns affecting the backtracking of the ECT, a popular local newspaper highlighted the China factor in the decision.[37]

## FAILED INVESTIGATIONS OF CHINESE PROJECTS

Pakistan and Sri Lankan leaders have raised concerns over Chinese projects in their respective nations—the CPEC in Pakistan by Khan's Tehreek-e-Insaaf (PTI) government and the Hambantota project by the Gotabaya government in Sri Lanka. The latter assured the public that it will 'make it a priority to revisit the already signed agreement' on the port lease for ninety-nine years signed by the previous government.[38]

Despite much hype and strident political rhetoric during both the elections, there has been no sign of significant amendments to either of these projects. Khan had accused the government of the then prime minister Nawaz Sharif 'of corruption in the management' of CPEC.[39] '[In] November 2019, the PTI government appointed former military spokesman Lieutenant General Asim Saleem Bajwa as head of a new CPEC Authority, giving the military greater control over the management of the project.'[40] Similarly in Sri Lanka, former General Daya Ratnayake was appointed as Chairman of the Port Authority by Gotabaya. Recently, after terminating India's ECT project, General Ratnayake commented in the media that the deal on Hambantota is in need of being revisited due to unclear clauses.[41] These appointments and the criticism of the Chinese, however, did not impact the Sino-Pak and Sino-Lanka relationship.

When Chinese President Xi Jinping made his maiden visit to Sri Lanka in September 2014 during the Mahinda's presidency, Sri Lanka elevated its bilateral relationship to a strategic cooperation partnership,[42] inking two dozen agreements in Colombo.[43] In the same manner, during Xi's maiden visit to Pakistan in April 2015, fifty-one MoUs were signed with the Sharif government.[44] Regardless of the change in governments, the two countries have continued with the previously signed bilateral commitments with China. The hostile position taken towards China during the elections, where the Chinese have been accused of corruption in their projects and infringing on the nation's sovereignty, is toned down post elections. Both Khan and Gotabaya turned around from the pre-election postures they took on the Chinese projects—from the rhetoric of the need to revisit and strike a better deal to absolute silence. In his election manifesto, Gotabaya promised that '[Sri Lanka] would abandon the economy based on foreign loans'.[45] Yet, Sri Lanka continued to borrow more from China. The 'frequency with which Khan u-turns' has also gone up.[46] Khan criticized the previous administration for the proverbial 'begging bowl' syndrome of going out to the world with requests for loans. But then, he too has been seeking funds from the IMF, China and the Arab nations.

China has defended Sri Lanka in the international arena, including the UNHRC, and will continue to do so. This assurance was given during the high-level visit of Senior Ambassador Yang Jiechi to Colombo and was demonstrated in practice at the UNHRC through the resolution submitted by the Chinese Permanent Representative in Geneva, Ambassador Chen Xu, explaining how 'China oppose(s) politicisation and double standards on human rights, as well as using human rights as an excuse for interfering in other countries' internal affairs', mentioning 'the clear lack of impartiality shown in the OHCHR's report to this session on Sri Lanka'.[47] Regardless of the outcome of the UNHRC resolution, the China–Sri Lanka axis will be further strengthened through China's unconditional support in this international forum.

Pakistan's support will also add extra weight to this axis. While China's sphere of influence will benefit from this exercise, Sri Lanka and Pakistan will work to find avenues to connect China's BRI infrastructure projects that, so far, have created huge economic burdens and little economic returns.

Both Khan and Gotabaya have reneged on their pre-election promises regarding Chinese projects in their countries. The unclear civil–military use of Sri Lankan and Pakistani ports in the respective agreements will also further exacerbate India's security concerns, which could also cause the India–Sri Lanka and India–Pakistan relationship to deteriorate if India's concerns are ignored. The absence of a regional security architecture is a cause of worry for all nations in South Asia. As evinced through its recent decisions on international projects, Sri Lanka's tilt away from countries such as India, Japan and the US, and the preference to bandwagon with China at the cost of its professed 'balanced' foreign policy posture, would have direct ramifications for its Western allies. Sri Lanka should recalibrate its foreign policy to 'balance' and benefit from both India and China, while strengthening its regional relationship with other nations, such as Pakistan. Overall, the expected success of Khan's visit to Colombo was overshadowed by Sri Lanka's 'critical turning point' at the UNHRC.[48]

## FOUR
## April 2021

### Sri Lanka's Rejection of the UNHRC Resolution: A Shift towards China?[49]

In Geneva, a tough resolution on promoting reconciliation, accountability and human rights in Sri Lanka was passed in March 2021, with twenty-two out of forty-seven countries supporting the resolution. This resolution gives more teeth to the Office of the United Nations High Commissioner for Human Rights (OHCHR) to investigate and collect evidence of human rights violations, not limited to the past unaddressed concerns by the government and also include the future concerns about President Gotabaya Rajapaksa's government. This is explained by Elisabeth Tichy-Fisslberger, speaking on behalf of the European Union at the UNHRC.[50] Backed by the US Secretary of State Anthony Blinken, she 'called on the Council to adopt resolutions due to Sri Lanka's lack of accountability for war crimes'. Sri Lanka's Foreign Minister Dinesh Gunawardena was quick to respond soon after the vote, 'The UN Core Group failed to secure 25 votes out of the 47 member UNHRC.'[51] Thus, taking into account the nations who did not support or abstained as one group, victory was projected using an illogical calculation. The result at UNHRC was quickly weaponized by the government in their favour, catering to their majoritarian voter base. The ultra-nationalist political view of the government is a readily available feature that could be used to call the UNHRC resolution an attempt by Western countries to bully countries such as Sri Lanka.[52]

This gives a bad start to the work towards the resolution. The need of the hour is to address minority concerns, not narrating an alternative view with unacceptable arguments and rejecting the UNHRC resolution.[53] Before the vote in Geneva, Sri Lankan foreign secretary assured that India would vote for Sri Lanka.[54] This was his own assessment and not a commitment that came from New Delhi. When the voting took place, India abstained. India's abstention from voting at the UNHRC was justified on several grounds—Tamil Nadu elections on the cards, internal pressure from the Tamilian polity, non-commitment from Sri Lankan government towards the devolution of power and the absence of a genuine reconciliation process. All this was clearly highlighted during Foreign Minister Jaishankar's visit in early January.[55]

It has been twelve years since the end of the civil war but all subsequent governments have failed to implement a domestic mechanism that could win over the Tamilian and the international community. The trust deficit has widened due to the complete withdrawal from the UNHRC resolution by the present government after its co-sponsorship in 2015 by the previous government. This was due to an inconsistent policy on reconciliation and multiple voices of several foreign ministers pledging support to different solutions, speaking at previous UNHRC sessions in Geneva. The present resolution, passed in March 2021, does not limit only to the civil war, and thus gives more emphasis to the last two years during which the human rights environment deteriorated further, adding new concerns such as the militarization of the present government.

There are two dangers of the March 2021 resolution. First, if the Sri Lankan government rejects the resolution completely, as C.A. Chandraprema, Sri Lanka's ambassador in Geneva explained, referring to the UNHRC resolution as 'unhelpful and divisive'[56] will invite a significant challenge from the West. A similar rejection was expressed after the vote by Foreign Minister Dinesh Gunawardena. President Gotabaya Rajapaksa expressed his displeasure, pointing out the geopolitics and India's devolution plea, 'I will not allow these countries to achieve their geopolitical needs by introducing separatism under the guise of power devolution.'[57] The complete rejection of the resolution could directly impact the relationship with the West and dilute Colombo's commitment towards international norms affecting the foreign policy balance. This would chart a path away from a *rules-based order*, and from Indo-Pacific and its allies. Second, it could also impact the country's exports to the Western nations—the EU and the US are Sri Lanka's largest export markets. This would also affect the country's image and the ability to attract Western investments, accelerating an inexorable drift of the country towards China.

### ANCHORAGE TO INDIAN OCEAN REGION

US Secretary of State Anthony Blinken and National Security Advisor Jake Sullivan met China's most senior diplomat Yang Jiechi and State Councillor Wang Yi in Anchorage, Alaska, marking the beginning of the Biden administration's China policy. Both parties were to exchange their views to ease the US-China tension that had exacerbated in the last few years. The US position on China was clearly articulated highlighting China's aggressive behaviour and violation of human rights in several geographies. According to senior US diplomat Richard Haass, the discussion was 'mishandled and a terrible start' to the de-escalation efforts where both sides accused each other about their respective policies.[58]

A day before the Alaska summit, the US increased its sanctions on China over its crackdown on people asking for more political freedom in Hong Kong. According to Wang Yi, 'Chinese people are outraged by this gross interference in China's internal affairs . . . this is not supposed to be the way one should welcome his guests . . .

this is miscalculated and only reflects the vulnerability and weakness inside the US. And this will not shake China's position.'[59] Adding to that, Yang Jiechi said, 'The time had passed when a small group of wealthy Western nations could dictate the shape of the global order and the US no longer represents world opinion.'

While both sides expressed similar level of hostility, the event is perhaps a deliberate recalibration, well-orchestrated by the US, to continue the antagonism with China to build strong relationships with US allies, which is a priority for the Biden administration. Japanese scholar Satoru Nagao argues, 'The more China escalates the situation, more the defence capabilities of the Quad will be institutionalised.'[60] In the meantime, due to US administration's unfavourable China policies, Beijing is charting a course ahead that depends less on the West with its 'dual circulation' economy, which is a more self-reliant economic model.[61] The tense US-China interaction in Anchorage will impact the Indian Ocean Region (IOR). China's belligerence could propel nations to expand their security footing in the IOR.

Strengthening Prime Minister Modi's Security and Growth for All the Region (SAGAR), Foreign Minister Dr Jaishankar made repeated visits to the Maldives to establish the coast guard naval operational base in at Sifvaru–Uthuru Thilafalhu (UTF), which will be developed and supported by Indian naval assistance, further extending US$50 million credit line for defence.[62] Sifvaru, which is situated close to the shore of south India, is a perfect location for Indian logistics, HADR efforts and maritime security operations. The Maldives had been a strategic location even in the British Empire where Gan (Addu Atoll) in the Maldives was used for a similar purpose by the Royal Navy and the Royal Air Force.

The second leg of Dr Jaishankar's visit was to Mauritius where security and defence cooperation between India and Maldives was further strengthened. The northern island of Agalega in Mauritius has already been developed by India for military use. A P-8I reconnaissance aircraft can easily land on the newly-built runway.[63]

All these and more security partnerships, such as those with Japan to access Djibouti, are clear security expansions made in the western IOR by India. The recent tripartite agreement between Sri Lanka, the Maldives and India is considered to be a move in the same direction of mini-lateral successes.

During the Quad leaders' summit consisting of India, US, Australia and Japan, Joe Biden, Scott Morrison, Yoshihide Suga and Narendra Modi pledged their commitment to safeguard the interests of democratic nations and to sustain a rules-based order in the Indo-Pacific where Chinese aggression is a concern for the Quad. The US commitment to a rules-based order in the Indo-Pacific was reiterated in Sri Lanka by the senior most US General, Kenneth S. Wilsbach, who visited the island after a decade. The US commitment and the role of the Quad has strengthened due to the aggressive behaviour of China in the periphery of India, the only Quad member who shares a land border with China.

In this geopolitical equation, it is vital that India strikes a balance and deters Chinese expansion, especially towards the IOR. Indian scholar Brahma Chellaney correctly observed, 'It is imperative that the Quad gain strategic heft so as to bring an expansionist China under pressure.'[64]

Sri Lanka's foreign policy posture is to balance the US and China, being a part of both BRI and the Indo-Pacific. Neither can Sri Lanka afford to move away from India nor the rules-based alliance where it could play an important strategic role rather than a passive partner, silently accommodating China's expansion in the island. However, there are clear signs that the Rajapaksa administration will continue to tilt in favour of China in certain sectors due to China's unconditional support in defending the Sri Lankan administration on its human rights record in Geneva and questioning the OHCHR report.[65] Along these lines, China will also support the domestic political position on minority concerns taken by the Rajapaksa regime to make strategic inroads in the politics of the island. A few days ago, President Gotabaya Rajapaksa thanked President Xi for

China's support at UNHRC during a telephonic concertation.[66] On this occasion, President Xi also gave a firm pledge to stand by Sri Lanka in case of undue pressure exerted by Western countries.

This growing Chinese space in India's periphery will be of great concern to New Delhi. Sri Lankan foreign policy bureaucrats and advisors should clearly understand the geopolitical concerns, not limiting to mere rhetoric of 'India first'[67] approach from the front door, while welcoming 'China preferred' approach from the back door. While the Sri Lankan government has drafted a twenty-point Foreign Policy Directive in an attempt to have a more consistent foreign policy,[68] this policy has been approved by the Cabinet without inputs from the Parliament, and is privy to only a few ministers. This needs a broader review and a collective approach to calibrate the balance.

## FIVE
## December 2021

### One Country One Law, China Circumventing a Sri Lankan Fertilizer Hazard[69]

The newly-appointed Chair of the high-level task force 'One Country One Law' in Sri Lanka, Ven Gnanasara, invited the youth who suffered due to 'racial, religious and provincial divisions' to submit their ideas and suggestions to the task force as it seeks to implements its objectives.[70] President Gotabaya has promised Sri Lanka 'vistas of prosperity and splendour'; prosperity is absent, with Sri Lanka going through a grave economic crisis, and hundreds of youth publicly displaying their displeasure by queuing up at the immigration and consular sections of foreign embassies to migrate out of Sri Lanka. The economic destitution and the daily struggle with high cost of living have worsened with the country's economic crisis, and the youth migration is a severe loss in terms of brain-drain for this developing nation. In the past, Sri Lanka faced two youth insurrections leading to the loss of thousands of lives. Today, a generation is fleeing the nation. The ultra-nationalism projected by the political parties will fuel the burning fire and not ease the present socio-political concerns. Adding to the domestic concerns is another external factor—the Chinese pressure on Sri Lanka.

CCP General Secretary Xi Jinping has championed an effort to build a new party–state legal system where the party rules and the state laws coexist as an organic whole. 'As paradoxical as it may seem, Xi's ideology is centred around the idea of ruling according to the law,' said Ling Li, a scholar of Chinese politics at the University of Vienna who argued that Xi might resurrect the Mao-era 'Party Chairman' title next year as he enters a third term.[71]

The influence of General Secretary Xi has grown and spread over the last few years to all levels and institutions. The Leninist centralization that Deng Xiaoping followed was the exact prescription Xi adopted, which has successfully worked in mainland China and there are now plans to expand the Chinese sphere of influence to the BRI nations including Sri Lanka. China is promoting this 'national rejuvenation' in full force, altering the playbook in many geographies, and Sri Lanka has become a victim due to its dependence on China.

### THE CHINESE FERTILIZER SHIPMENT

China blacklisted the People's Bank, a reputed Sri Lankan bank, over a US$42 million fertilizer shipment from China.[72] The Chinese embassy in Colombo tweeted the blacklisting.

In October 2021, the Sri Lankan authorities refused to accept a Chinese shipment of 20,000 tons of fertilizer due to the presence of harmful bacteria in the consignment. The Chinese authorities defended the quality of their export from Qingdao Seawin Biotech Company. Surprisingly, the same ship, *Hippo Spirit*, was rechristened *Seiyo Explorer* and entered Sri Lanka with the same consignment in November, this time closer to the southern Hambantota port built by the Chinese.[73] The ship deactivated its automatic identification system (AIS) and renamed itself in mid-sea. China is using its influence to get the contaminated fertilizer consignment offloaded on the island regardless of the rejection. The extent to which China would go, from blacklisting a reputed Sri Lankan bank to renaming the ship shows China's significant 'push' factor and depicts the apparent weakness in Sri Lankan institutional capacity—such as the foreign ministry—to defend the local bank and pressure China to adhere to the local test data. The Chinese wish to get a third-party assessment done on the fertilizer, undermining Sri Lankan expertise, which could be used for many future shipments to bypass the local process. China's capacity to manoeuvre supply chains is exemplified by this case, where Sri Lanka is being unreasonably pressured and is a victim of its heavy dependence on Chinese loans.

China is altering the rule book and standards to suit itself and pressure local policymakers in countries like Sri Lanka. The significant growth of Chinese influence over Sri Lankan elites, government institutions and media space was identified as 'high risk' by a recent comprehensive report titled *China's Influence in South Asia: Vulnerabilities and Resilience in Four Countries* by Carnegie Endowment.[74] The growing agitation amongst the public over Chinese loans is a serious indicator of this development. The report aptly highlights the high risk Sri Lanka faces from China when it comes to potential capture of 'influential elites and key individuals in Sri Lanka's vibrant and robust media, as an alternative to politicians, to get their view across to the public'. The report further states that, 'issue of captured or capturable elites by China is more relevant in Sri Lanka than in Bangladesh'.

Chinese influence over the ruling political party and government administration has impacted the state institutions and has been listed in the report as 'medium risk level'. This should be given serious consideration since it will alter the democratic process, inviting the alternative China model into Sri Lanka. Reversing China's belligerent behaviour will be impossible and will require diplomatic finesse, commercial innovation and institutional creativity on the part of many South Asian nations, and the report highlights essential recommendations for policymakers to consider. The fertilizer import dispute is an example of the quality standards nations such as Sri Lanka should be concerned with when it comes to Chinese exports. The far bigger issue is the complete lack of morals in getting the ship into Sri Lanka. Instead of facing the problem and solving it, a resolution was attempted by using dishonest means. It was all done with the Chinese government's connivance.

Sri Lanka should focus on the infrastructure standards and transparency of Chinese loans, and transfer key strategic projects back to Sri Lankan ownership.

However, the US view of a 'Chinese invasion' falls short of the actual ground situation in Sri Lanka. While there is a significant increase in Chinese influence due to infrastructure investment, vaccines supply and financial assistance, there is no 'China invasion' in Sri Lanka per se. China's expansion strategy has accelerated after multiple global and regional events such as the global financial crisis, the Trump presidency, Brexit and the Afghanistan exit by the US. However, it is too early to conclude a 'China invasion' as projected by several Pentagon officials, especially considering that regional power status is not always necessary to challenge a world power. Robert Gilpin argues, 'A rising power lacking regional hegemony could still challenge the hegemon globally over cross-cutting forms of control that sustain its global hegemonic order, such as economics, finance, tech and information.'

A few weeks ago, China displayed its military capacity in hypersonic missile capabilities, which General Mark Milley, Chairman of the Joint Chiefs of Staff, called a 'Sputnik moment'.[75] It may sound alarming due to the hyped-up fear, but it was not a Sputnik moment. Rush Doshi argues, 'What matters is not whether China has full regional hegemony but has built home region confidence that can manage the risk of hegemonic intervention if it pursues global expansion.'[76]

China has gradually built its confidence and its influence in Sri Lanka. Sri Lanka, with its present economic and political dysfunctionality, will be a lucrative ground for China's expansion in the region. It is a long game for the Middle Kingdom. In the next decade, the United States needs to help states in the Indo-Pacific develop their asymmetric capabilities to deter Chinese expansionist behaviour. Sri Lanka will face serious headwinds due to its strong China factor; the 'high risk' of capturability due to its political dysfunctionality will now spread to the most sensitive branch of government and law and order.

## SIX
## April 2022

### Political–Economic Turmoil in Sri Lanka: Competing Interests of China and India[77]

Even before its current economic crisis, Sri Lanka could be classified as a 'fragile state'. It had endured a multitude of internal and external shocks, including a three-decade civil war, Islamic terrorist attacks, accusations of human rights abuses by the government as well as political–economic dysfunctionality. In the present context, the fragile state has moved to a 'crisis state' in which its institutions face serious challenges and are unable to manage conflicts and shocks. The unmanageable economic crisis has triggered a political dysfunctionality. A violent protest on 1 April in which hundreds of people nearly succeeded in storming the president's residence[78] had a ripple effect as public demonstrations spread across the island calling for an end to the Rajapaksa family rule, corruption and the country's economic woes. Galle Face Green, a beachfront urban park that was once a popular weekend destination for families, is now occupied by protestors and resembles the Tahrir square during Arab Spring.

#### ECONOMIC CRISIS

Sri Lanka faces its worst financial crisis since its independence in 1948. Prolonged power cuts along with shortages of fuel, essential food and medicines, have increased public anger to unprecedented levels. On 3 April, a political crisis emerged as the entire Cabinet resigned, forcing President Gotabaya Rajapaksa to appoint a new Cabinet in order to ensure the continued functioning of his administration.

Sri Lanka's economic crisis has been triggered primarily by the country's longstanding liquidity and insolvency issues. Inadequate foreign reserves forced the government to suspend foreign debt repayment, defaulting for the first time in its history.

Other contributing factors include the government's tax cuts which led to a drop in state revenue, its unsustainable loans and a rejection of external expert advice due to its inward focused policy posture. The untimely occurrence of the Covid-19 pandemic had a devastating impact on tourism revenue and remittances from Sri Lankans working abroad. The country's economic problems were further aggravated by the government's sudden decision in April 2022 to ban chemical fertilizers and shift to organic farming.[79] The agricultural sector was wholly unprepared. The shortage of organic fertilizers led to a drop in crop yields and sent food prices soaring.

### CHINESE DEBT TRAP TO STRATEGIC TRAP

Sri Lanka's debt portfolio, particularly the proportion of Chinese loans, grew significantly under the Rajapaksa regime. Some academics have sought to dispel the popular notion of Chinese 'debt-trap diplomacy', arguing that China holds just 10 per cent of the country's total foreign debt, on par with Japan. However, Chinese interest rates—at more than 6 per cent—are significantly higher compared to other loans.

Apart from the debt trap, China is also engaging in 'strategic-trap diplomacy' in Sri Lanka, facilitated by the Rajapaksa regime's foreign policy.[80] The Rajapaksa-led political party—the SLPP—receives assistance from Beijing,[81] including political funding,[82] allowing it to strengthen its autocratic rule. The Chinese government also supported the Sri Lankan government over its alleged human rights abuses at the UNHRC,[83] leading Colombo to provide reciprocal support to Beijing over the latter's alleged mistreatment of Uighurs in Xinjiang.[84] In addition, China provided military and surveillance assistance to the Sri Lankan regime. By cooperating so closely with Beijing, Rajapaksa's foreign policy allowed Sri Lanka to fall deeper into the Chinese strategic trap. Furthermore, it was a shift from Sri Lanka's previous approach of maintaining balanced foreign relations with other nations, including its closest neighbour India.

China's growing influence over the island-nation has led to heightened geopolitical competition with India. In 2019, India objected to the development of wind farms by Chinese firms on three Sri Lankan islands as they were close to India's southern shores.[85] The project was subsequently terminated and awarded to India.[86] In 2021, Sri Lanka unilaterally withdrew from a tripartite agreement with India and Japan on the development of the strategic ECT at Colombo Port.[87] Though the Sri Lankan government subsequently offered India the development of the West Container Terminal as compensation, the *Sunday Times* of Sri Lanka reported earlier, 'New Delhi was worried that the rhetoric around the ECT initiative was promoted by Chinese Intelligence, with the objective of having it blocked.'[88]

Following the passing of the Colombo Port City Economic Commercial Bill in April 2021, approval was given for the establishment of China's extra-jurisdictional SEZ in Colombo Port City,[89] creating what one expert referred to derisively as 'a "Chinese province" in Sri Lanka'.[90] Further, a visit by Chinese ambassador Qi Zhenhong to Sri Lanka's Tamil-majority Northern province in December 2021 was seen as disregarding Indian sensitivities and an attempt to expand Chinese footprint in the area—a direct concern for India.[91]

## INDIA–CHINA COMPETING INTERESTS

Amidst the current economic crisis, India has stepped in to provide financial assistance to Sri Lanka. A four-pillar bilateral initiative was agreed between India and Sri Lanka which included lines of credit granted by India for food, medicines and fuel purchases, a currency swap agreement to deal with Sri Lanka's balance of payment issues, an 'early' modernization project of the Trinco oil farms and a Sri Lankan commitment to facilitate Indian investments in various sectors.[92]

Sri Lanka has borrowed from India and China multiple times to minimize the crisis.[93] In late 2021, New Delhi arranged a US$1.9 billion credit line with a US$500 million credit-line for fuel, while Beijing was requested to restructure debt repayments on US$3.5 billion. At around the same time, China provided Sri Lanka with a US$1.5 billion yuan-denominated swap. Since the start of the pandemic, Beijing has extended US$1.3 billion in syndicated loans to the country. More recently, Sri Lanka is seeking another US$1.5 billion credit-line from China as well as syndicated loans of up to US$1 billion.

Sri Lanka urgently needs around US$3 billion in bridge financing from the IMF to help restore supplies of essential items.[94] The IMF was the last resort and the only option due to the significant amount required to come out of the crisis. The IMF will push objective reforms to stabilize the situation, including restructuring of Sri Lanka's entire existing debt portfolio. India and China can both play a significant role in stabilizing Sri Lanka—an essential partner in the Indian Ocean for both nations. For India, the economic crisis might be an opportunity to reassert its influence and weaken China's grip over its neighbour. Yet, New Delhi would also have to carefully manage its engagement with Colombo, given how it has previously been accused of interfering in Sri Lanka's domestic politics.[95]

While the protestors want President Gotabaya Rajapaksa as well as his corrupt family members to be removed from power, the regime has launched a highly visible damage control campaign which includes admitting their policy failures.[96] However, this may not be sufficient to quell public anger. Protesters have not only called for an end to the Rajapaksa regime but also greater accountability and investigations into corruption, including that involving large-scale infrastructure projects. Such an investigation and the resulting actions will strain external relationships, especially with China. The previous administration of President Maithripala Sirisena had briefly suspended a US$1.4 billion development project with China Harbour Engineering Company in 2015 over bribery allegations involving Mahinda Rajapaksa (Gotabaya's brother and himself a former Sri Lankan president),[97] though the subsequent investigation had no conclusive outcome. Regardless, to avoid any potential prosecution, the Rajapaksa family will try to hold on to its political power for as long as possible.

The need of the hour is an effective interim government, one that can re-establish the nation's international credibility amidst the political–economic crisis, and smoothly navigate negotiations with the IMF for financial assistance. China and India are key players who could stabilize the situation, but they would need to set aside their competitive interests and focus on advising and assisting in objective reforms. A dysfunctional Sri Lanka is a risk to both India and China. What is immediately required is advice to carry out swift and sensible fiscal adjustments and recalibrate the country's dysfunctional policies, with assistance from the international community.

4

# Domestic Political Environment

## ONE
## December 2020

### Sri Lanka's Parliamentary Election: International and Security Challenges for the Rajapaksa Government[1]

Following Gotabaya's presidential victory in November 2019, his brother Mahinda became Sri Lanka's prime minister after a historical landslide victory in the August 2020 parliamentary elections. For the first time in the island's history, two siblings have taken over the executive and legislature, winning 145 seats in the 225-member Parliament. The United National Party (UNP) under former prime minister Ranil Wickremesinghe secured only one seat in the Parliament.

Geopolitical analyst Parag Khanna argues that politics is about sovereignty and transparency. He opines that the slightest manoeuvre to threaten sovereignty can bring down a government.[2] Mahinda's return to power in Sri Lanka after the 2015 defeat was on the promise of re-establishing the threatened national security and protecting the sovereignty of the country. National security was eroded by the Easter Sunday bombing in 2019, Sri Lanka's largest-ever terrorist attack after the end of the civil war.

Sovereignty was a hot topic during the presidential and parliamentary elections. Mahinda's party, the SLPP, raised the issue of the threat to the country's sovereignty during the elections. Other than the defining moment of the Easter Sunday attack, the 30/1 UNHRC resolution, co-sponsored by the Maithripala Sirisena–Wickremesinghe government to promote reconciliation, accountability and human rights in the country; the ninety-nine-year lease of Hambantota port to the Chinese; and the two US agreements (SOFA and MCC) were among the issues relating to the island's sovereignty that were raised during the elections. With Mahinda's victory, several questions arose in the international arena on democracy, rule of law, human rights, devolution of power, national reconciliation process, protecting minority communities and the China factor in Sri Lanka's foreign policy.

## INTENSE POWER RIVALRY: INDIA–CHINA AND US-CHINA

The incumbent administration's foreign policy is calibrated in a different and competitive environment in comparison to his brother Mahinda's presidential term from 2005 to 2015. There is now an intense power projection from three sides—China, India and the US—in Sri Lanka's vicinity. Sri Lanka, an island-nation sitting in a strategic location at the Sea Lines of Communications (SLOC) in the Indian Ocean, is directly influenced by external power rivalry.

Heightened India–China tension in India's northern border is not limited to the region. In the Indian Ocean space in the south of India, a maritime arms race is also slowly building up. Tension is brewing among the great powers in the area. The US did not win the Cold War on its own. It formed strong alliances with its Western partners in the North Atlantic Treaty Organization (NATO) and used containment as the primary foreign policy strategy. In the current situation, there is a militarization of the Quad (US, India, Australia and Japan). Moreover, the Quad is expanding to a 'Quad Plus' with the inclusion of South Korea, Vietnam and New Zealand. From quadrilateral security arrangements and joint military exercises to the signing of military logistics agreements such as the one between India and Australia, it is apparent that Containment 2.0 against China is fully at play.

Several Indian scholars have argued for the need for a NATO-like military alignment in the Indian Ocean. There is a significant danger in formulating such containment strategies against China as this will not bring stability to the existing order but will further destabilize the region and further strain the relationship between the US and China.

The external geopolitical tension has had a direct impact on the domestic affairs of the South Asian nations, including Sri Lanka. Sri Lanka has felt the simultaneous power projection of the US, China and India in its surrounding Indian Ocean space due to the containment strategies and growing mistrust among the great powers.

According to Chinese Foreign Minister Wang Yi, the US-China relationship is going on a downward spiral with a negative political agenda. He says that 'this is a political virus' designed by the US against China.[3] According to Indian professor Srikanth Kondapalli, 'Chinese assertive and aggressive responses have been a bid to cover up the Covid-19 disaster.'[4] China is expanding its geopolitical footprint in different geographies and retaliating in a tit-for-tat response as a show of its strength. The closing of the US consulate in Chengdu, China, this year by the Chinese government in response to the earlier shutting down of the Chinese embassy in Houston is an example of this strategy.

The heightened security environment cannot be contextualized as a 'Cold War'. Singaporean academic Kishore Mahbubani explains in his new book, *Has China Won? The Chinese Challenge to American Primacy*, 'In the Cold War, America's heavy defence expenditures proved prudent as they forced the Soviet Union, a country with a smaller economy, to match America's military expenses.'[5] The context is different with China. Wang Yi rightly explains, 'We reject any attempt to create a so-called "New Cold War" because it contravenes the fundamental interests of the Chinese and American peoples and the global trend toward development and progress.'[6] Sri Lanka will have to navigate its foreign policy in such a challenging geopolitical context, working closely with all the powers.

### GOTABAYA'S LEADERSHIP AMIDST A GLOBAL PANDEMIC

Shortly after the parliamentary election victory, the charge d'affaires of the Chinese embassy in Colombo, Hu Wei, met Prime Minister Mahinda Rajapaksa.[7] He handed over a congratulatory letter from the Central Committee of the Communist Party of China pledging continuous support to the SLPP, requesting to expedite the BRI projects, especially the Colombo Port City inaugurated by Chinese President Xi Jinping and then president Mahinda Rajapaksa in 2014.[8]

Sri Lanka received assistance in the fight against Covid-19 from China, and both nations have worked together to strengthen their bilateral ties during the pandemic. Sri Lankan authorities have neither accused nor viewed China as the cause of the pandemic. Gotabaya's successful leadership and management of the Covid-19 pandemic were well-received by the general public and contributed to the parliamentary election victory.

### THE MCC, SOFA, ECT AND MATTALA AIRPORT

There are several infrastructure and logistics agreements that were held up during Gotabaya's presidency. An estimated US$ 480 million from the US MCC grant to construct a transport corridor was held up after a presidential committee appointed by Gotabaya concluded in its report that the project would threaten national security and impede the sovereignty of the nation.[9] Another US agreement, the SOFA, which is a military logistics initiative, was put on hold since it was deemed a national security threat. The two US agreements are likely to be on hold for some time due to domestic political constraints that promote nationalism.

In another development, the Indian-led tripartite memorandum with the Japanese and Sri Lankan governments to develop Colombo Port's ECT, concluded during the previous Sri Lankan administration, is under review.[10] At the same time, the Chinese have built an international airport in Mattala. The new developments could be misconstrued as a pro-China position taken by the government and a drift away from Sri Lanka's balanced foreign policy. However, the government would like to project that there is no China consideration in these decisions; rather, there exists a greater national sentiment about protecting the sovereignty of the nation.

## THE RAJAPAKSAS' FOREIGN POLICY

Mahinda introduced his political manifesto, 'Mahinda Chinthanaya' (Mahinda's Vision), during his 2005 presidential campaign. In the manifesto, he spelt out a 'non-aligned' foreign policy. During his two terms in office, there were two significant achievements that received much attention in the international arena. The first was ending the almost three-decade war with the Liberation Tigers of Tamil Eelam (LTTE) in 2009.[11] The second was a Chinese-built port in the southern shores of the island known as the Hambantota port. The construction of the southern port was followed by many other Chinese infrastructure projects in the island. This was a clear indication of the Mahinda government's strong relationship with China. Th relationship was further cemented by Chinese President Xi's visit to the island in 2014, where the two sides signed multiple bilateral agreements and inaugurated the Colombo Port City project.[12]

India was concerned by the growing Chinese influence in Sri Lanka. The Chinese submarine visits to Sri Lanka during the last years of the Mahinda government were a turning point in the strained India–Sri Lanka relationship. India assessed the Chinese submarine visit as a direct national security threat to India. The relationship with India then deteriorated, with Rajapaksa himself accusing the Indian spy agency, the Research and Analysis Wing, for his election loss in 2015.[13]

The manifesto of the next president, Gotabaya, 'Vistas of Prosperity and Splendour', outlined a balanced and equidistant foreign policy for the island.[14] However, projecting equal distance in its relationship with all nations will be challenging due to the island's geographical proximity to India, a much larger geographical power in the region. A more 'multi-aligned' foreign policy will be visible in practice as Sri Lanka would like to work with all powers, thereby maintaining a balanced foreign policy in the coming years.

In November 2019, Gotabaya rightly explained, 'We don't want to get in between the power struggles of superpowers. . . . We are so small and we can't survive to get into [these] balancing acts.'[15] While Gotabaya may not want Colombo to be caught in the global power struggle, the question is, will these powers leave the country alone? Several analysts have already cautioned of a possible China-centric tilt due to an unmatched, continuous volume of assistance from China to Sri Lanka.[16] It is more likely that Gotabaya's foreign policy will continue on a similar trajectory as that of Mahinda, with a closer and stronger Chinese footprint. However, Sri Lankan foreign policy might recalibrate its India–Sri Lanka relationship, which was strained in the last years of the Mahinda presidency.

## INDIA–SRI LANKA RELATIONS

Indian Prime Minister Narendra Modi was the first global leader to congratulate Mahinda.[17] 'India is our friend and relation,' said Mahinda,[18] hoping to strengthen bilateral cooperation between India and Sri Lanka. With India's 'Neighbourhood First' policy, India could increase its assistance to the Sri Lankan economy and infrastructure. But as academic Constantino Xavier explains, India cannot take Sri Lanka's promises for granted and should 'deepen economic interdependence with Sri Lanka' as the island-nation will 'continue to welcome China's enthusiastic, generous and reliable financing for critical infrastructure'.[19]

Enhancing regional connectivity is presently one of India's top foreign policy priorities, whether it is with Nepal, Bhutan, Myanmar, Bangladesh or Sri Lanka. Building infrastructure to facilitate trade and enhance connectivity with these countries is a key element of New Delhi's 'Neighbourhood First' and 'Act East' policies, initiated by Modi when he assumed leadership.[20] India's Minister for External

Affairs, S. Jaishankar, explained, 'From the era when there were charges of [India] being overbearing, today the complaints are of doing too little. . . . Investing in South Asian connectivity is today the smartest move we can make. This is not just an issue of intent; it is even more of delivery. For good measure, that will be compared with the performance of China.'[21]

With Gotabaya's inaugural foreign visit to India, he has successfully managed to recalibrate the India–Sri Lanka relationship to a positive trajectory. During the last several months, Modi had several productive phone conversations with both Gotabaya and Mahinda, pledging assistance to Sri Lanka, which is undergoing a difficult time since the Easter Sunday terror attack. The Sri Lankan government has sought assistance from India, including for a US$1.1 billion special currency swap facility to add to the US$400 million SAARC currency swap to deal with the foreign exchange problem the country is facing right now. The Indian premier assured, 'We are ready to help under terms that are favourable to Sri Lanka.'[22]

The Sri Lankan economy has contracted, and the growth rate has slowed to less than three per cent of the gross domestic product, one of the lowest growth rates in South Asia.[23] For the India–Sri Lanka relationship to maintain its positive direction, there are several domestic political challenges the Sri Lankan government needs to address. These include the Tamil grievances on the devolution of power granted by the thirteenth amendment of the Constitution. While the 'thirteenth amendment plus',[24] a rhetorical political promise to go beyond the existing devolution of power, was made during Mahinda's presidency, it did not materialize due to strong alt-right ultra-nationalists backing the government. Sri Lanka's commitment to the 30/1 UNHRC resolution on reconciliation and accountability are both concerns for the Tamil polity in India and the larger Tamil diaspora in the West. The growing Chinese footprint in the island is a security concern for India. In addition, the US and India are uneasy about how Gotabaya will balance the Chinese sphere of influence in Sri Lanka with that of the other powers, the evolving domestic political landscape, the preservation of democratic values and not drifting towards a semi-autocratic regime.

## HAMBANTOTA: THE NEXT FINANCIAL CAPITAL

In the domestic political arena, while discussing the importance of the Chinese built and operated southern port of Hambantota in Sri Lanka during a recent interview, Mahinda's son, Namal Rajapaksa, who contested from his father's previous constituency, explained, 'Hambantota will become the next commercial city in the island; with highways, strategic port, international airport and all the logistics ready, we will make this happen.'[25] Namal's long-term view is to continue his father's vision of converting Hambantota into a modern city under his leadership, which has been perceived as a difficult and unachievable task by many in Colombo.

When looking at the massive Chinese infrastructure diplomacy carried out with two global connection hubs—the Hambantota port and Mattala airport, with other ancillary infrastructure, including an international convention centre, cricket stadium, highways, hotels and much more to come—this project of building another commercial city in the deep south perhaps could be completed under the leadership of the Rajapaksas.

## DEBT TRAP DIPLOMACY

Although the issue of the ninety-nine-year lease agreement of Hambantota port, signed during the previous administration of Sirisena–Wickremesinghe, was raised during the 2019 presidential election, it is very unlikely that the agreement will be amended by the new regime. Hambantota is not Djibouti and it is under Sri Lankan jurisdiction and control, while Djibouti was leased out initially as a multi-base facility to several other nations before it was leased to China for the latter's military purposes. The amount China loaned to Sri Lanka for its infrastructure projects was perhaps comparable to Djibouti. However, unlike Djibouti, the Chinese have assured the Sri Lankan government that the port will not be used for any military purpose. China needs a strategic location in the Indian Ocean to secure the transportation of its energy supplies like oil.

The growing Chinese debt to Sri Lanka is widely discussed. Beijing has been accused of trapping Sri Lanka through its large-scale lending. It should be noted that Sri Lanka's international sovereign bond debt is much higher than overall Chinese loans. However, the conditions in the Chinese loan agreements are not transparent and a matter of a concern. Sri Lanka has agreed to borrow further from China to sustain its economy due to its low foreign exchange reserves.[26]

The centralized nature of governance in Colombo left little room for public opinion on the matter and enabled purchases by Sri Lanka without competitive bidding, thus allowing very high prices to the sellers. Sri Lanka now needs to move out from these earlier practices. It can and should use its strategic location as a bargaining advantage for better terms with China. If Sri Lanka had more fallback options in place, it would certainly have obtained a better deal from China.[27] The absence of alternatives gives China the upper hand. Sri Lanka can use its infrastructure as a bargaining tool to obtain additional benefits. Of course, these would be at the expense of strategic and political risks associated with increased competition in the Indian Ocean.

The Gotabaya government claims that the surrounding land of the Hambantota port and port operation should not have been given on a ninety-nine-year lease to China. 'We were never to give control of the [Hambantota] port to China; that was a mistake,' according to Gotabaya.[28]

## TRIPLE SECURITY THREATS AND BALANCING THE TRIPLE SPHERES OF INFLUENCE

Gotabaya's government is likely to face three security challenges. First, there is growing extremist terrorism in the region as demonstrated by the deadly 2019 Easter Sunday attacks. Second, the LTTE ideology, which triggered cyber-attacks on several government websites, including the public administration by Tamil Eelam Cyber Force,[29] remains active. Third, there are external geopolitical fissures to Sri Lankan foreign policy. Balancing India, China and the US will be a top priority.

Gotabaya's challenges are daunting. In addition to balancing the triple spheres of influence from China, India and the US and preserving geopolitical equilibrium, Colombo will need to balance the infrastructure diplomacy carried out by external powers in the island. On the proposed 30/1 UNHRC resolution, instead of withdrawing from its own co-sponsored resolution, Sri Lanka should have engaged the UNHRC. Working on the post-conflict reconciliation process and building a genuine diaspora re-engagement strategy are important to ensure social cohesion in the country. Preserving and sustaining a transparent and democratic political environment will be integral to the government's success. Similarly, protecting sovereignty and ensuring national security are crucial to prevent a drift towards a semi-autocratic regime during these times of tight economic conditions and harmful mercantile practices. The constitutional amendment should include a devolution of power to the provinces. There should be checks and balances and separation of powers of the executive, legislature and judiciary to sustain democracy in the country.

## TWO
## June 2021

### The Coming Anarchy in Sri Lanka[30]

Autocratic governments usually supress the rule of law. They make its own rules unilaterally and enforce them. In such societies, people turn into unfree pawns as a result of worsening political conditions. The arrival of anarchy in the island-nation of Sri Lanka is due to a series of such factors. It is mainly driven by the worsening domestic political environment, curtailment of democracy, weaponizing the Sinhalese-Buddhist ultra-nationalism against the minority communities, and the exertion of undue influence on courts and judiciary. The recent political victimization of neutral agencies[31] is an attempt to rewrite rules by the politicians. In this backdrop, the worsening human rights conditions and arbitrary pardoning of criminals will weaken the rule of law. Such a dangerous tilt, away from democratic forms of governance, will drag the nation towards an autocracy.

Democracies 'can be dissolved in spectacular fashion like from a coup d'etat or a less dramatic but equally destructive manner' argue Steven Levitz and Daniel Ziblatt in their book *How Democracies Die*. The slow and equally destructive death of democracy has started in Sri Lanka.

Sri Lankans were confined to their homes during the lockdown following the government's 'disciplinary project',[32] while the government was engaged in releasing a convict using a prison side-door. 'The pardoning of Duminda Silva, whose conviction the Supreme Court upheld in 2018, undermines rule of law,'[33] explains US ambassador to Sri Lanka, Alaina B. Teplitz, referring to the presidential pardon given to the former member of Parliament and Rajapaksa political ally. The former justice minister Thalatha Athukorala questions, 'Today, those found guilty of the most serious crimes in our law enjoy presidential protection while the judges and police officers who brought them to justice have targets on their backs.'[34] The presidential pardon comes when the Sri Lankan government faces multiple challenges from the European Union (EU) pinpointing the abuses of the Prevention of Terrorism Act (PTA) and the growing human rights problems in the country. A warning to withdraw its GSP+ concession is already on the cards. The Office of the UN High Commissioner for Human Rights condemning the decision and expressing concern said, 'Presidential pardon of Duminda Silva, a former MP convicted of the murder of a fellow politician, is another example of selective, arbitrary granting of pardons that weakens rule of law and undermines accountability.'[35] Sri Lanka's bar association (BASL) questioned President Rajapaksa on the decision and raised severe concerns about the administration's position towards the rule of law.[36]

This was not an ad hoc decision of the government. The release was carried out along with the release of several other PTA detainees. Why was such a decision taken, especially at a time of significant external pressure, like that from EU?

## HUMAN RIGHTS CONCERNS

In a lengthy televised address on 25 June, days after the release of the former MP, President Gotabaya Rajapaksa talked of the progress of his development plan and continuous commitment to the rule of law, not referring to the PTA nor the pardoning act. The new European Union Parliament, adopting a resolution to withdraw the Generalized Scheme of Preferences (GSP+), is a clear warning to the Sri Lankan regime. The European Parliament adopted a resolution on 10 June calling for the repeal of Sri Lanka's draconian Prevention of Terrorism Act. Further, the resolution pointed out Sri Lanka's 'alarming path towards the recurrence of grave human rights violations . . . accelerating militarisation of civilian governmental functions, the reversal of important constitutional safeguards, political obstruction of accountability, exclusionary rhetoric, intimidation of civil society, and the use of anti-terrorism laws'.[37]

The regime has failed to address the human rights concerns highlighted multiple times, and procrastination in its addressal is the reason for this action by the EU Parliament. Earlier in March, the government rejected the UNHRC resolution,[38] giving a clear indication of the its position of 'no external interference' towards the reconciliation process.

Ironically, the real concern of many in the country is the absence of a reconciliation process. The departure from the internationally accepted process and continuous denial by the government on minority concerns is evident. The government has already lost its direction and moved from a progressive path towards a more autocratic one. Dr Jehan Perera correctly observes this fact and explains, 'The reality on the ground is that wounds of the country's 30-year war have not healed. The attempts to promote healing have lacked commitment. Thousands of acres of land in the North and East still continues to be under military control. This is the land that was once lived on and cultivated by Tamil people. Today it is being used by the military, some of it being cultivated, some it used for recreation purposes including hotels, and some of it for security purposes. Thousands of families still await news of the whereabouts of their loved ones despite an Office on Missing Persons which has yet to give a ruling on even a single missing person although four years have elapsed since it was set up. There are also still a few hundred persons in detention for a large number of years, some exceeding a decade in prison without trial.'[39] The government's denial and non-commitment will worsen the relationship with the EU and other Western democracies.

### GSP BENEFITS

Nearly 60 per cent of Sri Lankan exports benefit from preferential terms of trade of the EU's GSP+ and US's GSP schemes. The EU is Sri Lanka's largest export market with 30 per cent of the total, while the US is the largest single export market with 27 per cent of the total merchandize exports. Sri Lanka's exports, including apparel, fisheries, ceramic and rubber that use the GSP concession, will be directly impacted. Sri Lanka has duty-free access to 7,200 products with the EU GSP+ concession. It is estimated that the withdrawal of this concession would wipe out a significant chunk of foreign exchange earned through exports. 'We are concerned with the EU Parliament's resolution,' says Sri Lanka's Export Development Board chairman.[40]

The present state of the economy under the pandemic has been a challenge to Sri Lankan exports 'especially to the apparel industry', admitted even by President Gotabaya in his recent address, and GSP+ withdrawal will add significant pressure on the Sri Lankan economy. The government's senior ministers have ignored the impending GSP+ withdrawal warning saying that they are ready to move forward without the concessions. However, K.D. Vimanga, a policy analyst at Advocata, an economics think tank, explains that it is vital to retain the concession at present when the country is facing a severe economic crisis, especially with serious issues in debt repayments, lack of foreign exchange reserves and a balance of payment crisis. 'Understand the merits of it', the analyst warns the government.[41]

## DEMOCRATIC STABILITY

President Gotabaya's regime has developed a method of weaponizing unfavourable events in their favour by catering to the majoritarian Sinhalese-Buddhist voter base. The handling of the UNHRC resolution in Geneva in March and the withdrawal of the EU GSP+, saying we can do without them, or releasing the former member of Parliament convicted for murder in the name of justice, are all moves in the same direction. The political strategy of this administration is to cater to the majoritarian voter base by making claims of protecting the nation's sovereignty from foreign interference. Even this narrow-minded political strategy fails when certain decisions, such as ignoring rule of law to release a convicted murderer, are taken. The very act of conviction by one regime after following the constitutional process and arbitrary pardon by the next regime is a sign of weakness of the system, and reflects the moral standards of those in power. According to a senior political scientist in Sri Lanka, 'In the coming months, Sri Lanka's judicial sector will undergo significant reforms along with continuous interference despite a promise to amend the Constitution.'

Yale Professor Juan Linz, in his book *The Breakdown of Democratic Regimes*, talks of 'how regimes paint a rather bleak picture of their ability to survive'.[42] The Sri Lankan case provides ample examples of the political behaviour of the regime to survive. The public's loss of trust in its democratic institutions is a visible characteristic that can have a long-term impact on the country's stability. An essential ingredient, according to Linz, is 'the belief in the legitimacy of democratic institutions as a factor increasing the likelihood of stability in a democracy'. The coming anarchy in the entire nation is due to the breakdown of its democracy. This, for sure, will worsen economic conditions.

## THREE
## September 2021

### Rajapaksa's Dysfunctional Regime in Sri Lanka and Its Impact on South Asia[43]

Basic human rights and liberal democracy are ignored by the autocratic leadership in Sri Lanka. Such an environment discourages the public from exercising their democratic rights on a daily basis. The predominantly politically active Sinhalese Buddhists, who campaigned for and elected a Rajapaksa regime and supported autocratic sentiments earlier, now seem to be questioning the regime's behaviour. During the presidential election in 2019, which came in the immediate aftermath of the Easter Sunday attacks, national security was the top concern. However, at present, individual security is threatened more than ever before, owing to an economic crisis magnified by the pandemic. To survive in Sri Lanka's autocratic family rule requires remaining in greater fealty to the ultra-nationalistic ethos projected in no uncertain terms by the Gotabaya Rajapaksa regime.[44]

In this repressive environment, there will be no freedom of choice due to a deep fear that has crept into every household in the country. Shortage of essential food items at the height of the pandemic, with the highest number of deaths recorded on the island taking place at the same time, has led to the public battling a double crisis. President Gotabaya Rajapaksa declared emergency regulations[45] and appointed Major General M.D.S.P. Niwunhella (retired) to take over as Sri Lanka's Commissioner General of Essential Services amidst an economic emergency.[46] This is one more military appointment on the back of the earlier ones, and pushes the quasi-democracy towards a complete autocracy, expanding the regime's militarization programme. This was also a concern raised by the UNHRC.[47]

With the present dysfunctionality, hopefully Sri Lanka will not see another youth insurrection from its majoritarian Sinhalese Buddhists as was seen in the past in 1971 and 1989, triggered by economic failure and political injustice, when thousands of innocent lives were lost. The economic emergency allows authorities to control and seize stocks of staple foods; naturally, the current food shortage reminds the Sri Lankan public of the 1970s regime of Prime Minister Sirimavo Bandaranaike, which ended in 1977.

There is a steep devaluation of currency due to the foreign exchange crisis. The Sri Lankan rupee crossed a historical high at Rs231 to the US dollar, while 127 billion rupees were injected into the economy.[48] The Sri Lankan rupee has fallen 7.5 per cent against the US dollar this year.[49] The month-on-month inflation in the country rose to 6 per cent in August 2021, with government borrowings increasing significantly, especially due to continued borrowings from China. Around 80 per cent of the government's revenue goes to debt servicing. The government has reached out to many nations, including Bangladesh, which will provide US$200 million currency swap to assist the fast-depleting foreign exchange reserves of the country.[50]

Assessing the economic crisis, former deputy governor of the Central Bank, W.A. Wijewardena, says the economic situation has 'graduated from a crisis to a total catastrophe now',[51] a free-fall of the economy. The Central Bank acts as an advisory institution under such circumstances. A new governor of the Central Bank was appointed—former state minister Ajith Nivard Cabraal,[52] a close confidant of Prime Minister Mahinda Rajapaksa, to help control the situation.

## DYSFUNCTIONALITY AND THE CHINA TILT

A few weeks before the economic emergency, President Gotabaya Rajapaksa made a surprising Cabinet reshuffle of a few key ministries, including health and foreign affairs.[53] The health ministry was in a disastrous state with multiple interventions aimed at health professionals by the regime. Health Minister Pavithra Wanniarachchi was shifted out, to bring in Keheliya Rambukwella, a vociferous defender of the regime. The foreign affairs ministry was the other crucial ministry that was affected. During the time of the former foreign minister Dinesh Gunawardena, Sri Lankan foreign policy lost its balance and neutral posture, tilting toward China. There is no positive sign from the experienced new foreign minister, G.L. Peiris, that this situation will change and there will be a recalibration of the China bandwagoning policy.

The China tilt policy was reiterated at the recent 48th UNHRC session, where Sri Lanka defended China's human rights record, commenting, 'External forces should not seek to interfere in Xinjiang and Hong Kong, which are integral parts of the People's Republic of China (PRC).'[54] A few weeks earlier, the already strong bilateral economic cooperation was cemented at the diplomatic meeting between a high-profile delegation of the Parliament of the PRC and Sri Lanka, which took place in August 2021. The meeting was led by Basil Rajapaksa, the new Rajapaksa brother who joined the government, taking over as the finance minister. This meeting also included many other political heavyweights from the government, such as the new foreign affairs minister.

The Chairman of the National People's Congress (NPC) Standing Committee, Li Zhanshu, said, 'Chinese government will do its utmost to help overcome the economic challenge as well as the Covid challenge in Sri Lanka.'[55] Foreign Minister G.L. Peiris requested Chinese assistance in the international arena, saying, 'China has always stood by Sri Lanka as a close friend in the international arena' and that he 'looks forward to the continued support in the future as well'.[56] The foreign minister's request to protect the regime at the international forum will be taken up as a priority by the Chinese leadership.

The defence of Chinese human rights violations in a global forum is another ancillary ingredient, apart from China's 'debt trap' and 'vaccine dependence', towards realizing the Chinese 'strategic trap'. While the Chinese embassy expressed appreciation by saying, 'Well done! Sri Lanka the fastest vaccination speed in the world for the past week',[57] China is also working on the economic recovery, enlarging the Chinese debt and 'strategic trap' in Sri Lanka. Deborah Brautigam,[58] a professor at the School of Advanced International Studies at Johns Hopkins University, and Meg Rithmire,[59] an associate professor at Harvard Business School assess, 'After the construction of the port in Hambantota, for example, Chinese firms and banks learned that strongmen fall and that they'd better have strategies for dealing with political risk.'[60] Perhaps, China's risk assessment and learning have improved over time. But there is a 'strategic trap' orchestrated by China in Sri Lanka.

## DYSFUNCTIONAL STATES AND THE EXTREMIST THREAT

The dysfunctionality and the resulting frustrations caused by the country's mismanagement has created a fertile ground for multiple security threats to mushroom, including extremist terror. This threat comes from beyond our borders. A month after the attack in Christchurch, New Zealand, Sri Lanka's largest extremist terror attack took place. At that time, Sri Lanka's state minister of defence was quick to call the Easter Sunday attack a retaliation for the Christchurch attack.[61] Investigations into the attack are unearthing multiple new evidence. Cardinal Malcolm Ranjith revealed at a recent press conference, 'Sri Lankan military intelligence officer, through a local agent and an unspecified person in Indonesia, had forced the terrorist group ISIS to claim responsibility for the Easter Sunday attacks.'[62] This is a serious allegation, opening new dimensions about the attacks.

Ahamed Aathill Mohamed Samsudeen,[63] the Sri Lankan who committed the heinous act of stabbing innocent civilians in New Zealand in September 2021, perhaps had an indirect connection with terror cells in his hometown, Kattankudy, located in the Eastern Province of Sri Lanka, where Mohammed Zahran, the mastermind of the Easter Sunday attack, preached an increasingly extremist version of Islam. In order to subvert such a movement from taking root, the current regime in Sri Lanka set the draconian Prevention of Terrorism Act, which allows arrests and surveillance of suspects. The regime enforced many bans, including a ban on madrassas, ban on burqa and forced cremations for a limited time. The consequences of these actions will predictably be the spread of Islamophobia and the grooming of more extremists rather than the reverse.

With the US exit from Afghanistan and the re-Talibanization of the country, the regional security balance is under threat. This creates a stage for the return of extremism and terrorism. The void created by the absence of US counterterror operations will not be filled by China or Russia. For Beijing, with its close Taliban–Pakistan relations, it will be a test of Chinese leadership and their ability to maintain a balance. India faces serious security threats from all directions—on its western borders from Pakistan, on northern borders from China, on eastern borders from Bangladesh and in the south from Sri Lanka and Maldives. According to former Indian national security advisor Shivshankar Menon, 'Afghanistan is not a threat to us. It has to come through Pakistan.'[64]

The dysfunctional nature of many South Asian states presents a gap in robust counterterrorism mechanisms with a multi-jurisdictional approach. There is an absence of security architecture. This gap could make way for South Asia to become a hub of extremist and terrorist threats.

In the case of Sri Lanka, the absence of social security for minorities is the root cause that should be addressed. If counterterrorism mechanisms are used for arbitrary detention, as explained by UN Human Rights High Commissioner Michelle Bachelet in her recent update on Sri Lanka and how strict surveillance continues to be used,[65] it will invite dangerous security threats to the society and the region. In the absence of a holistic mechanism, Sri Lankan prisons will become breeding grounds for extremists and terrorists.

The knee-jerk decisions—the important Cabinet reshuffle, appointment of a new governor of the Central Bank,[66] increasing military appointments and arbitrary detentions—are definitely not moves in the right direction. The repressive policies of Rajapaksa overshadow everything else, including the new appointments for course correction. The crass act of the regime's own minister of prisons was clear evidence of a lack of moral values and dysfunctionality within the government.[67] While liberal democracy is suppressed by the Rajapaksa regime, the present dysfunctionality in Sri Lanka's political–economic environment and its pro-Chinese foreign policy will have a severe impact on the security of the entire South Asian region.

## FOUR
## December 2021

### Sri Lanka in Crisis: Repression, Protests and Geopolitical Tensions[68]

US President Joe Biden and his Chinese counterpart Xi Jinping met virtually in November 2021.[69] The tensions over Taiwan, bilateral trade and Indo-Pacific security have escalated over time. The meeting came on the backdrop of warnings by senior-level security experts against China's military build-up and its hypersonic missile capability. The virtual meeting failed to produce major breakthroughs, according to Amy Mackinnon,[70] but it did lower the temperature as geopolitical tensions rose. China is already assiduously securing its national interests, which may be detrimental to many South Asian nations, and Sri Lanka is a clear case of being in Chinese clutches due to its militaristic regime and the escalating economic crisis.

Sri Lanka, the island-nation close to the Indian sub-continent, is a good example to understand the consequences of China's large-scale infrastructure projects, vaccine diplomacy and Chinese loans. Being ruled by a regime with a military grip, headed by a former military officer Gotabaya Rajapaksa, Beijing found the present-day Sri Lanka more conducive to its objectives than earlier, when the first Rajapaksa regime in 2005–2015 was in power.

China has built two critical infrastructure facilities facing the Indian Ocean—the Hambantota port and the Colombo Port City. It has secured a long-term foothold through lease agreements signed by Sri Lanka without adequate evaluation, where these facilities could transform into military outposts. China cleverly claims that it has no negative intentions to make them military facilities by floating the idea that third countries could invest in the Chinese infrastructure. However, where are the third countries? This is more of a strategy to hide the military plans from the public.

A new Pentagon report highlights China's 'intention to establish a more robust overseas logistics and basing infrastructure to allow the People's Liberation Army (PLA) to project and sustain military power at greater distances'.[71] Beyond its base in Djibouti, China is pursuing additional military facilities to support naval, air, ground, cyber and space power projection. China has likely considered a number of countries, including Sri Lanka, as locations for PLA facilities.

With large financial borrowings from China, Sri Lanka has become heavily dependent on that country. This problem is further exacerbated by the pressure that China exerts on domestic politics. The pressure exerted on the regime is visible from the recent incident about the Chinese fertilizer shipment rejected by Sri Lankan authorities. The Chinese embassy tweeted about blacklisting of Sri Lanka's People's Bank, explaining the events leading to the aggressive decision. In a tweet, the mission said, 'Seawin [Chinese company] won the open bid, signed contracts, passed tests of China and Int'l agency designated by Ceylon Fertilizer, shipped before due. NPQ SL disagreed halfway, called toxic/harmful. Ship refused. Third-party test refused. L/C payment obligation refused. PBS blacklisted.'

The blacklisting was a clear warning of the extent of Chinese pressure on Sri Lanka. Ajantha De Silva, director-general of Sri Lankan Department of Agriculture, said, 'Our tests on the samples showed that the [Chinese] fertilizer was not sterile. We have identified bacteria which are harmful to plants like carrots and potatoes.'[72] The clear rejection was a black mark for the Chinese fertilizer company Qingdao Seawin, which defended itself by saying, 'The unscientific detection methods and conclusions of National Plant Quarantine Service (NPQ) in Sri Lanka obviously do not comply with international animal and plant quarantine convention,' and that they had falsely accused the Chinese company to slander the image of the Chinese enterprises and the Chinese government.

When the Sri Lankan authorities did not change their position, the Chinese said they would prefer a third party to retest the sample. The authorities rejected this attempt to retest. The question is, why is the Chinese ship *Hippo Spirit* still in Sri Lankan waters? After the Sri Lankan authorities rejected these shipments a month earlier, the ship was still seen close to the Sri Lankan waters in November. China is pressuring the Sri Lankan government to accept an alternative process (third-party test) to save the reputation of their global company Qingdao Seawin. The blacklisting of the bank was to exert pressure on the Sri Lankan regime. Another reason for the ship to remain in Sri Lankan waters was alleged by Nalinda Jayatissa, member of the JVP political party—due to a substantial underhand deal between the Prime Minister's office and the local agents of the Chinese company.[73]

The fertilizer incident was an eye-opener for the regime to recalibrate its posture and balance the China tilt and dependence. New Delhi stepped in to support Sri Lanka amidst the tussle between

Colombo and Beijing. Two Indian IAF C-17 Globemaster aircraft arrived in Colombo with 100,000 kg of nano nitrogen. India will be able to bounce back and reduce the Chinese footprint on the island now, and the Sri Lankan government can adjust its China bandwagoning foreign policy posture.

China presented its aggressive posture over the fertilizer incident when Sri Lanka is facing a severe economic crisis. The same aggressiveness of China is visible in India's immediate periphery, according to Rajeswari Rajagopalan.[74] China is building villages in Arunachal Pradesh which they are populating with, perhaps, military–civilian population. In Ladakh, there are at least nine patrol points in the Fingers-area and south of Demchok that India is no longer able to access. These are severe concerns for the security of India. Adding to this is China's pressure and expansion in Sri Lanka. Clearly, 'India's behaviour has been defensive in both diplomatic and military spheres, while China has adopted an extremely aggressive tone and engaged in similar military behaviour,' assess Rajagopalan.[75] This Indian posture could change if the present Chinese aggressiveness continues to escalate in India's periphery.

## PROTEST OVER ECONOMIC DYSFUNCTION IN SRI LANKA

Addressing the simultaneous insurmountable external foreign pressure and the domestic public frustration over the heightened economic crisis will be a formidable challenge for the Sri Lankan regime. The new budget presented by Finance Minister Basil Rajapaksa did not suggest any solution to the foreign exchange crisis the country is facing nor the food crisis stemming from the recent ban on chemical fertilizers. Thousands of people gathered at a rally in Colombo to demonstrate their frustration and anger over the economic hardships and the repressive regime of Gotabaya Rajapaksa.[76]

The economic crisis triggered multiple shocks, including a shortage of essential items of daily use and the rising cost of living, causing severe agitation in the public's minds. Despite numerous attempts by the government, including court orders, to prevent the protest march, the main opposition party SJB held the rally in Colombo. The regime has abused the pandemic restrictions to its benefit, to suppress the democratic rights of the people and to expand its autocratic rule. The massive protests depict the anger of the public, who risked their health to protect the democratic essence of the country.

The heavily militarized regime in Sri Lanka will face severe headwinds in the coming months due to the escalating economic crisis and the issues of human rights abuse. The majoritarian polity the Sinhalese-Buddhists shows signs of a clear shift, and a detachment from the Rajapaksa regime. The arbitrary detention of hundreds of people using the PTA[77] and handing over the crucial 'One Country One Law' task force to an ultra-nationalist Buddhist monk[78] was a disappointment for the minority community. The overall policy prescription of the regime shows all the signs of anarchy and a crisis worsening day by the day.

## FIVE
## December 2021

### Sri Lanka in 2021: Trouble Ahead for One of Asia's Oldest Democracies[79]

At the Biden administration's 'Summit for Democracy' this December, one of the oldest democracies in Asia, Sri Lanka, was kept off the invitation list.[80] The failure to receive an invitation reflects the ongoing backsliding in functional democracy under the semi-autocratic rule of one family.[81] Former military officer Gotabaya Rajapaksa and his brother Mahinda Rajapaksa hold the country's two highest offices of the president and prime minister, respectively. Along with serving other major roles in the administration themselves—Gotabaya is also the defence minister—several family members have been appointed to crucial Cabinet positions.

A majoritarian regime was formed in 2020 with a quick constitutional amendment to remove critical checks on executive power and bring more legislative controls under the president.[82] The brothers have also indicated a clear preference for the military by appointing twenty-eight current or former military and intelligence officials in the administration.[83]

The centralization of power under the Rajapaksa family underscores the regression of democracy in the country, which continued throughout 2021. This in part has resulted in the Rajapaksa tilt towards China, a move that will shape not only domestic politics but also Sri Lanka's economic future. As 2022 begins, the country finds itself facing a troubling set of challenges including an economic crisis and an increasing majoritarian rule.

## DOMESTIC POLITICS: DEEPENING DIVISIONS AND AN AUTHORITARIAN SLIDE

Over the past four decades, Sri Lanka has been engulfed by multiple internal and external security shocks. The two youth insurrections in 1981 and 1989, the protracted civil war ending in 2009 and the extremist terror attack in 2019,[84] all underscore the security threats driven by political–economic dysfunctionality. In South Asia, the Taliban's return to power after the US exit and the rise of extremist sentiments could spill over to vulnerable nations like Sri Lanka. The lynching and burning of a Sri Lankan worker in Pakistan may be an individual incident, but it has underscored the growing concerns about extremism.[85] In the absence of a regional security architecture and limited resources to curb extremist terror, Sri Lanka and other South Asian nations may face a daunting challenge in the coming years.

Amidst concerns of extremism and internal instability, the Sri Lankan government's hardline posture offers little hope of addressing minority concerns or pursuing a genuine reconciliation process promised since the end of the civil war. Minority communities, including Sri Lanka's Muslim and Tamil populations, have been troubled by several events that took place over the past year. In 2021, the government expanded the powers of the Prevention of Terrorism Act,[86] which has been used repeatedly to justify arbitrary arrests. The arbitrary detentions are likely to trigger extremist sentiments and Sri Lankan prisons could become breeding grounds for extremism. Three years after the brutal Easter Sunday attack, the government's ultra-nationalist posture with the military at the forefront has triggered more insecurity rather than curtailing it.

For Sri Lanka, 2021 began with a report by the UNHCR giving a severe warning on the alarming risks of human rights violations,[87] a report that the government rejected.[88] However, the concerns raised in the report came to the forefront later in the year with the appointment of the ultra-nationalist Buddhist monk Galagodaaththe Gnanasara Thero to lead the 'One Country One Law' Presidential Task Force.[89] Gnanasara had been imprisoned for contempt of court but was pardoned by President Rajapaksa shortly after the Easter Sunday terrorist attacks.

While touted as legal reforms to unite Sri Lanka, 'One Country One Law' has caused concerns among minorities given their lower representation in the task force and Gnanasara's leadership. Representing the Bodu Bala Sena (BBS), an ultra-nationalist Buddhist political movement,[90] Gnanasara, has been accused of stirring up anti-Muslim violence and the BBS has been seen as one of the reasons why Mahinda Rajapaksa lost the Muslim votes in 2015. According to the parliamentarian Shanakiyan Rasamanickam, 'The appointment of a criminal to lead this committee is a joke in itself.'[91]

Gnanasara has been periodically used as a proxy by several politicians, including Gotabaya Rajapaksa, to project and secure the ultra-nationalist sentiments for the regime. His appointment is a clear indication that the president wishes to ignore the international and domestic warnings on minority concerns in the country. The Buddhist priest's involvement in drafting recommendations for the nation's proposed legal body will drag the government further towards an ultra-nationalist Buddhist-centric autocratic path. As noted by Jehan Perera, this type of non-consultative approach presents a clear danger for the democratic institutions and processes.[92]

This approach has also been carried over to the process of drafting the new Constitution, which the prime minister promised will be ready for parliamentary approval in 2022.[93] Civil society has been markedly absent from the constitution-making process. Minority communities are particularly concerned about the impact the changes to the Constitution may have on their security. The visit of the Tamil National Alliance (TNA) delegation to the United States seeking external assistance is the only hope to address Tamil grievances due to the absence of a genuine consultative process.[94]

Along with shrinking space for oversight and independent inputs in government decision-making, the Rajapaksa administration has also undermined judicial independence on multiple occasions. In June 2021, a murder convict and former politician Duminda Silva, was released through a presidential pardon,[95] and subsequently appointed as the Chairman of a government institute.[96] In October 2021, the Attorney General declined to proceed in the case of a former Navy commander charged with the abduction and killing of eleven civilians. An year earlier, Sunil Ratnayake, charged and convicted of massacring Tamil civilians during the civil war, was also granted a presidential pardon.[97] Such instances not only 'rob victims of accountability and undermine the justice system' but also show the continued executive excesses across the government.[98]

## RAJAPAKSA FOREIGN POLICY AND THE CHINA TILT

With human rights, security assurance, vaccine diplomacy and extended assistance for the ailing economy, China made considerable inroads in Sri Lanka in 2021. Projects, including the terminal project in Colombo[99] and several large-scale loan packages[100] have made China the most important bilateral player for Sri Lanka.

Gotabaya Rajapaksa's foreign policy has so far been similar to the foreign policy of the Mahinda Rajapaksa administration. While the national policy framework of the present government espoused a policy drawing on principles of non-alignment,[101] it has in practice taken a 'China bandwagon' approach to geopolitics. Mahinda Rajapaksa's administration was a key supporter of China's BRI in Asia, and Gotabaya Rajapaksa has indicated similar support by accelerating the approval process for the Colombo Port City strategic project with China,[102] while using trade unions to help block a Japanese and Indian terminal project.[103] Sri Lanka has also come to China's defence in multilateral platforms, defending China on human rights violations in Xinjiang,[104] while China has pushed back against UNHRC efforts to challenge the Rajapaksa regime.

At the beginning of 2021, China acquired a SEZ with extra-jurisdictional rights in the Colombo Port City in less than thirty days despite Supreme Court concerns[105] and public displeasure. The pandemic environment was conducive to smoothly taking over the port without public protest and discourse. In November, China Harbour Engineering Company obtained another infrastructure contract closer to the acquired Port City of Colombo—the development of the ECT.[106]

China's inroads in Sri Lanka have been a growing concern for New Delhi. Towards the last quarter of 2021, the India–Sri Lanka relationship showed positive signs. For instance, after Sri Lanka banned contaminated fertilizer from China, India stepped in to provide the much-needed fertilizer.[107] Revisiting the trilateral military engagement at the Colombo Security Conclave[108] are strategies to stabilize India–Sri Lanka relations. However, beyond key port projects, such as Hambantota now operated under a ninety-nine-year lease by China, other critical infrastructure projects including telecommunication networks, surveillance for police and law and order enforcement are areas of concern for India.

China is Sri Lanka's largest trading partner and the country holds a significant volume of Chinese loans. The nation is clearly caught in a 'debt trap', with China taking control of strategic assets through 'debt to equity swaps' that no leader could revisit though promised during election campaigns.[109]

China also provided Sri Lanka with considerable amount of vaccine assistance as compared to other nations. Around 10 million Sri Lankans had received both doses of the Sinopharm vaccine by October 2021.[110] The vaccine diplomacy was also paired with more aggressive 'Wolf Warrior' diplomatic approach, with the Chinese embassy in Sri Lanka tweeting about the US blaming China for Covid-19, while ignoring its own failures and other such topics.[111] The continuous media propaganda has influenced the public and the local think tanks. One such think tank was engaged in printing and translating Chinese health guidelines.[112] They also signed MoUs with a CCP-affiliated think tank.[113] As aptly captured in the Carnegie South Asia report,[114] China has built critical ties with journalists, think tanks and political parties, including the SLPP—the political party of Rajapaksa.[115]

### ECONOMIC CRISIS

Sri Lanka faces a severe economic downturn that has 'graduated from a crisis to a total catastrophe'.[116] The pandemic, combined with inward-looking economic policies, has exacerbated the economic crisis. The country is also facing food shortage triggered in part by Sri Lanka's ongoing foreign exchange crisis and import restrictions.[117] Indicating the administration's preference for using the military, the president has appointed a senior military official as Commissioner General of Essential Services to control the distribution of essential consumer goods.[118]

The rising debt and the absence of a clear policy to handle it are clear signs of further economic downslide. The policy priorities in the 2021 Budget have made little attempt to address the deficit and debt sustainability—'missing the opportunity' for innovation or improving Sri Lanka's credit rating.[119] The government has also refused an IMF package[120] and limited external assistance.[121] With the rising cost of living and other public concerns over issues such as gas cylinder explosions,[122] protests and frustrations have increased. Many of Sri Lanka's youth are also looking to leave the country in search of opportunities elsewhere,[123] indicating a potential brain-drain challenge in the future.

In 2021, Sri Lanka's democracy continued its backward slide due to militarization, human rights abuses, arbitrary detentions and suppression of the minorities, which triggered multiple social, political, economic and foreign policy concerns. The ultra-nationalist, illiberal posture by the Rajapaksa sibling regime has spread all over into all sectors of the government. Thus far, the Gotabaya Rajapaksa administration has provided a lucrative environment for authoritarian external powers such as China to expand their influence. Under an increasingly anti-democratic government, Sri Lanka has faced multiple economic and domestic challenges in 2021—and these problems appear unlikely to go away unless the administration shifts its approach to key policies. With the absence of a genuine reconciliation process and ignoring human rights concerns, the regime may face more external pressure from the international community. Grievances from Sri Lanka's ethnic and religious minority populations could trigger domestic unrest, with social, political, economic and external shocks unlikely to disappear in the coming months.

# SIX
# February 2022

## Sri Lankan Economy Spiralling Out of Control: Requests IMF Assistance[124]

Sri Lanka's economic meltdown is one of the worst since its independence in 1948, pushing many families into poverty. The situation is rapidly spiralling out of control due to several ill-prescribed economic policies. The unstable economic crisis is clearly on the verge of igniting a dangerous political–economic crisis that can bring instability to the island-nation and the entire Indian subcontinent.

As a result of this crisis, which has been in the making for years, the government encouraged people to travel to work by bicycle,[125] perhaps not the best solution when the country is desperately trying to find answers to basic economic needs. The launch of Colombo Dunes in the Chinese Port city,[126] explains disconnect of policies and the priorities with the ordinary, general public.

The government's current policy on debt management is a concern for many citizens. Parliamentarian M.A. Sumanthiran questions, '[The] government's approach to resolving the crisis raises some serious questions. Its focus, almost solely on meeting foreign debt obligations, is draining the country of dollars needed for importing essentials for our people.'[127] The basic economic necessities of the individuals are far different from what the policy prescription addresses. The soaring prices of essential items have crippled many households. Several essential items are beyond the means of many. With the spread of Covid, many households are confronted with a two-front battle in the form of health and a dysfunctional economy.

Consumer prices in Sri Lanka shot up a record 14 per cent in December 2021, surpassing the previous high of 11.1 just a month earlier. According to the World Bank, 500,000 people in Sri Lanka have fallen below the poverty line since the Covid-19 pandemic struck.[128] Food inflation has hit a record 21.5 per cent. Supermarket shelves are almost bare, with minimum goods, and there is rationing of milk powder and other essentials. Restaurants can't serve meals. Apart from food scarcity, there are power cuts, further adding to the burden on the public. The inflation rate surged past Pakistan's to make it the highest in Asia, stoked by failed harvests and import restrictions to conserve dwindling foreign exchange reserves.[129]

The foreign exchange reserves fell from US$7.5 billion to US$$3.1 billion, enough to finance just a few months of imports. Presently, with US$1.6 billion foreign exchange reserves for imports and US$7.3 billion required for debt repayment within the next year, many are predicting that the country may slide down even further in the months ahead. Moody's downgraded Sri Lanka's credit rating to Caa2 from Caa1, and it will be difficult to attract investments in the future. Nishan de Mel, a Colombo based economist, assesses, 'It may take up to 5 years for Sri Lanka to get its rating back up.'[130]

India came forward to assist Sri Lanka by pledging US$400 million under the SAARC currency swap arrangement. It deferred a settlement of US$515.2 million to the Asian Clearing Union (ACU) by two months. Further, it extended a credit facility of US$1 billion to import essential items[131] and US$500 million for importing fuel from India, which will help the economy immensely to stabilize. The recent successful discussions between Finance Minister Basil Rajapaksa and Indian External Affairs Minister Jaishankar gave the cash-strapped economy some breathing space. However, Colombo's request to China for debt restructuring during the Chinese Foreign Minister Wang Yi's visit remains pending. Dushni Weerakoon, from the Institute of Policy Studies, said, 'It was advisable to go to the IMF, but a debt restructuring perhaps had cost.'[132]

Finance Minister Basil Rajapaksa's aspiration to approach IMF for assistance is a more realistic approach. But this is not easy given the ultra-nationalist forces in the government coalition. Another key barrier to an IMF programme is the Governor of the Central Bank, Ajith Nivard Cabraal, who seems to vehemently oppose the programme of reforms, including debt restructuring, for no logical reason. Former prime minister Ranil Wickremesinghe, pragmatic in his economic view, says, 'To solve the ongoing economic crisis the Finance Minister's approach to IMF must not be obstructed.'[133] Professor Ricardo Hausmann from Harvard Kennedy School, looking at the present management of Sri Lanka's macro economy, said it reminded him of Latin America in the 1980s and the direction of the Venezuelan economy in recent years. Sri Lanka had adopted ad hoc policies like capital controls and import restrictions, creating black-market premiums. Sri Lanka had not formulated a viable fiscal plan or a debt restructuring plan. Inflation was accelerating, and so were black market premiums. Under such circumstances of import restrictions and foreign exchange controls, the economic conditions would be unfavourable to attract new investments.[134]

The government remained undecided on an IMF loan at many Cabinet meetings during the last few months, ignoring multiple warnings from economic experts. As a prudent measure, Finance Minister Basil Rajapaksa has invited the IMF. He said, 'We have written to them and sought specialist advice from them,'[135] admitting that the only method of coming out of the crisis was to seek advice.

The finance minister perhaps senses a worse situation on the horizon. The concern is about the escalation of the economic crisis leading to a social uprising. In the past, Sri Lanka has encountered two youth insurrections launched by JVP in 1988 and 1971 when thousands of youth sacrificed their lives while protesting against the poor economic and political practices. George Town Economics Professor Santha Devaraja says, 'Most troubling is that the harsh economic conditions have led to violence in the streets.'[136] Though the context and socio-political drivers are not the same as in the 1980s, the present circumstances could trigger a security problem where the government tries to expand its military footprints and further reduces the democratic space during the economic crisis.

The government must follow more prudent and practical measures to manage the economic crisis and stabilize the economic environment before it escalates to a social crisis and, perhaps, an uprising. A more structured approach to stabilize the situation is a priority, and an IMF programme is perhaps the most viable option available.

## SEVEN
## April 2022

### People's Uprising in Sri Lanka: Sudden Rupture of the Rajapaksa Regime[137]

From its inception, Sri Lanka's leadership under President Gotabaya Rajapaksa was a perfect fit for Moises Naim's definition of a

'3P Autocrat'. These are 'political leaders who reach power through a democratic election and then set out to dismantle the checks on executive power through populism, polarisation and post-truth'.[138] Removing checks and balances through constitutional amendments and using populism and ultra-nationalist sentiments to polarize the society are forces used, further exacerbated by post-truth, which eventually deteriorates the nation's political systems.

The people's protests outside the president's house had a ripple effect on the entire nation.[139] The situation was further aggravated when the regime labelled the protesters as extremists and made multiple arrests. The false national security pretext backfired, with hundreds of lawyers appearing on behalf of the detained protesters.[140] Many, including students, judiciary members, farmers and their families, were voicing the same slogan, 'No more Rajapaksas'.

After the initial protest, the social media posts spewed hate towards the regime, seeing their actions as an attempt to further suppress democratic rights. To protect themselves from government action, the public turned to virtual private networks to access social media, multiplying domestic outreach and receiving global support. Within days, all the Cabinet ministers handed in their resignations—nobody wanted to be identified with the mismanaged, dysfunctional, political–economic systems. Senior ministers feared the retaliations by the Rajapaksa family, with the president's brother as the prime minister, another sibling as the finance minister and several family members holding key positions. This time, the people's power was able to dislodge the family reign. Some of the family members and their financiers are already fleeing the country.[141]

In an attempt to instil stability, Gotabaya appointed four new Cabinet members. This backfired, with the protestors calling his attempt 'a game of musical chairs' and continued demands for a fresh start with new faces and a new leadership. The newly appointed finance minister submitted his resignation within a day of being appointed. An immediate response to the people's demands would be for Gotabaya to step down rather than decide who to assign the handling of the past mismanagement. Another practical option is to dissolve the parliament and call for an election. If the protestors' demands are not met, the situation could spiral out of control and potentially lead to anarchy. South Asia is a place where installations of military regimes have taken place in such circumstances, and Sri Lanka is not far from this if the democratic wheels do not turn in the right direction.

The economic crisis has, however, overshadowed everything else. Currently, Sri Lanka faces its worst economic crisis, a by-product of the Covid-19 pandemic and the snowballing consequences of disastrous policy prescriptions from regime to regime. All this finally resulted in a liquidity problem, low foreign exchange reserves, the inability to repay accumulated debt and, eventually, insolvency. According to the *Economist*, 'A quieter disaster is breaking out in smaller international locations . . . Sri Lanka, Tunisia, Lebanon and Ghana are all candidates for mortgage programs from the International Monetary Fund.'[142] The pandemic has crippled most of these nations, especially due to the loss of tourism income and remittances from overseas citizens. Other factors in Sri Lanka, such as the accumulation of a massive debt and inward-looking economic policies like the chemical fertilizer ban, are factors directly contributing to the crisis.[143]

Weeks before the crisis, Sri Lanka secured multiple loans worth US$2.5 billion from China while also requesting assistance from the IMF. The Chinese loans will increase the debt payments and dependence on China, putting Sri Lanka's balanced foreign policy at risk. Chinese ambassador to Sri Lanka, Qi Zhenhong, mentioned that Beijing is considering a billion dollars' worth of buyers' credit to help the country.[144] Since 2020, China has provided the country US$2.8 billion, including US$1.5 billion in currency swap in 2021. Chinese companies have invested nearly US$1.05 billion in the Colombo Port City, and 43 companies have signed agreements to start businesses in the industrial zone in Hambantota.[145]

While the 'debt-trap diplomacy' is attempted to be debunked using specious arguments based on quantifying the volume of Chinese loans,[146] Gotabaya's regime has allowed the Chinese 'strategic-trap diplomacy' in Sri Lanka.[147] This trap manifests itself with the Chinese involvement in three areas. First, Sri Lanka's political sphere altered the democratic model by accepting autocratic sentiments. Second, China and Sri Lanka have mutually expressed support for each other in the face of allegations of human rights violations from the United Nations.[148] Third, Beijing has provided a lot of military and surveillance assistance to the island state.

Last year, I warned that the economic and political dysfunctionality would grow out of control.[149] The soaring prices of essential food items have become unbearable for many individuals.[150] Parliamentarian Harsha De Silva cautioned of a possible State Bank default and that the dollar could not be sold above LKR200.[151] His warning became a reality as the dollar rate has reached close to LKR300. The chain effect will be unmanageable for the domestic banking sector. Unfortunately, little has been done to address the problem.

Several people have died while waiting in long queues for fuel. Island-wide electricity blackouts have impacted manufacturing industries and the middle class, heightening the social narrative against the regime. The demonstrations and unhappiness have reached a level beyond government control. Against this backdrop, the Gotabaya regime has finally abandoned its inward-looking economic policies and appointed an advisory committee to address the debt crisis and seek IMF assistance.

Moving forward, what is required is an immediate course correction, engage the IMF, implement relevant economic measures and pursue restructuring efforts to stabilize the country. Political stability requires actions to end autocracy, restore democracy and build accountability measures to fight corruption. The rupture in Sri Lanka's political economy is also an opportunity to pursue objective choices and prudent economic policy that will strengthen the foundation of democracy.

# EIGHT
## 19 May 2022

### Economic and Political Crisis in Sri Lanka[152]

In autocracies, where rulers are above the law, the saying 'for my friends, everything; for my enemies, the law' is true.[153] In Sri Lanka, where the powerful Rajapaksa family expanded its autocratic control, the saying must be revised—'for my family, everything; for my enemies, the law'. Sri Lanka, Asia's oldest democracy, is struggling under the autocratic rule of the Rajapaksa family as the president continues to hold power despite mass protests. Mahinda Rajapaksa, however, was compelled to step down as prime minister on 9 May 2022.[154]

As the economic crisis worsened over the last few months, protests began to take place all over the island-nation. The Sri Lankan people began to realize that the power ultimately rests in their hands. However, the peaceful protestors were beaten up by the former prime minister's supporters,[155] and the protest site 'Gogotagama' was destroyed. Studying the ground reality,[156] Senior Political Scientist Jayadeva Uyangoda identified the protest site as a 'secular shrine of democracy',[157] further explaining that the 'political wind that blows through the "Gogotagama" of the Galle Face, Colombo, is truly refreshing. That is perhaps why so many citizens continue to visit the protest site to energize themselves and experience an inner transformation as citizens. This site must remain as a secular shrine of democracy's regeneration in Sri Lanka.'[158]

The thugs sent by the former prime minister attacked the 'secular shrine' and the retaliation was swift and brutal. The thugs were beaten back and a few were killed, including a member of Parliament. The Opposition leader was chased out of the protest site and hospital workers refused to treat the regime's supporters. For the second time in five weeks, President Gotabaya Rajapaksa declared a state of emergency in Sri Lanka.[159] The use of brute force by the police was witnessed as thousands of peaceful protestors were baton-charged and tear-gassed. The government's intention behind declaring a state of emergency remains questionable. Although it was attempted to be explained as a measure to ensure public safety and to be able to continue supplying essential goods and services smoothly,[160] it was clear that the underlying intention was to dismantle the island-wide protest using the security forces.

The regime has used national security and Prevention of Terrorism Act as a pretext to justify its suppression and the use of force. The US ambassador to Sri Lanka Julie Chung and many other diplomats raised concerns about the state of emergency declared to crush the peaceful protests.[161]

There is a danger in using excessive force and bringing the military to the forefront. Sri Lanka is a fragile society, rife with ethno-religious tensions from the past bloody insurrections and civil war. The short-sighted use of force could snowball into a full-fledged public agitation. People's anger could grow exponentially and further prolong the political–economic instability. In addition, given its military past, Sri Lanka could quickly move towards a military state, closer to the Myanmar model.

Sri Lanka is clearly facing an 'Arab Spring' moment to overthrow the autocratic rule, highlighting the rampant corruption and rising poverty. Protests at the president's house[162] and Galle Face had a contagion effect on the entire island. The government's actions of labelling the protesters as extremists and the police shooting in Rabukkana and attacking peaceful protestors at the protest site have only aggravated the situation.[163] Hundreds of lawyers are appearing on behalf of the protesters.[164] The regime's immediate family members[165] are fleeing the country as their properties are being burnt down.[166]

To quell this anarchy, the president should listen to the protestors and step down. The crisis could get out of control and many innocent lives will be lost, with the military at the forefront of attacking the protestors. Sri Lanka's ugly past could return if President Gotabaya does not step down and the Parliament does not immediately appoint a new leader of the nation's interim government to steer the nation to stability. Each hour is crucial, and Gotabaya should accept the reality.

On 11 May, the president addressed the nation and instead of resigning, outlined three actions to stabilize the crisis.[167] First, a new prime minister will be appointed from the Parliament. Second, the twentieth amendment will be amended, curtailing the executive powers and reverting to the previous amendment to empower the Parliament. Third, to accommodate the new regime, the executive presidency would be abolished.

The actions put forward by the president promise a power transition in which the new prime minister will require the support of the Parliament and the public, including the protestors. There will be a considerable burden on the new prime minister to function under the president for some time since the primary demand of the protestors is Gotabaya's resignation. Will President Gotabaya hand over national security and defence to the new prime minister? How will the new prime minister prosecute the various Rajapaksas for corruption and human rights abuse highlighted by the protestors, when the president is from the Rajapaksa family? How will the interim government win the trust of the public that the old government has lost? These are a few vital questions and challenges that the new prime minister, Ranil Wickremesinghe, will have to confront.[168]

Ranil Wickremesinghe's political party won only one seat, which is actually just the bonus seat offered to political parties for total votes received. His appointment as prime minister questions the fundamental democratic process and norms of institutional forbearance—the unwritten rule, that even if this is technically allowed by the Constitution, whether such a decision should be executed, undermining the norms of democracy.

## ECONOMIC CRISIS, THE IMF AND CHINA

The Rajapaksa government proved its inability to function even after appointing different Cabinets twice in the previous month, followed by Prime Minister Mahinda Rajapaksa's resignation. The president admitted his policy blunders and promised pragmatic reforms to satisfy the protestors.[169] But the protestors do not want to withdraw the critical demand, which is for the president to step down. With the worst economic crisis since its independence in 1948,[170] the nation has defaulted on its debt repayments, and its foreign-currency debt rating has fallen to 'selective default'. Finance Minister Ali Sabry alerted the Parliament that the usable foreign exchange reserves had dropped below US$50 million.[171] Food inflation has soared over 30 per cent in March. A significant fuel shortage means that power outages will continue for long hours and petrol pumps will run dry. The adverse effects of the economic crisis will be borne mostly by the low and middle income households.

The Sri Lankan government has approached the IMF for a rapid finance instrument and a bridge loan to stabilize the economic situation. Securing a loan from the IMF would require Sri Lanka to implement a debt restructuring programme. China's rejection of restructuring its debt is a concern—all the secret or opaque conditions of the loans will have to be revealed if IMF conditions are to be met.[172] Sri Lanka would lose a lot of time since its debt restructuring depends on support from the Paris Club—an IMF programme—and Chinese participation, and China may drag on the process. Confirming the Chinese reservation, the former Cabinet spokesman Nalaka Godahewa said the Government's 'only concern is the position of China'.[173]

Many nations have come forward to assist Sri Lanka. India has been assisting immensely in this economic crisis. Akhil Bery from Asia Society Policy Institute recommended a Quad humanitarian relief assistance to Sri Lanka.[174] It is an opportunity for India and the US to reduce China's influence on Sri Lanka and strengthen the 'partnership with New Delhi by supporting its central foreign policy objective of maintaining regional primacy and counteracting Chinese encirclement'.[175]

Sri Lanka's China bandwagoning foreign policy requires immediate recalibration. This is an opportunity for Sri Lanka to balance its foreign policy so that it is within the global rules-based order and to build more objective and prudent financial standards, moving away from the Chinese opaque, high-interest loans and unprofitable projects. Sri Lanka's commitment to the Indo-Pacific has been unclear so far due to its tilt towards China.[176] The recalibration will enable Sri Lanka to access funding from multiple channels, including Quad nations.

Sri Lanka would have to make improvements in democratic and human rights space if it hopes to re-enter the folds of the liberal world order and ask for global assistance to resolve its economic crisis. The country has an opportunity to re-embrace the democratic values lost due to autocratic manoeuvres in the past and re-democratize the nation's processes and institutions. For this, the country requires immediate stability with all of the Rajapaksas stepping down and allowing a new interim government supported by the protestors to operate until elections can take place in a few months to appoint new members to the Parliament for an overall system change.

## NINE
## 14 July 2022

### The Sri Lankan Crisis: The End of the Autocratic Regime[177]

The 9th of July was a momentous day in the history of Sri Lankan politics as protestors broke into President Gotabaya Rajapaksa's office and residence and demanded his resignation.

#### WHY THE RAJAPAKSA REGIME NEEDED TO END

Despite the worsening of the economic crisis over the past few months, Rajapaksa chose to retain his position as president by using the military to keep the protestors at bay instead of addressing the root causes of the crisis. There was a danger in this exercise of power and it clearly failed as protestors took over the president's residence and office and the prime minister's office. The president hoped for a quick solution by recruiting a liberal democrat, Prime Minister Wickremasinghe—who is the current president of Sri Lanka—after Gotabaya Rajapaksa took refuge in the Maldives.

The nation has come to a screeching halt as it faces fuel and food shortages. A two-week shutdown was announced for government offices and schools.[178] The economic crisis has triggered multiple social concerns and has led to an eruption of violence. A few weeks ago, soldiers fired shots into the air to control the situation at a fuel station in Sri Lanka as tensions flared up.[179] Six policemen were injured at another fuel station.[180] More than forty houses of parliamentarians were burnt by protestors last month.[181] Even though the protests were taking a turn for the worse, the newly appointed prime minister was more focused on rebuilding houses of the parliamentarians instead of addressing the food crisis and the deteriorating economic conditions. The Rajapaksa political strategist Basil Rajapaksa, former finance minister, resigned,[182] paving way for casino owner Dammika Perera to take his parliamentary seat, thus indicating that political favouritism continued despite the protests.

A strong warning was released by Wimal Weerawansa saying that if protestors' demands were not taken seriously, the next attack would target the country's affluent class.[183] 'They will attack everyone using luxury vehicles and those living in luxury homes. That is the inevitable future if the government keeps playing games with the crises,' he said.[184] This was a warning directed towards the possibility of a full-blown insurrection due to the dire humanitarian crisis. With the military in the forefront, multiple arrests of protestors[185] and the main opposition parties boycotting the Parliament,[186] the crisis in Sri Lanka is steadily getting out of control.

President Gotabaya has chosen the prime minister to be the housekeeper who cleans up the autocratic house and decorates it with democracy. Rajapaksa's authoritarian rule fits well with the five dimensions of authoritarian rule outlined by Steven Kotkin, a political science professor at Yale.[187] First, there is the use of a coercive mechanism with heavy militarization in more than fifteen sectors of the nation[188] and the stealthy operation of force and brutality using the Prevention of Terrorism Act—the anti-terror act—in a large number of arrests. Second, revenue streams to sustain the social contract between the government and the public were affected due to policies such as the sudden switch to organic farming. Though the regime understood that it had broken the social contract, it did not admit the policy blunders until the government fell. Third, the government controlled different facets of life by forcibly taking over minority land, making extra-jurisdictional arrests and interfering with law and order, handing over most duties of police to the military. The government cast a dark shadow in the lives of the public; any opposition or criticism of the regime was not well-received and adversely affected the individuals who chose to express dissent. Fourth, there were stories and narratives spun to weaponize nationalism to achieve the regime's political objectives, accusing internal and external forces and portraying them as national security threats. The narrative was constructed to project that national greatness was under threat and Rajapaksa was there to defend it. These stories were powerful and were effectively amplified using pro-Rajapaksa private media outlets. Fifth, the regime justified its China tilt by orchestrating a narrative that demonized the West for its continued questioning of the human rights violations by the Sri Lankan government.

The new leadership will have a Herculean task to rebalance the foreign policy and work on all the five dimensions to neutralize the problems and re-democratize the nation.

### DEMOCRACY AS A FACADE

President Gotabaya Rajapaksa made a three-way political agreement to survive. He appointed Ranil Wickremesinghe as the prime minister. Then, he got his own political party, the SLPP, to support the new prime minister. And in return, he got Ranil Wickremesinghe to secure his family—the Rajapaksas—political survival without any action being taken against them.

Wickremasinghe, an experienced politician with a good understanding of the internal dynamics of intra-party politics, immediately launched a campaign to win the confidence of the Parliament and the public for his own political survival. The new prime minister first blamed the media for appointing a president like Gotabaya, then he frontloaded a moral dilemma, putting the ball in the protestors court, making it clear that if the protestors disturbed him and the new regime, the situation would only worsen. The message was a carefully orchestrated strategy, warning everyone that a food security crisis was unavoidable if all political parties and the public did not support him—thus ensuring that anyone opposing him would be looked upon as a culprit.

There were a few immediate constitutional amendments made by the prime minister. The twentieth amendment that was introduced by Gotabaya Rajapaksa in 2020 to transfer power to the executive presidency was reversed by Wickremasinghe by the twenty-first amendment,[189] transferring considerable power back to the prime minister. However, according to a civil society activist and academic Dr Jehan Perera, 'The twenty-first Amendment does not significantly reduce the president's powers in the manner that was originally anticipated.'[190] Structural adjustments amidst the political and economic crisis are required to stabilize the situation. The concern is that the behind-the-scenes deal-making politics of Rajapaksa and Wickremasinghe provide no solution for the present crisis.

The protests continued with the primary demand unchanged—the 'GotaGoHome' slogan. Wickremasinghe has risked his political career siding with Rajapaksas, clearly understanding the difficulty of detaching and breaching the private agreement with the Rajapaksa brothers.

Rajapaksas came to Wickremasinghe with a huge baggage—the corruption scandals, human rights violations, and so on—all of which Wickremasinghe had to defend. To win political support in the Parliament, Wickremasinghe relied on the parliamentarians who backed the Rajapaksas. Wickremasinghe is walking on a political tightrope and requires immediate assistance from the IMF to stabilize the economy and simultaneously re-democratize the nation. However, the IMF is still on the staff-level agreement and there is much to be done before the funding agreement can come through.[191] Further delay in the IMF relief fund will cost lives and cause more public outrage.

Behind the change in leadership and the constitutional facade is an attempt to create the illusion of better governance through structural changes. What is immediately required is political stability to achieve economic stability, and the willingness to concede to the demands made by the protestors to bridge the trust deficit between the public and the policy-makers. The Opposition leader Sajith Premadasa and other opposition party leaders have announced that they are willing to give leadership to an interim, all-party regime. This could be the first step to re-democratize the nation.

5

# Security

## ONE
## April 2021

Twenty-Point Analysis of PCoI on Easter Sunday Attack[1]

A mother searching for her child identifies her daughter from the shoe she was wearing, her body lies covered under a white cloth. A lifeless foreigner being carried away. A body blown to pieces lying in the breakfast area on the ground floor. These are all life-changing images that I witnessed on 21 April 2019. By an act of fate, I, with my family, survived due to a delay of about three minutes while walking down to have Easter Sunday breakfast.

Two years have passed since the Easter Sunday terror attack that killed 260 innocent civilians, but still, for the entire month of April, the general public only heard different parliamentarians speak on the Presidential Commission of Inquiry (PCoI) report. In these two years, there have been three reports produced by two governments but there has been no prosecution nor vital information about the external factors.

The initial report immediately after the attack was prepared by a three-member committee headed by Justice Vijith Malalgoda (PC). Then came the Parliament Select Committee (PSC) report[2] and then the present Presidential Commission of Inquiry (PCoI),[3] warranted on 21 September 2019 by former president Maithripala Sirisena to empower a committee to take the required legal action. Interestingly, the committee appointed by President Sirisena found him guilty of negligence. Two years down the line, the public has lost faith in the authorities who promised to bring justice to the victims.

Malcolm Cardinal Ranjith called out to implement the recommendations put forward by the new report.[4] In this report, former president Maithripala Sirisena, former defence secretary, Inspector General of Police, director of State Intelligence Service and several others were clearly identified for prosecution under legal provisions for negligence of duty, while acquitting the former prime minister of all charges. Another six-member ministerial sub-committee headed by Minister Chamal Rajapaksa, appointed in February 2021, submitted a separate report on 15 March 2021 to President Gotabaya Rajapaksa,[5] identifying seventy-eight recommendations of the PCoI report for implementation, though it reportedly had different opinions on the original PCoI recommendations.[6]

The PCoI report, according to an earlier statement on 15 March by Malcolm Cardinal Ranjith, is 'incomplete'.[7] The Cardinal also finds a political hand (external), explaining, 'Our brethren were not attacked by religious extremism, but it was done by those who used religious extremism as a cat's paw to strengthen their political power.'[8] According to Minister Rear Admiral Sarath Weerasekera, it was Naufer Maulawi who was the mastermind behind the Easter Sunday attack and who is currently in the custody of the Sri Lankan Police.[9] However, this is old news, resurrected from the past, and not a new finding. The report also points to another person, Abu Hind. The question is, who was behind them—the external forces? Post attack, I worked to find answers about the external factors. While I discovered many vital pieces of information from terrorism experts and senior international diplomats and policymakers from other countries, there was an invisible hand which pushed me out diplomatically, and I was transferred to another country.

While studying the PCoI report, there are several areas where I found clear limitations and also positive trends. PCoI Volume 1, with 472 pages excluding the annexures, is a better assessment with much more information than the previous Parliament Select Committee (PSC) report published in 2019. The esteemed panel has collected diverse views and evidence from 457 witnesses. While the collection of all this information in a year was a Herculean task, the credit for the entire exercise has to be given to all the officers of PCoI. However, what PCoI lacks is rigorous analysis. Some important points hang in isolation without substantial connection to the relevant data points and some information fails to capture the existing knowledge in the security domain. This might be because the PCoI analysed the circumstantial evidence in a rush, while allocating more time for data collection. Here are a few limitations I would like to point out from the report:

1. PCoI recommends, on page 447, to prepare a National Defence Policy (NDP).
   The report says, 'It is recommended that a national security and defence policy be drafted and adopted.' The NDP was prepared by the Sirisena–Wickremesinghe government during 2015–2019 and approved by the Cabinet of Ministers on 14 November 2019.[10] It was prepared by the tri-forces, along with Chief of Defence Staff officers and INSS (Institute of National Security Studies) during my time as the Director-General (2016–2019). The NDP process commenced in 2016 and the present army commander and many distinguished officers from all the three forces were a part of the process and completed the task in 2019. However, there was a significant reduction of content in the final report. The first half of the initial document was stricken off. The importance of NDP was understood and fully supported and accelerated after the Easter Sunday bombing of 21 April 2019 since the initial document captured the possible extremist threat to the country. Although NDP was ready in 2017, multiple amendments and four defence secretaries, Karunasena Hettiarachchi, Kapila Waidyaratne, Hemasiri Fernando and General Shantha Kottegoda, kept the document in a preparatory mode for three years, not seeing the important areas of varied security threats the nation would face, such as extremism and

terror threats. The proposed structural adjustments to defence establishment including the National Security Council, to be instituted as a legal body to make better decisions and face the threats, were some of the fundamental reforms proposed. These could have strengthened Sri Lanka's preparedness to face an internal threat or event like the Easter Sunday bombings.

I have testified in writing in a thirteen-page submission and verbally in front of the PCoI for almost eight hours over two days. This was the NDP which was prepared earlier; this was not captured, instead the PCoI recommended a new NDP without any reference to the previous document. This recommendation has not been implemented yet and the existing NDP remains in force.

Rather than spending time to reinvent a new NDP, it's worthwhile to look at the existing NDP which was never shared with the general public. The document was declassified before sending it to the Cabinet so that it could be viewed by the public, but it never came out from the Cabinet office. NDP should have undergone a rigorous process of development with inputs from multiple stakeholders including the civil society, public experts and intellectuals, since national security is a topic that affects all sections of the society.

National Security Policy (NSP), which discusses the broader security challenges to the country including food security, health security, maritime security, environment security and most non-traditional security (NTS) domain concerns, was the preliminary document prepared to complement and further assess the NDP challenges. Without understanding the NSP challenges, an individual will not see the NDP challenges clearly. In the present National Defence Policy, the first half of the book (the NSP) was taken out, thereby weakening the defence policy. NSP and NDP should be handed over to the PCoI for their assessment. The PCoI recommendation which says, 'The party in power should have no control over the priority given to national security and national defence' is an important recommendation and should apply to the present government.

2. PCoI states on page 423 that 'Zahran spoke on lack of Good Governance and Judicial System' and therefore he committed suicide based on this fact. There is no rationality in this argument. Extremists don't commit suicide due to a lack of good governance. There are many social and ideological issues behind such a decision. The PCoI refers to the 'Staircase Model' of terrorism by Fathali M. Moghaddam, which I presented and explained to them.[11] This fact is not elaborated further nor given reference in the PCoI report on page 11. 'There is a staircase to terrorism' says the report, bringing a fact without further applying the model in its analysis. There is no connection. If you believe in incremental steps that the 'Staircase Model' of becoming a terrorist describes, then why refer to lack of good governance?
3. Professor Rohan Gunaratna's name is mentioned several times (pages 75, 147, 275) in the report and there is a reference to the Singapore model of countering extremism. Under 'missed opportunity' in Chapter 12, on page 147, there is a reference to a newspaper interview. Why is only the Singapore model of counterterrorism recommended by PCoI? This is a serious question. Why weren't any other suggestions or other examples and other leading experts on the issue of terrorism considered? Was Professor Rohan Gunaratna the only expert? Has the PCoI looked at other nations?
4. PCoI talks of implementing the Harmony Act of Singapore in Sri Lanka. Again, why only Singapore? Why all these recommendations from Singapore? Will you arrest everyone who speaks of religious disharmony as it happens in Singapore? Has the government considered how much this would impact the democratic space of the country? How much has the Harmony Act impacted democracy in Singapore? Have our security researchers done an analysis to find out the success of this Act in

Singapore? Under this Act, you can arrest without a warrant—is that correct? Is the government adding one more layer to the PTA which will further reduce the democratic space? Sri Lanka has a strong democratic model and using Singapore's unique governance model might not work in Sri Lanka.

5. Singapore is referred again on page 431 in the deradicalization programme. Again, why Singapore? Are there any other nations better than Singapore? Have we researched and analysed this data enough?
6. Terrorism Financial Act is a positive suggestion. In addition, introducing individual profiling software to analyse illegal wealth accumulation and strengthening the Financial Investigation Unit of Sri Lanka should be a priority. This point is a very important area that the PCoI has highlighted.
7. A unique idea, to teach all religions to all students as a new subject, is recommended, besides teaching religious reconciliation to all students in Grade 1–10. Can the education minister elaborate on how such a subject would be brought into the curriculum? And then, share the proposed curriculum with education experts? This is a good initiative but needs a properly thought-out, smooth implementation.
8. 'No foreigner should be allowed to work in Sri Lanka without security clearance'—page 439. This will further depict us as a military state. Such actions will portray an image of militarization in the international arena. Naturally, in any country, permission to work will not be given to criminals, those involved in terrorism, drug trafficking or illegal or immoral activities or those who are considered to be a threat to the safety, security and harmony of the country. Those refused under this rule will have a right to appeal.
9. On monitoring of hotels and motels check-ins referred in the PCoI, this information has to be considered as intelligence gathering and explaining it in detail in the PCoI document is not necessary. It would be appreciated if the PCoI refers to

INSS (Institute of National Security Studies) that recommended this in their earlier discussions several years before the Easter Sunday attack, and said that extremists could target hotels and highlighted the importance of hotel check-in information.

10. Creating a Sri Lankan identity is important as recommended in the report, but sanctions against religious practices of minorities, and bans on burka and madrasa will not help. We alienated our Muslim community due to forced cremation and we need to be extra careful with these culturally sensitive concerns. In France, where thirty attacks took place in eight years, President Macron is struggling with Islamophobia. It is very easy to ban but it is difficult to repair after the damage is done. In the present context, France is investing in a new French 'Institute of Islam' to promote understanding of the Islamic world's contributions to science, philosophy, art and literature. There is a price to be paid for taking strict measures and there is also a price to be paid for *not* taking strict measures early enough. National identity has to be above any religious or regional identity. 'Security analysts' inputs are essential in this regard. Sri Lanka has its own, unique society which we can't compare to France or Singapore.
11. Arabization and Wahabism ban—has the PCoI thought through enough about this sensitive area? There should be more discussion. When bringing in new regulations and actions, they should be in incremental steps. Some countries will have serious concerns about these actions.
12. INSS (Institute of National Security Studies) was recommended to work with the intelligence department (page 440). This is not the right thing to do. INSS is a think tank built for research on security. PCoI also recommended that the INSS head should be an expert on anti-terrorism and anti-extremism. In that case, what will happen to other areas of research which are also national security concerns, such as maritime, food, water, cyber, space and all other non-traditional security areas? Is this recommendation a

pre-orchestrated plan to bring an anti-terrorism expert from somewhere (like Singapore)?

13. Apart from the PCoI recommendations, an Integrated Threat Assessment Centre (ITAC) should be considered where all information will flow in one direction to better analyse it. The PCoI report highlights multiple stovepipes of information, but they are not flowing in one direction. The former director of State Intelligence Service (SIS) said, 'It's only information, not intelligence' which they got from India regarding the Easter Sunday attack; there was no sync between SIS/DMI/CNI/IGP and the political body. This was because there was no proper analysis of that information and a lack of coordination between the various intelligence agencies. Even after the 9/11 commission, ITAC was proposed by RAND corporation which was implemented in the US. I proposed the creation of an ITAC in May 2019 at the National Security Council meeting. The importance of this recommendation was discussed in the Parliament on 25 March 2021.
14. PCoI recommended that senior public officers should not hold more than one post, referring to former defence secretary Hemasiri Fernando (page 456). This observation is correct and should be immediately implemented. The same recommendation should be applied to the present government, to officers such as Admiral Professor Jayanath Colombage, who is the secretary foreign ministry and director general of INSS from February 2020. One can raise questions about conflict of interest, especially if such responsible officials are receiving two salaries. If any such officer has drawn one salary as secretary of foreign affairs and another as director general or director at a government institute, then this should be investigated by the auditor general and the public services commission.
15. The report states, 'A balance must be struck between ease of doing business and national security' ('supervision of annual reports', page 424). Under the guise of national security, is the

government trying to create a new militaristic model, unique to Sri Lanka? Who is going to go through the annual reports? Is it the ministry of defence? The ease of doing business is an index we should improve. Terrorists will use shadow companies or narco trade. It is the job of the intelligence and the financial intelligence agencies to find them. It has nothing to do with making a balance between ease of doing business and national security.

16. This PCoI report is titled 'Volume 1'. Where are the other volumes? Are we to study them one by one? If Volume 2 consists of evidence, then we need to see if it's sufficiently captured or partly captured. A rigorous analysis should be done by security researchers to ensure that.
17. This Easter Sunday attack is a unique case. In the morning of the day of the attack, there was an intelligence warning. After the attack, it took a few days to identify the claims of the ISIS. Why was there a delay? One suicide attacker didn't detonate at Taj—there was an incoming call at the time of the attempted detonation at Hotel Taj Samudra. This same detonation took place a few hours later in Dehiwala. Abu Hind was the person, according to the report, who gave instructions and advice. The report also says that he is a virtual person created by 'provincial Indian intelligence apparatus' (page 219). Is this correct? The former SIS director is the 'only witness to have testified impeding the identity of a possible foreign involvement' (page 218). Is this correct information? Out of 457 witnesses, was there only one person who talked about a foreign hand?
18. PCoI captures the threat forecast (Monthly Threat Forecast—MTF) written by me in January 2019, clearly identifying that there was a national security threat after the discovery of detonators in Wanathawilluwa, requesting to find the 'foreign connection behind the discovery' (pages 257 and 262) under President Maithripala

Sirisena's section and dysfunctional government section (page 352). Why was this limited to these sections? Wasn't the threat forecast a missed opportunity? The previous MTFs produced and discussed on video in 2017—are they not missed opportunities? What makes the Singaporean professor's comment so important compared to the local assessment?

19. The report also talks of politicization of intelligence. It says that intelligence reports had to contend with the political environment the administration in power and the president's personal impressions and preferences. President Maithripala Sirisena's statement on his assassination plot by Indian intelligence was one such incident which strained the relationship with the neighbour and was based on information with questionable credibility and accuracy.

The PCoI report contains SIS Director DIG Nilantha Jayawardena's comments that what the Indian intelligence shared about the Easter Sunday attacks was 'mere information' (page 158) and not intelligence, and his assessment of Indian Defence Secretary Sanjay Mitra's visit on the 7 April 2019 for the India–Sri Lanka Defence Dialogue, questioning 'whether the Secretary of Defence of India will visit the country if there was in fact a security threat as informed on 4th April 2019' (page 220). While the PCoI assesses that there was no credibility in the inputs from India and that the Indian secretary defence was a diversion from the intelligence provided as there was not enough actionable information to prevent the attack. But why did such vital information go unheard? Was it politicized by the regime?

To assess the degree of politicization of intelligence prior to the 4/21 attack, I presented Professor Eugene de Silva's model (STARR model) to the PCoI. The STARR model was applied to Vietnam Estimates in 1963, 9/11 and Iraq war 2003. According to Professor Eugene De Silva, 'The pathway to declaring war on Iraq was another classic case of politicization of intelligence.'

The STARR model has five facets that are considered in quantitative analysis:

*System*: This refers to the unit in charge of the intelligence process for a particular task.
*Timeline*: This refers to the total period, from the inception of the intelligence process to the final report and evaluation.
*Access*: This refers to the extent to which intelligence officers are provided with accessibility to operational activities.
*Resources*: This refers to the total resources used by the intelligence personnel throughout the intelligence cycle, until the completion of the task.
*Re-evaluation*: The reports produced are re-evaluated for accuracy and errors.

Modified Staple Scale is the range of scale, limiting to -2, -1, 0, +1 and +2. The value +2 denotes extreme polarization, either towards the objectives of the policy maker (+2) or away from the objectives (-2). The value of +2 is given when there is hard politicization and +1 when there is some politicization. Zero indicates that there is no politicization. The values do not measure whether the final intelligence report prepared favours the objectives of the policy maker or not. The values only indicate whether there has been any politicization towards or against the objectives of the policy makers.

The STARR model was applied by me to the Easter Sunday bombing after consultation with the creator of the model, Professor Eugene De Silva, to determine the degree of politicization of intelligence in the process (Table 5.1).[12]

The data analysis was taken from the day the first intelligence report was sent to the Sri Lankan authorities by the Indian authorities in the beginning of April 2019 and the subsequent warnings before the 21 April attack.

TABLE 5.1: Easter Sunday Data Applied to STARR Model Presented to PCoI by the Author

| Facet | Modified Staple Scale | Reason |
|---|---|---|
| System | +2 | Those who disagree on the extremism threat were forced to align with the politicized decisions. |
| Timeline | +2 | Indian secretary of defence visit on 7th April to Colombo with high terror alert—Indian Intelligence data is questionable |
| Access | +1 | Access was limited—Indian warning was circulated to few—communication gap |
| Resources | +2 | Access to the resources were controlled |
| Re-evaluation | +1 | No actual fact-based re-evaluation |
| Total Value | +8 | Highly politicized intelligence data |

Degree of Politicization according to modified Staple scale:
0: Non-politicized state
+1: Politicized to an extent towards the objectives of the policymaker
+2: Extremely politicized towards the objectives of the policymaker

According to this assessment, the total value of +8 signifies high politicization of intelligence. Higher the degree of politicization, lesser will be the space to take precise action due to adulteration of data from the political cycle.

The earlier plot about President Sirisena's assassination, accusing India and the trust deficit with India could have played a large role in decision-making, processing the available information and giving due weightage to the intelligence.

20. The PCoI report was correct in observing that the information provided was actual intelligence and there was enough actionable information for the authorities. At the PCoI, the esteemed council raised a question—If you were told of the 4 April 2019 intelligence information, what would you have done? My answer was that it would match perfectly with the January 2019 threat forecast I had written about, and I would immediately take actionable steps to prevent the

attack mentioned in the intelligence information. But unfortunately, there is always a shield to keep you out of such vital information loop, or keep you out of the entire establishment, by few individuals.

## TWO
## December 2021

### The Lynching of a Sri Lankan in Pakistan: Decluttering Religious Extremism[13]

The United States Commission on International Religious Freedom (USCIRF) report identifies Pakistan as the highest among the world's worst violators of religious freedom.[14] Adding to the account is the recent lynching and burning of a Sri Lankan factory manager in Sialkot, Pakistan. The brutal act was immediately condemned by Pakistan Prime Minister Imran Khan who tweeted, 'The horrific vigilante attack on factory in Sialkot & the burning alive of Sri Lankan manager is a day of shame for Pakistan. I am overseeing the investigations & let there be no mistake all those responsible will be punished with full severity of the law. Arrests are in progress.' The incident was connected to the 'hardline Tehreek-e-Labbaik Pakistan (TLP)'. The victim 'allegedly tore a poster of the hardline group in which Quranic verses were inscribed and threw it in the dustbin. The poster of the Islamist party was pasted on the wall adjoining the office of Kumara. A couple of factory workers saw him removing the poster and spread the word in the factory,' reports PTI.

Prime Minister Imran Khan made a U-turn in his policy decision on TLP. In April, the Pakistan Cabinet moved to ban the TLP under the anti-terrorism legislation, taking its leader Saad Rizvi into custody; in November, the same Cabinet revoked the declaration of the TLP as a banned group, and a provincial government moved to remove Rizvi's name from the anti-terrorism watchlist. The entire government was not in favour of this decision; Minister Fawad Chaudhry cautioned, 'Neither the Pakistani government nor the state is completely ready to fight extremism.'[15] Chaudhry also said, 'The way the state had to back off in the TLP's case, symbolises that the bomb (of extremism) is ticking.'[16]

While TLP denies its role in spreading extremism and Pakistan authorities debate over the subject, the lynching of the Sri Lankan is alarming, and points to uncontrolled and rising extremism, which could move beyond Pakistan's borders to the South Asia region. The ban on TLP was foreseen as an unfruitful exercise by Pakistani scholar Hussain Haqqani, who said, 'It is unlikely that banning one group (TLP) will diminish Pakistan's religious extremism problem.'[17] The problem was, 'While Pakistan's establishment has alternated between various Islamist factions, mainstreaming one while suppressing another, it has never thought about mainstreaming secularists who have been dubbed as traitors or unfaithful to the ideology of Pakistan.' The assassination of Salman Taseer,[18] former governor of Panjab, killed by his bodyguard for speaking against the blasphemy law, where the killer was garlanded with flowers by lawyers, depicts the clear position of Pakistan on blasphemy.

TLP has influenced Pakistan's foreign policy in the present environment, made conducive by PM Khan's administration. French President Macron was a clear target of the TLP and PM Khan for spreading Islamophobia. The recent summoning of France's ambassador by Pakistan's government is the result of the deep polarization of policymakers over extremism. President Macron explains, 'The problem is an ideology which claims its own laws should be superior to those of the Republic,'[19] and says he will always defend the laws of freedom of expression. In response, PM Khan says, '[Macron] has chosen to encourage Islamophobia by attacking Islam rather than the terrorists who carry out violence.' Turkish President Erdogan joins PM Khan in criticizing President Macron, clearly showing the division of world opinion.

The issues of making incorrect accusations of blasphemy and rising extremism have gone beyond the borders of Pakistan. In September, a Pakistani man was taken into custody in Paris by

French police for attacking and seriously wounding two people with a meat cleaver, allegedly over the issue of blasphemy.

Individual cases such as those in Paris or the Sri Lankan's murder in Pakistan are just one side of the story. The other side is the Pakistan's government and their military handlers accepting TLP's ludicrous demands and the TLP's ability to dictate terms to the government on its foreign policy and policy prescriptions. These are clear signs of concerns about the security of South Asia. What is required is that both France and Pakistan should work on reforming their laws to create a progressive society. France needs to respect its heterogeneous society and show respect and tolerance to all religions. Pakistan needs to reform its laws and make a consistent policy to develop religious harmony and curb extremist thinking. The Pakistan government has to manage its internal volatile security situation better. The TLP will influence the rise of far-right political parties that could further push the country towards extremism.

Indian and South Asian security are directly vulnerable to the rise of extremist forces.

Islamic State in Khorosan Province (ISKP) has claimed responsibility for the deadly explosions at Kabul airport, amid ongoing US evacuations where more than 160 people, including 13 United States troops, were killed.[20] Seeing the early signs of rising extremism in its periphery, India strongly condemned the terrorist strike in Afghanistan's capital, Kabul. India told the UN Security Council that these attacks reinforce the need for the world to stand united against terrorism and those who provide sanctuaries to terrorists. Subrahmanyam Jaishankar, minister for external affairs, called for adopting the Convention on Terrorism,[21] an important step to minimize the security threat.

In Afghanistan, with significant global financial assistance being stopped, poverty is on the rise and many people are suffering there. These are the exact conditions where terrorism and extremism thrive. This situation will further encourage right-wing extremist factions in Pakistan. The South Asian nations are vulnerable in this unfolding security environment, where Sri Lanka was the victim in the 2019 Easter Sunday terror attack.

Political and military actors orchestrate the Islamization and extremism campaigns for their political legitimization in the region. A policy prescription for moderate groups and religious harmony is a top priority for the region, where intertwined politically supported extremist structures must be dismantled to promote regional peace. The regimes in power should not be able to propagate and support extremist factions for political gain. The dual-faced policies that condemn extremism and yet promote it at the same time needs to end.

Unfortunately, the political narrative to propagate right-wing ultra-nationalist extremism is actively visible in Sri Lanka. Sri Lankan Minister Namal Rajapaksa tweeted, acknowledging the gravity of the situation, saying, 'We should be mindful that this could happen to anyone if extremist forces are allowed to act freely,'[22] forgetting the same Rajapaksa regime has elevated the extremist Buddhist force BBS to draft legal recommendations 'One Country One Law' for the nation, which is a concern for the minority community.

## THREE
## February 2022

### Fighting Economic Crime during the Pandemic: A Sri Lankan Perspective[23]

When assessing the pre-pandemic economic crime environment in Sri Lanka, in 2015, the island-nation went through its largest corruption scandal in its recent past, the Central Bank 'Bond Scam'.[24] The total value of the bond scam was in billions of rupees,[25] and a book with the title *The Great Bond Scam Cover-Up*[26] was authored and published by the present governor of the Central Bank, Ajith Nivard Cabraal. At the time of the bond scam, the Central Bank governor was Arjuna Mahendran and he faced the Presidential Commission of Inquiry. The accused governor was not a Sri Lankan citizen,[27] and he left for Singapore to avoid arrest.

The Sri Lankan Government has failed to extradite the governor since it has not met the documentation requirements of Singapore courts. The charges against the former prime minister for aiding and covering up the bond scandal were documented in 2019 in the book *The Great Bond Scam Cover-Up*, telling the public the 'period which will probably not exceed 12 months from the date of a new Government assuming office' was all that was needed to prosecute the culprits and bring them to justice. However, it has been two years, and the former governor and prime minister have not been brought to justice. The book, in the chapter 'Bringing Culprits to Justice', says that there are charges on sixteen counts against the former prime minister Ranil Wickremesinghe.[28] Several other accusations were against the governor and his nephew, the primary dealer involved in the bond purchases.

After returning to power, the new government formed a commission of inquiry. With enough evidence, why did the government fail to make any of the persons involved accountable? Who is harmed when the justice system fails to punish the guilty? Why did such high-level public officials support committing the crime and then covering up and not putting anyone behind bars? When will these questions be answered?

## DEMOCRATIC BACKSLIDING DURING PANDEMIC

The pandemic has allowed suppression of democratic values and norms in many nations. Some leaders tend to think inwards and have focussed on enhanced military strength to fight the pandemic. In Sri Lanka, the military has been at the forefront because of the regime's preference. For the first time, the island-nation has a president from a military background and a sibling regime with the president and prime minister from the same family. A total of six family members took up key ministerial portfolios such as finance, economics, defence and many others, making the regime the most prominent political–ministerial dynasty globally.

During the pandemic and lockdown, constitutional changes were done, moving power from the legislature to the executive president. The constitutional amendment took place without any public discussion. The concentration of political power with one individual raises many questions such as checks and balances and the independence of institutions, including the judiciary. The demotivation of the judiciary from acts such as the president pardoning a political criminal sentenced to life in prison by a tribunal raises public concerns.[29] The pardon was given during the lockdown when the public was following the government's 'disciplinary project' of pandemic health regulations. Thus, the democratic environment was misused by the authorities, as the public could not engage in demonstrations and public debate on important policy matters.

The Bill for a Chinese SEZ during the pandemic which gave extra-jurisdictional powers was quickly passed, taking full advantage of the Covid environment, is another such example.[30] The government suppressed the protest and criticism using the pandemic regulations and media censorship. US Ambassador Aliana Teplitz warned, 'Among those unintended consequences could be creating a haven for money launderers and other sorts of nefarious actors to take advantage of what was perceived as a permissive business environment for activities that would be illegal.' The China-backed Colombo Port City (SEZ) with easy business rules could be used as a money-laundering haven.[31]

Public perception of the 'rule of law' during pandemic and post-pandemic period will be an essential barometer to sustain democracy in many nations. According to Michel Foucault, 'In order to see perfect disciplines functioning, rulers dreamt of the state of plague.'[32] The pandemic environment allows governments to bring reforms for social discipline in their society. Unfortunately, the administration executed its 'disciplinary project' and political agenda during the lockdown to amplify the ultra-nationalist sentiments and populist policies. The US (with President Trump), Brazil (with President Bolsonaro) and several other nations, including Sri Lanka, are some examples of this.

In Sri Lanka, a major constitutional change to shift power from the legislature to the executive president was done during the pandemic. The primary structural reform in the Constitution through the twentieth amendment impacted the democratic fabric of the entire society; the independence of the independent commissions was a concern post this reform.

According to a CPA analysis, 'The notable changes from the amendment was, first, to the Constitutional Council overseeing appointments to key public service institutions, both at individual and institutional levels, which was to be replaced by the Parliamentary Council, which comprised only of Members of Parliament. Second, the Parliamentary Council was also limited in its influence in that it could only make observations to the President, who is not bound by them. Presidential immunity was bolstered under the provisions of the Bill. Third, the National Procurement Commission and the National Audit Commission were both to be abolished under the provisions of the Bill. Fourth, the President's powers over the Prime Minister, Cabinet, and the Parliament were also increased. Finally, there were changes to the law-making process including reintroducing the provisions relating to Urgent Bills and reducing the time duration a bill had to remain in the public domain prior to it being possible to table such bill in Parliament.'[33]

Sri Lanka also increased the role of the military in government administration. UNHRC highlighted this issue where military officers were appointed in twenty-eight positions,[34] including as foreign secretary, secretaries of several ministries and in Board positions.

The militarization agenda of the regime did not go well with the UNHRC. The government was expected to work on a demilitarization project and to address past human rights concerns of the Tamilians, on which it had been procrastinating because of the political pressure from the ultra-nationalist Sinhalese-Buddhists and the government catering to the majoritarian voter base. The EU's action in June 2021 to withdraw the GSP+ export concessions is a sign of its displeasure over the current human rights environment in the country.

Days after the EU announcement, the release of a political criminal from jail and his pardon by the president raises further concerns. This adds to the multiple apprehensions already existing over the rule of law, paving the way for economic crimes through political favours. The widening trust deficit among the people and the judiciary is a severe reaction to these acts. While the EU and UNHRC question the country's judicial mechanism to resolve human rights violations, the local trust deficit will add extra weight to the external pressure.

The exploitation of the lockdown and the disciplinary project for political gains by the government has significant consequences for Sri Lanka which already has multiple social issues regarding human rights. With its almost three-decade history of civil war and two full-scale youth insurrections where thousands of lives were lost, Sri Lanka is vulnerable to exploitative undemocratic practices, using ultra-nationalist sentiments to protect wrong-doers and not addressing concerns about large-scale corruption in the country.

The political interference in the working of the judiciary has two direct consequences for Sri Lankan. First, the minority distrust will increase, and so will the state of denial. The lack of independence and low credibility of the judicial system will create social distress between the minorities, the majority community and the international community. The semi-automatic militarized character will enlarge where fighting corruption in earlier democratic spaces will shift towards a new, more dangerous environment. This environment will have political clientelism protecting the economic crimes of the regime.

## TYPE OF REGIME AND DELEGATION OF POWER

Fukuyama argues that 'the major dividing line in effective crisis response will not place autocracies on one side and democracies on the other. Rather, there will be some high performing autocracies and some with disastrous outcomes. There will be a similar variance in outcomes among democracies, though likely smaller. The crucial determinant in performance will not be the type of regime, but the state's capacity and, above all, trust in government.'[35]

The type of regime was not a factor when comparing China and the US, Singapore and Taiwan, or any other democracy or autocratic power handling the pandemic. The criteria for efficiently controlling the pandemic was the state's delegation of powers and the trust of the public. The delegation to the military as the most efficient operating mode was seen in many nations, especially in Sri Lanka. The military played a pivotal role in bringing the pandemic to some level of control with the help of medical officials.

The concern now is to return the delegated power back to the government. In nations like Sri Lanka and the Philippines, the emergency powers given to the executive have not been returned. The same delegation of power is misused to enlarge the scope of the executive power of the government, moving towards an autocracy. The Sri Lankan president's former military role and his trust in the military played a pivotal role in appointing military officers to key government administrative positions. He also used the military for enforcing a primary price control of essential food items during the economic crisis amid the pandemic.

Similarly, the Prevention of Terrorism Act was misused by the government to detain hundreds of innocent civilians under the guise of national security. The abuse of power was because of institutional weakness, where checks and balances and the rule of law were further crippled. On being elected, one of the initial actions of the Gotabaya Rajapaksa regime was to transfer most of the legislative powers to the executive through a constitutional amendment. At the time of the amendment, the majoritarian regime said that the action was to stabilize the nation—definitely a false pretext and a move in the wrong direction.

After two years, the consequences are clear—breakdown of democratic processes and illiberal practices are visible throughout Sri Lanka. One of the oldest democracies in Asia, Sri Lanka was not invited to the global 'Summit for Democracy' because of the significant backsliding in democracy.[36] The summit has pushed the democratic agenda further to fight corruption, a critical ingredient identified by the present US administration. Despite the absence at the summit, significant investment and international assistance are required for nations like Sri Lanka to curb corruption, reduce the semi-autocratic footprint, bring back democratic values, and reduce political clientelism and economic crime.

The regime's power centre has a total of nine family members, including three influential family members holding the finance, economic and defence ministries, which could be compared to a Roman triumvirate model, with three brothers controlling the power in Sri Lanka. The political environment encourages political clientelism to flourish. Approvals from only one family are needed for political nominations for the business community to grow their businesses in many areas.

One example of political clientelism was the case of the regime's political associate who was accused on multiple counts and the attorney general had filed indictments on 7,573 charges in connection with arms trafficking and numerous economic crimes.[37] The case related to a company called Avant Garde, which operated a floating armoury and provided maritime security. The case was dropped, which raised grave public concerns about the regime's intention to fight economic crime.[38] The Attorney General who filed the case retired from his position soon after.[39]

Retired Attorney General De Livera PC said, 'The delays caused by Covid-19 are a curse to the justice system and stressed it will have serious repercussions and consequences in the administration of justice in the country.'[40] Highlighting fourteen high profile cases, including the Avant Garde and Central Bank bond scams, he said, 'When we refer to the High-Profile cases in Sri Lanka, the investigations are complex in nature and are delayed due to the slow pace of these investigations.'

The Attorney General admits there is a requirement to build capacity in the investigative mechanism, the judicial system and people's legal awareness to fight high profile economic crime in Sri Lanka. While this is understood by the present regime, political clientelism and direct interference by officials to protect their financiers and give them support become a priority for them. Political interference in the judiciary will undermine the fight against economic crime.

The pandemic was used to suppress justice for high profile cases in a semi-autocratic climate in Sri Lanka. The pandemic environment became a blessing for economic offenders, as health captured the public attention to the exclusion of almost all other concerns. One example of this was the recent sugar tender scandal which was reported by media for a brief period, until the pandemic news took precedence over the economic crime.[41]

The question to ask is, who was harmed and paid for all the economically-motivated crime during the pandemic? The direct impact, of course, was on the general public, suffering in a double crisis of health and economic crimes.

The ripple effect has also influenced the present dysfunctionality of the regime at a macro level, triggering an economic as well as a political crisis at the same time. Criminals engaged in financial crime with political backing will further exploit the economic crisis environment in Sri Lanka. The negative economic conditions[42] and the widening inequality could trigger civil unrest and a full-scale military takeover if the present crisis in Sri Lanka is not addressed immediately. There should be a considerable investment from the government to bring back a conducive environment to fight economic crime, restore democratic order and the independence of the judiciary.

# FOUR
## March 2022

The Wall of Strength against Aggression[43]

Out of the 193 United Nations member-states, 141 voted for the UN resolution on Russia's aggression against Ukraine (35 abstained and 5 voted against). Almost the entire world has shown solidarity and condemned the brutal aggression of Russia. President Biden gave the State of the Union address a day before the UN vote. Biden bluntly stated the miscalculation by President Putin, who 'sought to shake the foundations of the free world thinking he could make it bend to his menacing ways. But he badly miscalculated . . . he [Putin] met a wall of strength he never imagined.'[44]

War in Ukraine takes us back to the classic scholarship of Carl von Clausewitz's *On War* and Halford Mackinder's geopolitics of pivoting to the 'Heartland' ('Heartland' refers to Russia and its surrounding area) on the European nation-state's expansion in its immediate periphery. According to Robert Kaplan, Russia's fear of land-bound enemies is a principal theme of Mackinder's 'Heartland Theory'.[45] In 1762, the Ukrainian writer Semen Divovych authored *A Talk between Great Russia and Little Russia*. Little Russia was Ukraine. Divovych depicts with clarity the equal status Ukraine wished to maintain with Russia. This writing was produced centuries ago during the systematic integration of Ukraine by Empress Catherine II. The Tsarist Russification of Russia's immediate periphery has been a geopolitical characteristic of 'depicting strength' that Russia has displayed from time to time in its history. Under President Putin, the same Russification project has resurrected in the Ukraine invasion, with the miscalculation pointed out by Biden

Russia is one-sixth of the world's landmass and has eleven time zones. It is simply too large to be ignored. The Russians have pushed into Central and Eastern Europe to block nineteenth-century France, twentieth-century Germany and the twenty-first-century Western alliance, NATO. More than half of the twentieth century was defined by the Cold War between Russia and the United States. The twenty-first century is seeing aggression by Russia, with China to follow. Two Asian powers, Russia and China, are stepping up the escalation ladder in their respective geographical theatres—Ukraine in Europe and Taiwan in the Indo-Pacific.

Ukraine and Taiwan have long been peripheries of interest which Russia and China wish to annexe. China abstained from the UN resolution against the Russian invasion of Ukraine, just weeks before Beijing and Moscow declared a 'no limits' partnership after standoffs on Ukraine and Taiwan.[46] It came with a promise to collaborate more against the West by way of strategic designs. According to the Indian scholar Harsh Pant, 'The Russia–China axis is only going to get stronger as both nations prepare to take on the West, which is willing to accept [defeat] even without a fight.'[47]

In Ukraine, Russia has launched its biggest war since 1945. President Putin had alerted the nuclear deterrence force, foreseeing a NATO intervention in the coming days. Barry Pavel, senior vice president at the Atlantic Council, assesses a triple threat that will emerge and go beyond the Russia–Ukraine conflict. 'This Russian triple threat (conventional forces, hybrid warfare, and nuclear sabre-rattling) combined with a Russian leader willing to take risks means Europe and the US will face a level of insecurity and potentially instability.'[48] Ukraine's invasion is probably not only for regime change but also indicates what Russia wants to achieve in the global arena. But the question remains—What exactly does Russia want to gain from the invasion? And what characters will be different from their past warfare?

The Cold War created borders and boundaries in the Russian landmass and political space. Reclaiming land and escalating the conflict in Ukraine itself is also a bargaining strategy to achieve geopolitical objectives. Referring to the work of Herman Kahn during the Cold War, 'There are at least three ways in which a would-be escalator can increase, or threaten to increase his efforts: by increasing intensity, widening the area, or compounding escalation.'[49] In the next few days, the conflict in Ukraine, its quantitative increase in the intensity of firepower, and the territorial spill-over to nations neighbouring Ukraine could occur. While the area of growth of conflict is a concern, there is a significant increase in information and cyber warfare, which is a definite sign that this will spread across the modern military battle. The military muscle of Russia and Ukraine backed by the NATO-backed alliance, will have the qualitative and quantitative military force to engage in a full-scale war. Unlike in the wars in the past, information warfare will be the key to success.

The Russian intelligence services, feeling confident by the recent overwhelming victories in Ukraine cyberwar and potentially elsewhere, are likely to significantly ramp up cyberattacks and online disinformation according to a US White House security statement.[50] American and European leaders will have to prepare their citizens for significant, sustained increases in defence and homeland-security budgets and spending adequate amounts to protect shared interests and our democratic way of life.

In 2005 and 2014, the Ukrainian people toppled pro-Russian leaders who were ruling their nation. This trend will continue in the future with civilian unrest despite the brutal invasion and installation of a pro-Russian puppet regime. With their President Zelensky, the heroic Ukrainian people are fighting to secure the democratic values of their society. By all measures, it is an act of bravery against the oppressive Russian forces. For the first time in its history, the European Union has delivered weapons to the Ukrainian people to fight back. Almost the entire free world is with Ukraine in supporting its fight against the Russian autocrat. Soon, the Ukraine war could impact other geographies. The ramifications on geopolitics of other countries and especially on developing nations such as Sri Lanka in the form of high oil and commodity prices and loss of tourism income will be a serious economic concern.

While this geopolitical circumstance may be a generational challenge, in the end, the US and its NATO and Indo-Pacific allies will come out more united and robust than they have been in recent years. Over the last several decades, the US and its allies enjoyed an unusual luxury of reduced threats of invasion since autocratic regimes preferred to brew their military strength in the background and, instead of physical attacks, launched multiple cyber attacks and information warfare, threatening the democratic norms and values of liberal democracies.

Ukraine will be an opportunity to strengthen the liberal democratic alliance against oppressive regimes. The alliance's strength was seen when more than a hundred diplomats from forty Western countries and allies, including Japan, walked out of a speech by Russian Foreign Minister Sergey Lavrov at the UN human rights forum. President Putin has made uncomfortable all other aggressive nationalists worldwide who were on a similar track, as they find it difficult to support his misguided gambit. It is time President Biden sends a strong message to the natural partners who participated in the democratic summit in December 2021 to act on the promises they pledged. All other nations should also follow the path of building a *wall of strength*.

## FIVE
## March 2022

### Information Warfare between Ukraine and Russia[51]

The process of Russification of Russia's periphery during the ancient empire by the Tsars is continued today by President Putin. The invasion of Ukraine differs from previous Russification attempts due to a unique feature—information warfare. Unlike the Cold War, we live in a connected world with massive information overload. We are constantly trying to discern the truth from deception, sorting through misinformation and disinformation. Thomas Friedman rightly assesses that World Wide Web is actually 'World War Wired,'[52] and the West has dropped an 'economic nuclear bomb' on

Russia, thus crashing its currency and causing multiple economic impacts from Russia to spill over to many geographies.

'Information warfare,' as defined by the futurist, who is also the executive director of 'The Millennium Project', Jerome Glenn, is different from cyber warfare that attacks computers, software and command control systems. Information warfare focuses on manipulating information trusted by targets without their becoming aware, so that they make decisions against their interest and in the interest of the one conducting information warfare.[53]

Information warfare differs from misinformation and disinformation. Misinformation refers to false information presented as a fact, often without an inherent desire to deceive. Disinformation, on the other hand, also presents incorrect information as factual but is intended to mislead others. Disinformation relies on the same idea of intended deception as information warfare, but the main difference between these two is that information warfare specifically utilizes trusted sources to provide false information so that you are unaware you are being manipulated.

Information warfare is often confused with the term 'propaganda'. Propaganda is something that you are aware of and acknowledge, but with information warfare, you are often unaware that it is taking place. When propaganda is used in war, the main goal is to demoralize the enemy and convince them that their skills are lower than their opponents. Propaganda uses tools such as rumours, deception and false arguments. The main objective of information warfare is similar, as it is intended to mislead others and influence their opinion. The difference is that it is solely focused on gaining, destroying or changing information. In other words, the goal is information superiority as a means of gaining a hold over opponents and using it for nefarious purposes.

According to Brookings Fellow Jessica Brandt, information warfare is 'right out in the open on Russian state media, and Kremlin-backed accounts online. We also know that Moscow planned to fabricate a justification for an intervention by filming a gruesome video of purported war crimes, hiring Russian-speaking actors to play the part of mourners, and sending saboteurs into Eastern Ukraine to carry out a false flag operation.'[54] This may sound like propaganda but many believe it to be true. In response to Russian actions, there are multiple restriction and downgrades already imposed by online platforms such as Microsoft, Google, Facebook, Bing and Twitter on Russian Sputnik and RT content to counter disinformation.

When information warfare is coupled with cyber warfare and traditional tactics, it can have devastating effects on civilians and infrastructure. Russia wages a horrifying mix of psychological, cyber and traditional war against Ukraine. This is considered 'hybrid warfare' where non-traditional force-multipliers such as cyber and social media intelligence attacks are employed.[55] The use of network infiltration, denial of information and internet services and other advanced persistent threats (APTs) to achieve strategic political and military results are carried out in the hybrid warfare environment.

Russia's usage of information warfare in Ukraine results from a few factors. First, Russian attack on 22 February 2022 came swiftly. Within minutes of launching Putin's 'special military operation' to 'demilitarize' and 'denazify' the country, several explosions were reported near the Ukrainian capital of Kyiv. By not allowing the media much time to properly analyse the situation, Putin left the door open for rumours and misinformation to run rampant. Second, Putin's rhetoric in his address, specifically mentioning his intentions to 'denazify' the country, set the tone for this war. Ukraine's president, Volodymyr Zelenskyy, is Jewish and had family who died in the Holocaust, but if a person is not aware of this information, they might assume that Russia had a just cause for attacking the country. Third, Eastern Ukraine (also known as the Donbas region) has been controlled by pro-Russian, anti-government, separatist forces since the 2014 pro-Russian unrest in Ukraine. Having a pro-Russian region has made it significantly easier for Putin to utilize the Ukrainians in that region to promote propaganda and other acts of psychological warfare against the Ukrainian government, military and pro-government citizens.

Putin's aggressive usage of information warfare reinforces the belief that he aspires to use information warfare as an easily accessible, long-range, universal weapon to try and put his stamp on the international community.[56] By using propaganda and psychological warfare, Putin is trying to isolate Ukraine by creating chaos in Ukraine and the rest of the world.

Unfortunately for Ukraine, Putin's timing is in sync with recent developments. Moscow has developed innovative information and cyber tools to wage a long-term psychological war by combining its traditional use of state media, overt and covert propaganda and active measures alongside modern communications systems and social media.[57] Slovak Republic-based ESET and California-based Broadcom's Symantec, both cyber-security companies, observed a new type of malware that wipes out data, which was used against Ukraine in the 23 February attacks. The malware was novel because it attacks the master boot record (MBR) of computers.[58] Natalia Tkachuk, head of the Information Security and Cyber Security Service of the National Security and Defence Council of Ukraine, stressed at a joint briefing that there was 'a significant change in the purpose and mechanisms of the most recent cyber-attacks since there was a clear pivot away from obtaining intelligence information and personal data, to attempting to destabilize, discredit, and manipulate the country'.[59]

Cyber-attacks had severe destabilizing effects on 15 February 2022, when internet service providers reported massive interruptions in internet connectivity. The graph notes a particularly sharp decline at 2:00 pm, the same time the Ukrainian defence section went offline from distributed denial-of-service attacks (DDoS).[60]

Putin's usage of new cyber warfare tools is crucial to reinforce the efficacy of the psychological warfare aspect in the ongoing information war, because he is using it to create a war centred around distrust and betrayal. By combining psychological, electronic and physical warfare (three of the six components of information warfare),[61] Putin is constructing a hybrid war where only he controls the flow of information in Ukraine. If he can control the media by usurping communication centres and spreading propaganda via social media, he has the power to manage what the people of Ukraine—and the world—hear and see and, ultimately, how they react to it.

Now the big question—how can other countries help fight against information warfare and prevent such forms of hybrid warfare from recurring? Partnerships and collaborations are the key to generating a multi-jurisdictional and multipronged approach to combat information warfare. Michael Ruhle and Clare Roberts from NATO Security Challenges Division observe, 'Building close ties with like-minded nations across the globe is in itself a deterrent to would-be hybrid aggressors.'[62] Dr James Curtis, professor of Information Technology at Webster University in St Louis, recommends, 'Defense Department should partner with other agencies to fund and support a government-wide commitment to a cybersecurity education program for all Americans as early as the first days of school and continuing throughout adulthood.'[63] Cybersecurity education programmes will teach children how to protect themselves in cyberspace as well as promote a life-long interest, which can lead to increased employment and research in the field down the line. Additionally, 'Private military contractors and academic communities should team with the government via public-private partnerships to develop technical processes which identify and counter attacks such as deep fakes and other emerging digital social engineering methods.'[64] Public-private partnerships, particularly with the IW Executive Board (a committee created in 1995 to 'facilitate "the development and achievement of national information warfare goals"'),[65] could prove useful for educating the average citizen about the social engineering methods of the subject matter, as these are concepts people are often not aware of until they become victims of such activities.

Regarding the current situation in Ukraine, a multilateral defence effort is necessary to protect the Ukrainian people. Cybersecurity education, bans and downranking targeted media channels contributed to fighting the current information war. The proactive measure in early February to declassify documents pertaining to Russian intelligence by US President Joseph Biden proved to be a decisive action that caught Putin off-guard and impacted the Russian narrative in the information warfare. The US president's action won general public acclaim and exposed the hidden intentions of the Russian leader. This initiative was both defensive as well as offensive at the same time as it prevented Putin from unfavourable disinformation manoeuvres against the US, and it also provided factual, authoritative answers to the rest of the world. As the information is now publicly available to the Ukrainian government, they can better defend themselves from physical and potential cyber-attacks. Other countries could follow a similar strategy to prevent further manipulation of Russian and Ukrainian information, thereby assisting Ukraine in preventing information warfare and propaganda from spiralling out of control.

# SIX
# September 2022

## Ayman al-Zawahiri's Death and Political–Economic Fragility in South Asia[66]

Political and economic dysfunction is an invitation for terrorism to flourish in the least integrated region in the world—South Asia. P.R Chari, director at IPCS India,[67] captured this a year after the 9/11 attacks in a paper titled, 'Combating Terrorism: Devising Cooperative Countermeasures',[68] arguing that 'the war against international terrorism must rest on two pillars, viz. a holistic approach to countering the threat by addressing the allied threats to international security and devising of means to secure cooperation at all levels—international, regional and national. These are linked issues.' South Asia, at the moment, requires a particularly holistic approach.

When the autocratic president Gotabaya Rajapaksa fled Sri Lanka this summer, he left a dangerous military footprint. Would-be autocrats, who constantly warned that the Sri Lankan uprising would create chaos, had to prove that they were correct. The peaceful uprising on 9 July was systematically crushed by the military and the newly appointed president, Ranil Wickremesinghe, Rajapaksa's protege. The ousted autocrat could use political resources and proxies to create more dysfunction on the island; the purpose would be to convince Sri Lankans that life in the past was better and that his political return could restore it. Gotabaya's victory in the 2019 presidential race was based on a similar appeal—in the wake of the Easter Sunday terror attack, he guaranteed security and justice to the victims.

In nearby Pakistan, ex-prime minister Imran Khan has said, 'We are not far from the Sri Lanka moment when our public pours out into streets.'[69] Both Khan and Rajapaksa lost their positions in the same month. Other South Asian nations have obvious signs of political dysfunction, too—rampant corruption, arbitrary detention, militarization, human rights abuse and worse economic conditions. All this creates a safe haven for terrorism to flourish.

We must be careful with our analysis. Ethnic and religious divisions, for example, have not played a substantial role in Sri Lanka's recent turmoil. This suggests early signs of a coherent political ideology among the protestors. The Sri Lankan protest was effectively an Arab Spring moment. It had sprung up in protest against the same three problems that moved crowds in Tunis and Benghazi ten years ago—autocratic rule, rampant corruption and economic stagnation. In 2011, these revolts ended almost uniformly in more dysfunction than before. The protestors divided into bitter, warring camps and ideologies; some rallied to the Islamic State, while others became supporters of the kind of police states and illiberal governments they had once marched against.

Today, as Human Rights Watch warns,[70] Sri Lanka is such a police state, with over three thousand protestors arrested arbitrarily under the draconian emergency rule.[71] The other camp, the Islamist reaction, is in incubation. The country's present fragility is conducive to attracting terrorism from external sources, which devastated the country in 2019 and could resurface anytime again.

### TERRORISM IN SOUTH ASIA AND AYMAN AL-ZAWAHIRI'S DEATH

According to the Global Terrorism Index 2022,[72] 'South Asia recorded the highest number of terrorist explosive attacks in 2021 of any region in the world.' South Asia and sub-Saharan Africa have recorded more terrorism deaths than the entire Middle East and North Africa (MENA) in the last three years. South Asia remains the region with the worst average Global Terrorism Index (GTI) score (Figure 5.1).

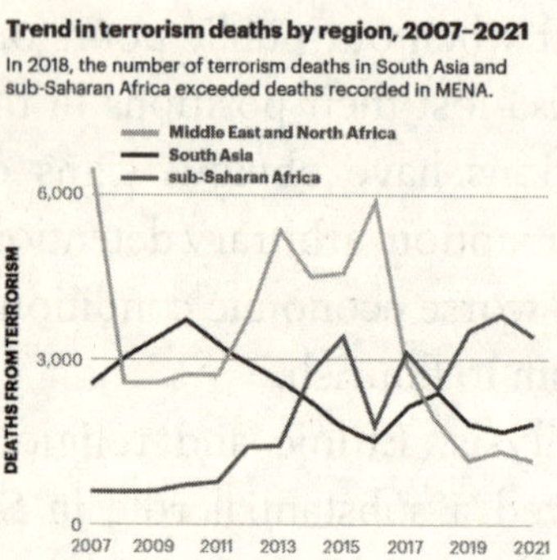


**GTI score, rank and change in score, 2011-2021**

| Country | Average Score | Change 2011-2021 | Change 2020-2021 |
|---|---|---|---|
| South Asia | 5.559 | -0.783 | -0.203 |
| North America | 4.421 | 1.507 | -0.298 |
| Middle East and North Africa | 3.547 | -0.616 | -0.294 |
| South America | 2.903 | 0.275 | -0.049 |
| sub-Saharan Africa | 2.400 | 0.433 | 0.004 |
| Asia-Pacific | 2.045 | -0.146 | -0.219 |
| Europe | 1.368 | -0.412 | -0.284 |
| Russia and Eurasia | 0.876 | -2.460 | -0.405 |
| Central America And the Caribbean | 0.202 | -1.132 | -0.052 |

FIGURE 5.1: Trends in Terrorism Deaths and GTI Score
(Source: Dragonfly Terrorism Tracker, IEP calculations)

Jeff Smith from the Heritage Institute rightly argues that despite the good news of the July 2022 assassination of Ayman al-Zawahiri, deputy of Osama bin Laden, there is also bad news. He says, 'One year after the chaotic [US] withdrawal from Afghanistan, Zawahiri's presence in the capital of Kabul confirms fears that the country again would become a safe haven for international terrorists.'[73] The precision strike on Ayman al-Zawahiri without any civilian casualties underscores the strength of the US to hunt down any terrorist in hiding. Biden administration's approval of a CIA-organized drone-launched Hellfire missile strike—the first since the American exit from Kabul a year ago—sent a clear message to nations providing safe refuge to terrorist leaders.

One week after Zawahiri's death, Abdul Wali, also known as Omar Khalid Khorasani, was killed.[74] It was a major blow to his armed group, known as the Tehreek-e-Taliban Pakistan (TTP). Khalid Khorasani had carried out some of the deadliest attacks in Pakistan, including the Easter Sunday attack in 2016,[75] killing seventy-five people from the Christian community. It was believed that he was close to Osama bin Laden and al-Zawahiri. He had a more tenuous relationship with IS.

On 29 April 2019, six months before the IS leader Abu Bakar al-Baghdadi's assassination, the IS chief appeared in his last video message,[76] claiming responsibility for the Sri Lankan Easter Sunday terror attack,[77] which killed 260 innocents. Member-state UN investigations revealed that the IS did not, in fact, direct or facilitate the attacks, nor did it know about them in advance. The UN Security Council report reads, 'In a video message in late April 2019, Abu Bakr al-Baghdadi confirmed that ISIL still aspires to have global relevance and expects to achieve this by continuing to carry out international attacks. The group is currently dependent upon ISIL-inspired attacks, such as the Easter Sunday bombings in Sri Lanka, which Abu Bakr al-Baghdadi mentioned but which ISIL leadership clearly knew nothing about in advance.'[78]

Clearly, locally inspired independent terror cells and their South Asian proxies remain, even if the terrorist leaders are killed, and the main groups are dismantled. It was clear from Ayman al-Zawahiri's death that Al Qaeda continues to cooperate closely with the Haqqani network. Zawahiri was living in a guest house in Kabul owned by Sirajuddin Haqqani at the time of the air strike.

There are four critical takeaways for South Asian leaders in the wake of the Zawahiri attack.

First, the weakening of the al-Qaeda network has forced violent extremist groups in Afghanistan to go underground, decentralize and join independent jihadi terror cells operating abroad, especially in other South Asian nations. Dysfunctional states like Pakistan and Sri Lanka will be lucrative grounds for their activities. Intelligence operatives, financiers, logisticians, couriers, and recruiters will sustain them. Since Afghanistan is cut off diplomatically from the West and ruled by an internationally unrecognized regime, addressing the longer-term counterterrorism in the region will be much more involved than the one-off killing of an individual.

Second, the single biggest success of the United States in Afghanistan was the US Special Operations Command (SOCOM) in over-the-horizon operations to take out most of the al-Qaeda leadership. But the capacity to deploy these operations without ground resources and directly hit the terrorists at will can lure the US into a false sense of security. Washington should find a solution to the limits of its over-the-horizon counterterrorism engagements, such as those due to the absence of local partners and operational support. The current limited reach of local engagements should be quietly expanded with a redefined and clear US–South Asia counterterrorism strategy.

Third, Washington should take strict measures against nations that safeguard terrorists and publicly question if those nations are living up to their counterterrorism commitments. At present, while the Taliban and US bicker, the former has guaranteed that Afghanistan would not harbour anyone who violated the 2020 Doha Accords. The United States, in turn, has assured them support for counterterrorism against al-Qaeda and the Islamic State-Khorasan Province (IS-K). Commitments may be tricky to uphold, but it's not an impossible task, and Washington must insist on it.

Finally, building trust in the region is the key. Major General Mahmud Ali Durrani (retired), in his paper on finding a common denominator to fight terrorism, says, 'The fundamental challenges to fighting terrorism, especially in South Asia, are the existing differences between various nations and the presence of serious mistrust due to the ongoing conflicts.'[79] A common denominator is absent—the critical ingredient of coordinating the counterterrorism strategies of the numerous South Asian nations. Multilateral engagement has to be strengthened. Sreoshi Sinha[80] is right to argue that strengthening the multilateral agenda is 'an option for nations like India to collaborate with the US and lobby for Washington to be admitted as an observer state to the Bay of Bengal Initiative for Multi-Sectoral Technical and Economic Cooperation (BIMSTEC)'.[81] Terrorist networks and modern economies have one thing in common—they are international affairs. Fighting one and building the other—the two faces of the same South Asian coin—cannot only be Washington's job, or Delhi's or Colombo's. Every country's discipline and perseverance count, and every weak link, every autocrat, weakens the chain.

# Annexure 1

## Rajapaksa Family Rule in Sri Lanka

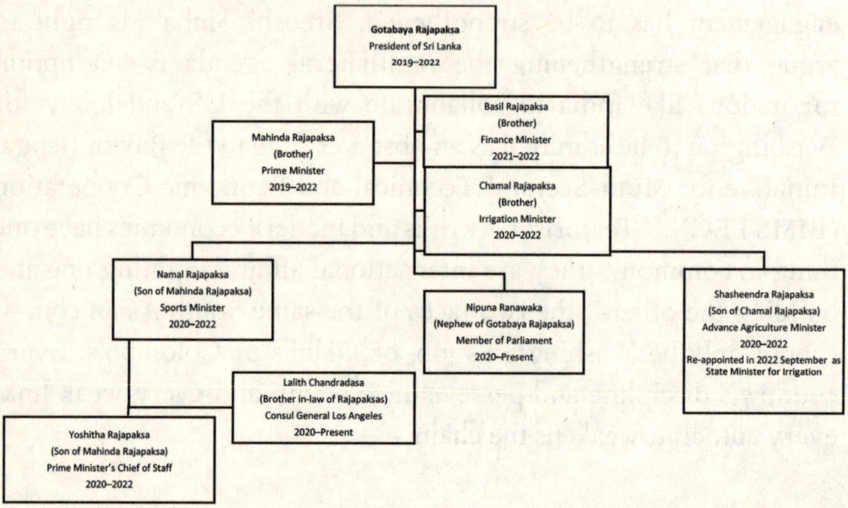


Rajapaksa Family Rule 2019–2022

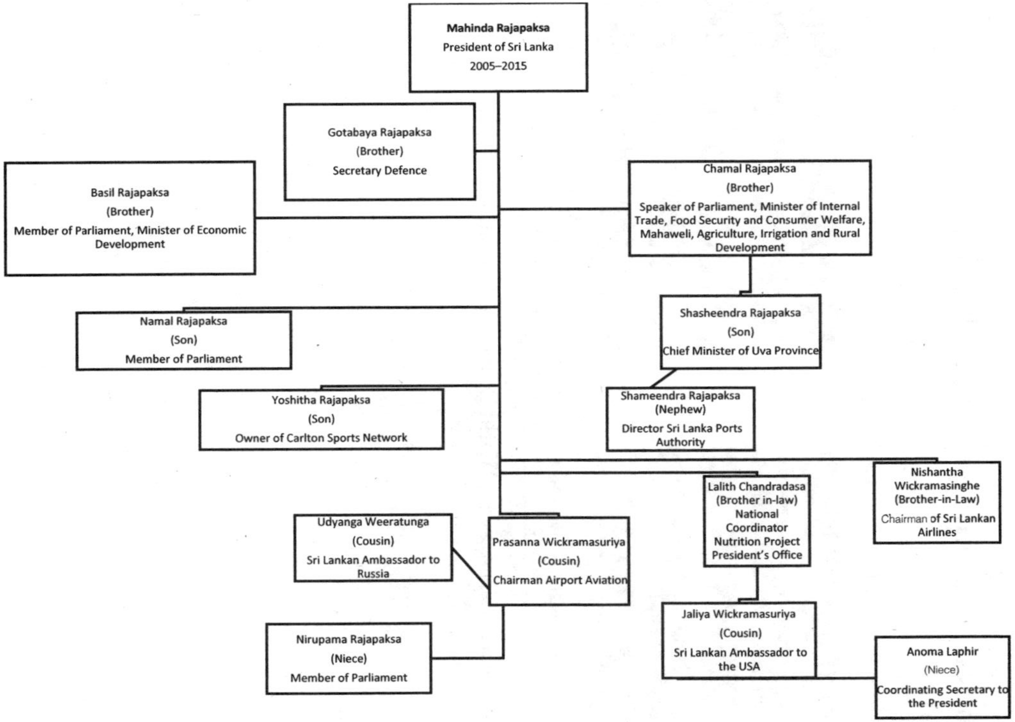


Rajapaksa Family Rule 2005–2015

# Annexure 2

Figure Showing the Most Severe Global Risk Factor

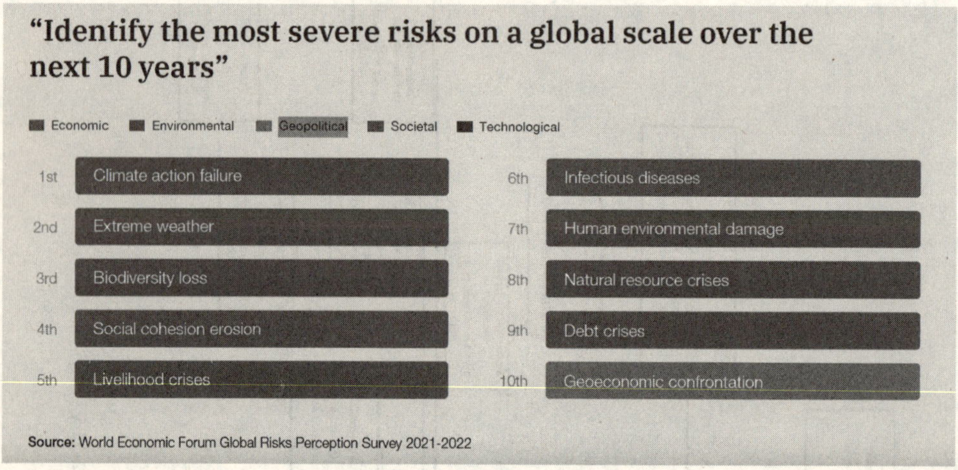


Source: *Global Risks Report 2022*, World Economic Forum, 14

# NOTES

INTRODUCTION

1 Paul Kelso, 'Sri Lanka Risks Running Out of "Food and Fuel" and Could Descend into "Anarchy" Former Energy Minister Says', Sky News, 7 May 2022, https://news.sky.com/story/sri-lanka-could-descend-into-anarchy-as-it-risks-running-out-of-food-and-fuel-former-energy-minister-says-12606983.

2 Sachini Perera, 'Tracking Militarization in Sri Lanka under the Gotabaya Rajapaksa Regime', Crowdsourced Document, https://docs.google.com/spreadsheets/d/1j50Lzq6ZfkWjNJ0SzU57X3iJQTz1uJXEwBrU5lrOT5c/edit#gid=0.

CHAPTER 1: CHINA IN SRI LANKA

ONE

1 Asanga Abeyagoonasekera, 'Sethusamudram to Samudra Manthan: Containing Chinese Influence in Sri Lanka', Observer Research Foundation, 28 July 2020, https://www.orfonline.org/expert-speak/sethusamudram-to-samudra-manthan-containing-chinese-influence-in-sri-lanka/.

2 K. Chandrasekaran, Sachin Bhardwaj, Shipra Jain, Rohit Singh Sahani, Akansha Baliga, Prashant Sarkar and G. Raghuram, 'Sethusamudram Shipping Canal Project: In Need of Divine Intervention', Emerald Insight, 10 July 2014, https://doi.org/10.1108/CASE.IIMA.2019.000033.

3 'DMK MP TR Baalu Writes to PM Modi, Requests to Revive Sethu Samudram Project', Times Now News, 10 July 2020, https://www.timesnownews.com/videos/times-now/india/dmk-mp-tr-baalu-writes-to-pm-modi-requests-to-revive-sethu-samudram-project/66952.

4 Namal Rajapaksa, 'Namal Reveals Facts about Sri Lanka's Second Commercial City', in Sinhala, YouTube, 18 July 2020, https://www.youtube.com/watch?v=CvuDf8WJnDQ.

5 Sidhant Sibal, 'America's Largest Warship Likely to Exercise with Indian Navy amid Chinese Aggression', WION, 19 July 2020, https://www.wionews.com/india-news/wion-exclusive-americas-largest-warship-likely-to-exercise-with-indian-navy-amid-chinese-aggression-314502.

6 CNBC-TV18, 'Geopolitics of Opportunity: As World Rebalances, How Should India Capitalise?', Facebook, 20 July 2020, https://fb.watch/cPx-m32GQg/.

7 Abhijit Singh, 'Make the Right Call on "Malabar" Going Quad', *The Hindu*, 20 July 2020, https://www.thehindu.com/opinion/lead/make-the-right-call-on-malabar-going-quad/article32132584.ece.

8 'Remarks by State Councilor and Foreign Minister Wang Yi at the China-US Think Tank's Media Forum', Ministry of Foreign Affairs China, 9 July 2020, https://www.fmprc.gov.cn/mfa_eng/wjb_663304/wjbz_663308/2461_663310/202007/t20200709_468780.html.

9 C. Raja Mohan, *Samudra Manthan: Sino-Indian Rivalry in the Indo-Pacific* (Washington, D.C.: Carnegie Endowment for International Peace, 2012).

10 Zulfick Farzan, 'MCC Contains Harmful Elements: Review Committee', NewsFirst, 25 June 2020, https://www.newsfirst.lk/2020/06/25/mcc-contains-harmful-elements-review-committee/.

11 'Do Not Recommend Sri Lanka Signing MCC in Its Current State: Review Committee Chair', EconomyNext, 3 July 2020, https://economynext.com/do-not-recommend-sri-lanka-signing-mcc-in-its-current-state-review-committee-chair-71661/.

TWO

12 Asanga Abeyagoonasekera, 'CCP Centenary and the Growing Chinese Footprint in Sri Lanka', Observer Research Foundation, 25 January 2021, https://www.orfonline.org/expert-speak/ccp-centenary-growing-chinese-footprint-srilanka/.

13 Andrew Greene, 'Suspected Chinese Submarine Drone Found by Indonesian Fishermen in Crucial Maritime Passage to Australia', ABC News, 31 December 2020, https://www.abc.net.au/news/2020-12-31/suspected-chinese-submarine-drone-found-by-indonesian-fishermen/13022488.

14 Jagannath Panda, 'India–China Relations to Stay Contrarian in 2021', *9DASHLINE*, 4 January 2021, https://www.9dashline.com/article/india-china-relations-to-stay-contrarian-in-2021.

15 Darshana M. Baruah, 'India in the Indo-Pacific: New Delhi's Theater of Opportunity', Carnegie Endowment for International Peace, 30 June 2020, https://carnegieendowment.org/2020/06/30/india-in-indo-pacific-new-delhi-s-theater-of-opportunity-pub-82205.

16 'US Strategic Framework for the Indo-Pacific', Trump White House Archives, 2021, https://trumpwhitehouse.archives.gov/wp-content/uploads/2021/01/IPS-Final-Declass.pdf.

17 Scott Detrow, 'Why Biden's National Security Advisor Plans to Focus on the U.S. Middle Class', NPR, 30 December 2020, https://www.npr.org/sections/biden-transition-updates/2020/12/30/951280373/why-bidens-national-security-adviser-plans-to-focus-on-the-u-s-middle-class.

18 Joseph R. Biden Jr, 'Why America Must Lead Again', *Foreign Affairs*, March–April 2020, https://www.foreignaffairs.com/articles/united-states/2020-01-23/why-america-must-lead-again.

19 'SLPP and China's CCP Hold Joint Seminar on "Governance Experience" ', NewsWire, 5 November 2020, http://www.newswire.lk/2020/11/05/slpp-and-chinas-ccp-hold-joint-seminar-on-governance-experience/.

20 'Pathfinder Ties Up with Communist Party of China', Daily News, 24 November 2020, http://www.dailynews.lk/2020/11/24/finance/234281/pathfinder-ties-communist-party-china.

21 'China Metallurgical's Construction of Sri Lanka's Central Expressway Has Started', Seetao, 16 September 2020, https://www.seetao.com/details/39120.html.

22 'Statement on Decision of Millennium Challenge Corporation Board', US Embassy in Sri Lanka, 17 December 2020, https://lk.usembassy.gov/statement-on-decision-of-millennium-challenge-corporation-board/.

23 'Jaishankar Expressed Concerns over China's "Influence in Indian Projects" ', *The Sunday Times*, 10 January 2021, http://www.sundaytimes.lk/210110/news/jaishankar-expressed-concerns-over-chinas-influence-in-indian-projects-427885.html.

24 Bilahari Kausikan, 'The Binary Fallacy: How Not to Think about Geopolitics in East Asia', CIRCD, 2018, https://www.cirsd.org/en/horizons/horizons-spring-2018-issue-no-11/the-binary-fallacy-how-not-to-think-about-geopolitics-in-east-asia.

25 Rory Medcalf, *Indo-Pacific Empire: China, America and the Contest for the World's Pivotal Region* (Manchester: Manchester University Press, 2020).

26 'India Calls on Sri Lanka to Fulfil Expectations of Tamil Minority', *Hindustan Times*, 6 January 2021, https://www.hindustantimes.com/india-news/india-calls-on-sri-lanka-to-fulfil-expectations-of-tamil-minority/story-V49Alanoa5X2O5BqoDNa3H.html.

27 'Deeply Saddened by Scenes at Jaffna University: UK Minister', *Daily Mirror*, 11 January 2021, http://www.dailymirror.lk/print/front_page/Deeply-saddened-by-scenes-at-Jaffna-University-UK-Minister/238-203525.

28 C. Raja Mohan, 'Delhi Must Manage Dynamic Interaction between Domestic Policies of India and Its Neighbours', *The Indian Express*, 12 January 2021, https://indianexpress-com.cdn.ampproject.org/c/s/indianexpress.com/article/opinion/columns/india-foreign-policy-subcontinent-politics-s-jaishankar-7142414/lite/.

THREE

29 Asanga Abeyagoonasekera, 'America and China Dock in Sri Lanka', in *President Biden and South Asia*, Edited by C. Raja Mohan and John Vater (Singapore: The Institute of South Asian Studies, January 2021), https://www.academia.edu/49131803/America_and_China_Dock_in_Sri_Lanka.

30 'No Compromise on Independence and Sovereignty, President Tells Pompeo', *Daily FT*, 29 October 2020, http://www.ft.lk/front-page/No-compromise-on-independence-and-sovereignty-Presidenttells-Pompeo/44-708220.

31 K.E. Haushofer, L.A. Tambs and E.J. Brehm, *An English Translation and Analysis of Major General Karl Ernst Haushofer's 'Geopolitics of the Pacific Ocean: Studies on the Relationship between Geography and History'*, edited and updated by Lewis A. Tambs, translated by Ernst J. Brehm (Lewiston, New York: Edwin Mellen Press, 2002).

32 Amanda Hodge, 'Mike Pompeo Tells Sri Lanka to Spurn "Predator" China', *The Australian*, 28 October 2020, https://www.theaustralian.com.au/world/mike-pompeo-tells-sri-lanka-to-spurn-predator-chi na/news-story/22085a62c825f9aae8342577206c19ca.

33 Rose Stephanie Justin, 'US Offers Sri Lanka a Different Vision, Accuses China of Being a Predator', Zenger, 30 October 2020, https://www.zenger.news/2020/10/30/us-offers-sri-lanka-a-different-vision-accuses-china-of-being-a-predator/.

34 Devirupa Mitra, 'Seven Years on, India Now Backs a Defence Pact between the US and Maldives', The Wire, 13 September 2020, https://thewire.in/south-asia/seven-years-on-india-now-backs-a-defence-pact-between-the-us-and-maldives.

35 'Frigate "P625" Gifted to Sri Lanka Navy by China', *Navy Recognition*, https://navyrecognition.com/index.php/news/defence-news/2019/august/7412-frigate-p625-gifted-to-sri-lanka-navy-by-china.html.

36 Sachin Parashar, 'Chinese Submarine Docking in Lanka "inimical" to India's Interests: Govt', *The Times of India*, 4 November 2014, https://timesofindia.indiatimes.com/india/Chinese-submarine-dockingin-Lanka-inimical-to-Indias-interests-Govt/articleshow/45025487.cms.

37 *Manifesto of the Sri Lanka Podujana Peramuna: Vistas of Prosperity and Splendour*, 2019, http://www.doc.gov.lk/images/pdf/NationalPolicyframeworkEN/FinalDovVer02-English.pdf.

38 Ada Derana, 'Get Real with Mahieash Johnney, Episode 58, Foreign Relations under President Gotabaya',

39 YouTube, 20 August 2020, https://www.youtube.com/watch?v=SoIkn3D47co&t=1461s. Ada Derana, 'Foreign Secretary Joins Indeewari Amuwatte', YouTube, 25 October 2020, https://www.youtube.com/watch?v=apUiGomqr5M&t=494s.
40 Gotabaya Rajapaksa @GotabayaR, '#SriLanka will always maintain a neutral stand in foreign policy and will not get entangled in struggles between power blocs', Twitter, 28 October 2020, 1:55 pm, https://twitter.com/gotabayar/status/1321367382376419328.
41 Devirupa Mitra, 'Sri Lanka Worried about Indian Ocean's Securitisation, Impact of Quad Military Alliance', The Wire, 30 October 2020, https://thewire.in/diplomacy/sri-lanka-worried-about-indianoceans-securitisation-impact-of-quad-military-alliance.
42 T.C. Schaffer and H.B. Schaffer, *India at the Global High Table: The Quest for Regional Primacy and Strategic Autonomy* (Washington, D.C.: Brookings Institution Press, 2016), p. 69.
43 Ambassador Shirley Amarasinghe took leadership of the 3rd UNCLOS, which gave birth to the present international codified law as the 'umbrella convention' in the world order of activities relating to the sea and maritime affairs in 1982, signed at Montego Bay.
44 'George Yeo: S'pore's "Chinese-ness" Promotes Strong Ties with China, but Must Set Itself Apart Politically', Mothership, 30 October 2020, https://mothership.sg/2020/10/george-yeo-singapore-china-30-years/.
45 'CoE Unimpressed by Singapore FTA', *Daily FT*, 31 December 2018, http://www.ft.lk/top-story/CoE-unimpressed-by-Singapore-FTA/26-669850.
46 Anja Manuel, *This Brave New World: India, China, and the United States* (New York: Simon and Schuster, 2016), p. 106.
47 Asanga Abeyagoonasekera, 'Sri Lanka and the Return of Geopolitics in the Indo-Pacific', Observer Research Foundation, 17 October 2020, https://www.orfonline.org/expert-speak/srilanka-return-geopolitics-indo-pacific/.
48 ISAS Events, 'Changing Geopolitics of South Asia', YouTube, 13 October 2020, https://www.youtube.com/watch?v=I78RqPGz4w8.
49 'Communist Party of China and SLPP Hold Virtual Advanced Seminar on Governance', *Daily FT*, 6 November 2020, http://www.ft.lk/news/Communist-Party-of-China-and-SLPP-hold-virtual-advancedseminar-on-governance/56-708551.
50 Salvatore Babones, 'Election 2020: Biden and Harris Could Be Bad News for India's Modi', *Foreign Policy*, 6 November 2020, https://foreignpolicy.com/2020/11/06/biden-harris-india-modi-election/.

51 Zulfick Farzan, 'No Thirteenth Amendment or Provincial Councils: Rear Admiral Sarath Weerasekera', NewsFirst, 30 September 2020, https://www.newsfirst.lk/2020/09/30/no-13th-amendment-or-provincial-councils-rear-admiral-sarath-weerasekera/.

FOUR

52 Asanga Abeyagoonasekera, 'Before the Phoenix Nest: Questions Surrounding the Port City of Colombo', Observer Research Foundation, 1 May 2021, https://www.orfonline.org/expert-speak/before-the-phoenix-nest-questions-surrounding-the-port-city-of-colombo/.

53 Thierry Pairault, 'China in Africa: Phoenix Nests versus Special Economic Zones', HAL Open Science, hal-01968812, 3 January 2019, https://hal.archives-ouvertes.fr/hal-01968812/document.

54 Ibid.

55 '"Port City Would Become a Chinese Colony through the Economic Commission Bill": MP Wijeyadasa Rajapakshe', Colombo Page, 15 April 2021, http://www.colombopage.com/archive_21A/Apr15_1618509702CH.php.

56 Ranjith Padmasiri, 'Port City Bill: ASG Presents Amendments: Petitioners See Threat to Sovereignty', *The Sunday Times*, 25 April 2021, http://www.sundaytimes.lk/210425/news/port-city-bill-asg-presents-amendments-petitioners-see-threat-to-sovereignty-441201.html.

57 Asanga Abeyagoonasekera, 'Bandwagoning with China: Geopolitics of a Container Terminal in Sri Lanka', Observer Research Foundation, 16 February 2021, https://www.orfonline.org/expert-speak/bandwagoning-china-geopolitics-container-terminal-srilanka/.

58 'Jointly Advance the China–Sri Lanka Friendship and Build the Great Wall Against Covid-19', Ministry of Foreign Affairs of the Peoples Republic of China, 1 April 2021, https://www.fmprc.gov.cn/mfa_eng/wjb_663304/zwjg_665342/zwbd_665378/202104/t20210401_9169593.html.

59 'Chinese-Built Railways Put Ethiopia on Track to Meet 2025 Development Goals', Embassy of the People's Republic of China in the Republic of South Africa, 10 May 2018, https://www.mfa.gov.cn/ce/cezanew/eng/znjl/t1558493.htm.

60 Abdi Latif Dahir, 'Thanks to China, Africa's Largest Free Trade Zone Has Launched in Djibouti', Quartz Africa, 9 July 2018, https://qz.com/africa/1323666/china-and-djibouti-have-launched-africas-biggest-free-trade-zone/.

61 Mordechai Chaziza, 'China's Military Base in Djibouti', The Begin-Sadat Center for Strategic Studies, Mideast Security and Policy Studies, no. 153

(August 2018), https://besacenter.org/wp-content/uploads/2018/08/153-Chaziza-Chinas-Military-Base-in-Djibouti-web.pdf.

62 'Touchroad Djibouti Special Economic Zone: African Fulcrum of Belt and Road', *China Daily*, 12 August 2016, https://www.chinadaily.com.cn/m/touchroad/2016-08/12/content_26451224.htm.

63 *Monica Wang*, 'China's Strategy in Djibouti: Mixing Commercial and Military Interests', in 'Asia Unbound' blog, Council on Foreign Relations, 13 April 2018, https://www.cfr.org/blog/chinas-strategy-djibouti-mixing-commercial-and-military-interests.

64 'Republic of Djibouti, High-Level Development Exchange: Launch of "Vision Djibouti 2035"', World Bank Group, 91695, June 2014, http://documents1.worldbank.org/curated/fr/870641468246040913/pdf/916950WP0DJIBO0x385342B00300PUBLIC0.pdf.

FIVE

65 Asanga Abeyagoonasekera, 'How China Won over Local Agency to Shackle Sri Lanka Using a Port City', Observer Research Foundation, 22 June 2021, https://www.orfonline.org/expert-speak/how-china-won-over-local-agency-to-shackle-sri-lanka-using-a-port-city/.

66 'Executive Order Addressing the Threat from Securities Investments That Finance Certain Companies of the People's Republic of China', The White House, 3 June 2021, https://www.whitehouse.gov/briefing-room/statements-releases/2021/06/03/fact-sheet-executive-order-addressing-the-threat-from-securities-investments-that-finance-certain-companies-of-the-peoples-republic-of-china/.

67 'Panama Cuts Ties with Taiwan in Favour of China', BBC, 13 June 2017, https://www.bbc.com/news/world-latin-america-40256499.

68 'Panama Awards $1.4B Bridge Project to Chinese Group', *Daily FT*, 7 December 2018, https://www.ft.lk/international/Panama-awards----1-4-b-bridge-project-to-Chinese-group/49-668318.

69 Ramon Martinez, 'China Plays Lead Role in Panama's First Digital Free Zone', Newsroom Panama, 16 July 2019, https://www.newsroompanama.com/news/china-plays-lead-role-in-panamas-first-digital-free-zone.

70 Mat Youkee, 'Has China's Winning Streak in Panama Ended?', Dialogo Chino, 25 March 2020, https://dialogochino.net/en/trade-investment/34472-has-chinas-winning-streak-in-panama-ended/.

71 'Opp. Leader Never Made Formal Request to Postpone Sessions: Speaker', *Daily Mirror*, 28 May 2021, http://www.dailymirror.lk/breaking_news/Opp-Leader-never-made-formal-request-to-postpone-sessions-Speaker/108-212937.

72 'Port Workers Engage in a Silent Protest Opposing the Sale of the ECT', NewsFirst, 17 December 2020, https://www.newsfirst.lk/2020/12/17/port-workers-engage-in-a-silent-protest-opposing-the-sale-of-the-ect/.
73 'Do Not Recommend Sri Lanka Signing MCC in Its Current State: Review Committee Chair', EconomyNext, 3 July 2020, https://economynext.com/do-not-recommend-sri-lanka-signing-mcc-in-its-current-state-review-committee-chair-71661/.
74 Robert D. Putnam, 'Diplomacy and Domestic Politics: The Logic of Two-Level Games', Cambridge University Press 42, no. 3 (22 May 2009), https://www.cambridge.org/core/journals/international-organization/article/abs/diplomacy-and-domestic-politics-the-logic-of-twolevel-games/B2E11FB757C4465C4097015BD421035F.
75 ' "Colombo Port City Economic Commission Act" Breeds Economic and Geostrategic Concerns', *The Financial Express*, 2 June 2021, https://www.financialexpress.com/world-news/colombo-port-city-economic-commission-act-breeds-economic-and-geostrategic-concerns/2263439/.
76 Liu Xin (@LiuXinin, 'Just point a finger at China and keep accusing even with no case, and #Xinjiang genocide is a so-called fact in Western discourse. Jayanath Colombage, DG of Institute of National Security of Sri Lanka, says if a lie is spread a thousand times, people begin to think it's true', Twitter, 6 June 2021, 3:20 pm, https://twitter.com/LiuXininBeijing/status/1401481490475536385?s=20.
77 Meera Srinivasan, 'Expect China-Style Development for Sri Lanka: Gotabaya', *The Hindu*, 9 October 2020, https://www.thehindu.com/news/international/expect-china-style-development-for-sri-lanka-gotabaya/article32816165.ece.
78 'No More Big Foreign Loan Projects: PB', NewsWire, 29 May 2021, https://www.newswire.lk/2021/05/29/no-more-big-foreign-loan-projects-pb/.
79 Ibid.
80 'Gotabaya Rajapaksa Thanks Xi Jinping for China's Vote against UNHRC Resolution against Sri Lanka', *The New Indian Express*, 30 March 2021, https://www.newindianexpress.com/world/2021/mar/30/gotabaya-rajapaksa-thanks-xi-jinping-for-chinas-vote-against-unhrc-resolution-against-sri-lanka-2283608.html.
81 'Sri Lanka, China Vow to Enhance Pragmatic Military Cooperation', CGTN, 29 April 2021, https://news.cgtn.com/news/2021-04-29/Sri-Lanka-China-vow-to-enhance-pragmatic-military-cooperation-ZQzRoJheVO/index.html.

82 'Sri Lanka Calls on US House Foreign Affairs Committee Not to Proceed with Resolution', *Daily FT*, 5 June 2021, https://www.ft.lk/front-page/Sri-Lanka-calls-on-US-House-Foreign-Affairs-Committee-not-to-proceed-with-Resolution/44-718881.

83 Ibid.

84 Kiran Sharma, 'Sri Lanka Remains in "State of Denial" over Alleged War Crimes', Nikkei Asia, 22 April 2021, https://asia.nikkei.com/Politics/Sri-Lanka-remains-in-state-of-denial-over-alleged-war-crimes.

85 'EU Parliament Adopts Resolution on Sri Lanka; Wants PTA Repealed, GSP+ Withdrawn', EconomyNext, 11 June 2021, https://economynext.com/eu-parliament-adopts-resolution-on-sri-lanka-wants-pta-repealed-gsp-withdrawn-82891/.

SIX

86 Asanga Abeyagoonasekera, 'The Rajapaksa Triumvirate and the CCP Backdoor in Sri Lanka', Observer Research Foundation, 10 August 2021, https://www.orfonline.org/expert-speak/rajapaksa-triumvirate-and-ccp-backdoor-in-sri-lanka/.

87 'Sri Lanka's Rajapaksa Family Tightens Grip with Ministerial Picks', Al Jazeera, 9 July 2021, https://www.aljazeera.com/news/2021/7/9/sri-lankas-rajapaksa-family-tightens-grip-with-ministerial-picks.

88 Shawn Yuan, 'Xi Says No More "Bullying" as China Marks Party Centenary', Al Jazeera, 1 July 2021, https://www.aljazeera.com/news/2021/7/1/china-xi-speech-100-years-ccp.

89 'Nipped in the Bud: The Suppression of the China Democracy Party', Human Rights Watch 12, no. 5 (September 2000), https://www.hrw.org/reports/2000/china/china009-01.htm#P104_9729.
Zhu Muzhi during a meeting organized by the Foreign Correspondents Club of China in April 1999, referring to people with views differing from the official CCP line.

90 Pingp, 'The Great Firewall of China: Background', Torfox, 1 June 2011, https://cs.stanford.edu/people/eroberts/cs181/projects/2010-11/FreedomOfInformationChina/the-great-firewall-of-china-background/index.html.

91 Rana Mitter and Elmira Bayrasli, 'The Communist Party of China at 100', Project Syndicate, 6 July 2021, https://www.project-syndicate.org/podcasts/the-communist-party-of-china-at-100?utm_source=Project%20Syndicate%20Newsletter&utm_campaign=9cb60ba8a4-contributor_newsletter_mitter_07_06_2021&utm_medium=email&utm_

term=0_73bad5b7d8-9cb60ba8a4-105011141&mc_cid=9cb60ba8a4&mc_eid=0a97a32d2f&barrier=accesspaylog.

92 'Address by Mahinda Rajapaksa at CPC and World Political Parties Summit', Embassy of the People's Republic of China in the Democratic Socialist [Republic] of Sri Lanka, 8 July 2021, https://www.fmprc.gov.cn/ce/celk/eng/xwdt/t1890684.htm.

93 Jonathan E. Hillman, Emperor's New Road: China and the Project of the Century (New Haven: Yale University Press, 2020).

94 Matthew Karnitschnig, 'Beijing's Balkan Backdoor', *Politico*, 13 July 2017, https://www.politico.eu/article/china-serbia-montenegro-europe-investment-trade-beijing-balkan-backdoor/.

95 'Lanka Issuing Coin to Mark Chinese Communist Party's Centenary', *The Sunday Times*, 27 June 2021, https://www.sundaytimes.lk/210627/news/lanka-issuing-coin-to-mark-chinese-communist-partys-centenary-447626.html.

96 'Chinese Govt's Commitment to Sri Lanka's Independence Greatly Appreciated: PM', *Daily News*, 19 June 2021, http://www.dailynews.lk/2021/06/19/local/251973/chinese-govt's-commitment-sri-lanka's-independence-greatly-appreciated-pm.

97 Colombo Gazette, 'Sri Lanka Signs China Sponsored Statement Raising Concerns on Human Rights in UK', NewsWire, 14 July 2021, https://www.newswire.lk/2021/07/14/sri-lanka-signs-china-sponsored-statement-raising-concerns-on-human-rights-in-uk/.

SEVEN

98 Asanga Abeyagoonasekera, 'Political Economic Instability and Wang Yi's Peripheral Diplomacy in Sri Lanka', Observer Research Foundation, 4 February 2022, https://www.orfonline.org/expert-speak/political-economic-instability-and-wang-yi/.

99 Ruwani Fonseka, 'People's Bank Pays USD 6.9 Million to Seawin Biotech', The Sunday Morning, 7 Jan 2022, https://www.themorning.lk/peoples-bank-pays-usd-6-9-million-to-seawin-biotech/.

100 Uditha Jayasinghe, 'Sri Lanka's President Asks China to Restructure Debt Repayments', Reuters, 10 January 2022, https://www.reuters.com/article/ousivMolt/idUSKBN2JJ092.

101 Bharatha Mallawarachi, Krutika Pathi and Joe McDonald, 'China Becomes Wild Card in Sri Lanka's Debt Crisis', The Diplomat, 20 May 2022, https://thediplomat.com/2022/05/china-becomes-wild-card-in-sri-lankas-debt-crisis/.

102 Meera Srinivasan, 'Jaishankar, Basil Rajapaksa hold "Detailed" Virtual Meeting', *The Hindu*, 15 January 2022, https://www.thehindu.com/

news/national/jaishankar-holds-talks-with-lankan-minister-discusses-india-assisted-projects-seeks-early-release-of-indian-fishermen/article38273834.ece.

103 Harsh V. Pant and Aditya Gowdara Shivamurthy, 'As India and China Compete, Smaller States Are Cashing In', *Foreign Policy*, 24 January 2022, https://foreignpolicy.com/2022/01/24/india-china-competition-investment-sri-lanka-maldives/.

104 Zulfick Farzan, ' "This Is Just the Beginning" Says Chinese Ambassador as Jaffna Visit Ends', NewsFirst, 17 December 2021, https://www.newsfirst.lk/2021/12/17/this-is-just-the-beginning-says-chinese-ambassador-as-jaffna-visit-ends/.

105 'Finance Minister Basil Rajapaksa Concludes a Successful Visit to New Delhi', High Commission of Sri Lanka in India, 3 December 2021, https://slhcindia.org/index.php?option=com_content&view=article&id=1154:finance-minister-basil-rajapaksa-concludes-a-successful-visit-to-new-delhi-&catid=50:demo-category&Itemid=1.

106 'China Suspends Energy Projects in Sri Lankan Islands Located Close to India over "Security Concern" from "Third Party" ', *The Economic Times*, 3 December 2021, https://economictimes.indiatimes.com/news/international/business/china-suspends-lanka-energy-project-over-security-concerns/articleshow/88067029.cms?from=mdr.

107 Ganeshan Wignaraja, 'Will China Rescue Sri Lanka's Economy in 2022?', Institute of South Asian Studies, 11 January 2022, https://www.isas.nus.edu.sg/papers/will-china-rescue-sri-lankas-economy-in-2022/.

108 'Chinese Foreign Minister's Sri Lanka Visit Highlighted Beijing's Relentless Drive in Indian Ocean Region, and India's Challenge', *The Indian Express*, 12 January 2022, https://indianexpress.com/article/opinion/editorials/wang-yo-to-sri-lanka-on-indian-ocean-region-7718355/.

109 NewsFirst, 'Minister Susil Premajayantha Interview', YouTube, 4 January 2022, https://www.youtube.com/watch?v=pziKapwbic8.

110 Zulfick Farzan, 'Maithripala Flays Government for Sacking Susil Premajayantha', NewsFirst, 4 January 2022, https://www.newsfirst.lk/2022/01/04/maithripala-flays-government-for-sacking-susil-premajayantha/.

EIGHT

111 Asanga Abeyagoonasekera, 'Sri Lankan Crisis between Debt Trap and Strategic Trap: The Chinese Stake', Institute for Security and Development Policy, 22 April 2022, https://isdp.eu/sri-lankan-crisis-between-debt-trap-and-strategic-trap-the-chinese-stake/.

112 Chinese Embassy in Sri Lanka @ChinaEmbSL, 'The Chinese "Debt Trap" Is a Myth', Twitter, 28 November 2021, 5:45 pm, https://twitter.com/

ChinaEmbSL/status/1464931016548630534?s=20&t=wT11iS90P_LM9Q1XnwaV3g.

113 Eric Olander, 'Deborah Brautigam: No Evidence of Chinese Debt Traps in Africa', 30 July 2019, China Global South Project, MP3 audio, https://chinaafricaproject.com/podcasts/podcast-china-debt-trap-africa-deborah-brautigam/.

114 'Sri Lanka on Alarming Path towards Recurrence of Grave Human Rights Violations: UN Report', United Nations Human Rights, 27 January 2021, https://www.ohchr.org/en/press-releases/2021/01/sri-lanka-alarming-path-towards-recurrence-grave-human-rights-violations-un.

115 'Port Workers to Rally against a Gang of Four: Work-to-Rule from the 29th: Rs. 15 Billion Commission in the Offing?', Lanka Leader, 28 January 2021, https://english.theleader.lk/news/1118-port-workers-to-rally-against-a-gang-of-four-work-to-rule-from-the-29th-rs-15-billion-commission-in-the-offing..

116 Ayeshea Perera, 'Sri Lanka: Protest at President Rajapaksa's Home Turns Violent', BBC, 1 April 2022, https://www.bbc.com/news/world-asia-60950266.

117 'Sri Lanka's New Finance Minister Ali Sabry Resigns a Day after Appointment', *Outlook*, 5 April 2022, https://www.outlookindia.com/international/sri-lanka-s-new-finance-minister-ali-sabry-resigns-a-day-after-appointment-news-190122.

118 'Sri Lanka President Expands Cabinet amid Economic Crisis Protests', Al Jazeera, 18 April 2022, https://www.aljazeera.com/news/2022/4/18/sri-lanka-president-expands-cabinet-amid-economic-crisis-protests.

119 PTI, 'Sri Lanka's Economy Worsens, Forex Reserves Plummeting to USD 500 Million', The Print, 4 April 2022, https://theprint.in/world/sri-lankas-economy-worsens-forex-reserves-plummeting-to-usd-500-million/902532/.

120 Bharatha Mallawarachi, 'China Mulls Package to Ease Sri Lanka's Economic Crisis', ABC News, 21 March 2022, https://abcnews.go.com/International/wireStory/china-mulls-package-ease-sri-lankas-economic-crisis-83574264.

121 Samantha Custer, Tanya Sethi, Jonathan Solis, Joyce Jiahui Lin, Siddhartha Ghose, Anubhav Gupta, Rodney Knight and Austin Baehr, *Silk Road Diplomacy: Deconstructing Beijing's Toolkit to Influence South and Central Asia* (Williamsburg, VA: AidData at William & Mary, 2019), https://docs.aiddata.org/reports/silk-road-diplomacy-2019.html.

122 Bharatha Mallawarachi, Krutika Pathi and Joe McDonald, 'China Becomes Wild Card in Sri Lanka's Debt Crisis', The Diplomat, 20 May 2022, https://

thediplomat.com/2022/05/china-becomes-wild-card-in-sri-lankas-debt-crisis/.

123 'US $ 1Bn Loan from China to Settle Previous Loans', *Daily Mirror*, 26 March 2022, https://www.dailymirror.lk/breaking_news/US-1Bn-loan-from-China-to-settle-previous-loans/108-233843.

124 Adnan Aamir, '$385 Bn of China's Belt and Road Lending Kept Undisclosed: Report', Nikkei Asia, 29 September 2021, https://asia.nikkei.com/Spotlight/Belt-and-Road/385bn-of-China-s-Belt-and-Road-lending-kept-undisclosed-report.

125 Wade Shepard, 'The Story Behind the World's Emptiest International Airport', *Forbes*, 28 May 2016, https://www.forbes.com/sites/wadeshepard/2016/05/28/the-story-behind-the-worlds-emptiest-international-airport-sri-lankas-mattala-rajapaksa/?sh=418bddd97cea.

126 Maria Abi-Habib, 'How China Got Sri Lanka to Cough Up a Port', *The New York Times*, 25 June 2018, https://www.nytimes.com/2018/06/25/world/asia/china-sri-lanka-port.html.

127 Brahma Chellaney, 'China's Debt-Trap Diplomacy', Project Syndicate, 23 January 2017, https://www.project-syndicate.org/commentary/china-one-belt-one-road-loans-debt-by-brahma-chellaney-2017-01.

128 Peter Fabricius, 'Will Mombasa and Port Sudan Be Ceded to Foreign Powers to Repay Debt?', Institute for Security Studies, 30 April 2020, https://issafrica.org/iss-today/is-covid-19-enabling-debt-trap-diplomacy.

129 *National Policy Framework: Vistas of Prosperity and Splendour*, 2019, http://www.doc.gov.lk/images/pdf/NationalPolicyframeworkEN/FinalDovVer02-English.pdf.

130 'Vice President Mike Pence's Remarks on the Administration's Policy towards China', Hudson Institute, 4 October 2018, https://www.hudson.org/events/1610-vice-president-mike-pence-s-remarks-on-the-administration-s-policy-towards-china102018.

131 Jeremy Mark, 'China's Real "Debt Trap" Threat', Atlantic Council Blog, 13 December 2021, https://www.atlanticcouncil.org/blogs/new-atlanticist/chinas-real-debt-trap-threat/.

132 Lee Jones and Shahar Hameiri, 'Debunking the Myth of "Debt-trap Diplomacy": How Recipient Countries Shape China's Belt and Road Initiative', Chatham House, August 2020, https://www.chathamhouse.org/sites/default/files/2020-08-25-debunking-myth-debt-trap-diplomacy-jones-hameiri.pdf.

133 Ganeshan Wignaraja, Dinusha Panditaratne, Pabasara Kannangara and Divya Hundlani, 'Chinese Investment and the BRI in Sri Lanka', Chatham House, March 2020, https://www.chathamhouse.org/sites/default/files/CHHJ8010-Sri-Lanka-RP-WEB-200324.pdf.

134 Ankit Panda, 'Sri Lanka Formally Hands Over Hambantota Port to Chinese Firms on 99-Year Lease', The Diplomat, 11 December 2017, https://thediplomat.com/2017/12/sri-lanka-formally-hands-over-hambantota-port-to-chinese-firms-on-99-year-lease/.

135 PTI, 'Report that Hambantota Port Deal Has Second 99-Year Lease Extension Runs Counter to Facts: China', *The Economic Times*, 24 February 2021, https://economictimes.indiatimes.com/news/international/world-news/report-that-hambantota-port-deal-has-second-99-year-lease-extension-runs-counter-to-facts-china/articleshow/81194141.cms?from=mdr.

136 Mohammed Rasooldeen, 'Pakistani PM Urges Sri Lanka to Join China Corridor', *Arab News*, 24 February 2021, https://www.arabnews.com/node/1815371/world

137 Colombo International Container Terminals Limited (CICT) is a joint venture Company between China Merchants Port Holdings Company Limited and Sri Lanka Ports Authority (SLPA), https://www.cict.lk/.

138 Natasha Gunaratne, 'Falling Port Volumes See Lacklustre Interest in Port Tender', *The Sunday Times*, 12 July 2009, https://www.sundaytimes.lk/090712/FinancialTimes/ft305.html.

139 'UN Human Rights Council Passes Resolution Mandating War Crimes Evidence Collection on Sri Lanka', Tamil Guardian, 23 March 2021, https://www.tamilguardian.com/content/un-human-rights-council-passes-resolution-mandating-war-crimes-evidence-collection-sri-lanka.

140 'Sri Lanka Supports China in Human Rights Issues', The-Quest, 27 June 2021, https://www.the-quest.org/news/sri-lanka-supports-china-in-human-rights-issues/.

141 Ambika Satkunanadan, 'Securitisation and Militarisation in Sri Lanka: A Continuum', *Daily FT*, 20 Jan 2021, https://www.ft.lk/columns/Securitisation-and-militarisation-in-Sri-Lanka-A-continuum/4-711827.

142 'Sri Lanka: UN Report Describes Alarming Rights Situation', Human Rights Watch, 3 March 2022, https://www.hrw.org/news/2022/03/03/sri-lanka-un-report-describes-alarming-rights-situation.

143 'Talk on China in Rajapakse 2.0: Ports and Geo-Political Challenges', Vivekananda International Foundation, 5 August 2021, https://www.vifindia.org/event/report/2021/august/05/talk-on-china-in-rajapakse-2-0-ports-and-geo-political-challenges.

NINE

144 Asanga Abeyagoonasekera, 'The Trap: China's Debt Restructuring and Strategic Manipulation in Sri Lanka', Institute for Security and Development Policy, 18 August 2022, https://www.isdp.eu/the-trap-chinas-debt-restructuring-and-strategic-manipulation-in-sri-lanka/.

145 Daniel Kliman, Rush Doshi, Kristine Lee and Zack Cooper, 'Grading China's Belt and Road', CNAS, April 2019, https://s3.amazonaws.com/files.cnas.org/CNAS+Report_China+Belt+and+Road_final.pdf.

146 Nicholas Casey and Clifford Krauss, 'It Doesn't Matter If Ecuador Can Afford This Dam. China Still Gets Paid', *The New York Times*, 24 December 2018, https://www.nytimes.com/2018/12/24/world/americas/ecuador-china-dam.html.

147 Elizabeth C. Economy, *The World According to China* (Medford, MA, USA: Polity, 2021).

148 PTI, 'Report That Hambantota Port Deal Has Second 99-Year Lease Extension Runs Counter to Facts: China', *The Indian Express*, 24 February 2021, https://indianexpress.com/article/world/hambantota-port-deal-china-7203319/.

149 'Sri Lanka Made "Dumb Bets" on China: CIA Chief on Crises-Hit Country', *Hindustan Times*, 21 July 2022, https://www.hindustantimes.com/world-news/sri-lanka-made-dumb-bets-on-china-cia-chief-on-crises-hit-country-101658368141545.html.

150 Asanga Abeyagoonasekera, 'Sri Lankan Crisis between Debt-Trap and Strategic Trap: The Chinese Stake', Institute for Security and Development Policy, 26 April 2022, https://isdp.eu/sri-lankan-crisis-between-debt-trap-and-strategic-trap-the-chinese-stake/.

151 Sumathi Bala, 'Sri Lanka "Can't Get Out of Crisis without China," Analyst Says', CNBC, 20 July 2022, https://www.cnbc.com/2022/07/20/china-can-play-critical-role-to-help-sri-lanka-with-its-debt-problems-analysts-say.html.

152 Andrea Shalal, Marc Jones, 'Yellen Says It's in China's Interest to Restructure Sri Lanka's Debt', Reuters, 14 July 2022, https://www.reuters.com/world/asia-pacific/yellen-says-its-chinas-interest-restructure-sri-lankas-debt-2022-07-14/.

153 Ibid.

154 'IMF Managing Director Kristalina Georgieva Urges G20 Leadership to Address "Exceptionally Uncertain" Global Outlook', International Monetary Fund, 16 July 2022, https://www.imf.org/en/News/Articles/2022/07/16/pr22261-md-g20-statement.

155 Uditha Jayasinghe, 'India to Support Crisis-Hit Sri Lanka's Economic Recovery', Reuters, 23 June 2022, https://www.reuters.com/world/asia-pacific/india-says-will-support-crisis-hit-sri-lankas-economic-recovery-2022-06-23/.

156 Aquilah Latiff and Anushka Wijesinha, 'Understanding China's Role in Sri Lanka's Debt Restructuring Efforts', The Diplomat, 2 August 2022,

https://thediplomat.com/2022/08/understanding-chinas-role-in-sri-lankas-debt-restructuring-efforts/.

157 Kallol Bhattacherjee, '"Opaque" Loans from China Hurt Sri Lanka: USAID Administrator', *The Hindu*, 28 July 2022, https://www.thehindu.com/news/international/opaque-loans-from-china-hurt-sri-lanka-usaid-administrator/article65690958.ece.

158 Weizhen Tan, 'About Half of China's Loans to Developing Countries Are "Hidden", Study Finds', CNBC, 12 July 2019, https://www.cnbc.com/2019/07/12/chinas-lending-to-other-countries-jumps-causing-hidden-debt.html.

TEN

159 Asanga Abeyagoonasekera, 'Chinese Spy Ship and Lanka's Tilt towards Beijing', Observer Research Foundation, 17 August 2022, https://www.orfonline.org/expert-speak/chinese-spy-ship-and-lankas-tilt-towards-beijing/.

160 Sandeep Dikshit, 'While Sri Lanka Denies Chinese Spy Ship to Dock, Pak Warship Heads towards Colombo', *The Tribune*, 8 Aug 2022, https://www.tribuneindia.com/news/nation/while-sri-lanka-denies-chinese-spy-ship-to-dock-pak-warship-heads-towards-colombo-420131.

161 IANS 'After Pressure from India, Sri Lanka Urges China to Defer Entry of Chinese "Spy" Ship', *The Economic Times*, 6 August 2022, https://economictimes.indiatimes.com/news/defence/after-pressure-from-india-sri-lanka-urges-china-to-defer-entry-of-chinese-spy-ship/articleshow/93394073.cms.

162 PTI, 'Sri Lanka Looks for Friendly Settlement of Chinese Research Ship Issue: PM Gunawardena', *The Economic Times*, 2 August 2022, https://economictimes.indiatimes.com/news/international/world-news/sri-lanka-looks-for-friendly-settlement-of-chinese-research-ship-issue-pm-gunawardena/articleshow/93304363.cms?from=mdr.

163 Ibid.

164 Rhea Mogul, 'Chinese Research Ship Yuan Wang 5 Docks at Sri Lanka's Hambantota Port', CNN, 16 August 2022, https://www.cnn.com/2022/08/16/asia/india-china-tensions-military-ship-docks-sri-lanka-intl-hnk/index.html.

165 Elizabeth C. Economy, *The World According to China* (Medford, MA, USA: Polity, 2021).

166 'China Reached 500 Kilometers from Kanyakumari, Know How It Happened and What Is India's Plan Now', NewsNCR, 29 May 2021, https://www.newsncr.com/national/china-reached-500-kilometers-from-kanyakumari-know-how-it-happened-and-what-is-indias-plan-now/.

167 Snehesh Alex Philip, 'The 3 Foundational Agreements with US and What They Mean for India's Military Growth', The Print, 27 October 2020, https://theprint.in/defence/the-3-foundational-agreements-with-us-and-what-they-mean-for-indias-military-growth/531795/.

168 Shihar Aneez and Ranga Sirilal, 'Chinese Submarine Docks in Sri Lanka Despite Indian Concerns', Reuters, 2 November 2014, https://www.reuters.com/article/sri-lanka-china-submarine/chinese-submarine-docks-in-sri-lanka-despite-indian-concerns-idINKBN0IM0LU20141102.

169 'Australia Says Chinese Spy Ship's Presence Off West Coast "Concerning" ', Reuters, 13 May 2022, https://www.reuters.com/world/asia-pacific/australian-defence-minister-says-chinese-spy-ship-waters-an-act-aggression-2022-05-13/.

170 Dzirhan Mahadzir, 'Chinese Navy Ship Operating Off Australia, Canberra Says', USNI News, 13 May 2022, https://news.usni.org/2022/05/13/chinese-navy-ship-operating-off-of-australia-canberra-says.

171 Christopher Walker and Jessica Ludwig, 'From "Soft Power" to "Sharp Power": Rising Authoritarian Influence in the Democratic World', *Sharp Power: Rising Authoritarian Influence*, National Endowment for Democracy, https://www.ned.org/wp-content/uploads/2017/12/Introduction-Sharp-Power-Rising-Authoritarian-Influence.pdf.

172 'How China Reacted to Sri Lanka Blocking Its Submarine with Eye on India, NDTV, 12 May 2017, https://www.ndtv.com/india-news/how-china-reacted-to-sri-lanka-blocking-its-submarine-with-eye-on-india-1692870.

173 Steven Feldstein, 'The Global Expansion of AI Surveillance', Carnegie Endowment for International Peace, 17 September 2019, https://carnegieendowment.org/2019/09/17/global-expansion-of-ai-surveillance-pub-79847.

174 Elias Biryabarema, 'Uganda's Cash-Strapped Cops Spend $126 Million on CCTV from Huawei', Reuters, 15 August 2019, https://www.reuters.com/article/us-uganda-crime/ugandas-cash-strapped-cops-spend-126-million-on-cctv-from-huawei-idUSKCN1V50RF.

175 China Will Agree to $4 Billion Aid for Sri Lanka "At Some Point": Bloomberg News', Reuters, 15 July 2022, https://www.reuters.com/world/asia-pacific/china-will-agree-4-billion-aid-sri-lanka-at-some-point-bloomberg-news-2022-07-15/.

176 Saibal Dasgupta, 'China Using Sri Lanka's Indebtedness to Show Military Muscle', VOA, 3 August 2022, https://www.voanews.com/a/china-using-sri-lanka-s-indebtedness-to-show-military-muscle-/6684873.html.

CHAPTER 2: GEOPOLITICS

ONE

1 Asanga Abeyagoonasekera, 'Sri Lanka and the Return of Geopolitics in the Indo-Pacific', Observer Research Foundation, 17 October 2020, https://www.orfonline.org/expert-speak/srilanka-return-geopolitics-indo-pacific/.
2 The Federal Government, *Policy Guidelines for the Indo-Pacific* (Berlin: Federal Foreign Office, August 2020), https://www.auswaertiges-amt.de/blob/2380514/f9784f7e3b3fa1bd7c5446d274a4169e/200901-indo-pazifik-leitlinien--1--data.pdf.
3 European Commission, 'EU-China: A Strategic Outlook', Joint Communication to the European Parliament, the European Council and the Council, 23 March 2019, https://ec.europa.eu/info/sites/default/files/communication-eu-china-a-strategic-outlook.pdf.
4 'U.S. Hopes to Institutionalize Quad Grouping to Counter China: Pompeo', Kyodo News, 10 October 2020, https://english.kyodonews.net/news/2020/10/aa9a15837419-us-hopes-to-institutionalize-quad-grouping-to-counter-china-pompeo.html.
5 David Wainer, 'Kissinger Warns US and China Must Set Limits to Avoid a Blowup', Bloomberg, 8 October 2020, https://www.bloomberg.com/news/articles/2020-10-07/kissinger-warns-u-s-and-china-must-set-limits-to-avoid-a-blowup.
6 Easwaran Ratnum, 'Sri Lanka Should Engage with China in Ways That Protect Its Sovereignty: Alaina B. Teplitz', *Daily Mirror*, 5 October 2020, http://www.dailymirror.lk/opinion/Sri-Lanka-should-engage-with-China-in-ways-that-protect-its-sovereignty-Alaina-B-Teplitz/231-197159.
7 'Media Statement 20201005', Embassy of the People's Republic of China in the Democratic Socialist [Republic] of Sri Lanka, 5 October 2020, http://lk.chineseembassy.org/eng/xwdt/t1822074.htm.
8 John Laidler, 'Memo to America: Not Everyone Wants to Be Like You', The Harvard Gazette, 6 November 2018, https://news.harvard.edu/gazette/story/2018/11/harvard-professor-stephen-walt-urges-shift-in-u-s-foreign-policy/.
9 Shihar Aneez, 'Sri Lanka's Economic Dependency Deepens after Moody's Rate Cut', *Daily FT*, 13 October 2020, https://www.ft.lk/columns/Sri-Lanka-s-economic-dependency-deepens-after-Moody-s-rate-cut/4-707393.
10 StratNewsGlobal, 'We Have an "India First" Policy on Strategic Security: Sri Lankan Foreign Secretary', YouTube, 24 August 2020, https://www.youtube.com/watch?v=VPgEp7nGCOk.

11 'Sri Lanka to Get US$ 500m Loan from China', NewsWire, 11 October 2020, http://www.newswire.lk/2020/10/11/sri-lanka-to-get-us-500m-loan-from-china/.

12 Saneet Chakradeo, 'How Does the India–China Rivalry Affect Secondary State Behaviour in South Asia?' Brookings Blog, 28 April 2020, https://www.brookings.edu/blog/up-front/2020/04/28/sambandh-blog-how-does-the-india-china-rivalry-affect-secondary-state-behaviour-in-south-asia/.

13 Ljiljana Grubic, 'Serbia's Increasing Importance for China's BRI', Emerging Europe, 25 June 2019, https://emerging-europe.com/voices/serbias-increasing-importance-for-chinas-bri/.

14 'China, Algeria Develop Fruitful Cooperation under BRI', CGTN Africa, 21 June 2019, https://africa.cgtn.com/2019/06/21/china-algeria-develop-fruitful-cooperation-under-bri/.

15 'UAE Signs Deals with China under Belt and Road Initiative', Economist Intelligence, 8 May 2019, http://country.eiu.com/article.aspx?articleid=1857968369&Country=United%20Arab%20Emirates&topic=P_7.

16 *Manifesto of the Sri Lanka Podujana Peramuna: Vistas of Prosperity and Splendour*, 2019, http://www.doc.gov.lk/images/pdf/NationalPolicyframeworkEN/FinalDovVer02-English.pdf.

17 Srikanth Kondapalli, 'Quad's No Longer Just Oceanic Foam', *Deccan Herald*, 11 October 2020, https://www.deccanherald.com/opinion/quad-s-no-longer-just-oceanic-foam-900277.html.

18 ISAS Events, 'Changing Geopolitics of South Asia', YouTube, 13 October 2020, https://www.youtube.com/watch?v=I78RqPGz4w8.

19 Asanga Abeyagoonasekera, *Conundrum of an Island: Sri Lanka's Geopolitical Challenges* (Singapore: World Scientific Publishing, 2021), https://worldscientific.com/worldscibooks/10.1142/12028.

TWO

20 Asanga Abeyagoonasekera, 'Sri Lanka and the Coming Biden Foreign Policy', Observer Research Foundation, 23 November 2020, https://www.orfonline.org/expert-speak/sri-lanka-and-the-coming-biden-foreign-policy-77271/.

21 Dayan Jayatilleka, 'US China and the Mutable Matrix of Authoritarianism and Tyranny', *Daily FT*, 29 October 2020, http://www.ft.lk/columns/US-China-and-the-mutable-matrix-of-authoritarianism-and-tyranny/4-708177.

22 Lauren Feiner, 'Read Joe Biden's First Speech as President-Elect', CNBC, 7 November 2020, https://www.cnbc.com/2020/11/07/read-joe-biden-acceptance-speech-full-text.html.

23 Srikanth Kondapalli, 'Between the Devil and the Deep Sea', *Deccan Herald*, 8 November 2020, https://www.deccanherald.com/opinion/between-the-devil-and-the-deep-sea-912737.html.

24 'Xi's SCO Speech Illustrates China's Commitment to Multilateralism, Regional Stability, Experts Say', Xinhuanet, 11 November 2020, http://www.xinhuanet.com/english/2020-11/11/c_139506967.htm.

25 'Executive Order on Addressing the Threat from Securities Investments that Finance Communist Chinese Military Companies', The White House, 12 November 2020, https://trumpwhitehouse.archives.gov/presidential-actions/executive-order-addressing-threat-securities-investments-finance-communist-chinese-military-companies/.

26 'Pathfinder and Huawei in Strategic Partnership to Develop ICT', *Daily FT*, 9 November 2020, http://www.ft.lk/front-page/Pathfinder-and-Huawei-in-strategic-partnership-to-develop-ICT/44-708648.

27 'Communist Party of China and SLPP Hold Virtual Advanced Seminar on Governance', *Daily FT*, 6 November 2020, http://www.ft.lk/news/Communist-Party-of-China-and-SLPP-hold-virtual-advanced-seminar-on-governance/56-708551.

28 'Basil Wants SLPP to Become Like China's CCP or India's BJP', NewsWire, 30 July 2020, http://www.newswire.lk/2020/07/30/basil-wants-slpp-to-become-like-chinas-ccp-or-indias-bjp/.

29 Shashi Tharoor, 'Constrain, Not Contain, China', *The Week*, 16 July 2020, https://www.theweek.in/columns/shashi-tharoor/2020/07/16/constrain-not-contain-china.html.

THREE

30 Asanga Abeyagoonasekera, 'Sri Lanka Facing the New Cold War in the Indo-Pacific Theatre', Observer Research Foundation, 20 December 2020, https://www.orfonline.org/expert-speak/srilanka-facing-new-cold-war-indo-pacific-theatre/.

31 Content is the intellectual property of ESRI and is used here with permission. Copyright © 2022 ESRI and its licensors. All rights reserved.

32 John Clancy, *'The Most Dangerous Moment of the War': Japan's Attack on the Indian Ocean, 1942* (Oxford: Casemate, 2015).

33 'U.S. Urges Sri Lanka to Make "Difficult" Choices over China Ties', Reuters, 22 October 2020, https://www.reuters.com/article/us-usa-srilanka-pompeo-idUSKBN2772R7.

34 Kelum Bandara, 'High Level Interaction and Commitment: The Way Forward on Path to Recovery', *Daily Mirror*, 10 December 2020, http://www.dailymirror.lk/opinion/High-level-interaction-and-commitment-the-way-foward-on-path-to-recovery/172-201525.

35 Uditha Jayasinghe, 'Up to the People to Give Us a Two-Thirds Majority: Basil', *Daily FT*, 29 July 2020, https://www.ft.lk/opinion/Up-to-the-people-to-give-us-a-two-thirdsmajority-Basil/14-703809.
36 John Ratcliffe, 'China Is National Security Threat No. 1', *Wall Street Journal*, 3 December 2020, https://www.wsj.com/articles/china-is-national-security-threat-no-1-11607019599.
37 Meera Srinivasan, 'India, Sri Lanka, Maldives Agree to Improve Intel Sharing', *The Hindu*, 28 November 2020, https://www.thehindu.com/news/national/nsa-doval-holds-bilateral-talks-with-maldivian-defence-minister/article33198873.ece.
38 '6th Indo-Sri Lanka Defence Dialogue', Ministry of Defence Sri Lanka, 8 April 2019, http://www.defence.lk/Article/view_article/329.
39 Sachin Parashar, 'Chinese Submarine Docking in Lanka "Inimical" to India's Interests: Govt', *The Times of India*, 4 November 2014, https://timesofindia.indiatimes.com/india/Chinese-submarine-docking-in-Lanka-inimical-to-Indias-interests-Govt/articleshow/45025487.cms.
40 'Analysis: Covert Israeli-Saudi Meeting Sends Biden a Strong Message on Iran', Reuters, 27 November 2020, https://www.reuters.com/article/uk-israel-saudi-analysis/analysis-covert-israeli-saudi-meeting-sends-biden-a-strong-message-on-iran-idUKKBN28714Q.

FOUR

41 Asanga Abeyagoonasekera, 'Bandwagoning with China: Geopolitics of a Container Terminal in Sri Lanka', Observer Research Foundation, 16 February 2021, https://www.orfonline.org/expert-speak/bandwagoning-china-geopolitics-container-terminal-srilanka/.
42 Truth with Chamuditha, 'Colombo Port Union Leaders Sanjaya Kumara Weligama and Shyamal Sumanarathna, Interview by Chamuditha Samarawickrama', YouTube, 21 January 2021, https://www.youtube.com/watch?v=wY_x-YAm-nw.
43 'Banded Together Only to Protect Port's ECT: Workers Association', *Daily News*, 25 January 2021, https://www.dailynews.lk/2021/01/25/local/239778/banded-together-only-protect-port%E2%80%99s-ect-workers%E2%80%99-association.
44 'Port Workers to Rally against a Gang of Four: Work-to-Rule from the 29th: Rs. 15 Billion Commission in the Offing?', Lanka Leader, 28 January 2021, https://english.theleader.lk/news/1118-port-workers-to-rally-against-a-gang-of-four-work-to-rule-from-the-29th-rs-15-billion-commission-in-the-offing.
45 S. Rubatheesan, 'India Fumes as China Gets Northern Power Projects', *The Sunday Times*, 7 February 2021, http://www.sundaytimes.

lk/210207/news/india-fumes-as-china-gets-northern-power-projects-431894.html.

46 Shihar Aneez and Ranga Sirilal, 'Chinese Submarine Docks in Sri Lanka Despite Indian Concerns', Reuters, 2 November 2014, https://www.reuters.com/article/sri-lanka-china-submarine-idINKBN0IM0LU20141102.

47 Stephen M. Walt, *The Origins of Alliances* (New York: Cornell University Press, 1990).

48 PTI, 'Report That Hambantota Port Deal Has Second 99-Year Lease Extension Runs Counter to Facts: China', *The Economic Times*, 24 February 2021, https://economictimes.indiatimes.com/news/international/world-news/report-that-hambantota-port-deal-has-second-99-year-lease-extension-runs-counter-to-facts-china/articleshow/81194141.cms.

49 Human Rights Watch, *World Report 2021: Events of 2020* (New York: Human Rights Watch, 2021), https://www.hrw.org/sites/default/files/media_2021/01/2021_hrw_world_report.pdf.

50 'Sri Lanka: UN Rights Chief Decries Mounting Abuses', Seven Stories Press, 29 January 2021, https://www.hrw.org/news/2021/01/29/sri-lanka-un-rights-chief-decries-mounting-abuses.

51 *NewsFirst*, 'Admiral Professor Jayanath Colombage, Interview by Asoka Dias', YouTube, 4 February 2021, https://www.youtube.com/watch?v=Vlwmokj6rwU&feature=youtu.be.

52 'Protest March by Tamil Political Parties & Civil Society Concludes, Thousands Attend Final Day March', NewsWire, 7 February 2021, http://www.newswire.lk/2021/02/07/rch-concludes-thound-final-dy-march/.

53 Sachini Perera, 'Tracking Militarization in Sri Lanka under the Gotabaya Rajapaksa Regime', Crowdsourced Database, https://docs.google.com/spreadsheets/d/1j50Lzq6ZfkWjNJoSzU57X3iJQTz1uJXEwBrU5lrOT5c/edit?usp=sharing.

SIX

54 Asanga Abeyagoonasekera, 'Russia and Sri Lanka's Role in Regional Security', Paper presented at the Nineth Conference on International Security, Moscow Russia, 21–24 June 2021, https://www.lankaweb.com/news/items/2021/09/20/russia-and-sri-lankas-role-in-regional-security-at-the-moscow-conference-on-international-security/.

55 'Study and Exploration', *Encyclopaedia Britannica*, https://www.britannica.com/place/Indian-Ocean/Study-and-exploration.

56 Yury Materiy, 'Bilateral Relations between Russia and Sri Lanka Have Developed a Good Pace', *Daily FT*, 12 June 2020, https://www.ft.lk/

Columnists/Bilateral-relations-between-Russia-and-Sri-Lanka-have-developed-a-good-pace/4-701510.

57 'Indo-Pacific: Council Adopts Conclusions on EU Strategy for Cooperation', Council of the European Union, 19 April 2021, https://www.consilium.europa.eu/en/press/press-releases/2021/04/19/indo-pacific-council-adopts-conclusions-on-eu-strategy-for-cooperation/.

58 Frederic Grare, 'The EU's Indo-Pacific Strategy: A Chance for a Clear Message to China and Europe's Allies', European Council on Foreign Relations, 22 April 2021, https://ecfr.eu/article/the-eus-indo-pacific-strategy-a-chance-for-a-clear-message-to-china-and-europes-allies/.

59 'Global Britain in a Competitive Age: The Integrated Review of Security, Defence, Development and Foreign Policy', HM Government, March 2021, https://www.gov.uk/government/publications/global-britain-in-a-competitive-age-the-integrated-review-of-security-defence-development-and-foreign-policy.

60 David Hutt, 'Why Southeast Asia Continues to Buy Russian Weapons', DW, 5 April 2022, https://p.dw.com/p/49TpG.

61 Ian Goldin and Mike Mariathasan, *The Butterfly Defect: How Globalization Creates Systemic Risks, and What to Do about It* (Princeton: Princeton University Press, 2012).

62 Kevin Liptak and Phil Mattingly, 'President Biden on Historic Putin Summit: "I Did What I Came to Do" ', CNN, 17 June 2021, https://edition.cnn.com/2021/06/16/politics/president-biden-president-putin-meeting/index.html.

63 'Sri Lanka Faces "Worst-Ever Beach Pollution" from Burning Ship', DW, 29 May 2021, sri-lanka-faces-worst-ever-beach-pollution-from-burning-ship/a-57712086.

64 'Crimario, Critical Maritime Routes Indo-Pacific', EU Crimario, https://www.crimario.eu/en/the-project/rationale-objectives/.

65 Sreeradha Datta, 'Colombo Port City Project and Indian Concerns', Vivekananda International Foundation, 11 June 2021, https://www.vifindia.org/print/8945.

66 William D. Davidson and Joseph V. Montville, 'Foreign Policy According to Freud', *Foreign Policy* 45, (1981), pp. 145–157, https://doi.org/10.2307/1148317.

67 Suzannah Jessep, 'Track II Diplomacy in the Time of Covid-19', Asia New Zealand Foundation, 11 May 2020, https://www.asianz.org.nz/track-2/track-ii-in-the-time-of-covid-19/.

FIVE

68 Asanga Abeyagoonasekera, 'Remembering a Military Quagmire: The Exit of the United States in Afghanistan and the Impact on the Small States', *South Asia Journal*, 5 September 2021, http://southasiajournal.net/remembering-a-military-quagmire-the-exit-of-the-united-states-in-afghanistan-and-the-impact-on-the-small-states/.

69 R.W. Apple Jr, 'Nation Challenged: News Analysis; Military Quagmire Remembered: Afghanistan Vietnam', *The New York Times*, 31 October 2001, https://www.nytimes.com/2001/10/31/world/nation-challenged-analysis-military-quagmire-remembered-afghanistan-vietnam.html.

70 Harsh V. Pant, 'Shaming of the Western Liberal Order', Observer Research Foundation, 18 August 2021, https://www.orfonline.org/expert-speak/shaming-of-the-western-liberal-order/.

71 Robert M. Gates, *Exercise of Power: American Failures, Successes, and a New Path Forward in the Post-Cold War World* (New York: Knopf, 2020).

72 Ullekh NP, '"The Return of the Taliban Will Have Grave Consequences for India," Says C. Christine Fair', *Open*, 23 July 2021, https://openthemagazine.com/feature/the-return-of-the-taliban-will-have-grave-consequences-for-india-says-c-christine-fair/?fbclid=IwAR1GOfL9ADTY3t-ebl9SyxIJ-GybCZuqRu80B2DxMgnEtSUlDXMrKx7OyQQ.

73 Sarah Chayes, 'The Ides of August', Blog, 2 September 2021, https://www.sarahchayes.org/post/the-ides-of-august?fbclid=IwARobCyQ2a5rEwV_JnuMeNFh9DEnmQIo1ljCuEUviduZCwoowAkhPpwIK4_o.

74 'China Says Taliban Expected to Play "Important" Afghan Peace Role', Reuters, 28 July 2021, https://www.reuters.com/world/china/taliban-delegation-visits-china-taliban-spokesperson-2021-07-28/.

SEVEN

75 Asanga Abeyagoonasekera, 'AUKUS, the Quad, China in Sri Lanka, and India's Security Concerns', *South Asia Journal*, 8 October 2021, http://southasiajournal.net/aukus-the-quad-china-in-sri-lanka-and-indias-security-concerns/.

76 'Remarks by President Biden, Prime Minister Morrison of Australia, and Prime Minister Johnson of the United Kingdom Announcing the Creation of AUKUS', The White House, 15 September 2021, https://www.whitehouse.gov/briefing-room/speeches-remarks/2021/09/15/remarks-by-president-biden-prime-minister-morrison-of-australia-and-prime-minister-johnson-of-the-united-kingdom-announcing-the-creation-of-aukus/.

77 'Fact Sheet: Quad Leaders' Summit', The White House, 24 September 2021, https://www.whitehouse.gov/briefing-room/statements-releases/2021/09/24/fact-sheet-quad-leaders-summit/.

78 Dhruva Jaishankar, 'Why Quad Leaders Would Likely Avoid Mentioning China in Public', CNBC, 24 September 2021, https://www.cnbc.com/video/2021/09/24/quad-summit-what-to-expect-as-us-india-japan-and-australia-meet.html.

79 The Print, 'C. Raja Mohan on How Quad Makes India Stronger & a More Vital Ally for Biden's US with China's Rise', YouTube, 26 September 2021, https://www.youtube.com/watch?v=v_fsOczACdk.

80 'Remarks by President Biden, Prime Minister Morrison, Prime Minister Modi, and Prime Minister Suga at Quad Leaders' Summit', The White House, 24 September 2021, https://www.whitehouse.gov/briefing-room/speeches-remarks/2021/09/24/remarks-by-president-biden-prime-minister-morrison-prime-minister-modi-and-prime-minister-suga-at-quad-leaders-summit/.

81 Carnegie Endowment, 'Special Address: Jayanath Colombage, Foreign Secretary for Sri Lanka', YouTube, 20 September 2021, https://www.youtube.com/watch?v=jHGHHo20ptg.

82 'SL Govt Decides Not to Sign $480mn MCC Agreement', *The Shillong Times*, 1 March 2020, https://theshillongtimes.com/2020/03/01/sl-govt-decides-not-to-sign-480mn-mcc-agreement/.

83 Carnegie Endowment, 'Special Address: Jayanath Colombage, Foreign Secretary for Sri Lanka', YouTube, 20 September 2021, https://www.youtube.com/watch?v=jHGHHo20ptg.

84 Press Trust of India, 'India Natural Ally of G7: PM Modi', *India Today*, 13 June 2021, https://www.indiatoday.in/india/story/india-natural-ally-of-g7-pm-modi-1814374-2021-06-13.

85 Rajeswari Pillai Rajagopalan, 'Does AUKUS Augment or Diminish the Quad?', Observer Research Foundation, 23 September 2021, https://www.orfonline.org/research/does-aukus-augment-or-diminish-the-quad/.

EIGHT

86 Asanga Abeyagoonasekera, 'A World Challenged by Geopolitical Tensions: The Global Risk Report 2022', *South Asia Journal*, 31 January 2020, http://southasiajournal.net/a-world-challenged-by-geopolitical-tensions-the-global-risk-report-2022/.

87 'Global Risks Report 2022', World Economic Forum, https://www.weforum.org/reports/global-risks-report-2022.

88 Ibid.

89 Ibid.

90 Ibid.

91 Ibid.

92 Ibid.

93 Anusha Ondaatjie and Asantha Sirimanne, 'Sri Lanka Asks China for Debt Restructuring During Wang Visit', Bloomberg, 9 January 2022, https://www.bloomberg.com/news/articles/2022-01-09/sri-lanka-asks-china-for-debt-restructuring-during-wang-visit.

94 Ibid.

95 Chinese Embassy Sri Lanka, 'AUKUS: Sword of Damocles that Is Hanging over Our Region', Embassy of the People's Republic of China in the Democratic Socialist Republic of Sri Lanka, 3 November 2021, http://lk.china-embassy.org/eng/xwdt/202111/t20211103_10440415.htm.

96 Ibid.

97 Klaus Schwab and Thierry Malleret, *The Great Narrative: For a Better Future* (Geneva: Forum Publishing, 2022).

NINE

98 Asanga Abeyagoonasekera, 'China in Sri Lanka and the Solomon Islands: Role of Littorals in the Geopolitical Competition', Institute for Security and Development Policy, July 2022, https://www.isdp.eu/publication/china-in-sri-lanka-and-solomon-islands-role-of-littorals-in-the-geopolitical-competition/.

99 Nathan Gardels, 'Brzezinski: America's Global Influence Depends on Cooperation with China', HuffPost, 23 December 2016, https://www.huffpost.com/entry/zbigniew-brzezinski-america-influence-china_n_585d8545e4b0d9a594584a37?section=us_world.

100 'China's Position Paper on Mutual Respect and Common Development with Pacific Island Countries', Embassy of the People's Republic of China in the United States of America, 30 May 2022, http://us.china-embassy.gov.cn/eng/zgyw/202205/t20220531_10694923.htm.

101 Ibid.

102 Ibid.

103 Associated Press, 'What's at Stake for China on South Pacific Visit?' U.S. News, 25 May 2022, https://www.usnews.com/news/world/articles/2022-05-25/explainer-whats-at-stake-for-china-on-south-pacific-visit.

104 'Projects under China-Proposed BRI Benefit PNG Significantly', Global Times, 31 May 2022, https://www.globaltimes.cn/page/202205/1267048.shtml.

105 Bonny Lin, Cristina L. Garafola, Bruce McClintock, Jonah Blank, Jeffrey W. Hornung, Karen Schwindt, Jennifer D.P. Moroney, Paul Orner, Dennis Borrman, Sarah W. Denton, and Jason Chambers, 'A New Framework for Understanding and Countering China's Gray Zone Tactics', RAND Corporation, 2022, https://www.rand.org/pubs/research_briefs/RBA594-1.html.

106 'Battle of Guadalcanal', *Britannica*, https://www.britannica.com/event/Battle-of-Guadalcanal.

107 John Clancy, *'The Most Dangerous Moment of the War': Japan's Attack on the Indian Ocean, 1942* (Oxford: Casemate, 2015).

108 Catherine Wilson, 'China–Solomon Islands Pact: Reading between the Lines', The Interpreter, 8 June 2022, https://www.lowyinstitute.org/the-interpreter/china-solomon-islands-pact-reading-between-lines.

109 Skandha Gunasekara and Mujib Masha, 'In Blow to Ruling Family, Sri Lanka's Prime Minister Quits in Face of Unrest', *The New York Times*, 9 May 2022, https://www.nytimes.com/2022/05/09/world/asia/mahinda-rajapaksa-resigns-sri-lanka.html.

110 'China Says It Has Signed Security Pact with Solomon Islands', Al Jazeera, 19 April 2022, https://www.aljazeera.com/news/2022/4/19/china-says-it-has-signed-security-pact-with-solomon-islands.

111 Shihar Aneez, 'U.S. Wants Military Cooperation Pact with Sri Lanka to Tackle Red Tape: TV', Reuters, 21 July 2019, https://www.reuters.com/article/us-sri-lanka-usa-defence/u-s-wants-military-cooperation-pact-with-sri-lanka-to-tackle-red-tape-tv-idUSKCN1UG062.

112 Asanga Abeyagoonasekera, 'China in Sri Lanka and Solomon Islands: Role of Littorals in the Geopolitical Competition', Institute for Security and Development Policy, 6 July 2022, https://www.isdp.eu/content/uploads/2022/07/Issue-Brief-July-6-2022-China-in-Sri-Lanka-and-Solomon-Islands.pdf.

113 Pentagon, 'Military and Security Developments Involving the People's Republic of China 2021', *Annual Report to Congress*, https://media.defense.gov/2021/Nov/03/2002885874/-1/-1/0/2021-CMPR-FINAL.PDF.

114 Chinese Embassy in Sri Lanka @ChinaEmbSL, 'Ambassador Qi Zhenhong and Madame Jin Qian started their 3-days visit', Twitter, 25 May 2022, 2:19 pm, https://twitter.com/ChinaEmbSL/status/1529384262914301954?s=20&t=RLH5AQXWsASjGY_zE72fgw.

115 Chinese Embassy in Sri Lanka @ChinaEmbSL, 'Ambassador Qi Zhenhong had a boat visit to the Trincomalee Harbour & China Bay', Twitter, 25 May 2022, 10:46 pm, https://twitter.com/ChinaEmbSL/status/1529511742534918144?s=20&t=ofB1p8cO5A9uPqQcKlYuQg.

116 China Aerospace Studies Institute, 'CASI Conference 2022: Great Power Competition and Deterrence', Air University, 3 May 2022, https://www.airuniversity.af.edu/CASI/Display/Article/3017368/casi-conference-2022-great-power-competition-and-deterrence/.

117 'Trendfield Holdings: 2 Uranium Research Permits Granted to China in Niger', Cision, 24 July 2006, https://www.prweb.com/releases/trendfield/holdings/prweb414973.htm.
118 Chinese Embassy in Sri Lanka@ChinaEmbSL, 'Ambassador Qi Zhenhong and Eastern Province Governor @Gyahampath co-chaired a business forum', Twitter, 25 May 2022, 5:12 pm, https://twitter.com/ChinaEmbSL/status/1529427597460791301?s=20&t=ofB1p8cO5A9uPqQcKlYuQg.
119 Robert Spalding, *Stealth War: How China Took over While America's Elite Slept* (New York: Penguin Random House, 2019), p. 76.
120 Kevin Rudd, *Avoidable War: The Dangers of a Catastrophic Conflict between the US and Xi Jinping's China* (New York: Public Affairs, 2022).
121 Kevin Rudd, 'How Ancient Chinese Thought Applies Today, HuffPost, 4 February 2015, https://www.huffpost.com/entry/chinese-strategic-thoughts_b_6417754.
122 Daniel Flitton, 'Who Really Killed the Quad 1.0?', The Interpreter, 2 June 2020, https://www.lowyinstitute.org/the-interpreter/who-really-killed-quad-10.
123 Tom Stayner, 'Anthony Albanese Says Quad Will Work More Closely with Indo-Pacific to Counter China's Influence', SBS News, 24 May 2022, https://www.sbs.com.au/news/article/anthony-albanese-says-quad-will-work-more-closely-with-indo-pacific-to-counter-chinas-influence/wkdumzwfk.
124 'In Asia, President Biden and a Dozen Indo-Pacific Partners Launch the Indo-Pacific Economic Framework for Prosperity', The White House, 23 May 2022, https://www.whitehouse.gov/briefing-room/statements-releases/2022/05/23/fact-sheet-in-asia-president-biden-and-a-dozen-indo-pacific-partners-launch-the-indo-pacific-economic-framework-for-prosperity/.
125 Asanga Abeyagoonasekera, 'Sri Lanka Crisis between Debt Trap and Strategic Trap: The Chinese Stake', Institute for Security and Development Policy, 26 April 2022, https://isdp.eu/sri-lankan-crisis-between-debt-trap-and-strategic-trap-the-chinese-stake/.
126 Dhruva Jaishankar and Tanvi Madan, 'The Quad Needs a Harder Edge', *Foreign Affairs*, 19 May 2022, https://www.foreignaffairs.com/articles/world/2022-05-19/quad-needs-harder-edge.
127 Kevin Liptak, Donald Judd and Nectar Gan, 'Biden Says US Would Respond "Militarily" if China Attacked Taiwan, but White House Insists There's No Policy Change', CNN, 23 May 2022, https://www.cnn.com/2022/05/23/politics/biden-taiwan-china-japan-intl-hnk/index.html.
128 Ibid.
129 Willy C. Shih. 'Testimony before the U.S.-China Economic and Security Review Commission Hearing on Supply Chains', USCC, 9 June 2022,

https://www.uscc.gov/sites/default/files/2022-06/Willy_Shih_Testimony.pdf.

CHAPTER 3 SRI LANKA'S FOREIGN POLICY

ONE

1 Asanga Abeyagoonasekera, 'Democracy and Equidistant Foreign Policy in the Majoritarian Government of Mahinda Rajapaksa', Observer Research Foundation, 11 August 2020, https://www.orfonline.org/expert-speak/democracy-equidistant-foreign-policy-majoritarian-government-mahinda-rajapaksa/.
2 Ajita Kadirgamar, *Lakshman Kadirgamar: The Cake that Was Baked at Home* (Sri Lanka: Vijitha Yapa Publications, 2015).
3 'Handout A: Montesquieu; Excerpts from the Spirit of Laws (1748)', Bill of Rights Institute, https://billofrightsinstitute.org/activities/handout-a-montesquieu-excerpts-from-the-spirit-of-laws-1748.
4 Krishan Francis, 'Rajapaksa Brothers Win by Landslide in Sri Lanka's Election', Yahoo!News, 6 August 2020, https://nz.news.yahoo.com/sri-lanka-polls-rajapaksa-brothers-221030832.html.
5 Asiri Fernando and Nuwan Senarathna, 'No Excuses Not to Deliver: SLPP', *Daily* FT, 8 August 2020, http://www.ft.lk/top-story/No-excuses-not-to-deliver--SLPP/26-704299.

TWO

6 Asanga Abeyagoonasekera, 'Perils of Power in Wounded Old Civilizations', Observer Research Foundation, 14 September 2020, https://www.orfonline.org/expert-speak/perils-of-power-in-wounded-old-civilizations/.
7 Aparna Pandey, *Making India Great: The Promise of a Reluctant Global Power* (Noida, India: HarperCollins, 2020).
8 V.S. Naipaul, *India: A Wounded Civilization* (Reprint, New York: Vintage, 2003).
9 S. Jaishankar, *The India Way: Strategies for an Uncertain World* (Noida, India: HarperCollins, 2020).
10 D.B.S. Jeyaraj, 'Controversial 20th Amendment to the Constitution Passed with a Two-third Majority', dbsjeyaraj.com, 22 October 2020, https://dbsjeyaraj.com/dbsj/archives/70705.
11 Ibid.
12 Francis Fukuyama, *Political Order and Political Decay: From the Industrial Revolution to the Globalization of Democracy* (London: Profile Books, 2015).
13 Matthew Lee, 'US Imposes Sanctions on Chinese Defense Firms over Maritime Dispute', Defense News, 26 August 2020, https://www.

defensenews.com/industry/2020/08/26/us-sanctions-chinese-defense-companies-over-south-china-sea-dispute/.

14 'Big Blow to China as Thailand Scraps KRA Canal Project', WION, 4 September 2020, https://www.wionews.com/world/big-blow-to-china-as-thailand-scraps-kra-canal-project-325142?fbclid=IwAR0oeykHX3H9boTrLgBb7jtRZfweog5_v1Q371op3iPVJTiW_Z_X_FtmgVE.

15 Navya Mudunuri, 'The Malacca Dilemma and Chinese Ambitions: Two Sides of a Coin', Diplomatist, 7 July 2020, https://diplomatist.com/2020/07/07/the-malacca-dilemma-and-chinese-ambitions-two-sides-of-a-coin/.

16 Berkeley Political Review, 'The Malacca Dilemma: A hindrance to Chinese Ambitions in the 21st Century', 26 Aug 2019, https://bpr.berkeley.edu/2019/08/26/the-malacca-dilemma-a-hindrance-to-chinese-ambitions-in-the-21st-century/.

THREE

17 Asanga Abeyagoonasekera, 'Pakistan in Sri Lanka's Changing Foreign Policy', ISAS, 1 April 2021, https://www.isas.nus.edu.sg/papers/pakistan-in-sri-lankas-changing-foreign-policy/.

18 'What the UNHRC Resolution Means for Sri Lanka', Al Jazeera, 25 March 2021, https://www.aljazeera. Com/news/2021/3/25/what-does-un-human-rights-resolution-mean-for-sri-lanka. The resolution allows the UN 'to collect, consolidate, analyse and preserve information and evidence, and to develop possible strategies for future accountability processes for gross violations of human rights or serious violations of international humanitarian law in Sri Lanka, to advocate for victims and survivors, and to support relevant judicial and other proceedings'.

19 Rahim Faiez, 'Pakistan's Prime Minister Khan on "Historic" First Visit to Afghanistan', The Diplomat, 20 November 2020, https://thediplomat.com/2020/11/pakistans-prime-minister-khan-on-historic-first-visit-to-afghanistan/.

20 S. Rubatheesan, 'India Fumes as China Gets Northern Power Projects', *The Sunday Times*, 7 February 2021, http://www.sundaytimes.lk/210207/news/india-fumes-as-china-gets-northern-power-projects-431894.html.

21 Mahinda Aluthgedara, '46th UNHRC Session: 18 Countries Pledge to Support Sri Lanka', *Daily News*, 25 February 2021, https://dailynews.lk/2021/02/25/local/242500/46th-unhrc-session-18-countries-pledgesupport-sri-lanka.

22 '46th Session of the Human Rights Council Report of OHCHR on Promoting Reconciliation, Accountability and Human Rights in Sri Lanka', United Nations Human Rights, 24 February 2021, https://www.ohchr.

org/en/2021/02/46th-session-human-rights-council-report-ohchr-promoting-reconciliation-accountability-and.

23 Kelum Bandara, 'Core-Group Working on SL Seeks Consensual Resolution at UNHRC: Foreign Secretary Admiral Professor Jayanath Colombage', *Daily Mirror*, 25 January 2021, http://www.dailymirror.lk/opinion/Core-group-working-on-SL-seeks-consensual-resolution-at-UNHRC-Foreign-Secretary-Admiral-Prof-Jaya/172-204396.

24 Meera Srinivasan, 'Modi's Address a Message to Our Govt: Wigneswaran', *The Hindu*, 15 March 2015, https://www.thehindu.com/news/international/south-asia/modis-address-a-message-to-our-govt-wigneswaran/article6994042.ece.

25 Meera Srinivasan, 'Sri Lanka Cancels Imran Khan's Parliament Address a Week Ahead of Visit', *The Hindu*, 17 February 2021, https://www.thehindu.com/news/international/sri-lanka-cancels-imran-khans-parliament-address-a-week-ahead-of-visit/article33857707.ece.

26 'Sri Lanka: Covid-19 Forced Cremation of Muslims Discriminatory', Human Rights Watch, 18 January 2021, https://www.hrw.org/news/2021/01/18/sri-lanka-covid-19-forced-cremation-muslims-discriminatory.

27 'Sri Lanka: Events of 2020', Human Rights Watch, https://www.hrw.org/world-report/2021/country-chapters/sri-lanka.

28 Zulfick Farzan, 'India Has No Right to Interfere with Internal Affairs: Sarath Weerasekera', NewsFirst, 9 October 2020, https://www.newsfirst.lk/2020/10/09/india-has-no-right-to-interfere-with-internal-affairs-sarath-weerasekera/.

29 Meera Srinivasan, 'Sri Lanka's Heightening War on the Drug Menace', *The Hindu*, 23 March 2019, https://www.thehindu.com/news/international/sri-lankas-heightening-war-on-the-drug-menace/article26620057.ece.

30 Shafqat Ali, 'Pakistan Sri Lanka Set 1 Billion Trade Target', *The Nation*, 25 February 2021, https://nation.com.pk/25-Feb-2021/pakistan-sri-lanka-set-dollar-1-billion-bilateral-trade-target.

31 Uditha Jayasinghe, 'Exporters Decry CB Order to Convert 25% Forex Earnings', *Daily FT*, 20 February 2021, http://www.ft.lk/top-story/Exporters-decry-CB-order-to-convert-25-forex-earnings/26-713543.

32 'Joint Communique', Foreign Ministry Sri Lanka, https://mfa.gov.lk/joint-communique-on-fm-24-02-2021/.

33 Mohammed Rasooldeen, 'Pakistani PM Urges Sri Lanka to Join China Corridor', *Arab News*, 24 February 2021, https://www.arabnews.com/node/1815371/world.

34 Shihar Aneez and Ranga Sirilal, 'Sri Lanka Rejects Chinese Request for Submarine Visit: Sources', Reuters, 11 May 2017, https://www.reuters.com/article/us-sri-lanka-china-submarine-idUSKBN1871P9.
35 'Sri Lanka to Get US$ 1500 Million from China', NewsWire, 6 February 2021, http://www.newswire.lk/2021/02/06/sri-lanka-to-get-us-1500-million-from-china/.
36 Stephen M. Walt, *The Origins of Alliances* (New York: Cornell University Press, 1990).
37 'Jaishankar Expressed Concerns over China's "Influence" in Indian Projects', *The Sunday Times*, 10 January 2021, http://www.sundaytimes.lk/210110/news/jaishankar-expressed-concerns-over-chinas-influence-in-indian-projects-427885.html.
38 *Manifesto of the Sri Lanka Podujana Peramuna: Vistas of Prosperity and Splendour*, 2019, http://www.doc.gov.lk/images/pdf/NationalPolicyframeworkEN/FinalDovVer02-English.pdf.
39 'China's Influence on Conflict Dynamics in South Asia', United States Institute of Peace, December 2020, https://www.usip.org/sites/default/files/2020-12/20201216-chinas_influence_on_conflict_dynamics_in_south_asia-report.pdf.
40 Ibid.
41 K.J.M. Varma, 'Report that Hambantota Port Deal Has Second 99-Year Lease', *The Times of India*, 24 February 2021, https://timesofindia.indiatimes.com/report-that-hambantota-port-deal-has-second-99-year-lease-extension-runs-counter-to-facts-china/articleshow/81194099.cms.
42 'Chinese President to Visit Sri Lanka', Ministry of Foreign Affairs—Sri Lanka, 9 September 2014, https://mfa.gov.lk/chinese-president-to-visit-sri-lanka/.
43 'Xi Jinping on Maiden Sri Lanka Visit to Boost Strategic, Economic Ties', *The Economic Times*, 16 September 2014, https://economictimes.indiatimes.com/news/international/world-news/xi-jinping-on-maiden-srilanka-visit-to-boost-strategic-economic-ties/articleshow/42636694.cms?from=mdr.
44 Irfan Haider and Mateen Haider, 'Economic Corridor in Focus as Pakistan, China Sign 51 MoUs', *Dawn*, 20 April 2015, https://www.dawn.com/news/1177109.
45 *Manifesto of the Sri Lanka Podujana Peramuna: Vistas of Prosperity and Splendour*, 2019, http://www.doc.gov.lk/images/pdf/NationalPolicyframeworkEN/FinalDovVer02-English.pdf.
46 Hussain Haqqani, 'Imran Khan's Populism Clashes with Pakistan's Economics', Hudson Institute, 11 August 2020, https://www.hudson.

org/research/16301-imran-khan-s-populism-clashes-with-pakistan-s-economic-realities.

47 Marwaan Macan-Markar, 'Sri Lanka Assured of China's Help in Burying Post-War Obligations', Nikkei Asia, 28 October 2020, https://asia.nikkei.com/Politics/International-relations/Sri-Lanka-assured-of-China-s-help-in-burying-post-war-obligations.

48 'Sri Lanka: UN Rights Chief Decries Mounting Abuses', Human Rights Watch, 29 January 2021, https://www.Hrw.org/news/2021/01/29/sri-lanka-un-rights-chief-decries-mounting-abuses.

FOUR

49 Asanga Abeyagoonasekera, 'Sri Lanka's Rejection of the UNHRC Resolution: A Shift towards China?', Observer Research Foundation, April 2021, https://www.orfonline.org/expert-speak/sri-lanka-rejection-unhrc-resolution-shift-towards-china/.

50 'Human Rights Council Strengthens Rights Office Probe into Sri Lanka's Long Civil War', UN News, 23 March 2021, https://news.un.org/en/story/2021/03/1088122.

51 Zulfick Farzan, 'Core Group Failed to Secure Majority at UNHRC: Dinesh', NewsFirst, 23 March 2021, https://www.newsfirst.lk/2021/03/23/video-core-group-failed-to-secure-majority-at-unhrc-dinesh/.

52 'Sri Lanka Slams Western Countries over Resolution at UNHRC', Xinhuanet, 24 March 2021, http://www.xinhuanet.com/english/2021-03/24/c_139832752.htm.

53 Chandani Kirinde, 'Dinesh Tells Parliament UNHRC Resolution Is Illegal', *Daily FT*, 26 March 2021, http://www.ft.lk/top-story/Dinesh-tells-Parliament-UNHRC-resolution-is-illegal/26-715380.

54 Rukshana Rizwie, 'India Assures of Its Support at UNHRC: Foreign Secretary', *Daily News*, 18 March 2021, http://www.dailynews.lk/2021/03/18/local/244328/india-assures-its-support-unhrc-foreign-secretary.

55 Press Trust of India, 'External Affairs Minister Jaishankar Wraps Up Official Visit to Sri Lanka', *Business Standard*, 7 January 2021, https://www.business-standard.com/article/current-affairs/external-affairs-minister-jaishankar-wraps-up-official-visit-to-sri-lanka-121010701368_1.html.

56 ' "Unhelpful and Divisive": Lankan Envoy Slams Resolution before Vote', *Daily FT*, 24 March 2021, https://www.ft.lk/news/-Unhelpful-and-divisive---Lankan-envoy-slams-Resolution-before-vote/56-715259.

57 'Will Not Betray Sovereignty of the Country, President Assures', Ada Derana, 27 March 2021, http://www.adaderana.lk/news/72623/will-not-betray-sovereignty-of-the-country-president-assures.

58 Joseph Bosco, 'Blinken and Sullivan Stand Up to China: Will Biden Back Them Up?' The Hill, 23 March 2021, https://thehill.com/opinion/international/544368-blinken-and-sullivan-stand-up-to-china-will-biden-back-them-up.

59 'Secretary Antony J. Blinken, National Security Advisor Jake Sullivan, Director Yang and State Councilor Wang at the Top of Their Meeting', US Department of State, 18 March 2021, https://www.state.gov/secretary-antony-j-blinken-national-security-advisor-jake-sullivan-chinese-director-of-the-office-of-the-central-commission-for-foreign-affairs-yang-jiechi-and-chinese-state-councilor-wang-yi-at-th/.

60 Satoru Nagao, 'Strike Capabilities of Japan, India, Australia Key for US-Led Counter-China strategy', *Sunday Guardian Live*, 27 February 2021, https://www.sundayguardianlive.com/news/strike-capabilities-japan-india-oz-key-us-led-counter-china-strategy.

61 Frank Tang, 'What Is China's Dual Circulation Economic Strategy and Why Is It Important?', SCMP, 19 November 2020, https://www.scmp.com/economy/china-economy/article/3110184/what-chinas-dual-circulation-economic-strategy-and-why-it.

62 Rezaul H. Laskar, 'India, Maldives Sign Agreements for Developing Naval Harbour, Boosting Defence', *Hindustan Times*, 21 February 2021, https://www.hindustantimes.com/india-news/india-maldives-sign-agreements-for-developing-naval-harbour-boosting-defence-101613921874713.html.

63 Samuel Bashfield, 'Agalega: A Glimpse of India's Remote Island Military Base', The Interpreter, 2 March 2021, https://www.lowyinstitute.org/the-interpreter/agalega-glimpse-india-s-remote-island-military-base.

64 Brahma Chellaney, 'The Quad: Hype vs Reality', *India Today*, 21 March 2021, https://www.indiatoday.in/magazine/up-front/story/20210329-the-quad-hype-vs-reality-1781502-2021-03-21.

65 'China Strongly Supports Sri Lanka During UNHRC Session', *Daily News*, 27 February 2021, http://www.dailynews.lk/2021/02/27/local/242672/china-strongly-supports-sri-lanka-during-unhrc-session.

66 'A Firm Pledge to Stand by Sri Lanka', *Daily News*, 30 March 2021, http://www.dailynews.lk/2021/03/30/local/245349/firm-pledge-stand-sri-lanka.

67 PTI, 'Sri Lanka Will Adopt "India-First Approach": Foreign Secretary Jayanath Colombage', *The Hindu*, 26 August 2020, https://www.thehindu.com/news/international/sri-lanka-will-adopt-india-first-approach-foreign-secretary-jayanath-colombage/article32447711.ece.

68 Disna Mudalige, 'A Challenging Year Ahead', *Daily News*, 6 January 2021, http://www.dailynews.lk/2021/01/06/features/237998/challenging-year-ahead.

FIVE

69 Asanga Abeyagoonasekera, 'One Country One Law, China Circumnavigating a Sri Lankan Fertiliser Hazard', Observer Research Foundation, 2 December 2021, https://www.orfonline.org/expert-speak/one-country-one-law/.

70 'Gnanasara Thero on Responsibility of Task Force for "One Country, One Law" ', ADA Derana, 1 November 2021, http://www.adaderana.lk/news/78107/gnanasara-thero-on-responsibility-of-task-force-for-one-country-one-law.

71 Christian Shepherd, 'China's Xi Jinping, Preparing for a Third Term, Shuts the Door on the Past', *The Washington Post*, 5 November 2021, https://www.washingtonpost.com/world/asia_pacific/china-xi-jinping-history/2021/11/05/387835c8-388f-11ec-9662-399cfa75efee_story.html.

72 'Fertiliser Shipment Row: Chinese Embassy Blacklists People's Bank of Sri Lanka', WION, 29 October 2021, https://www.wionews.com/south-asia/fertiliser-shipment-row-chinese-embassy-blacklists-peoples-bank-of-sri-lanka-424943.

73 ' "Hippo Spirit" to "Seiyo Explorer": Ship Carrying Rejected Chinese Organic Fertiliser to Lanka Changes Name', WION, 27 October 2021, https://www.wionews.com/south-asia/hippo-spirit-to-seiyo-explorer-ship-carrying-rejected-chinese-organic-fertiliser-to-lanka-changes-name-424364.

74 Deep Pal, 'China's Influence in South Asia: Vulnerabilities and Resilience in Four Countries', Carnegie Endowment, 13 October 2021, https://carnegieendowment.org/2021/10/13/china-s-influence-in-south-asia-vulnerabilities-and-resilience-in-four-countries-pub-85552.

75 Associated Press, 'China's Hypersonic Missile Test "Close to Sputnik Moment", Says US General', *The Guardian*, 28 October 2021, https://www.theguardian.com/us-news/2021/oct/28/chinas-hypersonic-missile-test-close-to-sputnik-moment-says-us-general.

76 Rush Doshi, *The Long Game: China's Grand Strategy to Displace American Order* (New York: Oxford University Press, 2021).

SIX

77 Asanga Abeyagoonasekera, 'Political-Economic Turmoil in Sri Lanka: Competing Interests of China and India', Centre on Asia and Globalisation, Lee Kuan Yew School of Public Policy, Singapore, April 2022, https://lkyspp.nus.edu.sg/cag/publications/center-publications/details/china-india-brief-202.

78 Ayeshea Perera, 'Sri Lanka: Protest at President Rajapaksa's Home Turns Violent', BBC, 1 April 2022, https://www.bbc.com/news/world-asia-60950266.

79 Ted Nordhaus and Saloni Shah, 'Sri Lanka, Organic Farming Went Catastrophically Wrong', *Foreign Policy*, 5 March 2022, https://foreignpolicy.com/2022/03/05/sri-lanka-organic-farming-crisis/.

80 Asanga Abeyagoonasekera, 'Sri Lankan Crisis between Debt-Trap and Strategic-Trap: The Chinese Stake', Institute for Security and Development Policy, 22 April 2022, https://isdp.eu/sri-lankan-crisis-between-debt-trap-and-strategic-trap-the-chinese-stake/.

81 'Sri Lankan Political Parties Mark CPC Centenary', Xinhuanet, 17 June 2021, http://www.xinhuanet.com/english/special/2021-06/17/c_1310013422.htm.

82 Maria Abi-Habib, 'How China Got Sri Lanka to Cough Up a Port', *The New York Times*, 25 June 2018, https://www.nytimes.com/2018/06/25/world/asia/china-sri-lanka-port.html.

83 'UN Human Rights Council Passes Resolution Mandating War Crimes Evidence Collection on Sri Lanka', Tamil Guardian, 23 March 2021, https://www.tamilguardian.com/content/un-human-rights-council-passes-resolution-mandating-war-crimes-evidence-collection-sri-lanka.

84 'Interview: No Evidence of Genocide or Detention Camp in Xinjiang, Says Sri Lanka's Foreign Secretary', Xinhuanet, 12 February 2021, http://www.xinhuanet.com/english/2021-02/12/c_139739459.htm.

85 'India to Build Sri Lanka Wind Farms after China Pushed Aside', *The Economic Times*, 29 March 2022, https://economictimes.indiatimes.com/industry/renewables/india-to-build-sri-lanka-wind-farms-after-china-pushed-aside/articleshow/90513780.cms.

86 Ravi Buddhavarapu, 'India Tries to Pry Sri Lanka Loose from China's Embrace', CNBC, 31 March 2022, https://www.cnbc.com/2022/04/01/india-tries-to-pry-sri-lanka-loose-from-chinas-embrace.html.

87 Arun Janardhanan, 'Why Sri Lanka Pushed India Out of Colombo Terminal Project, What's Being Offered as Compensation', *The Indian Express*, 4 February 2021, https://indianexpress.com/article/explained/explained-why-sri-lanka-has-pushed-india-out-of-colombo-terminal-project-and-whats-being-offered-as-compensation-7171502/.

88 'Jaishankar Expressed Concerns over China's "Influence in Indian Projects"', *The Sunday Times*, 10 January 2021, http://www.sundaytimes.lk/210110/news/jaishankar-expressed-concerns-over-chinas-influence-in-indian-projects-427885.html.

89 Asanga Abeyagoonasekera, 'Before the Phoenix Nest: Questions Surrounding the Port City of Colombo', Observer Research Foundation, 1 May 2021, https://www.orfonline.org/expert-speak/before-the-phoenix-nest-questions-surrounding-the-port-city-of-colombo/.

90 N. Sathiya Moorthy, 'Why New Bill Makes Colombo Port City a "Chinese Province" in Sri Lanka', Observer Research Foundation, 22 April 2021, https://www.orfonline.org/expert-speak/why-new-bill-makes-colombo-port-city-a-chinese-province-in-sri-lanka/.

91 Press Trust of India 'Sri Lanka: Chinese Envoy's Visit to Tamil-Majority Northern Province Sparks Concern', FirstPost, 29 December 2021, https://www.firstpost.com/world/sri-lanka-chinese-envoys-visit-to-tamil-majority-northern-province-sparks-concern-10243871.html.

92 Suhasini Haidar and Meera Srinivasan, 'Four-Pronged Plan on Sri Lanka Crisis', *The Hindu*, 3 December 2021, https://www.thehindu.com/news/national/four-pronged-plan-on-sri-lanka-crisis/article37816218.ece.

93 Devjyot Ghosal and Uditha Jayasinghe, 'Sri Lanka's Reluctance to Tap IMF Helped Push It into an Economic Abyss', Reuters, 18 April 2022, https://www.reuters.com/world/asia-pacific/sri-lankas-reluctance-tap-imf-helped-push-it-into-an-economic-abyss-2022-04-18/.

94 Ibid.

95 John Chalmers and Sanjeev Miglani, 'Indian Spy's Role Alleged in Sri Lankan President's Election Defeat', Reuters, 18 January 2015, https://www.reuters.com/article/us-sri-lanka-election-india-insight-idUSKBN0KR03020150118.

96 'Sri Lanka Crisis: President Rajapaksa Admits Mistakes, Says Fertiliser Ban Was Wrong', *Outlook*, 19 April 2022, https://www.outlookindia.com/international/sri-lanka-crisis-president-rajapaska-admits-mistakes-says-fertiliser-ban-was-wrong-should-ve-approached-imf-earlier-news-192136.

97 'Rajapaksa Comeback Bid Checked by Sri Lanka Bribery Probe', Reuters, 24 July 2015, https://www.reuters.com/article/sri-lanka-rajapaksa/rajapaksa-comeback-bid-checked-by-sri-lanka-bribery-probe-idUSL3N1043EF20150724.

CHAPTER 4: DOMESTIC POLITICAL ENVIRONMENT

ONE

1 Asanga Abeyagoonasekera, 'Sri Lanka's Parliamentary Election: International and Security Challenges for the Rajapaksa Government', *South Asia Discussion Papers* (Singapore: The Institute of South Asian Studies; Konrad Adenauer Stiftung, December 2020), https://www.academia.edu/44756693/Sri_Lanka_s_Parliamentary_Election_International_and_Security_Challenges_for_the_Rajapaksa_Government.

2 Parag Khanna, 'All Roads Need Not Lead to China', Noema, 13 July 2020, https://www.noemamag. com/all-roads-need-not-lead-to-china/.

3 Xinhua, 'Chinese FM Denounces Pompeo's Assertion of Failure of Engagement with China', *Free Press Journal*, 5 August 2020, https://www.freepressjournal.in/world/chinese-fm-denounces-pompeos-assertion-of-failure-of-engagement-with-china.

4 Srikanth Kondapalli, 'Beijing's Season of All-Round Assertion', *Deccan Herald*, 13 June 2020, https://www.deccanherald.com/opinion/beijing-s-season-of-all-round-assertion-849286.

5 Kishore Mahbubani, *Has China Won? The Chinese Challenge to American Primacy* (New York: Public Affairs, 2020).

6 'China Rejects Any Attempt to Create So-Called "New Cold War": FM', Xinhuanet, 5 August 2020, http://www.xinhuanet.com/english/2020-08/05/c_139267517.htm.

7 'China Congratulates Mahinda on Election Win', Ada Derana, 9 August 2020, http://www.adaderana. lk/news/66314/china-congratulates-mahinda-on-election-win.

8 Wu Jiao and Zhang Yunbi, 'Presidents Launch Port City Project', *China Daily*, 18 September 2014, https://www.chinadaily.com.cn/world/2014xisco/2014-09/18/content_18617323.htm.

9 Uditha Jayasinghe, 'Govt. Has Option Not to Sign MCC Agreement, Says Committee', *Daily FT*, 4 July 2020, http://www.ft.lk/front-page/Govt-has-option-not-to-sign-MCC-agreement-says-committee/44-702621.

10 Munza Mushtaq, 'Sri Lanka's India Ties Strained as Rajapaksa Rethinks Port Deal', *Nikkei Asia*, 10 July 2020, https://asia.nikkei.com/Politics/International-relations/Sri-Lanka-s-India-ties-strained-as-Rajapaksa-rethinks-port-deal.

11 Matthew Weaver and Gethin Chamberlain, 'Sri Lanka Declares End to War with Tamil Tigers', *The Guardian*, 19 May 2009, https://www.theguardian.com/world/2009/may/18/tamil-tigers-killed-sri-lanka.

12 Wu Jiao and Zhang Yunbi, 'Presidents Launch Port City Project', *China Daily*, 18 September 2014, https://www.chinadaily.com.cn/world/2014xisco/2014-09/18/content_18617323.htm.

13 'India's Spy Agency RAW behind My Poll Defeat, Says Former Sri Lankan President Mahinda Rajapaksa', *India Today*, 13 March 2015, https://www.indiatoday.in/world/story/sri-lanka-president-mahinda-rajapaksa-blames-india-raw-for-his-election-defeat-244216-2015-03-13.

14 *Manifesto of the Sri Lanka Podujana Peramuna: Vistas of Prosperity and Splendour*, 2019, http://www.doc.gov.lk/images/pdf/NationalPolicyframeworkEN/FinalDovVer02-English.pdf.

15 'Don't Want to Get between India–China Power Struggle: Sri Lanka President', *Hindustan Times*, 26 November 2019, https://www.

hindustantimes.com/world-news/don-t-want-to-get-between-india-china-power-struggle-sri-lanka-president-gotabaya-rajapaksa/story-2dP8rSFDCwOtEalEtTOECL.html.

16 Dr Paikiasothy Saravanamuttu, 'Needed: A Foreign Policy Beyond the Shackles of Necessity', Ground Views, 31 October 2020, https://groundviews.org/2020/10/31/needed-a-foreign-policy-beyond-the-shackles-of-necessity/

17 'Modi 1st to Congratulate Mahinda for His Victory', *The Times of India*, 7 August 2020, https://timesofindia. Indiatimes.com/india/modi-1st-to-congratulate-mahinda-for-his-victory/articleshow/77404562.cms.

18 'Sri Lanka Polls: Mahinda Rajapaksa Thanks PM Modi for Congratulatory Phone Call', Zee News, 7 August 2020, https://zeenews.india.com/world/sri-lanka-polls-mahinda-rajapaksa-thanks-pm-modifor-congratulatory-phone-call-2301139.html.

19 Aditi Phadnis, 'India Can't Take Promises Made to New Lanka Govt for Granted: Policy Expert', *Business Standard*, 5 December 2019, https://www.business-standard.com/article/current-affairs/india-can-t-take-promises-made-to-new-lanka-govt-for-granted-policy-expert-119113000881_1.Html.

20 Constantino Xavier and Riya Sinha, 'When Land Comes in the Way: India's Connectivity Infrastructure in Nepal', Brookings India, August 2020, https://www.brookings.edu/wp-content/uploads/2020/08/When-land-comes-in-the-way_M-1.pdf.

21 Ibid.

22 Meera Srinivasan, 'Gotabaya Seeks Additional $1.1 Billion SWAP Facility from Modi', *The Hindu*, 24 May 2020, https://www.thehindu.com/news/international/gotabaya-seeks-additional-11-billion-swap-facility-from-modi/article31662546.ece.

23 'The World Bank in Sri Lanka', The World Bank, https://www.worldbank.org/en/country/srilanka/overview.

24 Nirupama Subramanian, ' "Thirteenth Amendment Plus": India Sceptical of Sri Lankan Promise', *The Hindu*, 26 March 2011, https://www.thehindu.com/news/the-india-cables/lsquo13th-Amendment-Plusrsquo-India-sceptical-of-Sri-Lankan-promise/article14962436.ece.

25 'Namal Reveals Facts about Sri Lanka's Second Commercial City', YouTube, 18 July 2020. https://www.youtube.com/watch?v=CvuDf8WJnDQ.

26 Meera Srinivasan, 'Sri Lanka in Talks to Secure $500 Mn in Chinese Loans', *The Hindu*, 12 October 2020, https://www.thehindu.com/news/international/sri-lanka-in-talks-to-secure-500-mn-in-chinese-loans/article32837581.ece.

27 J.F. Nash, 'The Bargaining Problem', EconometricaI 18, no. 2 (April 1950), pp. 155–162, https://www.eecs.harvard.edu/cs286r/courses/spring02/papers/nash50a.pdf.

28 'President Rajapaksa Says Leasing H'tota Port Was a "Mistake", Calls for Renegotiation with China', *Daily FT*, 26 November 2019, http://www.ft.lk/front-page/President-Rajapaksa-says-leasing-H-tota-Port-was-a-mistake-calls-for-renegotiation-with-China/44-690388.

29 '2 Government Websites Hacked', NewsWire, 30 May 2020, http://www.newswire.lk/2020/05/30/2-government-website-hackeds/.

TWO

30 Asanga Abeyagoonasekera, 'The Coming Anarchy in Sri Lanka', *South Asia Journal*, 2 July 2021, http://southasiajournal.net/the-coming-anarchy-in-sri-lanka/.

31 'Open Wounds and Mounting Dangers: Blocking Accountability for Grave Abuses in Sri Lanka', Human Rights Watch, 1 Feb 2021, https://www.hrw.org/report/2021/02/01/open-wounds-and-mounting-dangers/blocking-accountability-grave-abuses-sri-lanka.

32 Michel Foucault, *Discipline & Punish: The Birth of the Prison*, translated by Alan Sherida (New York: Vintage Books, 1995), https://monoskop.org/images/4/43/Foucault_Michel_Discipline_and_Punish_The_Birth_of_the_Prison_1977_1995.pdf.

33 'Duminda's Pardon Undermines SL's Rule of Law: US Ambassador', *Daily Mirror*, 24 June 2021, https://www.dailymirror.lk/breaking_news/Danindas-pardon-undermines-SLs-rule-of-law-US-Ambassador/108-214761.

34 Aazam Ameen, 'Govt. Rewards Murderers While Punishing Police Officers, Former Justice Minister Responds to Duminda's Release', The Morning, 24 June 2021, https://www.themorning.lk/govt-rewards-murderers-while-punishing-police-officers-former-justice-minister-responds-to-dumindas-release/.

35 'UN Human Rights Office Condemns Presidential Pardon Granted to Duminda', NewsWire, 24 June 2021, https://www.newswire.lk/2021/06/24/un-human-rights-office-condemns-presidential-pardon-granted-to-duminda/.

36 'Bar Association Asks 06 Questions from President on Duminda's Pardon', NewsWire, 24 June 2021, https://www.newswire.lk/2021/06/24/bar-association-asks-06-questions-from-president-on-dumindas-pardon/.

37 'EU Parliament Adopts Resolution on Sri Lanka; Wants PTA Repealed, GSP+ Withdrawn', EconomyNext, 11 June 2021, https://economynext.

com/eu-parliament-adopts-resolution-on-sri-lanka-wants-pta-repealed-gsp-withdrawn-82891/.

38 'Statement by Valentin Zellweger, Vice-President of the Council, to the 10th Session of the Forum on Minority Issues', United Nations Human Rights, 30 November 2017, https://www.ohchr.org/en/statements/2017/12/statement-valentin-zellweger-vice-president-council-10th-session-forum-minority.

39 Jehan Perera, 'Can President and Prime Minister Work Together for Real Solution?', *Colombo Telegraph*, 22 June 2021, https://www.colombotelegraph.com/index.php/can-president-prime-minister-work-together-for-real-solution/.

40 Charumini de Silva, 'EDB Expresses Concern over EU Parliament Resolution to Withdraw GSP+', *Daily FT*, 14 June 2021, https://www.ft.lk/front-page/EDB-expresses-concern-over-EU-Parliament-resolution-to-withdraw-GSP/44-719186.

41 News 1st Newsline with Sharlan Benedict, 'Interview with Vimanga K.D.', *YouTube*, 22 June 2021, https://www.youtube.com/watch?v=bsijnolZny4.

42 Juan J. Linz, *The Breakdown of Democratic Regimes: Crisis, Breakdown and Reequilibration; An Introduction*, translated by Alfred Stepan (Baltimore: John Hopkins University Press, 1978).

THREE

43 Asanga Abeyagoonasekera, 'Rajapaksa's Dysfunctional Regime in Sri Lanka and Its Impact on South Asia', Observer Research Foundation, 23 September 2021, https://www.orfonline.org/expert-speak/rajapaksas-dysfunctional-regime-in-sri-lanka-and-its-impact-on-south-asia/.

44 'Sri Lanka's Rajapaksa Family Tightens Grip with Ministerial Picks', Reuters, 8 July 2021, https://www.reuters.com/world/asia-pacific/sri-lankas-rajapaksa-family-tightens-grip-with-ministerial-picks-2021-07-08/.

45 'Major General M.D.S.P. Niwunhella Appointed as Commissioner General of Essential Services. What's His Role?', NewsWire, 31 August 2021, https://www.newswire.lk/2021/08/31/major-general-m-d-s-p-niwunhella-appointed-as-commissioner-general-of-essential-services-whats-his-role/.

46 'Covid: Sri Lanka in Economic Emergency as Food Prices Soar', BBC, 1 September 2021, https://www.bbc.com/news/business-58390292.

47 'Oral Update on the Human Rights Situation in Sri Lanka', United Nations Human Rights, 13 September 2021, https://www.ohchr.org/en/2021/09/oral-update-human-rights-situation-sri-lanka.

48 'Sri Lanka Rupee Crosses 230 to Dollar, Rs127 Bn Printed Overnight to Sterilize SRR Hike', EconomyNext, 2 September 2021, https://

economynext.com/sri-lanka-rupee-crosses-230-to-dollar-rs127bn-printed-overnight-to-sterilize-srr-hike-85688/.

49 'Covid: Sri Lanka in Economic Emergency as Food Prices Soar', BBC, 1 September 2021, https://www.bbc.com/news/business-58390292.

50 'Currency Swap: Bangladesh Remits Another US$ 100 M', *Daily News*, 31 August 2021, https://www.dailynews.lk/2021/08/31/local/258052/currency-swap-bangladesh-remits-another-us-100-m.

51 'The Maligned Lakshman Shock: Patient Will Die Unless the New Governor Diffuses It Forthwith', *Daily FT*, 13 September 2021, https://www.ft.lk/opinion/The-maligned-Lakshman-shock-Patient-will-die-unless-the-new-Governor-diffuses-it-forthwith/14-722964.

52 'Mr. Ajith Nivard Cabraal Takes Office as the Governor of the Central Bank of Sri Lanka', Central Bank of Sri Lanka, 15 September 2021, https://www.cbsl.gov.lk/news/ajith-nivard-cabraal-takes-office-as-the-governor-of-cbsl.

53 'President Reshuffles Cabinet', Colombo Page, 16 August 2021, http://www.colombopage.com/archive_21B/Aug16_1629099284CH.php.

54 Easwaran Rutnam, 'Sri Lanka Tells UN Not to Interfere in Xinjiang and Hong Kong', Colombo Gazette, 16 September 2021, https://colombogazette.com/2021/09/16/sri-lanka-tells-un-not-to-interfere-in-xinjiang-and-hong-kong/.

55 Zulfick Farzan, 'US$ 1.5 Bn Currency Swap with China Stumbles on a Roadblock', NewsFirst, 2 September 2021, https://www.newsfirst.lk/2021/09/02/us-1-5-bn-currency-swap-with-china-stumbles-on-a-roadblock/.

56 Ibid.

57 Chinese Embassy in Sri Lanka @ChinaEmbSL, 'Well done! #SriLanka; The fastest #vaccination speed in the world for the past week', Twitter, 3 September 2021, 5:21 pm, https://twitter.com/ChinaEmbSL/status/1433759508585582594.

58 Deborah Brautigam and Meg Rithmire, 'The Chinese "Debt Trap" Is a Myth', *The Atlantic*, 6 February 2021, https://www.theatlantic.com/international/archive/2021/02/china-debt-trap-diplomacy/617953/.

59 Ibid.

60 Ibid.

61 'Sri Lanka Attack "Retaliation" for NZ Massacre: Minister', Al Jazeera, 23 April 2019, https://www.aljazeera.com/news/2019/04/sri-lanka-attacks-retaliation-christchurch-deputy-minister-190423082847025.html.

62 'Sri Lanka Church Unhappy about Probe into Easter Bombings', *Vatican News*, 16 August 2021, https://www.vaticannews.va/en/church/news/2021-08/sri-lanka-easter-church-bombings-government-probe-faulty-ranjith.html.

63 Natalie Chalk, 'Ahamed Samsudeen: New Zealand Knife Attacker Named as Sri Lanka Refugee Jailed over Extremist Material', ANI, 4 September 2021, https://inews.co.uk/news/ahamed-samsudeen-new-zealand-knife-attacker-sri-lanka-refugee-jailed-extremist-material-1183779.

64 *Rithika Siddhartha*, '"No Direct Terror Threat to India", Says Shivshankar Menon on Taliban', *Eastern Eye*, 3 September 2021, https://www.easterneye.biz/no-direct-terror-threat-to-india-says-shivshankar-menon/.

65 'Oral Update on the Human Rights Situation in Sri Lanka', United Nations Human Rights, 13 September 2021, https://www.ohchr.org/en/2021/09/oral-update-human-rights-situation-sri-lanka.

66 Anusha Ondaatjie, 'Sri Lanka Central Bank Chief Steps Down as Reserve Crisis Deepens', Al Jazeera, 10 September 2021, https://www.aljazeera.com/economy/2021/9/10/sri-lanka-central-bank-chief-steps-down-as-reserve-crisis-deepens.

67 'Sri Lankan Minister Accused of Abusing Political Prisoners Resigns', *The New York Times*, 15 September 2021, https://www.nytimes.com/2021/09/15/world/asia/sri-lanka-minister-abuse-prisoners.html.

FOUR

68 Asanga Abeyagoonasekera, 'Sri Lanka in Crisis: Repression, Protests, and Geopolitical Tensions', *South Asia Journal*, 2 December 2021, http://southasiajournal.net/sri-lanka-in-crisis-repression-protests-and-geopolitical-tensions/.

69 Evelyn Cheng, 'Biden-Xi Virtual Meeting Ends with Both Sides Calling for More Cooperation Amid Tensions', CNBC, 15 November 2021, https://www.cnbc.com/2021/11/15/biden-xi-kick-off-virtual-meeting-with-calls-to-increase-communication.html.

70 Amy Mackinnon, 'Biden and Xi Pause Saber Rattling for First Face-to-Face', *Foreign Policy*, 16 November 2021, https://foreignpolicy.com/2021/11/16/biden-xi-first-meeting-us-china-tensions/?utm_source=PostUp&utm_medium=email&utm_campaign=37508&utm_term=Editors%20Picks%20OC&tpcc=37508.

71 'Military and Security Developments Involving the People's Republic of China, 2021: Annual Report to Congress', Department of Defense, https://media.defense.gov/2021/Nov/03/2002885874/-1/-1/0/2021-CMPR-FINAL.PDF.

72 Anbarasan Ethirajan, 'Ship-Load of "Toxic" Chinese Fertilizer Causes Diplomatic Stink', BBC, 13 November 2021, https://www.bbc.com/news/world-asia-59202309.

73 Ruwani Fonseka, 'Why Is the Govt Desperate to Unload Chinese Fertiliser, Asks JVP', The Morning, 29 October 2021, https://www.themorning.lk/why-is-the-govt-desperate-to-unload-chinese-fertiliser-asks-jvp/.
74 Rajeswari Pillai Rajagopalan, 'Did China Create New Facts on the Ground Along the LAC With India?', Observer Research Foundation, 14 November 2021, https://www.orfonline.org/research/did-china-create-new-facts-on-the-ground-along-the-lac-with-india/.
75 Ibid.
76 'SJB Holds Rally in Colombo Despite Police Objection', NewsWire, 16 November 2021, https://www.newswire.lk/2021/11/16/watch-sjb-holds-rally-in-colombo-despite-police-objection/.
77 '2020 Country Reports on Human Rights Practices: Sri Lanka', U.S. Department of State, 30 March 2021, https://www.state.gov/reports/2020-country-reports-on-human-rights-practices/sri-lanka/.
78 Ibid.

FIVE

79 Asanga Abeyagoonasekera, 'Sri Lanka in 2021: Trouble Ahead for One of Asia's Oldest Democracies', South Asian Voices, 22 December 2021, https://southasianvoices.org/sri-lanka-in-2021-trouble-ahead-for-one-of-asias-oldest-democracies/.
80 Shannon Tiezzi, 'Which Asia-Pacific Countries Were (and Weren't) Invited to the US Summit for Democracy?', The Diplomat, 1 December 2021, https://thediplomat.com/2021/12/which-asia-pacific-countries-were-and-werent-invited-to-the-us-summit-for-democracy/.
81 Mujib Mashal, 'In Sri Lanka, the Government Looks Increasingly Like a Family Firm', *The New York Times*, 10 July 2021, https://www.nytimes.com/2021/07/10/world/asia/sri-lanka-basil-rajapaksa.html.
82 R.M. Lilani, 'Sri Lanka Debates Expanded Powers for President Rajapaksa', DW, 20 October 2020, https://www.dw.com/en/sri-lanka-president-parliament-powers/a-55331667.
83 'Sri Lanka on Alarming Path towards Recurrence of Grave Human Rights Violations: UN Report', United Nations Human Rights, 27 January 2021, https://www.ohchr.org/en/press-releases/2021/01/sri-lanka-alarming-path-towards-recurrence-grave-human-rights-violations-un.
84 Pamela Constable and Amantha Perera, 'Sri Lanka's President Says Intelligence Lapse Allowed Easter Bombings to Take Place,' *The Washington Post*, 26 April 2019, https://www.washingtonpost.com/world/asia_pacific/sri-lanka-leaders-promises-reorganization-of-security-services-

in-wake-of-easter-bombings/2019/04/26/84beda66-6792-11e9-a698-2a8f808c9cfb_story.html.

85 'Hardline Mob in Pakistan Lynches Lankan over "Blasphemy" ', *The Indian Express*, 4 December 2021, https://indianexpress.com/article/world/mob-lynching-blasphemy-sri-lankan-killed-7654648/.

86 'Sri Lanka: "Religious Disharmony" Order Threatens Minorities', Human Rights Watch, 16 March 2021, https://www.hrw.org/news/2021/03/16/sri-lanka-religious-disharmony-order-threatens-minorities.

87 'Sri Lanka on Alarming Path towards Recurrence of Grave Human Rights Violations: UN Report', United Nations Human Rights, 27 January 2021, https://www.ohchr.org/en/press-releases/2021/01/sri-lanka-alarming-path-towards-recurrence-grave-human-rights-violations-un.

88 ' "Political Move": Sri Lanka Urges Rejection of UNHRC Resolution', Al Jazeera, 24 February 2021, https://www.aljazeera.com/news/2021/2/24/sri-lanka-calls-un-rights-bodys-resolution-a-political-move.

89 Pavani Hapuarachchi, 'Gnanasara Thero to Lead New Task Force on One Country-One Law', NewsFirst, 27 October 2021, https://www.newsfirst.lk/2021/10/27/gnanasara-thero-to-lead-new-task-force-on-one-country-one-law/.

90 Tim Hume, ' "Fascists" in Saffron Robes? The Rise of Sri Lanka's Buddhist Ultra-Nationalists', CNN, 18 July 2014, https://www.cnn.com/2014/07/17/world/asia/sri-lanka-bodu-bala-sena-profile/index.html.

91 Meera Srinivasan, 'Hardline Monk to Head Legal Reforms Panel in Sri Lanka', *The Hindu*, 27 October 2021, https://www.thehindu.com/news/international/sri-lankan-president-appoints-task-force-led-by-controversial-buddhist-monk-for-one-country-one-law/article37189262.ece.

92 Jehan Perera, 'Non Consultative Decision-Making Will Not Work', Colombo Telegraph, 16 November 2016, https://www.colombotelegraph.com/index.php/non-consultative-decision-making-will-not-work/.

93 PTI, 'Sri Lanka's Draft of New Constitution Expected to Be Ready for Parliament's Nod by Early 2022: Minister', *The Hindu*, 19 October 2021, https://www.thehindu.com/news/international/lankas-draft-of-new-constitution-expected-to-be-ready-for-parliaments-nod-by-early-2022-minister/article37066704.ece.

94 Meera Srinivasan, 'TNA Seeks Joint U.S.-India Role for Sri Lanka Political Solution', *The Hindu*, 26 November 2021, https://www.thehindu.com/news/international/tna-seeks-joint-us-india-role-for-sri-lanka-political-solution/article37710230.ece.

95 Anbarasan Ethirajan, 'Duminda Silva: Anger As Sri Lanka Frees Politician Sentenced for Murder', BBC, 26 June 2021, https://www.bbc.com/news/world-asia-57608573.

96 'Duminda Silva Appointed Housing Development Authority Chairman', *Daily Mirror*, 17 July 2021, https://www.dailymirror.lk/breaking_news/Duminda-Silva-appointed-Housing-Development-Authority-Chairman/108-216350.

97 Bhavani Fonseka, 'When Impunity Becomes the Norm', Ground Views, 24 October 2021, https://groundviews.org/2021/10/24/when-impunity-becomes-the-norm/.

98 Ibid.

99 Meera Srinivasan, 'Sri Lanka Cabinet Clears China's Role in Terminal Project', *The Hindu*, 24 November 2021, https://www.thehindu.com/news/international/sri-lanka-cabinet-clears-chinas-role-in-terminal-project/article37670153.ece.

100 AFP, 'Sri Lanka Secures $1.5 Bn Chinese Loan', *The Hindu*, 23 March 2021, https://www.thehindu.com/news/international/sri-lanka-secures-15-bn-chinese-loan/article34144236.ece.

101 *National Policy Framework: Vistas of Prosperity and Splendour*, 2019, http://www.doc.gov.lk/images/pdf/NationalPolicyframeworkEN/FinalDovVer02-English.pdf.

102 Meera Srinivasan, 'Sri Lankan Parliament Passes Controversial Bill on China-Backed Port City', *The Hindu*, 20 May 2021, https://www.thehindu.com/news/international/sri-lankan-parliament-passes-controversial-bill-on-china-backed-port-city/article34608185.ece.

103 Asanga Abeyagoonasekera, 'In Sri Lanka, Unions Speaking Geopolitics, Rajapaksa Govt Adopting Protectionism', The Print, 17 February 2021, https://theprint.in/opinion/in-sri-lanka-unions-speaking-geopolitics-rajapaksa-govt-adopting-protectionism/606138/.

104 'Interview: No Evidence of Genocide or Detention Camp in Xinjiang, Says Sri Lanka's Foreign Secretary', Xinhuanet, 12 February 2021, http://www.xinhuanet.com/english/2021-02/12/c_139739459.htm.

105 PTI, 'Sri Lanka's Supreme Court Terms Chinese Port City Bill Inconsistent with Constitution: Parliament Told', *The Economic Times*, 18 May 2021, https://economictimes.indiatimes.com/news/defence/sri-lankas-supreme-court-terms-chinese-port-city-bill-inconsistent-with-constitution-parliament-told/articleshow/82734056.cms.

106 Meera Srinivasan, 'Sri Lanka Cabinet Clears China's Role in Terminal Project', *The Hindu*, 24 November 2021, https://www.thehindu.com/news/international/sri-lanka-cabinet-clears-chinas-role-in-terminal-project/article37670153.ece.

107 Anirban Bhaumik, 'India Steps in after Sri Lanka Bars Contaminated Fertilizer from China', *Deccan Herald*, 5 November 2021, https://

www.deccanherald.com/national/india-steps-in-after-sri-lanka-bars-contaminated-fertilizer-from-china-1047499.html.

108 'Colombo Security Conclave Obtains Operational Teeth with the Launching of "Focused Operation" ', *Financial Express*, 2 December 2021, https://www.financialexpress.com/defence/colombo-security-conclave-obtains-operational-teeth-with-the-launching-of-focused-operation/2380830/.

109 Ankit Panda, 'Will Gotabaya Revisit Sri Lanka's Hambantota "Debt Trap" with China?' The Diplomat, 19 November 2019, https://thediplomat.com/2019/11/will-gotabaya-revisit-sri-lankas-hambantota-debt-trap-with-china/.

110 Chinese Embassy in Sri Lanka @ChinaEmbSL, 'More than 10 million people in #SriLanka have received two doses of Sinopharm vaccine', Twitter, 15 October 2021, 9:13 am, https://twitter.com/ChinaEmbSL/status/1449219547081236484?s=20.

111 Chinese Embassy in Sri Lanka@ChinaEmbSL, 'The U.S. Intelligence Report on COVID-19 Origins: Ugly Agendas Under a Worn-Out Cover, Twitter, 1 September 2021, 11:35 am, https://twitter.com/ChinaEmbSL/status/1432947632079396866.

112 'Pathfinder Translates Chinese Covid-19 Prevention and Control Manual to Sinhala Launch Today', *Daily FT*, 30 July 2020, https://www.ft.lk/News/Pathfinder-translates-Chinese-COVID-19-prevention-andcontrol-manual-to-Sinhala-launch-today/56-703887.

113 'Pathfinder Ties Up with Communist Party of China', *Daily News*, 24 November 2020, http://www.dailynews.lk/2020/11/24/finance/234281/pathfinder-ties-communist-party-china.

114 Deep Pal, 'China's Influence in South Asia: Vulnerabilities and Resilience in Four Countries', Carnegie Endowment, 13 October 2021, https://carnegieendowment.org/2021/10/13/china-s-influence-in-south-asia-vulnerabilities-and-resilience-in-four-countries-pub-85552.

115 Zulfick Farzan, 'SLPP Members Attend Workshops by Chinese Communist Party: GL', NewsFirst, 28 April 2021, https://www.newsfirst.lk/2021/04/28/slpp-members-attend-workshops-by-chinese-communist-party-gl/.

116 W.A. Wijewardena, 'The Maligned Lakshman Shock: Patient Will Die Unless the New Governor Diffuses It Forthwith', *Daily FT*, 13 September 2021, https://www.ft.lk/opinion/The-maligned-Lakshman-shock-Patient-will-die-unless-the-new-Governor-diffuses-it-forthwith/14-722964.

117 Shihar Aneez, 'As Food and Energy Prices Soar, Sri Lankans Go Without', Al Jazeera, 17 November 2021, https://www.aljazeera.com/economy/2021/11/17/as-food-and-energy-prices-soar-sri-lankans-go-without.

118 'Sri Lanka Declares Economic Emergency to Contain Food Prices amid Forex Crisis', Reuters, 31 August 2021, https://www.reuters.com/world/asia-pacific/sri-lanka-declares-economic-emergency-contain-food-prices-amid-forex-crisis-2021-08-31/.

119 *K.D.D.B. Vimanga*, 'Did We Miss the Opportunity to Formulate "A Non-traditional Budget"?', Advocata, 13 November 2021, https://www.advocata.org/commentary-archives/2021/11/13/did-we-miss-the-opportunity-to-formulate-a-non-traditional-budget.

120 Srimevan Colombage, 'Denying IMF Support Is No Solution for Sri Lanka's Economic Woes', *Daily FT*, 3 August 2021, https://www.ft.lk/columns/Denying-IMF-support-is-no-solution-for-Sri-Lanka-s-economic-woes/4-721234.

121 PTI, 'Sri Lanka Will Not Default on Debt Repayments Despite Forex Crisis: Finance Minister', *The Economic Times*, 11 December 2021, https://economictimes.indiatimes.com/news/international/world-news/sri-lanka-will-not-default-on-debt-repayments-despite-forex-crisis-finance-minister/articleshow/88224928.cms?from=mdr.

122 'Sri Lanka's Mysterious Gas Explosions Become Nobody's Baby', EconomyNext, 18 December 2021, https://economynext.com/sri-lankas-mysterious-gas-explosions-become-nobodys-baby-88920/.

123 Amani Nilar, 'Long Queues for Passports: Sri Lankans Opting to Leave the Country?', NewsFirst, 23 October 2021, https://www.newsfirst.lk/2021/10/23/long-queues-for-passports-sri-lankans-opting-to-leave-the-country/.

SIX

124 Asanga Abeyagoonasekera, 'Sri Lankan Economy Spiralling Out of Control: Requests IMF Assistance', Vivekananda International Foundation, 14 February 2022, https://www.vifindia.org/2022/february/14/sri-lankan-economy-spiralling-out-of-control-requests-imf-assistance.

125 Zulfick Farzan, 'Sri Lanka to Promote Cycling to Work: Cabinet Paper Ready', NewsFirst, 26 January 2022, https://www.newsfirst.lk/2022/01/26/sri-lanka-to-promote-cycling-to-work-cabinet-paper-ready/.

126 Shirajiv Sirimane, 'Port City Sports New Ventures', *Sunday Observer*, 31 October 2021, https://www.sundayobserver.lk/2021/10/31/opinion/port-city-sports-new-ventures.

127 'Can Our People Eat? Sri Lankan Politicians Meet amidst "Unprecedented Economic Crisis"', Tamil Guardian, 31 January 2022, https://www.tamilguardian.com/content/can-our-people-eat-sri-lankan-politicians-meet-amidst-unprecedented-economic-crisis.

128 'Explained: Why Sri Lanka Is on Brink of Bankruptcy and What the Government Is Doing', FirstPost, 27 January 2022, https://www.firstpost.com/world/explained-why-sri-lanka-is-on-brink-of-bankruptcy-and-what-the-government-is-doing-10325191.html.

129 Anusha Ondaatjie, 'Sri Lanka Raises Rates to Fight Asia's Second-Fastest Inflation', Bloomberg, 20 January 2022, https://www.bloomberg.com/news/articles/2022-01-20/sri-lanka-raises-rates-to-fight-one-of-asia-s-fastest-inflation.

130 'Sri Lanka Debt Re-structuring: Opinion Divided among Think Tanks', Verite Research, 7 December 2021, https://www.veriteresearch.org/2021/12/07/sri-lanka-debt-re-structuring-opinion-divided-among-think-tanks/.

131 Meera Srinivasan, 'Jaishankar, Basil Rajapaksa Hold "Detailed" Virtual Meeting', *The Hindu*, 15 January 2022, https://www.thehindu.com/news/national/jaishankar-holds-talks-with-lankan-minister-discusses-india-assisted-projects-seeks-early-release-of-indian-fishermen/article38273834.ece.

132 'Sri Lanka Debt Re-structuring: Opinion Divided among Think Tanks', Verite Research, 7 December 2021, https://www.veriteresearch.org/2021/12/07/sri-lanka-debt-re-structuring-opinion-divided-among-think-tanks/.

133 'Basil's IMF Approach Must Not Be Obstructed: UNP Leader', Lanka News Web, 31 January 2022, https://lankanewsweb.net/archives/3406/basils-imf-approach-must-not-be-obstructed-unp-leader/.

134 Shenal Fernando '2019 Tax Cuts Led to Rating Downgrades, Made Borrowing Harder', The Morning, 8 December 2021, https://www.themorning.lk/2019-tax-cuts-led-to-rating-downgrades-made-borrowing-harder/.

135 'Sri Lanka Seeks Technical Support from IMF: Basil', EconomyNext, 2 February 2022, https://economynext.com/sri-lanka-seeks-technical-support-from-imf-basil-90135/.

136 Pathfinder Foundation, 'The Nightmare Scenario: A Default on Sovereign Debt', The Morning, 30 December 2021, https://www.themorning.lk/the-nightmare-scenario-a-default-on-sovereign-debt/.

SEVEN

137 Asanga Abeyagoonasekera, 'People's Uprising in Sri Lanka: Sudden Rupture against the Rajapaksa Regime', ISAS Briefs, 11 April 2022, https://www.isas.nus.edu.sg/papers/peoples-uprising-in-sri-lanka-sudden-rupture-against-the-rajapaksa-regime/.

138 Moises Naim, *The Revenge of Power: How Autocrats Are Reinventing Politics for the 21st Century* (New York: St. Martin's Press, 2022).

139 Ayeshea Perera, 'Sri Lanka: Protest at President Rajapaksa's Home Turns Violent', BBC, 1 April 2022, https://www.bbc.com/news/world-asia-60950266.

140 'Over 300 Sri Lanka Lawyers Flock to Represent 53 Arrested Protestors', EconomyNext, 2 April 2022, https://economynext.com/over-300-sri-lanka-lawyers-flock-to-represent-53-arrested-protestors-92397/.

141 'Avant-Garde Chairman, Family Left the Country?' *Daily Mirror*, 4 April 2022, https://www.dailymirror.lk/latest_news/Avant-Garde-chairman-family-left-the-country/342-234477.

142 'Despite Bulging Debt Everywhere, the IMF Is Struggling to Be Helpful', *The Economist*, 26 February 2022, https://www.economist.com/finance-and-economics/2022/02/26/despite-bulging-debt-everywhere-the-imf-is-struggling-to-be-helpful.

143 Ted Nordhaus, 'In Sri Lanka, Organic Farming Went Catastrophically Wrong', *Foreign Policy*, 5 March 2022, https://foreignpolicy.com/2022/03/05/sri-lanka-organic-farming-crisis/.

144 Shihar Aneez, 'China May Give Sri Lanka US$2.5 Bn in Loans, Trade Credits', EconomyNext, 21 March 2022, https://economynext.com/china-may-give-sri-lanka-us2-5bn-in-loans-trade-credits-91884/.

145 'Sri Lanka Seeks USD 2.5 Billion Massive Loan from China', *News Wire*, 21 March 2022, https://www.newswire.lk/2022/03/21/sri-lanka-seeks-usd-2-5-billion-massive-loan-from-china/.

146 Deborah Brautigam and Meg Rithmire, 'The Chinese "Debt Trap" Is a Myth', *The Atlantic*, 6 February 2021, https://www.theatlantic.com/international/archive/2021/02/china-debt-trap-diplomacy/617953/.

147 Ravi Buddhavarapu, 'India Tries to Pry Sri Lanka Loose from China's Embrace', CNBC, 31 March 2022, https://www.cnbc.com/2022/04/01/india-tries-to-pry-sri-lanka-loose-from-chinas-embrace.html.

148 'Interview: No Evidence of Genocide or Detention Camp in Xinjiang, Says Sri Lanka's Foreign Secretary', Xinhuanet, 12 February 2022, http://www.xinhuanet.com/english/2021-02/12/c_139739459.htm.

149 Asanga Abeyagoonasekera, 'Rajapaksa's Dysfunctional Regime in Sri Lanka and Its Impact on South Asia', Observer Research Foundation, 23 September 2021, https://www.orfonline.org/expert-speak/rajapaksas-dysfunctional-regime-in-sri-lanka-and-its-impact-on-south-asia/.

150 Ruth Pollard, 'How Four Powerful Brothers Broke an Island Nation', Bloomberg, 18 March 2022, https://www.bloomberg.com/opinion/

articles/2022-03-17/the-rajapaksa-brothers-power-isn-t-enough-to-stop-sri-lanka-going-broke.

151 Zulfick Farzan, 'State Bank on Verge of Default: Harsha Tells Parliament', NewsFirst, 24 March 2022, https://www.newsfirst.lk/2022/03/24/state-bank-on-verge-of-default-harsha-tells-parliament/.

EIGHT

152 Asanga Abeyagoonasekera, 'Economic and Political Crisis in Sri Lanka', Observer Research Foundation, 19 May 2022, https://www.orfonline.org/expert-speak/economic-and-political-crisis-in-sri-lanka/.

153 Luis Felipe Lopez-Calva, 'To My Friends, Anything; To My Enemies, the Law', UNDP Blog, 21 February 2019, https://www.undp.org/latin-america/blog/"-my-friends-anything-my-enemies-law".

154 'Sri Lanka PM Mahinda Rajapaksa Resigns As Crisis Worsens', Al Jazeera, 9 May 2022, https://www.aljazeera.com/news/2022/5/9/sri-lanka-pm-mahinda-rajapaksa-offers-to-resign-as-crisis-worsens.

155 'Lanka PM's Supporters Attack Anti-Govt Protesters, 23 Injured', The Federal, 9 May 2022, https://thefederal.com/international/lanka-pms-supporters-attack-anti-govt-protesters-23-injured/.

156 Jayadeva Uyangoda, 'Decoding Political Messages from the Citizens', *Daily Mirror*, 9 May 2022, https://www.dailymirror.lk/recommended-news/Decoding-political-messages-from-the-citizens/277-236535.

157 Ibid.

158 Ibid.

159 Iqbal Athas, 'Sri Lanka President Declares New State of Emergency As Protests Roil Island', CNN, 7 May 2022, https://www.cnn.com/2022/05/07/asia/sri-lanka-president-rajapaksa-state-of-emergency-hnk-intl/index.html.

160 'Govt Explains Why State of Emergency Was Imposed', NewsWire, 7 May 2022, https://www.newswire.lk/2022/05/07/govt-explains-why-state-of-emergency-was-imposed/.

161 'US, EU, UK Raise Concerns over State of Emergency in Sri Lanka', NewsWire, 7 May 2022, https://www.newswire.lk/2022/05/07/us-eu-raise-cver-state-of-emergency-in-sri-lanka/.

162 Ayeshea Perera, 'Sri Lanka: Protest at President Rajapaksa's Home Turns Violent', BBC, 1 April 2022, https://www.bbc.com/news/world-asia-60950266.

163 'Sri Lanka Crisis: One Killed after Police Fire Live Bullets at Protesters', BBC, 20 April 2022, https://www.bbc.com/news/world-asia-61151037.

164 'Over 300 Sri Lanka Lawyers Flock to Represent 53 Arrested Protestors', EconomyNext, 2 April 2022, https://economynext.com/over-300-sri-lanka-lawyers-flock-to-represent-53-arrested-protestors-92397/.
165 'Namal's Wife, In-Laws Leave Country', *Daily Mirror*, 3 April 2022, https://www.dailymirror.lk/top_story/Namals-wife-in-laws-leave-country/155-234384.
166 Hannah Ellis-Petersen, 'Sri Lanka Troops Rescue Ex-PM as Houses Torched in Deadly Night of Unrest', *The Guardian*, 10 May 2022, https://www.theguardian.com/world/2022/may/10/troops-rescue-outgoing-sri-lanka-pm-as-houses-torched-in-deadly-night-of-unrest.
167 'President Will Not Resign', NewsWire, 11 May 2022, https://www.newswire.lk/2022/05/11/president-ready-to-abolish-executive-presidency-after-discussing-with-the-ent/.
168 'Ranil Wickremesinghe Sworn in As PM of Crisis-Hit Sri Lanka', Al Jazeera, 12 May 2022, https://www.aljazeera.com/news/2022/5/12/ranil-wickremesinghe-to-be-new-pm-of-crisis-hit-sri-lanka-party.
169 Ibid.
170 Emily Schmall, 'Sri Lanka Economy Has Hit Rock Bottom Putting Pressure on President', *The New York Times*, 25 March 2022, https://www.nytimes.com/2022/03/25/world/asia/sri-lanka-economic-crisis.html.
171 'Sri Lanka Foreign Reserves Dip below $50 Million, Minister Waves Red Flag', *The Business Standard*, 4 May 2022, https://www.tbsnews.net/world/south-asia/sri-lanka-foreign-reserves-dip-below-50-million-minister-waves-red-flag-413458.
172 Vanya Gautam, 'Friend or Foe? Before $2.5 Billion "Help", China Had Rejected Sri Lanka's Loan Rescheduling Appeal', India Times, 24 March 2022, https://www.indiatimes.com/worth/investment/china-refuses-sri-lankan-appeal-for-rescheduling-debt-repayment-565226.html.
173 Jorgelina Do Rosario, 'Analysis: Complex Web of Creditors, Politics Threatens Sri Lanka Restructuring', Reuters, 28 April 2022, https://www.reuters.com/world/asia-pacific/complex-web-creditors-politics-threatens-sri-lanka-restructuring-2022-04-28/.
174 Akhil Bery, 'U.S. Should Push the Quad to Help Sri Lanka', *Asia Nikkei*, 5 May 2022, https://asia.nikkei.com/Opinion/U.S.-should-push-the-Quad-to-help-Sri-Lanka.
175 Ibid.
176 'Indo-Pacific Strategy of the United States', The White House, February 2022, https://www.whitehouse.gov/wp-content/uploads/2022/02/U.S.-Indo-Pacific-Strategy.pdf.

NINE

177 Asanga Abeyagoonasekera, 'The Sri Lankan Crisis: The End of the Autocratic Regime', Observer Research Foundation, 14 July 2022, https://www.orfonline.org/expert-speak/the-end-of-the-autocratic-regime/.

178 AFP, 'Sri Lanka Schools, Govt Offices to Shut As Transport Grinds to Halt', *The Times of India*, 17 June 2022, https://timesofindia.indiatimes.com/world/south-asia/sri-lanka-schools-govt-offices-to-shut-as-transport-grinds-to-halt/articleshow/92286109.cms?from=mdr.

179 'Shots Fired into Air As Tension Flared Up in Vishwamadu', *Daily Mirror*, 18 June 2022, https://www.dailymirror.lk/breaking_news/Shots-fired-into-air-as-tension-flared-up-in-Vishwamadu/108-239327.

180 'Six Cops Injured in Athurugiriya Petrol Shed Clash: Nine Arrested', *Daily Mirror*, 18 June 2022, https://www.dailymirror.lk/breaking_news/Six-cops-injured-in-Athurugiriya-petrol-shed-clash-Nine-arrested/108-239314.

181 Hannah Ellis-Petersen, 'Sri Lanka Troops Rescue Ex-PM As Houses Torched in Deadly Night of Unrest', *The Guardian*, 10 May 2022, https://www.theguardian.com/world/2022/may/10/troops-rescue-outgoing-sri-lanka-pm-as-houses-torched-in-deadly-night-of-unrest.

182 Uditha Jayasinghe, 'Sri Lanka Tycoon Dhammika Perera to Replace President's Brother in Parliament', Reuters, 10 June 2022, https://www.reuters.com/world/asia-pacific/sri-lanka-tycoon-dhammika-perera-replace-presidents-brother-parliament-2022-06-10/.

183 '"It'll Be Worse Next Time," Says Weerawansa', *The Island*, 12 June 2022, https://island.lk/itll-be-worse-next-time-says-weerawansa/.

184 Ibid.

185 'Sri Lankan Police Arrest 21 Anti-Government Protesters', World Socialist Web Site, 20 June 2022, https://www.wsws.org/en/articles/2022/06/21/vktc-j21.html.

186 'Sri Lanka's Main Opposition Parties Boycott Parliament This Week', NewsWire, 21 June 2022, https://www.newswire.lk/2022/06/21/sri-lankas-main-opposition-to-boycott-parliament-this-wk/.

187 Stanford CDDRL, 'Modern Authoritarianism and Geopolitics: Thoughts on a Policy Framework', YouTube, 11 April 2022, https://www.youtube.com/watch?v=E7ZtsajvV98&t=1597s.

188 Bhavani Fonseka, 'When Impunity Becomes the Norm', Ground Views, 24 October 2021, https://groundviews.org/2021/10/24/when-impunity-becomes-the-norm/.

189 PTI, 'Sri Lankan Cabinet Passes 21st Amendment Aimed at Empowering Parliament over President', *The Hindu*, 20 June 2022, https://www.thehindu.com/news/international/sri-lankan-cabinet-passes-21st-

amendment-aimed-at-empowering-parliament-over-president/article65545784.ece.

190 Jehan Perera, 'Government Has to Change for Protest to End', Colombo Telegraph, 5 April 2022, https://www.colombotelegraph.com/index.php/government-has-to-change-for-protests-to-end/#comments.

191 'IMF Team Arrives in Sri Lanka As Crisis Worsens', Al Jazeera, 20 June 2022, https://www.aljazeera.com/economy/2022/6/20/imf-team-arrives-in-sri-lanka-as-crisis-worsens.

CHAPTER 5 SECURITY

ONE

1 Asanga Abeyagoonasekera, 'Twenty-Point Analysis of PCoI on Easter Sunday Attack', Colombo Telegraph, 21 April 2021, https://www.colombotelegraph.com/index.php/twenty-point-analysis-of-pcoi-on-easter-sunday-attack/.

2 'Easter Sunday Attacks Parliamentary Select Committee Report: Full Text', Colombo Telegraph, 23 Oct 2019, https://www.colombotelegraph.com/index.php/easter-sunday-attacks-parliamentary-select-committee-report-full-text/.

3 'Final Report of PCoI on Easter Sunday Attacks Handed over to President', Presidential Secretariat, 1 Feb 2021, https://www.presidentsoffice.gov.lk/index.php/2021/02/01/final-report-of-pcoi-on-easter-sunday-attacks-handed-over-to-president/.

4 Disna Mudalige, 'Easter Sunday Probes: Cardinal Calls for Decisive Action', *Daily News*, 7 April 2021, http://www.dailynews.lk/2021/04/07/features/246041/cardinal-calls-decisive-action.

5 Darshana Sanjeewa Balasuriya, 'Cabinet Sub Committee Report on Easter Sunday Attacks Handed over to President', *Daily Mirror*, 5 April 2021, http://www.dailymirror.lk/breaking_news/Cabinet-Sub-Committee-report-on-Easter-Sunday-attacks-handed-over-to-President/108-209378.

6 Ibid.

7 Camelia Nathaniel, 'Easter Sunday Attacks PCoI Report Incomplete: Cardinal', *Daily News*, 16 March 2021, http://www.dailynews.lk/2021/03/16/local/244112/easter-sunday-attacks-pcoi-report-incomplete-cardinal.

8 'Cardinal Sees Political Hand behind Easter Sunday Terror Attacks', *Daily FT*, 19 April 2021, http://www.ft.lk/front-page/Cardinal-sees-political-hand-behind-Easter-Sunday-terror-attacks/44-716410.

9 Mihi Perera, 'We Have Decided that Naufer Moulavi Is the Mastermind of Easter Attacks: Sarath Weerasekera', The Morning, 6 April 2021, https://

www.themorning.lk/we-have-decided-that-naufer-moulavi-is-the-mastermind-of-easter-attacks-sarath-weerasekera/.

10 The approval was given to Cabinet Paper No. 19/313211031173 on 14 November 2019. This was the final cabinet meeting of President Maithripala Sirisena.

11 Fathali M. Moghaddam, 'The Staircase to Terrorism: A Psychological Exploration', *American Psychologist* 60, No. 2 (2005), pp. 161–169, https://www.academia.edu/3450594/The_staircase_to_terrorism_a_psychological_exploration.

12 Prof. Eugene De Silva was consulted by the author to develop and apply the STARR model on Easter Sunday terror attack.

TWO

13 Asanga Abeyagoonasekera, 'The Lynching of a Sri Lankan in Pakistan: Decluttering Religious Extremism', *South Asia Journal*, 11 December 2021, http://southasiajournal.net/the-lynching-of-a-sri-lankan-in-pakistan-decluttering-religious-extremism/.

14 'USCIRF Releases Groundbreaking Report on the Enforcement of Blasphemy Laws Globally', USCIRF, 9 December 2020, https://www.uscirf.gov/news-room/releases-statements/uscirf-releases-groundbreaking-report-enforcement-blasphemy-laws.

15 Asad Hashim, 'Pakistan Frees Far-Right TLP Chief after Deal Following Protests', Al Jazeera, 19 November 2021, https://www.aljazeera.com/news/2021/11/19/pakistan-releases-tlp-chief-saad-rizvi.

16 Shumaila Jaffery, 'Pakistan: Islamists against Muhammad Cartoons Stage Comeback', BBC, 1 December 2021, https://www.bbc.com/news/world-asia-59456545.

17 Husain Haqqani, 'Pakistan's Religious Extremism Didn't Start with TLP. It Won't End with Banning It', The Print, 17 April 2021, https://theprint.in/opinion/pakistans-religious-extremism-didn't-start-with-tlp-it-wont-end-with-banning-it/641311/.

18 Atish Taseer, 'A Murderer and Also a Victim of Place', *The New York Times*, 20 November 2015, https://www.nytimes.com/2015/11/21/opinion/a-murderer-and-also-a-victim-of-place.html.

19 Asad Hashim, 'Pakistan Says Macron "Encourages Islamophobia", Summons Envoy', Al Jazeera, 26 October 2020, https://www.aljazeera.com/news/2020/10/26/pakistan-accuses-macron-of-encouraging.

20 'UN Condemns "Abhorrent" Terrorist Attack at Kabul Airport', United Nation, 27 August 2021, https://news.un.org/en/story/2021/08/1098602.

21 'India Calls for Adoption of Convention on Terrorism, As Security Council Considers Fears that Fighters Will Return to Afghanistan, Surge in Africa',

United Nations, 19 August 2021, https://www.un.org/press/en/2021/sc14608.doc.htm.

22 Namal Rajapaksa @RajapaksaNamal, 'On Brutal Murder of Priyantha Diyawadana in Pakistan', Twitter, 4 December 2021, 12:26 am, https://twitter.com/RajapaksaNamal/status/1466843834940203010?s=20.

THREE

23 Asanga Abeyagoonasekera, 'Fighting Economic Crime during the Pandemic: A Sri Lankan Perspective, *Journal of Financial Crime*, February 2022, https://www.emerald.com/insight/content/doi/10.1108/JFC-01-2022-0009/full/html.

24 'Sri Lanka Arrests Ex-Central Bank Deputy Governor, Four Other over Alleged Bond Scam', Reuters, 26 March 2021, www.reuters.com/article/us-sri-lanka-bondarrests-idUSKCN1R62D8.

25 'Central Bank Bond Fraud Case to Be Heard on March 18', ColomboPage, 19 February 2021, http://www.colombopage.com/archive_21A/Feb19_1613719693CH.php.

26 Ajith Nivard Cabraal, *The Great Bond Scam Cover-Up: The Mother of All Cover-Ups*, (Colombo: Ajith Nivard Cabraal, 2019).

27 Lahiru Pothmulla, 'Bandula to Go to SC on Mahendran's Citizenship', *Daily Mirror*, 9 May 2017, https://www.dailymirror.lk/Breaking-News/Bandula-to-goto-SC-on-Mahendran-s-citizenship/108-128611.

28 Ajith Nivard Cabraal, *The Great Bond Scam Cover-Up: The Mother of All Cover-Ups* (Colombo: Ajith Nivard Cabraal, 2019).

29 Anbarasan Ethirajan, 'Duminda Silva: Anger As Sri Lanka Frees Politician Sentenced for Murder', BBC, 26 June 2021, www.bbc.com/news/world-asia-57608573.

30 Krishan Francis: Associated Press, 'Sri Lankan Court: China-Built Port Board Needs Public Assent', ABC News, 19 May 2021, https://abcnews.go.com/International/wireStory/court-china-built-port-city-commission-public-assent-77752415.

31 ANI, 'US Cautions China-Backed Port City Could Turn into Money-Laundering Haven', *Sunday Island*, 2 April 2021, https://island.lk/us-cautions-china-backed-port-city-could-turn-into-money-laundering-haven/.

32 Michel Foucault, *Discipline and Punish: The Birth of the Prison*, translated by Alan Sherida (New York: Vintage Books, 1995), https://monoskop.org/images/4/43/Foucault_Michel_Discipline_and_Punish_The_Birth_of_the_Prison_1977_1995.pdf.

33 'A Brief Guide to the 20th Amendment to the Constitution', Centre for Policy Alternatives, 19 July 2021, https://www.cpalanka.org/a-brief-guide-to-the-20th-amendment-to-the-constitution/.

34 'Sri Lanka on Alarming Path towards Recurrence of Grave Human Rights Violations: UN Report', United Nations Human Rights, 27 January 2021, https://www.ohchr.org/en/NewsEvents/Pages/DisplayNews.aspx?NewsID=26695&LangID=E.

35 Francis Fukuyama, 'The Thing that Determines a Country's Resistance to the Coronavirus', *The Atlantic*, 30 March 2020, https://www.theatlantic.com/ideas/archive/2020/03/thingdetermines-how-well-countries-respond-coronavirus/609025/.

36 'The Summit for Democracy', U.S. Department of State, https://www.state.gov/summit-for-democracy/.

37 Dilshan Tharaka, 'Senadhipathi, Others Acquitted from Avant-Garde Case', *Daily News*, 21 May 2021, https://www.dailynews.lk/2021/05/21/law-order/249896/senadhipathi-others-acquitted-avant-garde-case.

38 Zulfick Farzan, 'Nissanka Senadhipathi Acquitted & Released in the High Seas Arms Trafficking Case', NewsFirst, 21 May 2021, https://www.newsfirst.lk/2021/05/21/nissanka-senadhipathi-acquitted-released-in-the-high-seas-arms-trafficking-case/.

39 Imesh Ranasinghe, 'Sri Lanka's Outgoing Attorney General Turns Down Diplomatic Posting', EconomyNext, 6 May 2021, https://economynext.com/sri-lankas-outgoingattorney-general-turns-down-diplomatic-posting-81526/.

40 Zulfick Farzan, 'Exclusive: Rule of Law Has Suffered Due to Delays in Justice System: Retiring AG De Livera', NewsFirst, 24 May 2021, https//www.newsfirst.lk/2021/05/24/exclusive-rule-of-law-has-suffered-due-to-delays-in-justice-system-retiring-ag-de-livera/.

41 Pia Krisnankutty, 'Sri Lanka's Sugar Prices at Record High, Opposition Alleges It's a Govt "Scam"', The Print, 8 September 2021, https://theprint.in/world/sri-lankas-sugar-prices-at-record-high-opposition-alleges-its-a-govt-scam/730100/.

42 Minoli de Soysa and Hannah Ellis-Peterson, '"There Is No Money Left:" Covid Crisis Leaves Sri Lanka on the Brink of Bankruptcy', *The Guardian*, 2 January 2022, https://www.theguardian.com/world/2022/jan/02/covid-crisis-sri-lanka-bankruptcy-poverty-pandemic-food-prices.

FOUR

43 Asanga Abeyagoonasekera, 'The Wall of Strength against Aggression', Near East South Asia, 7 March 2022. https://nesa-center.org/the-wall-of-strength-against-aggression/.

44 'Remarks of President Joe Biden: State of the Union Address As Prepared for Delivery', The White House, 1 March 2022, https://www.whitehouse.gov/briefing-room/speeches-remarks/2022/03/01/remarks-of-president-joe-biden-state-of-the-union-address-as-delivered/.

45 Robert D. Kaplan, *The Revenge of Geography: What the Map Tells Us about Coming Conflicts and the Battle against Fate* (New York: Random House, 2012).
46 Tony Munroe, Andrew Osborn and Humeyra Pamuk, 'China, Russia Partner Up against West at Olympics Summit', Reuters, 5 February 2022, https://www.reuters.com/world/europe/russia-china-tell-nato-stop-expansion-moscow-backs-beijing-taiwan-2022-02-04/.
47 'Inflection Point for a Western-Led Global Order', Bharat Times, 26 February 2022, https://news.bharattimes.co.in/inflection-point-for-a-western-led-global-order/.
48 Barry Pavel, ' "We Are in New, Dangerous Territory": Here's How NATO Must Respond to a Russian "Triple Threat" That Goes beyond Ukraine', Market Watch, 23 February 2022, https://www.marketwatch.com/story/we-are-in-new-dangerous-territory-heres-what-to-expect-from-nato-in-response-to-a-russian-triple-threat-that-goes-beyond-ukraine-11645646568?mkt_tok=NjU5LVdaWCowNzUAAAGCoVEPs7T6-QkRrtcSCTI9ekg82lxVvfehJ-or9aionS1uzFyde4BkIZde9wB3iUcqe9J9RVmEEC6ZOnI_p-EL035V-xwOZBQLmde-K3Dn.
49 Herman Kahn, *On Escalation: Metaphors and Scenarios* (New York: Praeger, 1965).
50 'Fact Sheet: Act Now to Protect against Potential Cyberattacks, The White House, March 2021, https://www.whitehouse.gov/briefing-room/statements-releases/2022/03/21/fact-sheet-act-now-to-protect-against-potential-cyberattacks/.

FIVE

51 Asanga Abeyagoonasekera and Alexandra Moore, 'Information Warfare between Ukraine and Russia', NIICE, 13 March 2022, https://niice.org.np/archives/7696.
52 Thomas L. Friedman, 'Putin Had No Clue How Many of Us Would be Watching', *The New York Times*, 3 April 2022, https://www.nytimes.com/2022/04/03/opinion/ukraine-russia-wired.html.
53 'Global Challenge 10', The Millennium Project, https://www.millennium-project.org/challenge-10/.
54 Jessica Brandt and Adrianna Pita, 'How Is Russia Conducting Cyber and Information Warfare in Ukraine?' Brookings, 3 March 2022, https://www.brookings.edu/podcast-episode/how-is-russia-conducting-cyber-and-information-warfare-in-ukraine/.
55 Olivia Savage and Anika Torruella, 'Behind the Veil: Information Warfare in Ukraine Paves a Shadowy Path to War', Janes, 25 February 2022, https://www.janes.com/defence-news/news-detail/behind-the-veil-information-warfare-in-ukraine-paves-a-shadowy-path-to-war.

56 Jolanta Darczewska, 'The Anatomy of Russian Information Warfare. The Crimean Operation, a Case Study', OSW, 22 May 2014, https://www.osw.waw.pl/en/publikacje/point-view/2014-05-22/anatomy-russian-information-warfare-crimean-operation-a-case-study.

57 Ben Sohl, 'Ukraine Is the Front Line in Russia's Information War', Newlines Institute, 21 February 2022, https://newlinesinstitute.org/russia/ukraine-is-the-front-line-in-russias-information-war/.

58 Olivia Savage and Anika Torruella, 'Behind the Veil: Information Warfare in Ukraine Paves a Shadowy Path to War', Janes, 25 February 2022, https://www.janes.com/defence-news/news-detail/behind-the-veil-information-warfare-in-ukraine-paves-a-shadowy-path-to-war.

59 Ibid.

60 Jonathan Greig, 'Ukraine Ministry of Defense Confirms DDoS Attack: State Banks Lose Connectivity', ZDNet, 15 February 2022, https://www.zdnet.com/article/ukraine-ministry-of-defense-confirms-ddos-attack-state-banks-loses-connectivity/.

61 'What Type of Threat Is Information Warfare?', NSTEC, https://www.nstec.com/technology/what-type-of-threat-is-information-warfare/#qa_10.

62 Michael Ruhle and Clare Roberts, 'Enlarging NATO's Toolbox to Counter Hybrid Threats', *NATO Review*, 19 March 2021, https://www.nato.int/docu/review/articles/2021/03/19/enlarging-natos-toolbox-to-counter-hybrid-threats/index.html.

63 James Curtis, 'How to Defeat the Info-Warfare "Triad of Disruption" ', *National Defense*, 5 August 2021, https://www.nationaldefensemagazine.org/articles/2021/8/5/how-to-defeat-the-info-warfare-triad-of-disruption.

64 Ibid.

65 Roger C. Molander, Andrew Riddile and Peter A. Wilson, *Strategic Information Warfare: A New Face of War*, (Santa Monica, CA: RAND Corporation, 1996), https://www.rand.org/pubs/monograph_reports/MR661.html.

SIX

66 Asanga Abeyagoonasekera, 'Ayman al-Zawahiri's Death and Political-Economic Fragility in South Asia', Near East South Asia Center for Strategic Studies, 15 September 2022, https://nesa-center.org/ayman-al-zawahiris-death-and-political-economic-fragility-in-south-asia/.

67 Institute of Peace and Conflict Studies, http://www.ipcs.org/.

68 S.K. Khatri, and G.W. Kueck, Eds., *Terrorism in South Asia: Impact on Development and Democratic Process* (Delhi: Shipra Publications, 2003), https://rcss.org/2003/01/26/research_volume/terrorism-in-south-asia/.

69 'Pakistan Not Far from "Sri Lanka Moment": Imran Khan', *Business Recorder*, 23 July 2022, https://www.brecorder.com/news/40187702.

70 'Sri Lanka: Heightened Crackdown on Dissent', Human Rights Watch, 2 August 2022, https://www.hrw.org/news/2022/08/02/sri-lanka-heightened-crackdown-dissent.
71 Amani Nilar, 'Stop Arresting Peaceful Activists under "Imaginary Charges": Medical Professionals', NewsFirst, 10 September 2022, https://www.newsfirst.lk/2022/09/10/stop-arresting-peaceful-activists-under-imaginary-charges-medical-professionals/.
72 'Global Terrorism Index 2022', ReliefWeb, 2 March 2022, https://reliefweb.int/report/world/global-terrorism-index-2022.
73 Jeff M. Smith, 'Good Riddance: The Elimination of Al-Qaeda's Top Terrorist and the Troubling Questions It Raises', The Heritage Foundation, 3 August 2022, https://www.heritage.org/terrorism/commentary/good-riddance-the-elimination-al-qaedas-top-terrorist-and-the-troubling.
74 'Top Pakistan Taliban Leader Killed in Afghanistan Roadside Attack', Al Jazeera, 8 August 2022, https://www.aljazeera.com/news/2022/8/8/top-pakistan-taliban-leader-killed-in-afghanistan-roadside-attack.
75 'Pakistan Taliban Faction Claims Park Attack on Lahore Christians', BBC, 28 March 2016, https://www.bbc.com/news/world-asia-35909677.
76 Nayera Abdallah Mahmoud and Ali Abdelaty, 'Islamic State Airs Video Purporting to Be Leader Al-Baghdadi', Reuters, 29 April 2019, https://www.reuters.com/article/us-mideast-crisis-baghdadi/islamic-state-airs-video-purporting-to-be-leader-al-baghdadi-idUSKCN1S51QB.
77 Katie Mettler, Lauren Tierney and Shelly Tan, 'Sri Lanka Timeline: How Eight Explosions Wrought Devastation on Easter Sunday', *The Washington Post*, 21 April 2019, https://www.washingtonpost.com/world/2019/04/21/sri-lanka-timeline-how-eight-explosions-wrought-devastation-easter-sunday/?itid=tf_sri-lanka-bombings.
78 'Letter Dated 15 July 2019 from the Chair of the Security Council Committee', United Nations Security Council, 15 July 2019, https://www.securitycouncilreport.org/atf/cf/%7B65BFCF9B-6D27-4E9C-8CD3-CF6E4FF96FF9%7D/s_2019_570.pdf.
79 Institute for Defence Studies and Analyses, *Combating Terrorism: Evolving Asian Perspectives*, Edited by Shruti Pandalai (New Delhi: Pentagon Press 2019), https://idsa.in/system/files/book/book_combating-terrorism.pdf.
80 Sreoshi Sinha, 'The al-Zawahiri Strike and U.S. Counterterrorism in Afghanistan', South Asian Voices, 24 August 2022, https://southasianvoices.org/the-al-zawahiri-strike-and-u-s-counterterrorism-in-afghanistan/.
81 Ibid.

# INDEX

A
Abeywardena, Mahinda Yapa, 26
aircraft carrier warships, 3
Albanese, Anthony, 105
Andaman and Nicobar Islands, 3
Apple, R.W., 86
ASEAN weapons trade, 83
Asia Cooperation Dialogue, 81
Asian Clearing Union (ACU), 175
Aspen Security Forum, 48
*A Talk between Great Russia and Little Russia*, 212
Atlantic Council, 213
Atlantic–Pacific Ocean, 26
Australia–UK–US (AUKUS), 94, 97
autocratic governments, 153
automatic identification system (AIS), 137

B
Baalu, T.R., 1
Bachelet, Michelle, 77, 78, 122
Baglay, H.E. Gopal, 70
Bandaranaike, Sirimavo, 10, 159
Bar Association of Sri Lanka (BASL), 21
Basic Exchange and Communication Agreement (BECA), 12, 63, 65
begging bowl syndrome, 129
Belt and Road (BRI), xix, 6
  agenda, 22
  beneficiaries, 47
  projects, 67, 113, 125
Biden, Joe, 11, 25, 83, 90, 91, 94, 106, 134, 163, 212
bilateral military relations, 13
Bing, 217
Bodu Bala Sena (BBS), 169
Brautigam, Deborah, 41, 160
BRICS, 81
British Empire, 8
Brzezinski, Zbigniew, 98
Bush, George W., 87

C
Central Bank bond scam, 210
Central Committee of the Communist Party, 7, 147
Centre for Security, Strategy and Technology (CSST), 70
Centre for Strategic and International Studies (CSIS), 91
Ceylon Fertilizer, 164
Chandraprema, C.A., 131
Chatham House, 44
Chellaney, Brahma, 43
China Aerospace Security Institute (CASI), 104
China Civil Engineering Construction Corporation (CCECC), 99
China Communications Construction Company (CCCC), 25, 66, 117
China Development Bank, 50
China Harbour Engineering Company (CHEC), 25, 143, 171
China Merchants Group, 23
China Metallurgical Group Corporation, 8
China–Myanmar Economic Corridor (CMEC), 76, 119, 126
China–Pakistan Economic Corridor (CPEC), 76, 119, 125, 126, 128
China policy, 25
China Reform Forum (CRF), 7

China's Exim Bank, 50
*China's Influence in South Asia: Vulnerabilities and Resilience in Four Countries*, 137
China's Strategic Support Force (SSF), 52
Chinese Communist Party (CCP), 7, 35, 48, 67
  agenda, 36
  model, 28, 33
Chinese dual-use spy vessel, 52
Chinese fertilizer shipment, 136
Chinese infrastructure
  diplomacy, 3
  portfolio, 25
  projects, 26
Chinese multinational group, 23
Chinese Permanent Representative, 129
Chinese PLAN submarine port, 75
Chinese political model, 21
Chinese State Councillor, 29
Chinese technologies, 53
Chinese-tilted foreign policy, 55
Churchill, Winston, 100
Coastal belt, 8
Coast Guard, 13
Cold War, 83, 117, 145, 213
Colombage, Jayanath, 60, 93
Colombo East Container Terminal, 8
Colombo East Port Terminal (ECT), 121
Colombo International Container Terminal (CICT), 9
Colombo Port City, 19, 21, 22, 24, 28, 34, 37, 67, 75, 92, 148, 164, 178, 206
Colombo Port City Economic Commission Bill, 26–27
Colombo Port City project, 22
Colombo Port's Eastern Container Terminal, 5
Colombo Security Conclave, 171
Colombo's foreign policy, 40, 54
Communications Compatibility and Security Agreement and Logistics Exchange Memorandum of Agreement, 12
Communist Party of China (CCP), 18, 56
Communist rule, 87
*Conundrum of an Island*, 82

D
Dalian Port Authority, 23
Dawson, William Francis, 8
debt-trap diplomacy, 41, 43, 46
*Decision Point*, 87
Director National Intelligence, 71
Djibouti International Free Trade Zone (DIFTZ), 23
Djibouti Port, 23
dollar trade target and SAARC, 124–125
Doval, Ajit, 13, 72
'dual circulation' economic model, 24

E
East Container Terminal (ECT), 73
Economic, Scientific and Technological Cooperation, 81
*Economist*, 178
Economy, Elizabeth C., 47, 52
European Union (EU), 30, 59, 155
Excess Defense Articles Program, 13
*Exercise of Power*, 87

F
Facebook, 217
Fast Aircraft Carrier Strike Force, 68
Feldstein, Steven, 55
Fenghe, Wei, 29
financial dependence on China, 42
Five Eyes, 71
foreign policy analysis, 9
Free and Open Indo-Pacific (FOIP), 91
Friedman, Thomas, 215

G
Gates, Robert M., 87
geo-intelligence alliances, 71
geopolitical analyst, 144
geopolitical fissures, 6

geopolitics, 75
George Town Economics, 176
Georgieva, Kristalina, 50
German Maritime Warfare Command, 68
G20 finance officials meeting, 50
Gilpin, Robert, 138
Global Risk Report, 95
Global Risks Perceptions Survey (GRPS), 95
Global Terrorism Index (GTI), 222
Google, 217
GSP benefits, 156
Gunaruwan, Lalithasiri, 5, 93
Gunawardena, Dinesh, 11, 47, 52
Gwadar Port, 125, 126

H
Hambantota Port City, 3, 21, 29, 31, 34, 41, 43, 45, 47, 52, 80, 90, 92, 119, 126
  development, 42
  project, 44, 128
Hameiri, Shahar, 44
Harnage, Oren Bartholomew, 86
Harris, Kamala, 18, 64
*Has China Won? The Chinese Challenge to American Primacy*, 146
Haushofer, Karl, 11, 58
Hegel, Chuck, 64
Hong Kong Special Administrative Region, 29
*How Democracies Die*, 154
Huawei's 5G, 53
Human Rights Watch Report 2021, 77

I
India–Maldives–Sri Lanka agreement, 85
Indian Defence Secretary, 198
Indian Foreign Minister, 9
Indian foreign policy, 76
Indian Ocean Island, 3, 4, 5, 6, 10, 15, 16, 17, 39, 84, 94, 95, 101, 125, 145
Indian Ocean Region (IOR), 131
Indian Ocean Rim Association, 16
Indian Ocean Zone for Peace, 10
Indian Peacekeeping Force (IPKF), 114
India–Sri Lanka
  accord, 38
  bilateral security cooperation, 2
  relation, 10, 148
  security, 72
Indo-Pacific configuration, 95
Indo-Pacific Economic Framework (IPEF), 105, 108
  clean economy, 105
  connected economy, 105
  resilient economy, 105
Indo-Pacific region, 4
Indo-Sri Lanka Defence Dialogue, 71
information warfare, 216
Institute of National Security Studies (INSS), 5, 195
Intergovernmental Commission on Trade, Economic, Scientific and Technological Cooperation, 81
International Monetary Fund (IMF), 17, 50, 51, 175, 178
  programme, 49, 183
*International Relations in a Globalized World*, 109
Iran's nuclear programme, 72
Islamic State in Khorosan Province (ISKP), 203
IW Executive Board, 219
IZP group, 23

J
Jaffna University, 10
Jaishankar, Dhruva, 91
Jaishankar, S., 4, 9, 37
Jamaat-ul-Mujahideen Bangladesh (JMB), 89
Japan's Light Rail project, 18
Jayasundara, P.B., 29
Jayewardene, J.R., 112, 115
Jiechi, Yang, 14, 22
Jones, Lee, 44
JVP political party, 165

K
Kadirgamar, Lakshman, 109
Kandyan Kingdom, 8
Kausikan, Bilahari, 9
Khanna, Parag, 144
Kissinger, Henry, 59
Kohonna, Palitha, 51
Kondapalli, Srikanth, 17, 145
KRA Canal Project, 118
Kumaratunga, Vijaya, 115

L
Latiff, Aquilah, 51
Lavrov, Sergey, 215
Law of the Sea, 15
Leninist political structure, 7
Liberation Tigers of Tamil Eelam (LTTE), 123, 148

M
Mackinder, Halford J., 80
Mahinda, 150
Malalgoda, Vijith, 189
Malleret, Thierry, 98
Manuel, Anja, 17
Maritime Great Power strategy, 102
Maritime Security Cooperation, 71
Marxist Communist system, 32
Mattala Airport, 3, 5, 43
memorandum of cooperation (MoC), 74
Menon, Shivshankar, 17
Microsoft, 217
Middle East and North Africa (MENA), 222
military logistics agreements, 5, 101, 145
Millennium Challenge Compact (MCC) grant, 5
Minister of External Affairs, 4
Ministry of Defence, 5, 29
Ministry of Public Security, 32
Mitra, Sanjay, 198
Modi, Narendra, 1, 54, 90, 94, 117, 122, 127, 149
Mohan, C. Raja, 5, 10, 92
Moody's Investors Service, 60
Moramudali, Umesh, 50
Morrison, Scott, 105
Myanmar model, 181
Myanmar port, 119

N
Naipaul, V.S., 114
National Defence Policy (NDP), 192
National People's Congress (NPC), 160
National Plant Quarantine Service (NPQ), 165
National Security Advisor (NSA), 7, 13, 17, 72, 87, 132, 162
National Security and Defence Council of Ukraine, 218
National Security Council, 196
National Security Policy (NSP), 192
National Tohweed Jamath (NTJ), 89
New Cold War, 68, 90, 146
Nikitin, Afanasy, 80
North Atlantic Treaty Organization (NATO), 145
intervention, 213
like military alignments, 4
security challenges division, 219

O
Office of the United Nations High Commissioner for Human Rights (OHCHR), 130
Overseas Economic and Commercial Cooperation Zones (OECCZ), 19–20

P
Pacific Islands, 107
Pacific Ocean, 4–5
Panama Canal, 26
Paris Climate Summit, 64
Paris Club, 183
Parliamentary Council, 207
Parliament Select Committee (PSC), 189, 190

Peiris, G.L., 111, 160
Pence, Mike, 43
Pentagon Report, 45
People's Liberation Army (PLA), 52, 164
People's Liberation Army Navy (PLAN), 3, 13, 24, 45
affiliated Chinese Naval Research Institute, 24
People 's Republic of China (PRC), 66, 160
Perera, Jehan, 156, 170
Pillai, Rajeswari, 95
PLASSF, 55
political and economic dysfunction, 220
Pompeo, Mike, 10
Port City Bill, 21, 29, 30, 34
Port City Development Project, 8
Port City legislation, 29
Premadasa, Sajith, 188
Premajayantha, Susil, 40
Presidential Commission of Inquiry (PCoI), 189, 190, 192, 195
Prevention of Terrorism Act, 154, 162, 181, 186, 209
Progressive Workers Association for Commercial Industry and Services (PWACIS), 73
Putnam, Robert, 27

Q

Qingdao Seawin Biotech Group, 36
Quadrilateral partnership (Quad), 12
dialogue, 93
Quadrilateral Security Dialogue, 104

R

Rajagopalan, Rajeswari Pillai, 95
Rajapaksa, Basil, 31, 36, 37, 38, 160, 166
Rajapaksa, Gotabaya, 5, 6, 10, 13, 28, 29, 30, 31, 36, 48, 55, 62, 65, 74, 75, 76, 94, 115, 127, 128, 130, 131, 134, 135, 140, 142, 149, 150, 157, 158, 164, 166, 167, 169, 170, 171, 176, 180, 184, 185, 187, 190, 221
Rajapaksa, Mahinda, 3, 22, 31, 33, 35, 44, 53, 61, 65, 73, 100, 103, 109, 110, 122, 143, 147, 167, 169, 170, 180
Rajapaksa, Namal, 3, 109, 151, 204
Rajapaksa, Wijeyadasa, 21
*Rajapaksa's Dysfunctional Regime in Sri Lanka*, 158
Rama-Setu, 1
Ratnayake, Daya, 128
Reciprocal Access Agreement (RAA), 71
reconciliation process, 18, 112
*rules-based order*, 63
Russia–Sri Lanka diplomatic relationship, 81
Russia–Ukraine border, 96

S

Sabry, Ali, 52
Samagi Jana Balawegaya (SJB), 110
*Samudra Manthan*, 5, 6
Schwab, Klaus, 98
Sea Lines of Communications (SLOC), 145
Second World War, 58, 68, 106
Security and Growth for All the Region (SAGAR), 133
Sethusamudram Canal, 2
Sethusamudram Project, 1
Sethusamudram Shipping Canal Project, 1
'Silver Fox', 39
Singh, Abhijit, 4
Sinhalese-Buddhist constituency, 121
Sinhalese-Buddhist ultra-nationalism, 154
Sino-Djibouti cooperation projects, 23
Sino-Lanka diplomatic and security relationship, 22
Sirisena, Maithripala, 40, 54, 115, 143, 189, 190
Solomon Islands, 98, 99, 100, 101, 107
Songavare, Manasseh, 100
South Asian Association for Regional Cooperation (SAARC), 125

process, 125
South Pacific Islands, 99
Special Economic Zone (SEZ), 19
Sri Lanka
bar association, 155
debt distress, 44
democracy, 173
economic crisis, 139–140
economic dysfunction in, 166
intelligence and communications network, 54
neutral foreign policy, 14
Rajapaksa Family Rule, 226
Singapore free trade agreement, 16
UNHRC resolution, 18–19
*Sri Lanka at Crossroads*, 80, 82
Sri Lanka Freedom Party (SLFP), 40, 110
Sri Lanka Mahajana Party (SLMP), 115
Sri Lankan foreign policy, 9, 29, 30, 149, 152
Sri Lankan foreign policy establishment, 15
Sri Lankan military intelligence officer, 160
Sri Lankan Parliament, 26, 27, 122
Sri Lanka Podujana Peramuna (SLPP), 7, 17–18, 28, 147
'Staircase Model', 193
STARR model, 198, 199, 200
State Intelligence Service (SIS), 196
Status of Forces Agreement (SOFA), 5, 12, 18, 77, 102
*Stealth War*, 103
strategic-trap diplomacy, 41, 45
Sumanthiran, M.A., 174
'Summit for Democracy', 210
*Sunday Times*, 74, 141

T
Tamil community, 38, 39, 121
Tamil Eelam Cyber Force, 152
Tamil geography, 39
Tamilian grievances, 10
Tamil National Alliance (TNA), 78, 170
Tamil war memorial, 10
Taylor, Alfred Dundas, 1
Tehreek-e-Labbaik Pakistan (TLP), 201
Tehreek-e-Taliban Pakistan (TTP), 223
Teplitz, Alaina B., 154
*The Avoidable War*, 104
*The Breakdown of Democratic Regimes*, 157
*The Cake That Was Baked at Home*, 109
*The Emperor's New Road*, 34
*The Great Bond Scam Cover-Up*, 204, 205
*The Great Narrative*, 98
'The Millennium Project', 216
*The Origins of Alliances*, 76, 127
*The Spirit of the Laws*, 111
*The World According to China*, 47, 52
Tichy-Fisslberger, Elisabeth, 130
Trade Union Association, 73
triple security threats, 152
Trump, Donald, 11, 63
Trump presidency, 138
Twitter, 217

U
Ukraine cyberwar, 214
ultra-nationalist political elements, 19
UN Core Group, 129
UN High Commissioner for Human Rights, 77, 119, 122, 154
UN Human Rights High Commissioner, 162
United National Party (UNP), 110, 144
United Nations Convention on the Law of the Sea (UNCLOS), 11, 16
United Nations Human Rights Council (UNHRC), 9, 10, 14, 18, 30, 39, 62, 64, 65, 78, 119, 121, 122, 123, 129, 131, 141, 150, 153, 155, 158
United States Agency for International Development (USAID), 51
United States Commission on International Religious Freedom (USCIRF), 201

unmanned underwater vehicle (UUV), 6
UN Security Council report, 223
USS *Nimitz*, 3
USS *Ronald Regan*, 3
USS *Theodore Roosevelt*, 3
US-China Economic and Security Review Commission, 108
US House Foreign Affairs Committee (HFAC), 29
US-Indo-Pacific report, 7
US MCC grant, 21
US Pacific Command (USPACOM), 69
US Special Operations Command, 224

V
Vimanga, K.D., 157
'Vistas of Prosperity and Splendour', 62

W
Walt, Stephen M., 76, 127
Wanniarachchi, Pavithra, 160
Weerawansa, Wimal, 185
West Container Terminal, 141
Western democracies, 156
Western diplomatic toolkit, 91
Wickremesinghe, Ranil, 48, 49, 144, 175, 182, 185, 187, 188, 205, 221
Wignaraja, Ganeshan, 39
Wijesinha, Anushka, 51
Wijewardena, W.A., 158
Wilsbach, Kenneth S., 134
World Bank, 19
World Political Future summit, 34

X
Xiaoping, Deng, 136

Y
Yahampath, Anuradha, 102
Yeo, George, 16
*Yuan Wang 5*, 52, 53, 54, 55, 56

# ABOUT THE AUTHOR

Asanga Abeyagoonasekera is an international security and geopolitics analyst and strategic adviser from Sri Lanka. He is a senior fellow at the Millennium Project in Washington, DC. He has led two government think tanks providing strategic advocacy on foreign policy and security in Sri Lanka. He was the founding director-general of the national security think tank under the Ministry of Defence (INSSSL). He was also the executive director at the foreign policy think tank Kadirgamar Institute.